Palgrave Studies in the History of the Media

Palgrave Studies in the History of the Media publishes original, high quality research into the cultures of communication from the middle ages to the present day. The series explores the variety of subjects and disciplinary approaches that characterize this vibrant field of enquiry. The series will help shape current interpretations not only of the media, in all its forms, but also of the powerful relationship between the media and politics, society, and the economy.

More information about this series at
http://www.palgrave.com/gp/series/14578

Thomas S. Freeman · David L. Smith
Editors

Biography and History in Film

palgrave
macmillan

Editors
Thomas S. Freeman
University of Essex
Colchester, UK

David L. Smith
University of Cambridge
Cambridge, UK

Palgrave Studies in the History of the Media
ISBN 978-3-319-89407-2 ISBN 978-3-319-89408-9 (eBook)
https://doi.org/10.1007/978-3-319-89408-9

Cover credit: Shutterstock/Bikeworldtravel

This Palgrave Macmillan imprint is published by the registered company Springer Nature Switzerland AG
The registered company address is: Gewerbestrasse 11, 6330 Cham, Switzerland

For Dr. Susan Doran
and in memory of
Patricia Margery Smith (1925–2017)
and David Martin Bevington (1931–2019)

Contents

Notes on Contributors

David Bevington was the Phyllis Fay Horton Distinguished Service Professor in the Humanities at the University of Chicago. His books include *From 'Mankind' to Marlowe* (1962), *Tudor Drama and Politics* (1968), *Action Is Eloquence* (1984), *Shakespeare: The Seven Ages of Human Experience* (2005), *This Wide and Universal Theater: Shakespeare in Performance, Then and Now* (2007), *Shakespeare's Ideas* (2008), *Shakespeare and Biography* (2010), and *Murder Most Foul: Hamlet Through the Ages* (2011). He was the editor of *Medieval Drama* (1975), the Bantam Shakespeare, and *The Complete Works of Shakespeare* (7th edition, 2014). He was the senior editor of the Revels Student Editions and a senior editor of the Revels Plays, *The Norton Anthology of Renaissance Drama* (2002), and *The Cambridge Edition of the Works of Ben Jonson* (7 vols., 2012). He died on 2 August 2019.

Samantha A. Cavell is the Visiting Assistant Professor in Military History at Southeastern Louisiana University. Her publications include *Midshipmen and Quarterdeck Boys in the British Navy* (2012), and contributions to *The Battle of New Orleans Reconsidered* (2015) and *Yankees in Nelson's Navy* (forthcoming). She is also a member of the Historian General's Committee for the Naval Order of the United States.

Klaus Dodds is Professor of Geopolitics in the Department of Geography at Royal Holloway, University of London. He is the author of a number of books including *Ice: Nature and Culture* (2018), and co-author of *The Scramble for the Poles* (2016). He is a Fellow of the

Academy of Social Sciences and holds a Major Research Fellowship courtesy of the Leverhulme Trust.

Thomas S. Freeman is a Lecturer in the Department of History at the University of Essex. He is the co-author of *Religion and the Book in Early Modern England: The Making of John Foxe's 'Book of Martyrs'* (2011), and the co-editor of five essay collections on early modern British History, including *The Tudors and Stuarts on Film* (2009).

Bart K. Holland is Associate Professor in the Department of Medicine at Rutgers New Jersey Medical School. He is a working scientist who teaches epidemiology while maintaining a strong interest in the historical development of medical practice. His publications include 'Treatments for Bubonic Plague: Reports from Seventeenth-Century British Epidemics' (*Journal of the Royal Society of Medicine*, 2000), and a translation of Patrice Bourdelais' *Les épidémies terrassés: une histoire de pays riches* (2006).

Sean M. Kelley is Senior Lecturer in History at the University of Essex. He is the author of two monographs on Atlantic slavery and is a contributing editor of *Freedom Narratives*, an international collaborative project that collects and publishes autobiographical testimonies of Africans from the era of the slave trade.

Jon Lawrence is Associate Professor in History at the University of Exeter. His books include *Speaking for the People: Party, Language and Popular Politics in England, 1867–1914* (1998) and *Electing Our Masters: The Hustings in British Politics from Hogarth to Blair* (2009). He is most recently the author of *Me, Me, Me? Individualism and the Struggle for Community in Post-war England* (2019).

Kate Masur is an Associate Professor of History at Northwestern University. She is the author of numerous books and articles on the Civil War and Reconstruction in the United States. Her books include *An Example for All the Land: Emancipation and the Struggle Over Equality in Washington, D.C.* (2010); *The World the Civil War Made* (2015), co-edited with Gregory P. Downs; and a re-release of John E. Washington's 1942 classic, *They Knew Lincoln.*

Andrew Priest is Senior Lecturer in Modern United States History at the University of Essex. He is the author of *Kennedy, Johnson and NATO: Britain, America and the Dynamics of Alliance* (2006), and co-editor of *US Presidential Elections and Foreign Policy: Candidates, Campaigns, and Global Politics from FDR to Bill Clinton* (2017).

William B. Robison is Head of the Department of History and Political Science at Southeastern Louisiana University. He is the editor of *History, Fiction, and 'The Tudors': Sex, Politics, Power, and Artistic License in the Showtime Television Series* (2016), co-author of *The Tudors on Film and Television* (2013), and co-editor of *Historical Dictionary of Late Medieval England* (2002) and *Historical Dictionary of Stuart England* (1996).

David L. Smith is Fellow, Director of Studies in History, and Graduate Tutor at Selwyn College, Cambridge. His books include *Constitutional Royalism and the Search for Settlement, c. 1640–1649* (1994), *A History of the Modern British Isles, 1603–1707: The Double Crown* (1998), *The Stuart Parliaments, 1603–1689* (1999), and (with Patrick Little) *Parliaments and Politics During the Cromwellian Protectorate* (2007).

Florence Sutcliffe-Braithwaite is Lecturer in Twentieth-Century British History at University College London. Her first book, *Class, Politics and the Decline of Deference in England, 1968–2000*, was published in 2018.

Elisabeth van Houts is Fellow and Director of Studies in History at Emmanuel College, Cambridge, and Honorary Professor of European Medieval History in the University of Cambridge. Her books include *The Gesta Normannorum Ducum of William of Jumièges, Orderic Vitalis and Robert of Torigni* (2 vols., 1992–1995), *Memory and Gender in Medieval Europe, 900–1200* (1999), *History and Family Traditions in England and the Continent, 1000–1200* (1999), *The Normans in Europe* (2000), and as co-editor with Julia Crick, *A Social History of England, 900–1200* (2011), with Patricia Skinner, *Medieval Writings on Secular Women* (2011), and with Rosalind Love, *The Warenne (Hyde) Chronicle* (2013).

'Movies That Exist Merely to Tell Entertaining Lies'?: Biography on Film

Thomas S. Freeman and David L. Smith

In contrast to an explosion of interest in historical films over the past quarter century or so, biographical films, or biopics as they are often casually termed, have attracted very little academic attention. There are, in fact, currently only a handful of books dealing with the topic of biographical films, most notably the pioneering study of George Custen and also Dennis Bingham's more recent study, which argues that biopics form an underappreciated, but valid film genre.[1] The reason for this neglect is the low regard in which biographical films are generally held. Some of this disdain is aesthetic: biographical films have been criticized for their reliance on formula, their unoriginality, their superficial treatment of people and their predictable plots. Biographical films have also been scorned for their reckless mingling of fact and fiction. In an interview for the journal *Film and History*, John Tibbetts, the author

T. S. Freeman (✉)
University of Essex, Colchester, UK
e-mail: tfreeman@essex.ac.uk

D. L. Smith
Selwyn College, Cambridge, UK
e-mail: dls10@cam.ac.uk

T. S. Freeman and D. L. Smith (eds.), *Biography and History in Film*, Palgrave Studies in the History of the Media,
https://doi.org/10.1007/978-3-319-89408-9_1

of a monograph on biographical films about composers, was asked the following question: 'The biopic is a mendacious genre that may have little to do with historical or biographical truth. Can you justify your interest in movies that exist merely to tell entertaining lies?'[2]

Yet while biographical films may not, as a class of film, be particularly admired, they date back to the earliest days of the American film industry and they remain popular to the present day. And this is the major reason why scholars, especially historians, need to examine and analyse biopics: film has been, and continues to be, the most popular and accessible form of public history in the twentieth and twenty-first centuries. Robert Rosenstone observes that:

> Each day it becomes clearer to even the most academic of historians that the visual media are the conveyer of public history in our culture. That for every person who reads a book on a historical topic about which a film has been made, especially a popular film such as *Schindler's List* (1993), many millions of people are likely to encounter that past on screen.[3]

Studies undertaken in the United States and Australia have confirmed Rosenstone's assertion and unsurprisingly revealed that more people in those countries drew their knowledge of history from films and television than from reading about it.[4] And, of course, this was as true of biographical films as it was of historical films. George Custen has pointed out that while it almost certainly was not the intention of filmmakers to provide a definitive account of an individual, they nevertheless did exactly this as they were the only source of information that many people would have about a historical figure.[5]

Historical myths have been created by film. For example, the popular image of the storming of the Winter Palace in 1917, in which a mob of workers, soldiers and sailors batter their way, in broad daylight, against strenuous opposition, into the palace is factually incorrect; there was little resistance to the attack, which actually took place at night.[6] The popular image was established by Sergei Eisenstein's great propaganda film, *October: Ten Days That Shook the World* (1927) and it has burned into public consciousness. A series of interviews of high school students and their families, conducted in Seattle in 1996, demonstrated how powerfully film could mould perceptions of the past, even the recent past. Asking the subjects of the interview about their memories of the Viet Nam war, the researchers found that the film *Forrest Gump* was cited by about 60% of those interviewed as a source for a particular aspect of the war years. And even more importantly, many of the participants in the study, created memories of the period that were unconsciously based on incidents in the film.[7] Examples like this, explain the concern of the eminent historian Eric Foner, that audiences believe too readily that what they see in historical films is true.[8]

A striking example of how false historical information can be disseminated, and readily accepted, is provided by the circulation of the story that Thomas Jefferson shot a man for treason on the White House lawn. This was originally a casual remark made by a character played by John Travolta in the 2001 film *Swordfish*, but it rapidly gained a place in popular culture, with the fictitious victim of Jefferson even acquiring a name and identity: he was supposedly one Rodney Cox from North Carolina who was executed for divulging naval secrets. There is now a website, refuting the 'very persistent story', which is maintained by the museum at Monticello, Jefferson's former estate and also a Wikipedia site on the 'Rodney Cox myth'.[9] The role of biographical films as the paramount source of biographical information, as well as the power of film in shaping images, and even memories, of the past, gives the film an extraordinary power in forming popular perceptions of historical figures. It is due to film, for example, that Henry VIII is perceived as a riotous glutton and has become the patron saint of Renaissance Fairs. And it is for this reason, as well as the popularity of biographical films, that historians cannot afford to ignore them.

But this begs the questions of what a biographical film is and what its relationship to biographical fact should be. A number of scholars have defined biographical films in terms that emphasize the consanguinity of biography and biographical film. Ellen Cheshire has maintained that a biopic depicts 'the life of an important real person' and she also draws a distinction between such films and films which portray real people in an invented story such as *Mrs. Brown* (1997) or *The Terminal* (2004).[10] The insistence that a biopic should be about an important person is problematic—biographical films have been made about figures such as Monty Stratton, Ed Wood, Bob Crane, Andy Kaufman or Bettie Page whose fame and importance are arguably minimal—but Cheshire's insistence that the lead figure in a biopic should be a real person and the film should deal with real events is a helpful guide. Custen similarly defines a biopic as being about real, not fictional people, and urged that films which might be based on real people, but used different names for their subjects, should not qualify as biopics, which are the versions of an actual life.[11] (Examples of such diaphanously veiled biographies—*films à clef*—include films such as *The Bad and the Beautiful* [1953], whose protagonist shares numerous biographical and personal details with the producer David Selznick, but bears the name of Jonathan Shields or *Dreamgirls* [2006] in which the eponymous, fictitious singing group for whom the film is named is closely based on 'The Supremes'.)

The views of Cheshire and Custen, insisting that the biopics should have a factual core, have, however, been challenged. Dennis Bingham argues that *Citizen Kane*, the greatest *film à clef*, is a biopic although there is not a historical figure in the film. He also opines that 'biopics are not history' instead they 'are attempts of individual artists to understand public people through dramas'.[12] Bingham's opinion has some substance. As we shall discuss below, there are ways in which historical films cannot replicate print histories and biographical films cannot replicate print biographies. But it is specious to maintain that the biopic does not have to be about real people and that it does not need to have any biographical content at all. If a film has as its subject fictitious people and if the film does not have any historical content, what makes it a biopic as opposed to a generic drama?

Yet even if a film is centred on historical figures, that does not necessarily make it a biopic. *Jesse James* (1939), for example, is about a genuine historical figure, but almost everything in the film, except for James' murder at the end of it, is complete fiction. *Jesse James* did not really claim to be a biography, but MGM's *Till the Clouds Roll By* (1946), purports to be a biography of the American songwriter Jerome Kern. However, the plot of the film is complete fiction. MGM's *Words and Music* (1948) also claims to be a biography of the song-writing team of Richard Rogers and Lorenz Hart, but not only is the plot a travesty of their lives but the two protagonists are radically different from the actual people the film portrays: in the film, Hart is straight and Rogers is warm, likable and continually supportive of his partner. This is a tricky point because the vast majority of biopics have some fictional moments—sometimes wildly fictional moments—and fictional characters: the older friend/mentor/confidant, often a composite of a number of real people, is almost a cliché of the genre.

Our definition of a biographical film is that it is a film dealing with the life, or the portion of a life of a figure or figures, usually historical figures, otherwise figures of some prominence. It should at least appear to be factual; a film such as *Churchill: The Hollywood Years* (2014), which is about a historical figure, is also an overt parody and should not be considered as a biopic. Similarly, a film about a historical figure, whose plot depends on fantasy and the supernatural, such as *Abraham Lincoln: Vampire Hunter* (2012) should also not be considered a biopic. A biographical film may include some fictional characters and some fictional events, but it should make an overall effort to adhere to the known facts and to present its subjects and their careers with some accuracy. It should also depict how its central character or characters influenced, and responded to, the times and circumstances in which they lived.

Our approach in this volume is to analyse biographical films as biographical documents. We define a biographical document as a work—in any medium—which presents the life or the portion of a life of a prominent or historic figure. The difference between a biographical document and a biography is that that the former may legitimately mix fact and fiction together but the latter may not. A biographer who knowingly relates falsehoods or invents material loses credibility and their works lose authority. In 1999, Edmund Morris, author of a respected biography of Theodore Roosevelt, sailed into a maelstrom of criticism when he wrote a biography of Ronald Reagan, which had a fictitious narrator, some fictitious characters and fabricated footnotes to document their existence.[13] These practices are standard in a biographical film, which is a biographical document, but unacceptable in a biography. The contributors to this volume examine the topics essential to the assessment of any biographical document: who created it, why it was created and the circumstances in which it was created. They also examine the inaccuracies in the biographical document. This may seem like pedantry to some, but inaccuracies are often deliberate and comparing these with historical knowledge, *at the time when the biographical document was created*, often casts light on the motives behind the document. Finally the contributors analyse the impact that various biographical films have had on popular perceptions of the subjects of these films.

II

Before looking more closely at biographical films, we should say more about biography itself. First of all, we need to explore the question of biography as a method, and how it relates to history as a discipline. Biography has often been seen as distinct from history—even as its poor relation—and professional historians have frequently looked down upon biography. In their celebrated controversy over the nature of history as a discipline, this was one point on which E.H. Carr and G.R. Elton found themselves in broad agreement. Carr wrote that

> It is tempting to make a distinction between biography which treats man as an individual and history which treats man as part of a whole, and to suggest that good biography makes bad history. ... We are entitled by convention...to reserve the word 'history' for the process of enquiry into the past of man in society.[14]

Elton echoed him, arguing that 'even at its best biography is a poor way of writing history'. This, he asserted, was because

> The biographer's task is to tell the story, demonstrate the personality, and elucidate the importance of one individual; he should not be concerned with the history of that individual's times except insofar as it centres upon or emanates from him. In measure as he deserts his proper subject for what concerns the historian, that subject's age, he fails in his own task.

As a result, Elton concluded that 'biography is not a good way of writing history. The historian should know the histories and characters of many men, as he should know much else, but he should not write biography – or at least should not suppose that in writing biography he is writing history'.[15] In other words, the biographical method, by its very nature, raises inherent problems of perspective and risks exaggerating the significance of the individual whose life it recounts.

Many scholars have shared the reservations of Carr and Elton. The renowned philosopher and literary theorist, Roland Barthes, famously called biography 'the fiction that dare not speak its name'.[16] David Nasaw, the author of a number of admired biographies, has observed that 'biography remains the profession's unloved stepchild, occasionally but grudgingly let in the door, more often shut outside with the riffraff'.[17] Biography has never formed part of professional academic training for historians, and it does not figure in any doctoral training programmes. Many biographies have been written by journalists or popular writers rather than by historical scholars. In an article on 'writing the modern British monarchy' entitled 'from biography to history', David Cannadine suggested that royal biographies often illustrated 'the limitations of the genre'.[18] Ian Kershaw, introducing his monumental two-volume biography of Hitler, acknowledged that an 'inbuilt danger in any biographical approach is that it demands a level of empathy with the subject which can easily slide over into sympathy, perhaps even hidden or partial admiration'.[19] This raises a further charge often levelled against biographers, namely that they are liable to become too sympathetic towards their subjects. Although there are some notable exceptions, such as Hugh Trevor-Roper's life of Archbishop William Laud,[20] most biographies are probably more in danger of being too sympathetic than the reverse. Yet this need not necessarily be an insurmountable obstacle to good historical practice for, as Kershaw observes, it may be the case that 'comprehensive repulsion more than the possibility of sympathy poses the greater drawback to insight'.[21]

Kershaw makes a further telling point regarding the problem of perspective when he writes that: 'Biography also runs the natural risk of over-personalizing complex historical developments, over-emphasizing the role of the individual in shaping and determining events, ignoring or playing down the social and political context in which those actions took place'. He regards 'avoiding this pitfall' as his major challenge in undertaking a biography of Hitler, and it is undoubtedly a danger in any biography.[22] Tony Badger, in examining the New Deal, similarly argues that 'the emphasis on Roosevelt inherent in the biographical approach ... distorts more than it illustrates', and suggests that 'the biographical approach does not help understand just how many of the consequences of the New Deal were unintended, how the major trends in American social and economic developments were not the ones desired by Roosevelt'.[23] We shall see that the same hazards—of over-emphasis upon one individual and undue sympathy with, or even hostility towards, them—also surface in relation to biographical films.

There is, perhaps, a further danger with biography as a method, namely that of anachronism. Because biographies generally describe lives that have been completed, the ending of which is known, there is a hazard that they might read episodes during that life, and the subject's aims, attitudes and perspectives, in the light of that. There is a corresponding danger of under-estimating how open their choices might have been—or at least appeared to be—and of making insufficient allowance for the fact that the subject could not foresee the future. The temptation to employ hindsight, always a double-edged tool for historians, is perhaps especially great for those writing biographies.[24] Here again, we run up against a problem that is true also of biographical films: the audience knows how the subject's life would unfold and end, whereas the subject did not. Similarly, readers and audiences are aware of the outcomes of past events and processes in a way that the historical actors who were living through those events and processes could not have been. Hindsight inevitably provides a different perspective on historical developments and their consequences and legacies that was not available to people alive at the time.

Despite all these reservations, however, biography remains a perennially popular form of writing, and one that continues to excite the fascination of scholars and readers alike. Biography forms an important strand within the Classical and Christian traditions, and can be traced back to works as diverse as the 'lives' written by Suetonius and Plutarch or the Gospels and the Acts of the Apostles. The genre of medieval 'saint's lives' consciously built upon this tradition, albeit in ways that raised difficult questions about the boundary between biography and hagiography. The humanist rediscovery of the classics ensured that biography—whether as individual biographies or in collections of lives—became a prominent trope of the Renaissance.[25] Thereafter, biography remained a consistently popular genre, to a point where Emerson could write in the nineteenth century that 'there is properly no history only biography'.[26] Benjamin Disraeli expressed a similar sentiment in his novel *Contarini Fleming* (1834): 'Read no history, nothing but biography, for that is life without theory'.[27] Other nineteenth-century voices were less enthusiastic, and Thomas Carlyle's assertion that 'a well written Life is almost as rare as a well spent one'[28] anticipated the later aspersions by professional historians discussed above. Nevertheless, historical biographies have continued to command a wide readership down to the present day, and a growing number of historians have advanced arguments in defence of the biographical method.

This has become especially significant during the twentieth century when a number of the most fashionable frameworks for historical interpretation, including Marxism and the *Annales* School, stressed the power of impersonal forces in shaping historical developments. In their different ways, both Marxists and the *Annalistes* played down the role of individual agency in causing historical change. Within a Marxist framework, human history is conceived in terms of the formation of classes, defined by their economic relationship to the means of production, which periodically conflict with each other in such a way as to bring about the transitions from feudalism to capitalism and ultimately to communism.

Class is thus the organizing principle, constructed culturally and socially as well as economically, and individual identity is subordinated to collective.[29] Similarly, in the writings of the *Annales* School, 'events and innovations...are almost never the simple creation of particular individuals'.[30] Rather, the goal of these historians has been to pursue a 'total history' in which the study of collective *mentalités* dwarfs the variations that might exist between particular individuals and their beliefs and motivations.[31] Although they have often disagreed with each other, one thing that Marxists and *Annalistes* have in common is that their work rests on impersonal paradigms that deny the importance of the individual personalities that are the very essence of biography.

Against this, Derek Beales has asserted that 'it must be remembered on the other side, first, that the juggernauts are powered and directed by men; secondly, that history is concerned with trends as they affect people; and thirdly, that individuals' reactions to trends, even the reactions of those who never gain the woods of freedom, constitute the historian's prime material'.[32] Beales takes as the starting-point for his defence of biography a feeling of dissatisfaction with the work of the French historian Fernand Braudel, whose massive history of the Mediterranean in the age of Philip II is one of the most influential products of the *Annales* School.[33] Braudel eschewed mere 'biographical history' in favour of 'the history of structures and ... expanses'.[34] He developed an immense tripartite scheme comprising the *longue durée* (the study of *structures*), the moyenne *durée* (*conjonctures*) and *the courte durée* (*événements*). This framework had the effect of reducing human beings to small players within a much broader and longer historical process, and Braudel wrote that 'confronted by man, I am always tempted to see him as enclosed in a destiny which he scarcely made, in a landscape which shows before and behind him the infinite perspective of the *longue durée*'. Such an interpretation, with its emphasis on impersonal forces, is, as Antonia Fraser has written, 'definitely not the biographer's credo'.[35] By presenting people as subordinate to wider forces and trends, Braudel downplayed the role of free choice, and he argued that 'all efforts against the prevailing tide of history, which is not always obvious, are doomed to failure'.[36] Not the least of the purposes of biography is to reassert the role of the individual and the possibility of freely made decisions.

Beales and Fraser have also challenged the idea that biography is incompatible with the writing of good history. Beales argues that 'biography has been too much disparaged', and he feels that 'one of the principal uses of a biography is to help us appraise the evidence left by the subject'.[37] That appraisal is subject to the same rigorous standards as any form of historical writing. As Fraser writes, it is essential to 'avoid anachronistic moral judgements as well as anachronistic statements', and she insists that 'it is simply not the duty of a biographer to clean up the act of a character long dead and gone, according to the values of the present time'. Rather, 'one should keep faith with history itself, and the record, and ... recreate the excitement of the life as it was once lived', and that to her 'is the value of biography in history'.[38]

This readiness to defend biography as a valuable form of historical writing has gathered momentum in recent years. In *History in Practice*, Ludmilla Jordanova argues that 'biography can cut across arbitrary divisions between historical fields and approaches', and adds that 'whereas biographies used to be thought of as conventional and frumpy, it is now becoming clear how rich in historical insights they can be'.[39] John Tosh has likewise affirmed the value of the biographical approach. He suggests that 'biography is indispensable to the understanding of motive and intention', and that 'it is for this reason that during the present century biographers have increasingly stressed the private or inner lives of their subjects as well as their public careers'. He concludes that 'from this perspective, the personal development of important individuals in the past is a valid subject of historical enquiry in its own right'.[40] Two recent studies of biography as a genre, by Barbara Caine and Hermione Lee, have taken a similarly positive view of its scholarly value. In particular, Caine and Lee have both demonstrated the extraordinary flexibility and inclusiveness of the biographical method and its responsiveness—indeed openness—to new agendas and areas of study.[41] As Caine puts it, because biography is 'always a form of contingent narrative' it 'has a particular appeal at a time when historical interest is extending beyond the national and even the imperial to the transnational and the global'.[42]

Scholars have also shown a growing confidence that the issues of perspective and sympathy that have so preoccupied the critics of biography are surmountable. Hayden White's argument that all narrative is biased undermines one of the major foundations for privileging history over biography, namely the idea that history is objective whereas biography is subjective.[43] Barbara Taylor writes that 'we now possess many historical biographies that do a superb job of integrating their subjects into their historical contexts; life histories are no longer a genre apart'.[44] Provided that sufficient attention is paid to the contexts within which an individual lived, many of the hazards of excessive concentration on one life can be overcome. As Jochen Hellbeck has observed, 'there are ways of writing biography that retain the inherent interest and excitement of exploring how it felt for historical subjects to live their lives, while also maintaining a critical distance and observing the shaping influences of context and structure'. He even goes as far as to claim that biographies 'are what historians should write insofar as they believe that it is their vocation to understand the human condition in its historically variable forms'.[45] Similarly, Shirley A. Leckie has argued convincingly that

> Biography matters because we need it for inspiration, consolation, and companionship, which we derive when 'a living being walks off the pages' and we feel that we actually know another human being more intimately than we know many of the individuals with whom we interact daily. ... We also value biography as a way of encountering the personal myths of others [and] we want to understand the extent to which history molds individuals and, in turn, is influenced by individuals.

She concludes that 'all these are popular and important reasons that biography matters to the general public and will continue to matter for the foreseeable future'.[46]

The inherent immediacy and human appeal of biography, and its capacity to illuminate motivation and agency, all help to explain its enduring popularity. Indeed, it is striking that the popular appetite for the genre extends even to very lengthy, extremely detailed, multi-volume biographies. In the nineteenth century, such works often still had something of the edifying purpose that had persisted from earlier periods. For example, in the 1870s Theodore Martin's five-volume biography of Prince Albert presented Queen's Victoria's beloved consort in almost reverential terms as both a selfless public figure and a model husband and father.[47] Public interest in monumental biographies has survived long after the decline of Victorian values and pieties. One only has to look at Martin Gilbert's six-volume biography of Winston Churchill to see the continuing public interest in intricately detailed accounts of the lives of major political figures.[48] Nor is this interest confined to those who are generally seen in positive and heroic terms. Even the life of so antipathetic an individual as Adolf Hitler remains enduringly fascinating, as the great success of Ian Kershaw's two-volume biography of the Führer demonstrates.[49] It seems very likely that biographies of Churchill or

Hitler command much greater interest—and a much wider readership—than would more general histories of their respective countries during their lifetime. Much the same appears to be true in the United States, as Robert Caro's multi-volume life of Lyndon B. Johnson demonstrates.[50] Four volumes have appeared to date, running down to the presidential election of 1964, with a fifth and final volume currently in progress. These few examples of large-scale biographies could easily be multiplied at considerable length, and they suggest that the public appetite for biographical information is still as healthy as ever.

This popular appeal is true also of the sub-genre of collective biography. Recent years have seen the publication of the 60-volume *Oxford Dictionary of National Biography* (Oxford, 2004) and the 9-volume *Dictionary of Irish Biography* (Cambridge, 2009). As Keith Thomas has written of the *Oxford DNB*, 'one cannot read these lives without hugely enhancing one's sense of the range of human possibility'. The purpose of biography may have changed over the centuries, and Thomas notes that 'since classical times, the commemoration of the virtuous dead has been seen as a moral duty and an incentive to their emulation by the living'.[51] Such high-minded aims may be less in vogue today than they once were but the capacity of biographies to encourage role-modelling should not be under-estimated. Lois W. Banner has observed that 'in a present-day world fraught with peril', her students 'are looking for role models after whom to pattern their own lives': 'empathizing with others through biography' is a helpful aspect of this process.[52] A biography offers the intrinsic interest of allowing its readers to engage with the successes and failures, and the trials and tribulations, of another human being. As Jordanova has argued, 'a key feature of all historical writing is made manifest in' biographies, namely 'the desire, even the need, to identify with our objects of study'.[53] It is no wonder, then, that biography continues to hold such a wide appeal and that as a genre it looks unlikely to fall from popular favour any time soon.

It would also be fair to say that biography can address certain themes and aspects of human experience that history commonly does not. Some of the most enduringly popular subjects for biographies include criminals, sports men or women and entertainers. These are all areas of human activity and achievement that have a broad and continuing appeal. Yet they are also topics to which professional historians have tended, at any rate until recent times, to devote relatively little attention. Insofar as the histories of crime, or sport, or entertainment have been explored by professional historians, it has been by relating them to broader social and economic trends rather than by reconstructing the lives of individual exponents. History has usually set these subjects within larger thematic frameworks, and offered accounts on a wider scale in terms of mass movements and developments, while leaving the stories of specific individuals to biographers. Here again, biography can present the past with a vividness and a human immediacy that eludes the broader but less personal style of writing that is characteristic of professional historians.

III

Whatever scholars' varying estimations of the merits of biography or of biographical films, filmmakers have consistently, not to say ceaselessly, insisted on the accuracy of their product. Ever since Hollywood began making historical and biographical films, considerable efforts have been made, in studio publicity, to extoll the accuracy of their films.[54] The films themselves were often prefaced by written or spoken assertions of their authenticity and the reality of what they depicted.[55] These prefaces could be elaborate, sweeping and exaggerated. In the opening of the film *Nell Gwyn* (1934), the credits state that the dialogue between Charles II and Nell Gwyn is either taken from Samuel Pepys' diaries or by Miles Malleson, the scriptwriter. The film begins with Pepys writing his diary (the title is clearly shown) and starting to describe the main characters in the film. The implication is, of course, that despite the earlier acknowledgement of Malleson, the film, and what is spoken in the film, are based on the contemporary testimony of Pepys. In her chapter in this volume, Elisabeth van Houts describes a similar ploy: in this case beginning the film with shots of the medieval manuscript records of Joan of Arc's trial. Similar practices still exist and overstated claims are still made. The 2004 film *King Arthur* is prefaced by this assertion:

> Historians agree that the classical 15th century tale of a King Arthur and his Knights rose from a real hero who lived a thousand years earlier in a period often called the Dark Ages. Recently discovered archaeological evidence sheds light on his true identity.

Apart from advancing the dubious proposition that there is a historical consensus about Arthur's existence, much less his identity, this preface misleadingly implies that the film is a historically accurate account of Arthur's life, based on new archaeological discoveries. With even greater cunning, *Braveheart* (1996), which provides a profoundly inaccurate account of the Scottish hero William Wallace, begins with a narrator declaring, 'I shall tell you of William Wallace. Historians from England will say I am a liar, but history is written by those who hang heroes'. There are no claims made here that the film gives an accurate account of Wallace's life; instead it pre-emptively dismisses anyone who criticizes its accuracy as having been biased by English propaganda.

Film studios have also distributed promotional materials that boasted of the historical research that went into certain films. MGM produced a booklet for their prestige film *Marie Antoinette* (1939) which proudly claimed that 1538 books and 5000 pages of manuscripts were consulted for the film.[56] A year earlier, a souvenir book was created for another MGM film, *The Buccaneer*, a biopic of Jean Lafitte. The book maintained that Cecil B. DeMille, the film's director, at the head of a large research team, had 'crossed 280 miles through the swamps of Louisiana, where descendants of Lafitte's pirates still live' gathering oral testimonies and artefacts relating to the pirate.[57] Not infrequently, studio efforts to promote the historical accuracy of their films appropriated the appearance, style and even function of academic works. An extreme example of this occurred when the studio research for Cecil B. DeMille's *The Ten Commandments* was published by the University of Southern California Press, as *Moses and Egypt: The Documentation to the Motion Picture 'The Ten Commandments'*. (DeMille paid for the publication which particularly targeted clergy and newspaper writers and editors.)[58] A related studio practice, which persisted throughout the twentieth century, consists of study guides (often thinly disguised press kits) being sent out to schools.[59] The practice, at least in certain instances, caused controversy. In 1991, Warner Brothers attracted heated criticism for distributing to history departments in high schools and universities, a study guide designed by Oliver Stone to accompany his divisive and provocative film *JFK*.[60] Six years later, Dream Works Studios, which produced the film *Amistad*, a drama about the famous mutiny on a slave ship in 1839, triggered controversy from respected academics and pundits, because of a study guide, based on the film, which was distributed to teachers in 20,000 American high schools and colleges. The study guide was sharply criticized for erasing 'the distinction between fact and fabrication', particularly for its asking students to study a composite figure created for the film as if he was a real person, and also for its presentism.[61]

The insistent, and sometimes extravagant, truth claims for historical and biographical films and the imitation of academic practice in marketing them, might seem to indicate a certain respect for historical accuracy by filmmakers, or, at least, a sense that audiences desire accuracy in historical and biographical films and that the appearance of it, at least should be conveyed. In fact, the situation has been much more complex. George Custen has observed that, for 'the producers of biopics, historical accuracy was not the foremost concern....For producers, historicity and accuracy were attractive as long as they remained selling points'.[62] In fact, studio executives and their employees have often been dismissive of criticisms of the veracity of their films that have come from their audiences. Admittedly there have been a few cases where protests caused changes to be made to a film. The portrayal of Gustavus Adolphus as an inebriated oaf in *Cardinal Richelieu* (1935) drew protests that led to the deletion of scenes portraying the king after the film's premiere.[63] (And even this concession to veracity was probably made because the Swedish government, irked by this cavalier portrayal of a national hero, also protested.) Another rare attempt to placate audiences over inaccuracies in a film is revealing because of the paltry effort made by the studio. Scottish newspapers and politicians mounted a campaign on behalf of the citizens of Dalbeattie, denouncing the portrayal in the film *Titanic* of William Murdoch (a native of Dalbeattie and an officer on the doomed ocean liner) who was falsely depicted as first accepting bribes from wealthy passengers to allow them into lifeboats, then shooting poor passengers rushing to get into the lifeboats and finally committing suicide. Twentieth Century Fox, which distributed *Titanic*, refused to admit that the depiction of Murdoch was inaccurate but they donated a less than princely £5000 to the prize fund of the town's school.[64]

Almost invariably, however, filmmakers have brushed off objections to the accuracy of historical or biographical film, whether these objections were made while the film was in production or after it was released. When an associate producer complained to Daryl Zanuck, then Vice President of Production at Twentieth Century Fox, about inaccuracies in the studio's forthcoming film *Lloyds of London* (1936). Zanuck lectured him that:

> Technicalities of this type never cause any trouble. In Rothschild[65] I made [Nathan] Rothschild an English Baron and there never was a Rothschild a Baron. I had the King of England give him the honour, and at the time there was no King of England as the king was in the insane asylum-and the Regent had the gout and couldn't stand up, but I used Lumsden Hare[66] and the picture in England got the same wonderful reviews it received in America and no one ever mentioned these technical discrepancies.[67]

In fact, filmmakers regarded the right to alter factual details as absolutely necessary to success. When George M. Cohan objected to inaccuracies in a projected film biography of him, the producer of the film wrote to him, stating that the artistic license to change facts is 'the only way in which a biographical picture can be made interesting and worthy'.[68] And, while occasionally there have been strident and widespread objections to the inaccuracies in historical films such as *Birth of a Nation* (1915), *Mississippi Burning* (1988), *JFK* (1991) and *U-571* (2000), no efforts were made by the makers of these films to change, or even apologize for their content. And for the most part, audiences have had little objection to deviations from historical reality in films; significantly all of the films listed in the previous sentence enjoyed considerable box-office success.

IV

While accuracy in historical films and biopics is something that both filmmakers and their audiences at least claim to value, a number of academic writers believe that such accuracy is not possible in history, much less in historical films. These scholars cite the influential work of Hayden White to maintain this position; one declares that 'The once arcane lesson of White's *Metahistory*---that historiography is about arranging and telling stories, not about delivering objective truth—is, by now, also common knowledge'.[69] Elsewhere the same author claims that a work of history has no greater claims to truth than a historical film.[70] However, what these scholars are doing is to oversimplify White's argument. White did maintain that History is a form of narrative and that to present his or her interpretation of the past, a historian must select the data to be used in the narrative. This necessary process of selection is inherently subjective and ensures that historical writing cannot be objective.[71] But nowhere does White say that the factual content of the stories historians tell is insignificant or that they can legitimately relate stories without factual content. It is also important to remember that subjectivity is not the same thing as invention. The work of historians and biographers must be perceived to conform to fact in order to have any credibility. As a historian deeply interested in the historical film has observed: 'Scholars must defend against the notion that history is no more than narration and the historian no more than a "storyteller", stringing together dates and details'.[72]

There are also scholars who argue that since objective fact is an impossible goal then biographies and biopics must also liberate themselves from the restrictions of factual accuracy. Dennis Bingham, for example, has urged that the 'biopic stopped being thought of as strictly factual, and became more commonly understood as a genre with recognizable conventions and the licence to invent creatively, while adhering to the fundamental truth of the actuality'.[73] One would think that preserving the factual basis of biopics would be an important step in preserving their distinctiveness as a genre but that is not a concern of this introduction. What is of interest is that Bingham has also reproved Lytton Strachey for writing biographies that were not based on original research.[74] Clearly Bingham feels that between biography and biographical films, there is, and should be, a great gulf fixed. In fact, there are few objections to the makers of biopics indulging in some creative licence (and none from the editors of this volume); the question is how far one can go in altering fact and yet 'adhere to the fundamental truth of the actuality'.

The relative willingness to accept a degree of fiction in biographical films is rooted in a recognition, shared by scholars in many disciplines, that, because of the nature of film as a medium, all film depictions of the past inevitably employ fiction. A number of aspects of the artificiality of films in depicting the past, such as the rendering of dialogue in films in the language of the filmmakers, rather than the language that would have been used (e.g., in films about Cleopatra, the actors do not speak in Greek, Latin or Egyptian) or the compression of years of time into several hours are readily accepted by audiences with, at best, minimal thought. Even less regarded, however, are the exorbitant demands film make on the limited data we have about the past. In every scene set in the past, the appropriate objects must be shown; but what are they? The characters must speak, but what do they say? We may have reports of some remarks or even speeches, but never enough for a film. David Herlihy has used the example of Charlemagne's coronation on Christmas night in the year 800 to illustrate the problem. While chronicles describe the event, they do not describe the interior of old St. Peter's, where the coronation took place, what the participants looked like and what they were wearing, what music was heard and what was said.[75] For events that took place before photography and film, the need for the invention of detail in depicting a historical scene is omnipresent. And even for events in the twentieth and twenty-first centuries, this need is still pressing as many events are not filmed or photographed and films and photographs are not transparent windows onto the past.

Even depicting people or physical objects accurately can be problematic because they can be difficult to place in their context. For example, Roberto Rossellini, learning that Louis XIV was only about five feet, five inches tall, cast Jean-Marie Patte, an actor of that height, to play the Sun King in his *The Taking of Power by Louis XIV*. But while this was an average height in seventeenth-century France, it is significantly below average today, and the film created a misleading impression of a small, insecure king, surrounded by people who loomed over him.[76] Conversely, while there have been many films about Henry VIII, none have yet shown the king, who was about two inches over six feet, towering over his contemporaries as Henry actually did.

But the nature of film as a medium distorts historical and biographical films far more profoundly than this. A historical or biographical film may depict an event in more vivid and memorable detail than a print account can but it cannot detail the debates over whether the event took place as pictured or whether it even took place at all. A striking example of the inability of historical and biographical films to evaluate the sources on which they are based came with Oliver Hirschspiegel's *Downfall* (2004), a film about the fall of Berlin and the last days of Hitler. The film depicts Albert Speer, Hitler's Minister for Armaments and favoured architect, defying the Führer in order to save Germans from Hitler's reprisals for their failure to win the war. A number of historians objected that Speer was the only source for this incident and that he had every reason to lie in order to rehabilitate his reputation. Hirschspiegel responded that he based his film on eye-witness accounts and the incident depicted on screen was recounted in Speer's memoirs.[77] And this is an important limitation of film in presenting history: there is no practical way to evaluate the sources on which the content of the film is based. A printed work can discuss this in the text or in footnotes but how can these crucial issues be discussed within a historical film without compromising the film's aesthetic and dramatic qualities?

The inability of films to enumerate, much less evaluate, their sources also means that films cannot present or assess different interpretations of events. As Ian Jarvis has observed, a particular viewpoint or interpretation presented in a film cannot be defended with citations of sources and objections to that viewpoint cannot be maintained.[78] A film can show Luther nailing his 95 theses to a church door in Wittenberg (and it is worth noting that there is a debate as to whether this happened) but it is virtually impossible to present the myriad varying analyses of why he defied the Church or why Luther's defiance led to the Reformation. And this is a serious objection to claims that films can truly be histories or biographies. As Ian Kershaw has observed—he is speaking of television but his remarks apply with equal force to cinema-film is least effective

> where an issue is highly contentious and subject to widely differing interpretations. The lifeblood of a history seminar is disagreement and problems of interpretation...Television history is far more directive. Problems of interpretation tend to muddy the waters and leave the viewer, confused, baffled or at least unable to decide which of variant interpretations is most valid...in a ratings-led medium, there is no room for this approach.[79]

David Herlihy has argued that the limitations inherent in the medium of film mean that historical and biographical films cannot follow historical methodology and thus should not be used to teach history and, presumably should not be regarded as historical sources: 'I do not see how films can carry a critical apparatus....If the film is intended to achieve an aesthetic response then there is no need for a critical apparatus. But if it is meant to teach history, that apparatus is indispensable'.[80]

Yet if some historians feel that the limitations of film as a medium disqualify films as a suitable means for communicating history, other scholars, most notably Robert Rosenstone, have argued that films are as valid and trustworthy a means for communicating history as print. Rosenstone expressly demands that historians:

> stop expecting films to do what (we imagine) books do. Stop expecting them to get the facts right, or to present several sides of an issue or to give a fair hearing to all the evidence on a topic, or to all the characters or groups represented in a particular situation, or to provide a detailed

> historical context for events. Stop, also, asking them to be a mirror of a vanished reality that will show us the past as it really was. Dramatic films are not and never will be 'accurate' in the same way as books (claim to be), no matter how many academic consultants work on a project and no matter how seriously their advice is taken.[81]

Earlier in the same volume, Rosenstone criticizes Natalie Davis for her comments on particular historical films because:

> Her judgements contain too much that derives from the standards of academic evidence. This puts as much of a burden on filmmakers as one would put on historians if we were to judge their renderings of the past in filmic terms and then to ask why are such works, compared to the colour, movement and excitement of the screen, so slow, stuffy, measured, colourless and silent?[82]

Another historian, Robert Toplin has concurred, stating that '*Accurate* strikes me as a troublesome and inaccurate word to employ in these discussions about cinematic history'.[83]

However neither Rosenstone nor Toplin are consistent in their views on the importance of accuracy in historical and biographical films. Rosenstone's discomfort with invented material in historical films has been commented on and he has maintained that 'To be taken seriously the historical film must not violate the overall data and meanings of what we know of the past. All changes and inventions must be apposite to the truths of discourse, and judgement must emerge from the accumulated knowledge of the world of historical texts into which the film enters'.[84] Elsewhere Rosenstone asserts that measuring whether invention in film is 'true' or 'false' has to be determined 'from the existing body of historical texts, from their data and arguments'.[85] Similarly, Toplin, despite finding accuracy a troublesome concept in discussing historical films, frequently evaluates historical films on the basis of their accuracy or inaccuracy, as when he writes of *Mississippi Burning*, *Amistad* and *The Hurricane*: 'these motion pictures contain so many elements of fictional excess and gross simplification they *deservedly* were attacked by historians and pundits in the media'.[86] And elsewhere Toplin is wary of Rosenstone's dismissal of accuracy in historical films:

> Rosenstone and other historians have awakened us to the value of being open to cinematic history, but there is a danger in pursuing their logic to

> an extreme. A consistently open-minded view of the filmmaker's efforts to fictionalise would leave us unprepared to discriminate between an admirably filmed presentation and a poor one. It would lead us toward treating almost *any* fabrication or distortion as a legitimate exercise as long as it contributed to how an audience thought about the past.[87]

Even historians who are anxious to emphasize the importance of film as histories and the role of filmmakers as historians have to take into account the accuracy of films, as they do of any depiction of the past in any medium.

Even those scholars who are most sceptical about the value of films as a means of depicting history or biography, readily admit the potency with which film uses visual imagery, and to a lesser extent, sound, to create vivid portrayals of the past. Film can let its viewers experience life as a slave or in the trenches of the First World War, to visualize the grandeur of the Colosseum rising above the houses of Rome or the myriad workers labouring on the Pyramids, with an immediacy and power no printed history can match. Occasionally, film goes even further and uses its visual resources to depict and dramatize history. In *Cabaret* (1972), for example, which is set in Germany in 1931, the protagonists go to a beer-garden in the country. A handsome boy, seen in close up, is singing a *gemütlich* song about the beauties of nature. As the camera pans down, the audience sees, for the first time, that the singer is wearing a brown uniform with a swastika armband. While the ballad becomes an anthem, promising that soon the world will belong to the singer, nearly everyone in the garden rises and joins in the singing. When the song is finished, the boy dons a Hitler Youth cap and lifts his arm in a Nazi salute. Through control of what the audience sees, and adroit manipulation of the camera, the film gives us a sense of the appeal of the Nazis, in a manner that no printed text could equal.

The capabilities of film for visual presentation have always tempted filmmakers to develop sets and props, such as James Cameron's elaborate, detailed recreation of the *Titanic*, which strive for the most authentic period detail. This quest for veracity in settings and material objects often occurs in films where concern with historical accuracy is otherwise conspicuously absent. For *Night and Day*, a 1946 biopic of Cole Porter, which brazenly rearranged or suppressed the facts of its subject's life, the Warner Bros. research department meticulously investigated minutiae such as the correct placement of the Yale insignia on a megaphone and the year when electric Christmas ornaments were first used.[88] With a similar diligence, the costumes for the medieval epic *El Cid* were all painstakingly dyed with vegetable dyes, rather than modern mineral dyes, to give the costumes a suitably authentic appearance.[89] At times the trouble taken by filmmakers to recreate the material objects used in historical and biographical films can appear obsessive. For his 2002 film, *Gangs of New York*, Martin Scorsese constructed buildings, on a set outside Rome, made of bricks, imported from the United States, which matched the appearance of nineteenth-century buildings in New York.[90] And Scorsese was trumped by Alan Pakula, who not only built a replica of the newsroom of the *Washington Post* for *All the President's Men* (1976), but also had 'authentic *Washington Post* newsroom garbage' shipped to the set of his film and used to fill the wastebaskets in the ersatz newsroom.[91] Such examples are less eccentric than they might seem to be. These gestures are not designed to impress those who watch the films: a member of the audience scanning the litter baskets surrounding Robert Redford and Dustin Hoffman is even less likely than one who is a specialist in New York bricks. These details are intended to form part of the studio's publicity campaigns. Such attention to detail is another part, like film prologues and study guides sent to teachers, of the truth claims made by filmmakers, who hope that potential audiences would be won over by such attention to accuracy. In fact, very often when the publicity for a film boasts of the careful research expended on a film, it is speaking of research on the costumes, furnishings and buildings of the time when the films are set. (The somewhat deprecatory nickname of 'costume films' for historical films is a reflection of this perceived priority for filmmakers.)

To many historians, this concern with the material culture of the past, while not entirely misplaced, reflects an undesirable set of priorities, an elevation of the values of the museum gift shop over the values of the museum itself. There is a danger that a fixation on the accuracy of props, sets and costumes can blind, not only audiences, but also critics and scholars, to the more substantive errors in a historical or biographical film. For example, Robert Burgoyne has praised Martin Scorsese's *Gangs of New York* for its accuracy because of the verisimilitude of its depiction of the Five Points in mid-nineteenth-century Manhattan and of life within the notorious slum. But Burgoyne says nothing about the film's many errors of fact, most notably its whitewashing of the violence and racism of the Draft Riots in New York City in 1863.[92] As a result of this obsession with accuracy in material objects, even a historian as enthusiastic about the ability of film to present the past as Rosenstone, bristles at 'the mistaken notion' held by filmmakers that 'history is no more than a "period look"' and its 'baleful Hollywood corollary: as long as you get the look right, you may freely invent characters and incidents and do whatever you want to the past to make it more interesting'.[93] Robert Toplin has described what historians would like to see in a historical or biographical film:

> All the details may be in place, but the historian hopes the product reflects a deep interest in the subject, a feeling for the people, the culture and the era, and a commitment to recreating the past in a responsible way.[94]

The differences between print and film have affected the portrayal of people in biographical films in different ways due to the inherent strengths and limitations of print and film. But the purposes of biographical film, didactic and commercial, have led to further pressures on how people from the past are portrayed on film.

V

Biographical films can certainly run into some of the same dangers as written biographies, but they also offer many of the same attractions. As a medium, as we have just seen, film has the advantage over the printed page of having greater potential for drama, colour and excitement. Film may even intensify both the strengths and the weaknesses inherent in written biographies, as the essays in this collection demonstrate.

Nevertheless, it is equally true that biographical films also possess the appealing qualities of biography as a genre, with the intrinsic human interest of following an individual life through all or part of its course. Above all, they have the potential to dramatize, in a vivid and accessible medium, the lived experience of prominent figures. The films discussed in this book all deal with individuals who achieved great prominence and even mythic status. They have been widely admired but in some cases also vilified, and the films about them can be closely related to these issues of popular perception and public reputation. In this collection, the reputation of an individual is sometimes closely associated with a specific set of values or beliefs, and praise or criticism of the person necessarily has implications for validating or questioning those values.

This is perhaps especially true where the individual is a widely revered public figure, as with Joan of Arc or Lincoln. In other cases, the individual and their beliefs have had a strongly polarizing effect, for example Margaret Thatcher and her policies, and a film treatment necessarily has to take some kind of stand on highly contested and controversial issues. In still other instances, it has not always been immediately clear what values a film is seeking to promote, and this can in turn provoke debate and dispute, as is evident in the essay on *El Cid*.

What is apparent is that the power and immediacy of film as a medium can provide a dramatic intensity that goes well beyond that of written biographies. Rosenstone makes this point very persuasively when he writes that

> Film may lack the ability to provide deep psychological insight, or extensive descriptions of particular intellectual or political milieus, but it can suggest with a terrifying immediacy how the past looked, and how people moved, felt, spoke and acted – in time. Unlike the written word, the biofilm, even in its flashbacks always functions in the present tense, suggesting, even making you feel as if you have lived through those moments yourself.[95]

In this way, biographical films not only offer an enjoyable and rewarding form of entertainment but also have the capacity to provoke, unsettle, shock or to reassure or console. For example, the scenes of Joan of Arc's death, or the depiction of the extreme Antarctic landscapes in *Scott of the Antarctic*, evoke the appalling nature of their subjects' sufferings with a dramatic power that is greater than the written word alone can achieve. The emotional impact of film can be heightened by appeal to the aural as well as visual senses. The ability of the soundtrack to arouse the chosen emotions of the audience potently shapes the ways in which an audience views the protagonist of biographical film. Ralph Vaughan Williams' music highlights the heroism of Scott in traversing an alien and hostile landscape, while the score in *Braveheart* powerfully creates audience empathy for William Wallace.[96] The most impassioned prose cannot stir emotions as directly and powerfully as film can and when this emotional power is used to relate the life of an individual, then the life will be presented with a drama and influence that the written word cannot match.

The power of film to dramatize and to provoke emotional responses is particularly potent in biographical films because of their focus on individuals. It is easier, both emotionally and intellectually, to identify with a person, than with a group or a cause. One scholar, contrasting the global success of *Gladiator* with the relative failure of *The Fall of the Roman Empire*, a film on which it was based and with which it shared a very similar plot, observed that one reason why *Gladiator* was far more successful than its predecessor was because of its unblinking focus on the film's hero.[97] And while many brilliant and moving films have been made about the Holocaust, the film with the greatest popular impact has been *Schindler's List*, in large part because it presents the Holocaust through the attitudes and activities of Schindler.[98] The life and lived experiences of one individual have provided the most accessible way to understand a vast and monstrous event in history.

The focus on individuals in biographical films obviously means that these films face many of the same challenges of perspective, sympathy and anachronism that biographical texts do. They run the same risk of focusing too narrowly on an individual life and losing sight of broader social and political contexts. There is perhaps a natural tendency for biographical films to exaggerate the significance and achievements of their subjects. This is often a particular danger with political figures, as the essays on Abraham Lincoln, Margaret Thatcher and John F. Kennedy below indicate, but the cases of Louis Pasteur and Robert Falcon Scott reveal that it is no less true of scientists or explorers. It is difficult to avoid the inherent problem of teleology when the end point of a life is already known in a way that it was not to the individual or their contemporaries.[99] Most films seek to achieve some kind of satisfactory closure in a way that a human life usually does not permit. Some lives ended in a particularly dramatic way, as was the case with Joan of Arc or El Cid, and the presentation of this on film raises issues of sympathy and perspective. Equally, where the subject was assassinated a decision has to be taken about whether to show that episode in sometimes gory detail or to concentrate on an earlier portion of the person's life (as in the depiction of John F. Kennedy in *Thirteen Days*).

In common with written biographies, there is also the constant danger of exaggerating the agency of a particular individual and of overemphasizing both their freedom of choice and the magnitude of their legacy. The issue of legacy is often particularly challenging when the nature of the individual's achievement is contested, as in the case of the two films about William Shakespeare, or when attitudes on key issues exemplified by the person's life have altered radically not only since their own lifetime but also since they were portrayed on film, as with *The Trials of Oscar Wilde* in 1960. Such hazards make it particularly difficult to know what perspective to adopt, and they led George F. Custen to write disparagingly that 'Hollywood biography is to history what Caesar's Palace is to architectural history: an enormous, engaging distortion, which after a time convinces us of its own kind of authenticity'.[100]

Yet the very act of making the past accessible, which historical and biographical films do so effectively, in itself distorts the past. The eminent historian Carlo Ginsburg has asserted that

> The historian's task is just the opposite of what most of us were taught to believe. He must destroy our false sense of proximity to the past because they come from societies very different to our own. The more we discover about these people's mental universes, the more we should be shocked by the cultural distance that divides us from them.[101]

Or, as the equally eminent Robert Darnton reminds us, 'We constantly need to be shaken out of a false sense of familiarity with the past'.[102] Nevertheless, as the example of the unprecedented success of the musical *Hamilton* demonstrates, making history apposite to the present is the philosopher's stone that turns the past into gold. And throughout the decades in which biographical and historical films have been made, filmmakers have diligently sought to remove contexts and material that are alien to modern audiences. A striking example of this is the way in which films consistently downplay the religiosity common to past eras. Thus, in notable, but not atypical, examples, *A Man for all Seasons* explains Thomas More's defiance of Henry as motivated by a reassuringly modern concern with freedom of conscience rather than religious conviction and *Kingdom of Heaven* sees the Crusaders, apart from a handful of extremists, as moderate and religiously tolerant.

In the vast majority of cases, biographical films insist on presenting not only an accessible past but virtuous, and more importantly, sympathetic heroes. (Interesting exceptions to this are a few notorious figures, such as Al Capone and Richard Nixon, who have been the subjects of numerous biopics, yet have not been portrayed as either sympathetic or admirable.) This means that there is a propensity for biographical films to intensify certain weaknesses of biography which have already been discussed: a bias in favour of the subject of a biography or biopic and a tendency to magnify the subject's importance. The need for likeable and virtuous heroes can obviously lead to an overt rewriting of history, but it can also have more subtle but equally important effects. The people of pre-modern eras often held beliefs and values that moderns find rebarbative; the medievalist Nancy Caciola, defending the fictionalization of characters in *Kingdom of Heaven*, stated that 'I, as a professional, have spent much time with medieval people, so to speak, in the texts that I read, and quite honestly there are very few of them that if I met [them] in the flesh I feel that I would be very fond of'.[103] The need for sympathetic subjects can present filmmakers with a stark choice of fictionalizing the attitudes, beliefs and actions of their subjects or reducing the range of people that they can present in their films. The quest for likeable protagonists can also dictate what the sources for a film are; for example, the writer of a BBC series on Charles II admitted that she chose to base the series on a biography of the king by Antonia Fraser, ignoring more recent and more critical biographies of Charles, because Fraser, unlike the others, presented her with a historical figure who could be sympathetically dramatized.[104]

The desire for biopics to be centred on people that audiences can root for, has also led to a conspicuous emphasis on marital love or romance in biographical films, no matter how much imagination is required. *Braveheart* not only supplies William Wallace with a fictitious wife, but also provides him with a passionate romance with a French princess. Similar flights of invention gave Carthage's famous general a fictitious Roman noblewoman as a lover in *Hannibal* (1960). When the subject of a biopic was as unlikely a figure for a conventional screen romance as Brigham Young, the enterprising creators of *Brigham Young-Frontiersman* (1940), simply shifted the focus of the film from Brigham Young to a fictitious young couple-played by Tyrone Power and Linda Darnell-who travel in the same wagon train as Young, to Salt Lake City. Like the animals entering Noah's Ark, the subjects of biographical films have been compelled to journey in pairs.

Yet all human lives are to a greater or lesser degree inaccessible to audiences, because human lives are complicated and disorderly. They rarely possess clear narrative arcs and often lack clear dramatic moments; they are instead seemingly rambling and unfocused. To translate human lives into biographical films often involves compressing, rearranging or even eliminating untidy facts. Of course, this is also true for translating human lives into print biographies. But there is a crucial difference. The author of a print biography can emphasize or minimize, even exclude, factual material from his or her narrative. A print biographer can condense events and to a limited degree, re-structure the events of his subject's lives. But the biographer cannot invent material, at least not without destroying his reputation. Yet the makers of biographical films will do this frequently and egregiously. For example, the film *Frost/Nixon* features a phone call from Nixon to David Frost, in which the inebriated ex-president bares his psyche to the British television personality. The phone call never occurred. And no filmmaker who has done a film on Mary Stuart has ever been able to resist filming a fictitious conversation between Mary and her cousin, Elizabeth I of England, although, in fact, the rival queens never met.

There is particular pressure on filmmakers to alter facts, or provide novel emphases to the subject's biography, in order to give the biographical film a happy ending. Robert Toplin relates a revealing example of how great this pressure can be. Toplin was 'principal creator' of a PBS film on Denmark Vesey, who was convicted of leading a slave revolt and executed in Charleston, South Carolina, in 1822. Toplin and his colleagues were concerned that because the revolt failed and Vesey died on the gallows, 'the drama would prove depressing rather than inspiring and *that audiences would reject the film because of its gloomy ending*'.[105] A fictitious ending was devised in which Vesey's son meets his mother at his father's grave and she assures him that Denmark Vesey will never be forgotten.[106] This conclusion was invented to alleviate concerns over the reception of a non-profit film; the pressure on filmmakers with budgets of tens of millions of dollars must be geometrically more intense.

Certainly some filmmakers have pole-vaulted over the inconvenient obstacles of fact in order to land on the desired happy ending. *The Virgin Queen* (1955) concludes with Walter Raleigh and his wife, Bess Throckmorton, sailing off to the New World to settle there, a denouement which ignores Raleigh's imprisonment in the Tower from 1603 to 1613, his execution in 1618 and the fact that neither he nor Bess Throckmorton ever set foot in North America. Occasionally the defeat and violent death of the subject of a biographical film is so well known that it is impossible to ignore or omit. Yet even in these circumstances, filmmakers have worked to provide a satisfactory ending, by transforming defeat into triumph and presenting death as a necessary, indeed almost planned, step in the achievement of the subject's goals. For example, the final scene to *They Died with Their Boots On*, a biopic of George Armstrong Custer, produced by Warner Bros in 1941, shows Custer's widow visiting his commander, General Philip Sheridan, after Custer's defeat and death at the Little Bighorn. She reads a letter by her late husband to the general. In the letter, Custer demands that the government honour its treaties with the Sioux and that the Indians be allowed to live in their own lands, protected by the US army. Sheridan assures Libby Custer that the government would honour Custer's wishes and he tells her, in the final line of the film, 'your soldier won his last battle after all'. Similarly ***Braveheart*** shows-in some detail-the execution of William Wallace, but it also, at the end of the film, depicts the memory of Wallace inspiring Robert the Bruce and the Scottish soldiers to fight the English and secure Scotland's liberty. The pressure on filmmakers to highlight romance and triumph in the lives of the subjects of their biopics is also present for biographers working in print. Yet the crucial difference remains: a biographer cannot invent material, even if it supports the overall interpretation which the biographer wishes to convey, while the makers of biopics have the freedom to rewrite the past to convey whatever larger messages they wish.

This is perhaps the essential difference between biography in print and biography on film, but there are others. Print biographers have chosen as their subjects people from around the globe and throughout history; in practice the same has been less true for the makers of biographical films. In the first half of the twentieth century studios in the United States and Europe dominated the film industry. This was also a time when ethnocentrism and outright racism flourished in those countries and the historical figures depicted in films tended overwhelmingly to be those from 'civilized' countries. And while important film industries developed in countries such as China, Japan and India, as a general rule (there are significant exceptions) the films made in these countries have tended not to be biographical films. As a result, the cinematic equivalent of the Mercator projection has resulted, in which certain areas of history have been unnaturally enlarged and certain others unnaturally reduced. For example, the number of biographical films about the denizens of the American West far exceeds the number of biographical films made about the inhabitants of China throughout its history.

Non-whites from within the United States and Europe have also been rarely the subject of biographical films. As one scholar has observed,

> From an African-American perspective...the generic progress of the biopic occurred in the motion picture equivalent of an all-white neighbourhood.

> While the Hollywood biopic tradition is varied and complex, the specifically African American models are sparse and one dimensional. The few exceptions prove the rule: *The Jackie Robinson Story* (1950), *The Joe Louis Story* (1953) and *St. Louis Blues*, the story of W. C. Handy, were all noteworthy products of a postwar atmosphere congenial to human rights, but though there was a *Glenn Miller Story* in 1955 and a *Benny Goodman Story* [that same year], there was no *Duke Ellington Story* in 1957.[107]

Nor has the situation greatly changed. In the past twenty-six years since *Malcolm X* was released in 1992, there have only been a handful of biopics with a black person as the protagonist: notably *Ali* (2001), *Ray* (2004), *Twelve Years a Slave* (2013) and *Mandela: Long Walk to Freedom* (2013).[108]

Women have also been underrepresented in biographical films. But that is also only part of what has been a systematic misrepresentation of women. For one thing, until at least the 1980s, the female subjects of biopics were limited to social elites-often queens and noblewomen who obtained their status through birth or marriage-religious figures, entertainers or criminals or 'loose' women. Even with a rare exception such as *Madame Curie* (1943), the focus is more on Marie Curie's marriage and relationship with her husband than it is on her scientific work. (By comparison, while *The Story of Louis Pasteur*, discussed in detail in Bart Holland's chapter in this volume, allots an important role to Pasteur's wife, it is not fixated on Pasteur's marriage.) Rigid conventions mandated that women in public life were portrayed as suffering because they abandoned their domestic role in order to pursue a career outside the home. (These attitudes may be present in even so recent a film as *The Iron Lady*.) The conventions surrounding biopics have been so intractable that Dennis Bingham has argued, not unpersuasively, that biopics about men and biopics about women should properly be regarded as forming separate genres.[109]

Yet if women were confined to the kitchen in biopics, gay people were locked in the attic. The total exclusion of even the mention of any non-heterosexual passions in the protagonists of biographical films reached truly farcical levels in films devoted to the openly gay lyricist Lorenz Hart (*Words and Music* [1948]) and the all but openly gay composer Cole Porter (*Night and Day* [1946]). A biopic of Michelangelo, *The Agony and the Ecstasy*, made in 1965, grants the artist a chaste affair (she is willing, he less so) with a daughter of Lorenzo de Medici, but completely omits any mention of his homosexual passions. Charlton

Heston, who played Michelangelo, insisted in press conferences that the artist was straight, intoning that 'There is no record of his [Michelangelo] being gay'.[110] (This ignores Michelangelo's love poetry to Tommaso dei Cavalieri and other men.) This situation has changed dramatically in the past few decades with biopics such as *Gods and Monsters* (1998), *Kinsey* (2004), *Capote* (2005) and *Milk* (2008) providing sympathetic and frank portraits of gay protagonists.

The silence of biopics on blacks, women and gays, arguably reflected traditional attitudes which affected print biographers as well as film biographers, although it can also be argued that these attitudes took longer to change in film than in print. There are subjects that are given different levels of coverage in film and print biography: for example, film biography tends to give less coverage to scientists, philosophers, writers, economists, statesman, artists and musicians than print biography does. Perhaps the most important difference in coverage is that it is rather rare for film biography to present the childhood of its subject, while this is territory very few print biographers will ignore.

An additional complication that affects film, as opposed to print, biography is the importance of the actors who portray the characters in a biopic. As George Custen observed, biopics present their audiences with a double image of a historical figure: that of the figure being portrayed and that of the actor portraying him or her.[111] Often, the actor was better known to the public than the person he or she was portraying, which often facilitated the public perceiving the historical figures as possessing the personas of the actors who played them. This could be managed to serve the messages that the biopic was supposed to send. When Henry Fonda played Abraham Lincoln or Charlton Heston played the Cid, their casting led audiences to perceive these figures as quintessentially mid-American or quasi-Biblical heroes. When Kevin Costner played Jim Garrison in *JFK*, his casting subliminally enhanced the validity of Garrison's controversial theories about Kennedy's assassination. Sometimes an actor has given added credibility to a role by playing it several times as Flora Robson and Cate Blanchett did with Elizabeth I or Judi Dench has done with Victoria.

Ellen Cheshire has argued that the striking resurgence of biographical films in the past few decades-a resurgence which incidentally shows no sign of abating-is that they are a safe, reliable type of film, which while often lacking in innovation, are often popular and profitable.[112] It might be added to this that they are often prestigious, frequently winning Oscars, Golden Globes, BAFTAs and other awards. However, there are signs that the biopic is changing or that, at a minimum, some filmmakers have been pushing against the well-defined conventions of biopics. Roberto Rossellini in *The Taking of Power by Louis XIV* (1966) and Kevin Brownlow and Andrew Mollo in *Winstanley* (1975), cast non-professionals in most of the roles and avoided such audience pleasing plot devices as romances and happy endings in their films. Alex Cox, in *Walker* (1987) used anachronistic props-computers, cans of Coca-Cola, copies of *Time* magazine and Mercedes automobiles-in narrating the story of William Walker, a nineteenth-century American adventurer who briefly ruled Nicaragua. More radically, Hans-Jürgen Syberbergs, in *Hitler, a Film from Germany* (1978), used dolls and puppets to portray Hitler in many guises, including Frankenstein's monster and Parsifal. Somewhat similarly, *I'm Not There* (2007), a biopic of Bob Dylan, had the singer portrayed by various actors including Heath Ledger and Cate Blanchett, who represented different aspects of Dylan's persona at different points in his career. These films were all critically praised and commercially unsuccessful. It will be interesting to see if the biopic stays rooted in its traditional, profitable soil or becomes more radical and also less tied to biography. Indeed, there may come a time when the biopic has become an increasingly abstract form of filmmaking which has increasingly less concern with realism or even seemingly accurate detail. But at the moment when this is being written, the biopic is a popular, usually seemingly realistic, but often inaccurate way of representing the past.

VI

Banner has written that 'reading biographies is fun', and the public 'seems to have a never-ending taste for reading about the lives of others'.[113] That point holds good for biographical films as well. Like written biographies, they continue to exercise an extraordinarily potent appeal for large numbers of people, and the essays that follow explore a series of major examples of this appeal in action. The chronological settings range from the ancient world to the present day, and the subjects are as different as politicians, scientists, explorers, authors and warriors. Biographical films thus have the capacity to portray an extremely wide variety of human experience. Far from being the poor relation of history, biography—whether in books or on film—provides a remarkably effective medium through which a broad cross-section of the population can explore and engage with the historical past.

The popularity of biographical films, combined with the copious, and largely inevitable, amounts of misleading or inaccurate historical material in them, creates a challenge for the historian. There are a number of people, both inside and outside of academia, who question the need for historians to be concerned. One scholar has mocked the tendency of 'historians to become a branch of the police and file charges of inauthenticity' at historical films.[114] It is a little difficult to understand why this scholar should feel harassed. In discussing the inaccuracies and misrepresentations in historical or biographical films, historians are not assessing or evaluating the overall worth of these films. A film, like any other artistic representation of the past, can be flawed as a depiction of history, yet admirable on aesthetic or other considerations. Historians can and do appreciate this; it is unlikely that a historian will stand up during a performance of *Macbeth* and cry out that it is an inaccurate portrayal of eleventh-century Scotland. Filmmaking is the most collaborative of all the arts and it is foolish for anyone, with expertise in any field, to evaluate a film entirely on the basis of that expertise.

Yet historians are committed to the belief that all representations of the past are significant and it would be a dereliction of their profession to ignore the contents of the most accessed sources of information about the past. As specialists in research about the past, and as people professionally concerned with how it is presented, it is natural that they comment on this. And this is generally accepted, at least where other art forms are concerned. There are historical studies of the representation of the past in dramas, paintings, statues, operas and other forms of art. Since the historical content of the history plays of Shakespeare, or the novels of Sir Walter Scott are scrutinized by historians why should this not be done for the films of, say, Cecil B. DeMille or Steven Spielberg? Moreover, casually dismissing the content of a historical or biographical film is, in effect, trivializing the film. The filmmakers' choice to make a film about particular historical events or figures is in itself a decision with significance, and should not be disregarded in assessing a historical or biographical film. Departures from accuracy, whether deliberate or unconscious, provide valuable clues as to the purposes that these films were meant to achieve and the messages that they contain. Colin McArthur's observation, writing of *Braveheart*, is true for historical and biographical films in general:

> The question of *Braveheart's* historical inaccuracies and omissions is far from unimportant, but to note them and then celebrate the film or, on the other side of the coin, note them and traduce it on that account, is to close off discussion of the crucial interface between cinema and historiography, of what it means for cinematic institutions of our own time to represent cultures distant in time and space.[115]

The contributors to this volume are concerned with precisely the interface between cinema and historiography. In order to understand how biographical films represent people of the past, we have looked at the factors that shape these representations. A first factor is to examine the political, cultural and social context in which a biopic was made and the messages about the present that these depictions of the past are trying to send. Secondly we examine the sources on which these films are based. Although it may sometimes seem like it, no biopic has ever been purely a product of invention, there is always some reference to history and this means that there is some consultation of historical sources, no matter how rudimentary. Examining the variations between these sources and the content of biopics facilitates, as has already been said, an understanding of why these biopics have been made and of the times in which they were made. The production of a biopic, from its financing to its casting, to its filming and its editing, all mould its contents; any analysis of the content and meanings of a film that ignores these details is necessarily incomplete. We also look at the reception of a biopic. This goes beyond describing its popularity to looking at its place within the historiography of its subject and its influence on the ways in which the subject and his times have been viewed.

Our approach then uses questions of historical accuracy as a starting point to examine a biopic as a part of the historiography of its subject. There are other approaches to studying biographical and indeed historical films and we would not claim for a moment that our's is the only, or indeed, the definitive methodology. But as historians, vitally interested in the transmission and receptions of perceptions of the past, we feel that it is a valid one. We hope that this volume, in a small way, might help guide the enthusiasm about the past that biographical films undoubtedly generate into reflection on, and perhaps further study of, both history and biography.

Notes

1. Custen, 1992; Bingham, 2010.
2. Welsh, 2005, p. 87.
3. Rosenstone, 2018, p. 12.
4. Hughes-Warrington, 2006, p. 1.
5. Custen, 1992, p. 7.
6. Rabinowitch, 2004, pp. 299–301.
7. Wineburg, 2001, pp. 239–42, 251–52.
8. 'Conversation Between Eric Foner and John Sayles', in Carnes, 1995, pp. 11–28.
9. See www.monticello.org/site/research-and-collections/execution-white-house-lawn.
10. Cheshire, 2015, pp. 5–6.
11. Custen, 1992, pp. 6–8.
12. Bingham, 2010, pp. 50–51, 127.
13. Morris, 1999; for examples of criticisms of this book see Dowd, 1999; Kakutani, 1999.
14. Carr, 2001, pp. 41–42.
15. Elton, 1969, pp. 169–70.
16. Quoted in Rosenstone, 2007, p. 13.
17. Nasaw, 2009, p. 573.
18. Cannadine, 2004, p. 295.
19. Kershaw, 1998, p. xxi.
20. Trevor-Roper, 1940.
21. Kershaw, 1998, p. xxi.
22. Kershaw, 1998, p. xxi.
23. Badger, 1996, pp. 256, 261.
24. Fraser, 2000, pp. 6–9.
25. See especially Caine, 2010; Lee, 2009; and the essays in France and St. Clair, 2002. Also still useful are Nicolson, 1927; Merrill, 1932.
26. Fraser, 2000, p. 5.
27. Quoted in Rollyson, 2004, p. 42.
28. Fraser, 2000, p. 4.
29. See, for example, the helpful overview in Burrow, 2009, pp. 486–93.
30. Stoianovich, 1976, p. 217.
31. Useful introductions to the *Annales* School can be found in Stoianovich, 1976; and in Burke, 1990.
32. Beales, 1996, p. 283.
33. Braudel, 1949.
34. Beales, 1996, pp. 268–69.
35. Fraser, 2000, p. 4.

36. Quoted in Beales, 1996, p. 268.
37. Beales, 1996, pp. 281–82.
38. Fraser, 2000, pp. 7, 9.
39. Jordanova, 2006, p. 46.
40. Tosh, 2015, pp. 55–56.
41. Caine, 2010; Lee, 2009.
42. Caine, 2010, p. 124.
43. See especially White, 1987.
44. Taylor, 2009, p. 641.
45. Hellbeck, 2009, p. 615.
46. Leckie, 2004, p. 13.
47. Martin, 1875–1880.
48. Gilbert, 1971–1988.
49. Kershaw, 1998, 2001.
50. Caro, 1982–2012.
51. Thomas, 2005, pp. 17, 51.
52. Banner, 2009, p. 585.
53. Jordanova, 2006, pp. 45–46.
54. Custen, 1992, pp. 34–35; Eldridge, 2006, pp. 127–28.
55. Custen, 1992, pp. 51–55.
56. Custen, 1992, p. 38.
57. Custen, 1992, p. 267, n. 7.
58. Eldridge, 2006, p. 148.
59. Custen, 1992, pp. 12–13; Toplin, 2009, p. 70.
60. Toplin, 2009, p. 69.
61. Foner, 1997; Briley, 1998, p. 393.
62. Custen, 1992, p. 128.
63. Custen, 1992, pp. 36–37.
64. Freeman, 2009, pp. 8–9.
65. Actually the title of the film was *The House of Rothschild* (1934).
66. Lumsden Hare (1874–1964) was an Irish character actor who played the Prince Regent but bore no great physical resemblance to him.
67. Quoted in Custen, 1992, p. 38.
68. Behlmer, 1986, p. 183. The film that resulted was the heavily fictionalised and very successful *Yankee Doodle Dandy* (1942).
69. Sobchack, 1996, p. 4.
70. Sobchack, 1990, p. 26.
71. White, 1975, 1978.
72. O'Connor, 1990, p. 3.
73. Bingham, 2010, p. 155.
74. Bingham, 2010, p. 32.
75. Herlihy, 1988, p. 1189.

76. Sorlin, 1990, p. 44.
77. Doran and Freeman, 2009, pp. 23–24.
78. Jarvie, 1978, p. 378.
79. Kershaw, 2004, p. 121.
80. Herlihy, 1988, p. 1192.
81. Rosenstone, 2018, p. 33.
82. Rosenstone, 2018, p. 27.
83. Toplin, 2007, p. 129.
84. Rosenstone, 1995, p. 79. Also see Burgoyne, 2008, pp. 9–10.
85. Rosenstone, 1995, p. 71. On Rosenstone's distinction between 'true' and 'false' invention see Rosenstone, 2018, p. 54.
86. Toplin, 2002, p. 203 (our emphasis).
87. Toplin, 2009, p. 17.
88. Custen, 1992, p. 128.
89. Fraser, 2004, p. 180.
90. Doran and Freeman, 2009, p. 15.
91. Carnes, 2004, p. 47.
92. Burgoyne, 2008, pp. 44–45. For criticisms of the presentation of history in *Gangs of New York*, see Gallman, 2003, pp. 1125–26; Henkins, 2003, p. 620.
93. Rosenstone, 1995, p. 60.
94. Toplin, 1988, p. 1225.
95. Rosenstone, 2018, p. 95.
96. There is an excellent discussion of the impact of the music in *Braveheart* on audiences in McArthur, 2003, pp. 160–72.
97. Rose, 2004, pp. 170–71.
98. For discussion of the impact of *Schindler's List*, see Burgoyne, 2008, pp. 100–102.
99. Brown and Vidal, 2014, pp. 3–11.
100. Custen, 1992, p. 7.
101. Quoted in Wineburg, 2001, p. 10.
102. Darnton, 1984, p. 12.
103. Prof. Caciola's comments are in the featurette 'Creative Accuracy: The Scholars Speak' in the DVD of the Director's Cut of *Kingdom of Heaven*.
104. Hutton, 2009, p. 256.
105. Toplin, 2002, p. 155 (our emphasis).
106. Toplin, 2002, pp. 155–56.
107. Doherty, 2000, p. 44.
108. Perhaps arbitrarily, we are not counting *Endgame* (2008), *Invictus* (2009) and *Mandela and De Klerk* (2013) as biopics.
109. Bingham, 2010, pp. 23–24, 213–22.

110. Elliot, 2017, p. 252.
111. Custen, 1992, p. 34.
112. Cheshire, 2015, pp. 6–7.
113. Banner, 2009, p. 586.
114. Lynch, 2003, p. 87.
115. McArthur, 1998, p. 169.

Bibliography

Ambrosius, L. E. 2004. *Writing Biography: Historians and Their Craft*. Lincoln: University of Nebraska Press.

Badger, Tony. 1996. 'The New Deal Without FDR: What Biographies of Roosevelt Cannot Tell Us', in T. C. W. Blanning and David Cannadine (eds.), *History and Biography: Essays in Honour of Derek Beales*, pp. 243–65. Cambridge: Cambridge University Press.

Banner, L. W. 2009. 'Biography as History', *American Historical Review*, 114 (2009), pp. 579–86.

Beales, D. 1996. 'History and Biography: An Inaugural Lecture', in T. C. W. Blanning and David Cannadine (eds.), *History and Biography: Essays in Honour of Derek Beales*, pp. 266–83. Cambridge: Cambridge University Press.

Behlmer, R. (ed.). 1986. *Inside Warner Bros. (1935–1941)*. London: Weidenfeld and Nicholson.

Bingham, B. 2010. *Whose Lives Are They Anyway? The Biopic as Contemporary Film Genre*. New Brunswick, NJ: Rutgers University Press.

Blanning, T. C. W., and Cannadine, David (eds.). 1996. *History and Biography: Essays in Honour of Derek Beales*. Cambridge: Cambridge University Press.

Braudel, F. 1949. *La Mediterranée et le monde méditerranéen à l'époque de Philippe II*. Paris: Armand Colin.

Briley, R. F. 1998. 'The Study Guide *Amistad*: A Lasting Legacy', *The History Teacher* 31 (1998), pp. 390–94.

Brown, T., and Vidal, Belén, eds. 2014. *The Biopic in Contemporary Film Culture*. London: Routledge.

Burgoyne, R. 2008. *The Hollywood Historical Film*. Malden, MA and Oxford: Wiley-Blackwell.

Burke, P. 1990. *The French Historical Revolution: The* Annales *School, 1929–89*. Stanford: Stanford University Press.

Burrow, J. 2009. *A History of Histories: Epics, Chronicles, Romances and Inquiries from Herodotus and Thucydides to the Twentieth Century*. London: Penguin.

Caine, B. 2010. *Biography and History*. Basingstoke: Palgrave.

Cannadine, D. 2004. 'From Biography to History: Writing the Modern British Monarchy', *Historical Research* 77 (2004), pp. 289–312.

Carnes, M. (ed.). 1995. *Past Imperfect: History According to the Movies*. New York: Henry Holt.

Carnes, M. 2004. 'Shooting (Down) the Past: Historians vs. Hollywood', *Cinéaste* 29 (2004), p. 47.

Caro, R. A. 1982–2012. *The Years of Lyndon Johnson*, 4 Vols. New York: Alfred A. Knopf.

Carr, E. H. 2001. *What Is History?* Basingstoke: Palgrave.

Cheshire, E. 2015. *Bio-pics: A Life in Pictures*. London and New York: Wallflower.

Custen, G. F. 1992. *Bio/pics: How Hollywood Constructed Public History*. New Brunswick, NJ: Rutgers University Press.

Darnton, R. 1984. *The Great Cat Massacre and Other Episodes in French Cultural History*. London: Penguin.

Doherty, T. 2000. 'Malcolm X in Print, on Screen', *Biography* 23 (2000), pp. 29–48.

Doran, S., and Freeman, T. S. 2009. *Tudors and Stuarts on Film*. Basingstoke: Palgrave Macmillan.

Dowd, M. 1999, 'Forest Gump Biography', *The New York Times*, 22 September. Accessed at www.nytimes.com/1999/09/22/opinion/liberties-forrest-gump-biography.html.

Eldridge, D. 2006. *Hollywood's History Films*. London and New York: I.B. Tauris.

Elliot, M. 2017. *Charlton Heston: Hollywood's Last Icon*. New York: HarperCollins.

Elton, G. R. 1969. *The Practice of History*. London: Fontana.

Foner, E. 1997. 'Hollywood Invades the Classroom', *New York Times*, 20 December. Accessed at www.nytimes.com/1997/12/20/opinion/hollywood-invades-the-classroom.html.

France, P., and St. Clair, William (eds.). 2002. *Mapping Lives: The Uses of Biography*. Oxford: Oxford University Press.

Fraser, A. 2000. 'The Value of Biography in History', *The Historian* 66 (2000), pp. 4–9.

Fraser, J. 2004. *Close Up: An Actor Telling Tales*. London: Oberon Books.

Freeman, T. S. 2009. 'It's Only a Movie!' in S. Doran and T. S. Freeman (eds.), *Tudors and Stuarts on Film*, pp. 1–28. Basingstoke: Palgrave Macmillan.

Gallman, J. Matthew. 2003. *Journal of American History* 90 (2003), pp. 1124–26.

Gilbert, M. 1971–1988. *Winston S. Churchill*, 6 Vols. London: Heinemann.

Hellbeck, J. 2009. 'Galaxy of Black Stars: The Power of Soviet Biography', *American Historical Review* 114 (2009), pp. 615–24.

Henkins, D. 2003. *American Historical Review* 108 (2003), pp. 620–21.

Herlihy, D. 1988. 'Am I a Camera? Other Reflections on Film and History', *American Historical Review* 93 (1988), pp. 1186–92.

Hughes-Warrington, M. 2006. *History Goes to the Movies: Studying History on Film*. London and New York: Routledge.

Hutton, R. 2009. 'Why Don't the Stuarts Get Filmed?' in S. Doran and T. S. Freeman (eds.), *Tudors and Stuarts on Film*, pp. 246–58. Basingstoke: Palgrave Macmillan.

Jarvie, I. 1978. 'Seeing Through Movies', *Philosophy of the Social Sciences* 8 (1978), pp. 374–97.

Jordanova, L. 2006. *History in Practice*. London: Hodder.

Kakutani, M. 1999. 'A Biographer Who Claims a License to Blur Reality', *The New York Times*, 2 October 1999. Accessed at www.nytimes.com/1999/10/02/books/critic-s-notebook-a-biographer-who-claims-a-license-to-blur-reality.html.

Kershaw, I. 1998. *Hitler, 1889–1936: Hubris*. London: Penguin.

Kershaw, I. 2001. *Hitler, 1936–1945: Nemesis*. London: Penguin.

Kershaw, I. 2004. 'The Past and the Box: Strengths and Weaknesses', in D. Cannadine (ed.), *History and the Media*, pp. 118–23. Basingstoke: Palgrave.

Leckie, S.A. 2004. 'Biography Matters: Why Historians Need Well-Crafted Biographies More Than Ever', in L. E. Ambrosius (ed.), *Writing Biography: Historians and Their Craft*, pp. 1–26. Lincoln, NE: University of Nebraska Press.

Lee, H. 2009. *Biography: A Very Short Introduction*. Oxford: Oxford University Press.

Lynch, D. 2003. '*Clueless:* About History', in S. R. Pucci and J. Thompson (eds.), *Jane Austen and Co.: Remaking the Past in Contemporary Culture*, pp. 71–92. Albany: State University of New York Press.

McArthur, C. 1998. '*Braveheart* and the Scottish Aesthetic Dementia', in T. Barta (ed.), *Screening the Past: Film and the Representation of History*, pp. 168–87. Westport, CT: Praeger.

McArthur, C. 2003. *Brigadoon, Braveheart and the Scots: Distortions of Scotland in Hollywood Cinema*. London: I.B. Tauris.

Martin, T. 1875–1880. *The Life of His Royal Highness the Prince Consort*, 5 Vols. London: Smith, Elder.

Merrill, D. K. 1932. *The Development of American Biography*. Portland, ME: Southworth Press.

Morris, E. 1999. *Dutch: A Memoir of Ronald Reagan*. New York: Random House.

Nasaw, D. 2009. 'History and Biography: Introduction', *American Historical Review* 114 (2009), pp. 573–78.

Nicolson, H. 1927. *The Development of English Biography*. London: Hogarth Press.

O'Connor, J. 1990. 'Introduction', in J. O'Connor (ed.), *Image as Artifact: The Historical Analysis of Film and Television*, pp. 1–9. Malabar, FL: Robert E. Kreiger.

Rabinowitch, A. 2004. *The Bolsheviks Come to Power*. London: Pluto Press.

Rollyson, C. 2004. *Reading Biography*. Lincoln, NE: Universe.

Rose, P. 2004. 'The Politics of Gladiator', in Martin W. Winkler (ed.), *Gladiator: Film and History*, pp. 150–72. Maldon, MA and Oxford: Blackwell.

Rosenstone, R. A. 1995. *Visions of the Past: The Challenge of Film to the Idea of History*. Cambridge, MA: Harvard University Press.

Rosenstone, R. A. 2007. 'In Praise of the Biopic', in Richard V. Francaviglia, Jerry Rodnitzky, and Peter C. Rollins (eds.), *Lights, Camera, History: Portraying the Past in Film*, pp. 11–29. College Station: Texas A&M University Press.

Rosenstone, R. A. 2018. *History on Film/Film on History*, 3rd edition. Abingdon and New York: Routledge.

Sobchack, V. 1990. '"Surge and Splendor": A Phenomenology of the Hollywood Historical Epic', *Representations* 29 (1990), pp. 24–49.

Sobchack, V. 1996. 'Introduction: History Happens', in V. Sobchack (ed.), *The Persistence of History: Cinema, Television and the Modern Event*, pp. 1–14. New York and London: Routledge.

Sorlin, P. 1990. 'Historical Films as Tools for Historians', in John E. O'Connor (ed.), *Image as Artifact: The Historical Analysis of Film and Television*, pp. 42–68. Malabar. FL: Robert E. Kreiger.

Stoianovich, T. 1976. *French Historical Method: The Annales Paradigm*. Ithaca and London: Cornell University Press.

Taylor, B. 2009. 'Separations of Soul: Solitude, Biography, History', *American Historical Review*, 114 (2009), pp. 640–51.

Thomas, K. 2005. *Changing Conceptions of National Biography: The Oxford DNB in Historical Perspective*. Cambridge: Cambridge University Press.

Toplin, R. B. 1988. 'The Filmmaker as Historian', *American Historical Review* 93 (1988), pp. 1210–27.

Toplin, R. B. 2002. *Reel History: In Defense of Hollywood*. Lawrence: University Press of Kansas.

Toplin, R. B. 2007. 'In Defense of the Filmmakers', in P. V. Francaviglia, J. Rodnitzky, and P. C. Rollins (eds.), *Lights, Camera, History: Portraying the Past in Film*, pp. 113–36. College Station, TX: Texas A&M Press.

Toplin, R. B. 2009. *History by Hollywood*, 2nd edition. Urbana and Chicago: University of Illinois Press.

Tosh, J. 2015. *The Pursuit of History: Aims, Methods and New Directions in the Study of History*. London and New York: Routledge.

Trevor-Roper, H. R. 1940. *Archbishop Laud*. London: Macmillan.

Welsh, J. 2005. 'Musical Biography and Film: John Tibbetts Interviewed by Jim Welsh', *Film and History* 35 (2005), p. 87.

White, H. 1975. *Metahistory: The Historical Imagination in Nineteenth-Century Europe*. Baltimore: Johns Hopkins University Press.

White, H. 1978. *Tropics of Discourse: Essays on Cultural Criticism*. Baltimore: Johns Hopkins University Press.

White, H. 1987. *The Content of the Form: Narrative Discourse and Historical Representation*. Baltimore: Johns Hopkins University Press.

Wineburg, S. 2001. *Historical Thinking and Other Unnatural Acts: Charting the Future of Teaching the Past*. Philadelphia, PA: Temple University Press.

Filming a Legend: Anthony Mann's *El Cid* (1961)

Thomas S. Freeman

On first glance, *El Cid* is not a complicated film. It purports to relate the exploits of Rodrigo Díaz, an eleventh-century Castilian soldier who was given the honourific title of 'el Cid', and who, after a successful career as a mercenary, seized the city of Valencia and established himself as a territorial prince.[1] The film follows a straight-forward linear beginning-to-end order in depicting the Cid's life, without flashbacks or narrative movement backwards and forwards in time. *El Cid* is an epic which, like most epic films, focuses on spectacle and on large-scale conflict between clearly demarcated adversaries. The film's two leads, Charlton Heston, who portrays Rodrigo, and Sophia Loren, who portrays Rodrigo's wife Jimena, give impressive performances, but the characters they portray are uncomplicated, strong-willed models of rectitude and honour. The other characters in the film are similarly good or evil, morally black or white, without shadings of grey. (Admittedly two figures in *El Cid*, Count Garcia Ordóñez—in the film a romantic rival of Rodrigo's—and King

T. S. Freeman (✉)
University of Essex, Colchester, UK
e-mail: tfreeman@essex.ac.uk

T. S. Freeman and D. L. Smith (eds.), *Biography and History in Film*, Palgrave Studies in the History of the Media,
https://doi.org/10.1007/978-3-319-89408-9_2

Alfonso VI of León-Castile begin as morally flawed adversaries of the Cid and end as his faithful allies, but these transformations are presented as sudden Damascene conversions and not as the results of complex character developments.) As for the Cid, as will be discussed below, in the film he is not only lionized as a hero, he is practically deified.

Nor is there any doubt that, like many films, *El Cid* contains messages intended to address political and social issues of the time (1960–1961) in which it was made. But at this point simplicity vanishes, for the messages discerned in *El Cid* are not only disparate, they are almost contradictory. A number of scholars have maintained that *El Cid* is an attack on totalitarianism as well as racial intolerance.[2] Other scholars, however, have rejected this claim and at least one scholar has argued that *El Cid* was propaganda on behalf of Francisco Franco, the dictator of Spain at the time the film was made, and has gone so far as to say that the film portrays the Cid as the head of a 'Fascist leadership cult'.[3] Intriguingly, it has even been argued that it is impossible to determine from the film whether the Cid is an 'icon of racial integration or a figure of racial segregation'.[4] In this chapter, I will argue that the film works, and was intended to work, as both propaganda for Franco and as propaganda for racial equality. These different messages were the result of the different goals of those involved in the collaborative enterprise of making an epic film. Samuel Bronston, the producer of *El Cid*, wished to make a profit on the film and also to establish a major film studio based in Spain; both goals necessitated gaining Franco's support. Other people involved in the film—the director, the scriptwriters and probably its star—wished, for ideological reasons, to depict the Cid as a champion of racial equality and racial harmony. It was possible for these two messages to co-exist within the same film because they had crucial elements in common: they both depended on portraying the Cid as an altruistic leader who united the people of Spain, both Christian and Moor, to work together in a common cause. The difference in the interpretations was whether the cause was defending Europe from Communism or the struggle for Civil Rights.

II

The reasons for the co-existence of these disparate messages in *El Cid* lie in the production of the film and the people involved its making. Before discussing these, however, it is useful to look at the sources on which

El Cid was based. Here also, the film is not as straight-forward and uncomplicated as it appears to be on the surface. There are four contemporary or nearly contemporary, accounts of the Cid. Two of these are accounts by Moslem historians, one written before the Cid's death in 1099 and the other in 1109.[5] These are largely hostile to the Cid, and while important to historians, they were not used in the making of *El Cid*. The other two are by Spanish Christians: a Latin poem, the *Carmen Campi Doctoris* ('The Song of the Campeador'), celebrating the Cid's exploits and very probably written in his lifetime, and the *Historia Roderici* ('The History of Rodrigo'), a Latin prose life of the Cid, probably written in the first quarter of the twelfth century.[6] These last two, largely laudatory, accounts are the beginning of an extensive literary outpouring which transformed Roderigo Díaz into a legendary hero whose achievements, real and imagined, were celebrated for centuries. However, they were also relatively little used for *El Cid*.

The flood of literature honouring the Cid, which included chronicles, hagiographies, ballads, and eventually plays and film, crested with the great medieval Spanish epic, the *Poema de Mio Cid* ('The Poem of my Cid') written in the years 1201–1207.[7] It has been commonly assumed—not least by Charlton Heston—that *El Cid* is based on the *Poema de Mio Cid*, but this is not the case.[8] A few episodes, in the film are loosely based on the *Poema*, and there are quotations from or close paraphrases from the *Poema* in *El Cid* but much of the film was derived from other sources.[9]

One of the primary sources for *El Cid* is not a medieval work at all, but Pierre Corneille's popular and influential drama, *Le Cid*, which was first performed in Paris in 1636. This work drew much of its content from some early seventeenth-century works of literature on the Cid, which in turn drew on traditional ballads about him. Yet despite literary roots that go back to the late Middle Age, Corneille's play contains almost no historically accurate material.[10] However circumstances led to its inclusion in *El Cid*. Shortly before the filming was scheduled to begin, both Heston and Loren expressed their dissatisfaction with the existing script; in fact, Loren had threatened to abandon *El Cid* unless the script was rewritten. Ben Barzman, a blacklisted writer, was hired to revise the script on short notice. According to Barzman's wife Norma, her husband remembered having seen Corneille's play performed in Paris and hurriedly adapted it for the film. Barzman's new script met with the approval of both Heston and Loren.[11]

Yet while the first half of *El Cid* closely follows Corneille's play, there are interesting alterations and embellishments. In Corneille, a young Rodrigo is betrothed to Jimena, the daughter of the king's champion, the Count Gormas.[12] However, Rodrigo's father, in a quarrel with Gormas, calls the Count a liar. Gormas strikes Rodrigo's father. Rodrigo asks that Gormas apologise to his father, but Gormas refuses. Since his father is too old to fight, Rodrigo feels impelled by honour to challenge Gormas to a duel. Rodrigo kills Gormas in the duel. Jimena, despite being passionately in love with Rodrigo, feels impelled by honour to avenge *her* father. The Moors attack and Rodrigo distinguishes himself in battle against them. Jimena then approaches the king and demands justice for her father. She requests that a single combat between her champion and Rodrigo be arranged and although she dislikes her champion, she publicly offers to marry him if he kills Rodrigo. The king, sympathizing to an extent with Jimena, but unwilling to lose Rodrigo's services, agrees but adds a stipulation of his own: if Rodrigo wins, Jimena will marry him. After the duel, Jimena's champion comes to her carrying a bloody sword, and she assumes that he has killed Rodrigo. Without giving her champion, a chance to speak, Jimena, thinking that Rodrigo is dead confesses her love for him. Her champion then reveals that Rodrigo had disarmed him but spared his life. The king orders that Jimena wed Rodrigo. She agrees, but asks for a year's delay in order to mourn her father properly. The king agrees to this and Rodrigo departs joyfully.

In the film, Gormas also hits Rodrigo's father, Rodrigo demands an apology, Gormas refuses, a duel ensues and Gormas is killed. In the film, Jimena also swears vengeance although she deeply loves Rodrigo. The emotional relationships of Corneille's play are maintained through all of this, with Gormas admiring Rodrigo's sense of honour in wishing to avenge his father, Jimena torn between love for Rodrigo and her duty as a daughter and with Rodrigo admiring and understanding Jimena's sensed of honour and consequent desire to avenge her father. But instead of having Rodrigo go off to fight the Moors, the film has Rodrigo act as the king's champion (replacing the deceased Gormas) in a single combat with the champion of the king of Aragon over possession of the city of Calahorra.[13] Rodrigo is the victor and asks the king to grant him Jimena's hand in marriage. The king agrees. Jimena promises Ordóñez that she will marry him if he kills the Cid. Ordóñez conspires with some Moors to ambush Rodrigo, but the Cid's friend the emir al-Mu'tamin rescues him. The marriage takes place but Jimena remains hostile to

Rodrigo and informs him that she conspired with Ordóñez to have him killed. Their marriage is not consummated and Jimena's enmity only turns back to love when Alfonso VI unjustly exiles Rodrigo.

The sections of *El Cid* which are based on Corneille's drama take up just under half of the running time of the film. Thus a substantial part of *El Cid* is based on a seventeenth-century play, which was significantly revised by the screenwriters. A major alteration, the continuation of Jimena's animosity to the Cid, even after their marriage, was a concession to audience expectations. Corneille's solution of the dramatic conflict between Jimena and Rodrigo is to have the king order their marriage. This is unsatisfactory to modern audiences, who expect (at least in fiction) that marital relations be based on love. Barzman needed to resolve Corneille's dilemma in a way that had Jimena willingly renew her love for the Cid, and, at the cost of some plausibility, he did so. But while the first part of the film is ahistorical, it is also, in dramatic terms, successful.

El Cid can be divided into three parts. The first is the section largely based on Corneille's play and it runs from the estrangement between the Cid and Jimena through their unconsummated wedding. Then there is what might be viewed as a bridging section, which begins with King Fernando's death and the ensuing struggle for power between his sons Sancho and Alfonso and which ends with the victorious Alfonso ordering the Cid into exile. The next scene, in which the Cid departs into exile, begins the third section. In this scene, the Cid reconciles with Jimena and brings what could be called the Corneille storyline, that of tragic love and hatred between the couple, to an end. A new theme starts at the end of this scene as the Cid's followers demand that he lead them and he reluctantly leaves Jimena. This third section of the film moves largely away from the personal and focuses on the Cid's evolution from hero into national legend. The eminent film scholar Jeanine Basinger has observed that *El Cid* is nearly unique among film epics in that the human story is maintained along with the spectacle. Much of this is due to the dominance of the material from Corneille in the first half of *El Cid*. 'Because the human, intimate portion of El Cid's story is so well developed and believable, the audience accepts Rodrigo as a human being who actually is transformed into a legend. This gives the ending of the film its power'.[14]

The two later sections of the film employ information gathered by, and were also shaped by, Ramón Menéndez Pidal, the historical consultant for *El Cid*. In hiring the venerable scholar (Menéndez Pidal was born in 1869), the filmmakers were getting the services of the Cid's most influential biographer and one of the greatest authorities on eleventh-century Spain. They were also hiring a scholar whose pronounced views on the Cid while according well with the interpretation of the filmmakers rendered much of the film's accuracy problematic to later historians of medieval Spain.[15]

Menéndez Pidal was the son of a magistrate who lost his position because he refused to swear allegiance to the Spanish constitution of 1869, a liberal document established after the Revolution of 1868 toppled the monarchy. Although Menéndez Pidal's family was not wealthy, it was well connected. Menéndez Pidal's uncle, the Marqués de Pidal, owned the oldest extant manuscript of the *Poema de Meo Cid* and Ramón made it the gateway to his life's work. Ultimately, Menéndez Pidal would publish an authoritative edition of the *Poema* and in 1896, he published the first of many works on the medieval Spanish epic. In 1900 he married and during the honeymoon (which was spent retracing the Cid's travels in exile), the newly married couple heard a provincial washerwoman singing a ballad, hitherto unrecorded, about the death of a Spanish prince in the late fifteenth century. They recognized that even though the prince had died nearly four centuries previously the ballad contained accurate historical information. This incident confirmed Menéndez's conviction that medieval ballads and poems contained authentic information even though they had been in oral circulation for long periods of time.[16] Menéndez Pidal felt confident in drawing on these literary sources as valid historical evidence for events that took place long before they were committed to writing. He also dated the composition of the *Poema de Mio Cid* to 1140; most scholars today date the work to the first decade of the thirteenth century.[17] Menéndez Pidal's earlier dating of the *Poema* would, if accepted, enhance its value as a historical source by moving it closer in time to the events it recounts.

Richard Fletcher has observed that there are 'three important features which differentiate the Cid of the poem from the Rodrigo Díaz of history'.[18] The *Poema* portrays the Cid as a Castilian hero, as a crusading hero (it does not mention his services as a mercenary to Moslem employers) and as consistently loyal to Alfonso VI of Castille. These qualities were seen as particularly necessary and admirable at the time when the *Poema* was written and the kingdom of Castile was locked in a bitter struggle with the Almohads, a new wave of Moslem invaders from

North Africa.[19] But these same qualities were also qualities that Menéndez Pidal felt were necessary and admirable in Spain in the last half of the nineteenth century and the first half of the twentieth century. Self-sacrificing loyalty to Castille, to the Church and to the monarchy were required to see Spain through weak governments and internal strife. In a heartfelt passage in his masterwork on the Cid, written in the tumultuous year of 1929, Menéndez Pidal wrote that the Cid's heroic example could dispel the cynicism and apathy that had engulfed Spain 'desde el amago 98' [since the bitter year of 1898] when Spain had lost its empire and been humiliated in the eyes of the world.[20] Modern scholars, lacking the particular biases that permeated Menéndez Pidal's work, have tended to see the Cid as an adventurer, who allied with Christian and Moslems to suit his own interests and whose conquest of Valencia was motivated by personal ambition, not a desire to serve his king.

Menéndez Pidal, aware of the film's potential to present his interpretation of the Cid's life and times to a global audience, threw himself into the project with zeal. He worked with Barzman and with Charlton Heston, in order to see that his interpretation of the Cid and his career reached the screen.[21] (Menéndez Pidal, going beyond what is normally expected of a historical consultant, spent a month with Miklós Rózsa, who composed the score for *El Cid*, examining and discussing thirteenth-century *cantigas*, which Rózsa drew on to lend a medieval Spanish flavour to the score.)[22] But Menéndez Pidal's influence can be seen most clearly on Charlton Heston. Before meeting the venerable scholar, Heston wrote in his journal:

> My research on El Cid is going slowly, but usefully. There's a hell of a lot more in the man than there is in the script, more than the bloodless ideal of medieval chivalry that the legend leaves us with. He seems, as I read the rather meagre material the Paramount research department turned up, to have been nearly as often a bad man as a good one.[23]

But when the time came to write his autobiography, Heston had a different view of the Cid:

> Some modern historians, trying to clear the cloud of Arthurian legend that obscures him, have cast the Cid simply as a ruthless mercenary. Certainly they were endemic a few centuries later, the Italian *condotieri* [sic], the Spanish conquistadores who conquered South America....I don't think

> that it's a realistic view of the Cid. Even if we strip away a thousand years of mythic excess, history still gives us a battered, striving man, loyal to the king who exiled him and imprisoned his wife and daughters.[24]

This new perspective on the Cid certainly reflects the viewpoint of Menéndez Pidal who created a favourable impression on Heston when he met the actor. Heston would later describe the Spanish scholar's 'blazingly vigorous mind' and marvelled at the 'fervour with which he led me through his subject'.[25] It has been observed that as a result of the historian's involvement in *El Cid*, 'Menéndez Pidal's Cid has been made known to millions'.[26] Yet if *El Cid* presented Menéndéz Pidal's interpretation of the Spanish hero, it was because it was an interpretation that was useful to the filmmakers. As we shall see, all of the different messages that the film sought to convey depended on the heroism of the Cid. And a heroic champion struggling for his king and his country against disloyalty, ingratitude and powerful enemies provides the dramatic cohesion for the second half of the film.

Menéndez Pidal's influence on *El Cid* went beyond his validation of a heroic Rodrigo Díaz, which the filmmakers wanted, indeed, needed to portray. The scholar's decades of research into the medieval literature on the Cid, provided numerous colourful and dramatic anecdotes that were cleverly woven into the screenplay of *El Cid*. For example, in the film, the Cid rescues Alfonso, the future king of Castile, from the imprisonment to which his brother Sancho has consigned him, singlehandedly besting thirteen knights in the process. The rescue of Alfonso is entirely the invention of the scriptwriters, but the tale of the Cid defeating fifteen (not thirteen) knights in a single fight appears in the *Historia Roderici*.[27] Later in *El Cid*, the Cid and Jimena, going into exile, are looking for shelter but their search is fruitless as Alfonso VI had ordered that no one aid them. A young girl comes up to the Cid and tells him that her father cannot give him and Jimena shelter because the king would have their hands cut off. She then softly adds that if they wait until dark and move slowly, no one will see them enter her father's barn and they could spend the night there. Surprisingly, this scene is based on an episode in the *Poema de mio Cid*. Here the Cid, riding into exile, comes across an isolated house. There is no response to his shouted inquiries whether anyone is there, even though he kicks at the door. Finally a nine year old girl comes out and says that her family has been told that if they give him shelter, their eyes will be put out. She asks God's blessing on the Cid and then goes back into the house and shuts the door.[28]

Stories of the legendary Cid, drawn from poems, ballads, monastic chronicles and other sources, are adapted and inserted throughout *El Cid*. The choice of anecdotes for inclusion seems not to have been based on the perception that one particular source was more accurate or more complete than the others. Instead, anecdotes were cherry picked from all manner of sources, based on their dramatic or aesthetic usefulness.

The most striking example of this is the episode at the very end of *El Cid*, where the dead body of the hero is strapped to his horse and he rides into battle for one last time. This is very loosely based on a pious legend, now known as the *Leyenda de Cardeña*, written in the monastery of Cardeña in 1272. The Cid was buried at the monastery and a cult venerating his memory flourished. The *Leyenda* is the culmination of this cult. It relates that St. Peter—the patron of the monastery—appeared in a vision to the Cid shortly before the hero's death. The saint informs the Cid that God loves him so much that He will grant him victory in battle even after the Cid is dead. The Cid's body is embalmed, clothed, booted, spurred and mounted on his charger. It is led in procession towards Castile. At this time the Castilian troops win a victory, with the celestial aid of St. James, over the forces of 'the king of Tunis'.[29] A less reliable source could hardly be found, but this story (with the supernatural elements purged) exerted a powerful appeal to the filmmakers. Anthony Mann, the director of *El Cid*, stated that the reason that he wanted to make that film was that he loved the concept of an ending where a dead man rides to victory on his horse.[30]

There were yet other reasons to glean anecdotes from the vast harvest of literature on the Cid, reasons related to the example the Cid presented and virtues which were considered relevant to the world the Cid had left nearly nine hundred years before. Which virtues these were and the ways in which they were relevant would vary radically among the different filmmakers and were also a reflection of how and why *El Cid* came to be made.

III

In the years following World War II, Hollywood faced a deepening crisis from the threat of a new technology: television. By 1953, there were televisions in two-thirds of American households, while film audiences had declined by twenty-five percent from 1946.[31] Hollywood's strategy for countering the threat television presented was to give audiences what television could not: full-colour, wide-screen spectacles.

Fortunately for Hollywood, big screen westerns, historical epics and Biblical epics proved to be very popular with audiences in this period. Unfortunately for Hollywood, these lavishly produced films were expensive to make at a time when the studios were suffering from diminished revenues, thanks not only to television but also to a Supreme Court decision, made in 1948, which forced the studios to divest themselves of the theatre chains that they once owned. In fact, the studios could no longer maintain many of their production facilities.[32]

The decline of the studios facilitated the rise of independent producers. These were usually successful directors or actors—such as Jimmy Stewart, Kirk Douglas, Burt Lancaster and Stanley Kramer—and they supplied much of the funding for their films. Major studios might invest additional funding and generally managed publicity and the distribution of the independent pictures, but it was the independent producers who took the lion's share of the financial risks in making them.[33] These producers lacked the extensive resources of the studios and as a result, 'in the feverish atmosphere of Hollywood in the 1950s, the search by independent producers for the cheapest production costs rose virtually to the level of a holy quest.'[34] A very effective way to reduce the expenses of film production was to make the picture overseas, where labour was markedly cheaper than in the USA. Other factors also made filming outside of the US attractive. Some governments provided incentives, such as tax concessions and even subsidies, to encourage foreign producers to film there.[35]

The factors that made other countries attractive for US filmmakers were the existence of equipment and facilities for film production, low wages along with low costs in general and a government's willingness to aid a filmmaker. The number of countries meeting these criteria was finite, particularly since the Cold War made filming beyond the Iron Curtain an arduous prospect for Western filmmakers, at least in the 1950s and early 1960s. Britain was a popular destination for US filmmakers as it possessed first-rate production facilities and an almost bottomless pool of actors who spoke, more or less, the same language as Americans. But the strong pound and strong unions made filming there only somewhat less expensive than filming in America.[36] Production costs in France steadily rose through the postwar years while the French governments had ambivalent attitudes towards, and provided fluctuating levels of support for, foreign filmmakers.[37] Italy had a thriving film industry of its own and an excellent film infrastructure, while its government encouraged foreign filmmaking in the country. But the costs of filmmaking in Italy were steadily rising.[38] Another popular overseas venue for filmmaking was Mexico. Expenses were low there, it was conveniently close to the USA and it had production facilities and trained technicians. But powerful unions pushed the production costs upwards and recurring strikes paralyzed film production; at the same time political and cultural strains periodically created tensions between American film crews and the Mexicans.[39]

And so, ultimately, filmmakers began to look to Spain, which possessed a basic film infrastructure, wonderful scenery and a weak currency. Yet there were considerable drawbacks to filming in Spain. The most obvious was that under Francisco Franco's dictatorship, a gimlet eye was fixed on films that were made in Spain. For example, wariness about the glorification of proletariat rebellion led to Franco's regime initially refusing to allow *Spartacus* to be filmed there.[40] Even films of which the Spanish government approved, did not escape oversight. Stanley Kramer's *The Pride and the Passion*, a film about Spanish partisans and English army officers allying to wage a guerrilla war against Napoleon's armies in Spain, had the support of Franco himself. Nevertheless, this did not stop the Minister of Information and Tourism from reproving Kramer for depicting the Spanish army in the film as completely shattered and demoralized by their defeats. Kramer was not only told that this 'inappropriate presentation is completely false'; he was also warned that it 'is incompatible with a request for the co-operation of that same army'. Kramer duly made the requested changes.[41]

The possibility of reprisals against non-compliant filmmakers was a very real one. In 1963, Columbia Pictures sought permission to film *Behold a Pale Horse* in Spain. After the script, about a Spanish anarchist's one man campaign opposing Franco's rule over the Basques, had been read by the Ministry of Information and Tourism, they not only refused to allow the film to be made in Spain, they also threatened to close Columbia's subsidiary in Spain if the film was made anywhere. The film was made in France and Columbia Pictures was expelled from Spain. The ban on Columbia was lifted in 1966, but the point had been made. The Franco regime also objected to a planned film of *The Royal Hunt of the Sun*, a successful West End and Broadway play about Francisco Pizarro's capture and execution of the Inca emperor Atahualpa, and threatened MGM with closure of its operations in Spain. Mindful of what had happened to Columbia, MGM pulled out of *The Royal Hunt of the Sun*.[42]

Aside from pervasive government supervision, another serious drawback to filming in Spain was the fact that while Spain did have existing film facilities, they were rudimentary. A report from the US embassy in 1960 noted that Spain did not have the film, cameras, sound equipment and lights available that US filmmakers required.[43] But the very low cost of filming in Spain was an ace that trumped all other disadvantages. Stanley Kramer's *The Pride and the Passion* cost 3.5 million dollars to make, but as Kramer noted 'It would have cost twice that much if we'd made it anywhere else....The country has almost no facilities for film production for making movies. That sounds expensive at first. But in the long run we saved money—big money.'[44] Ted Richmond, the producer of *Solomon and Sheba*, a Biblical epic filmed in Spain in 1958–1959, which was driven over schedule by the death of its star Tyrone Power during production—a tragedy which sent the film at least a million dollars over budget—stated 'I know that if we had finished "Solomon and Sheba" with Ty Power, we would have been $300,000 under budget'.[45] The low cost of filming in Spain ensured that both of these films made substantial profits. This lack of expense was so attractive that Robert Rossen, Stanley Kramer and Kirk Douglas filmed there in the years 1955–1960, despite Franco's notoriously conservative dictatorship and their well-known liberal politics.

Having American films made in Spain was also becoming increasingly attractive to Franco's regime. Spain had been an international pariah since Franco's close alliances with the Fascist governments of Germany and Italy during and after the Spanish Civil War (1936–1939). Only the Cold War and Spain's possession of ideal locations for American air and submarine bases allowed Franco to gain a limited acceptance from the Western powers. But while Franco's position was secure by 1953, when he and President Eisenhower agreed to the Madrid Pact, which entailed de facto US recognition of Franco's rule, the dictator still presided over a country with a stagnant economy. A major goal of the Franco regime was to boost tourism to Spain as this would bring much needed hard currency into the country.[46] Films shot in Spain could powerfully assist in promoting tourism, first by giving Madrid a reputation as a locale habituated by celebrities and secondly by showing international audiences Spanish castles and scenic marvels. At the same time, films could emphasize the cultural heritage of Spain and present suitably heroic episodes, such as resistance to the Napoleonic invasion, from Spanish history.[47] A letter of March 1956, from the Information and Tourism minister to the minister of the Spanish Army made the importance Franco's government attached to these objectives clear. After informing the head of the army that *The Pride and the Passion* would soon begin filming in Spain and that it had Franco's personal support, the letter continued:

> Given the magnitude of producing this film, and that the film emphasizes the heroic comportment of the Spanish people against Napoleon's troops, this producer requests to the greatest extent possible as determined by the Army Ministry, facilities of troops and materiél in order to achieve the ambition of this film. Permit me, General, to state that this Ministry finds itself extremely interested that the realization of the film under discussion will achieve the most brilliant result in order to emphasize to the world these facets of our history.[48]

And soon a producer would appear who would establish an even tighter and more symbiotic relationship with the Franco regime.

Until 1959, filming in Spain was done by individual independent producers who were based overseas. In the late 1950s, however, Samuel Bronston, after a chequered career in Hollywood, arrived in Spain and began to pursue his dream of establishing a major studio in Spain.[49] Bronston's first film made in Spain, *John Paul Jones* (1959), was neither a critical nor a financial success. But Bronston's next film, the Biblical epic *King of Kings* (1961), was a considerable hit. Bronston's third film would be *El Cid*. Basing a film on Spain's national hero was very shrewd. It fitted in perfectly with the Franco regime's goal of glorifying the Spanish past. At the same time, Franco personally, and publicly, identified himself with the Cid; a film about *el Campeador* offered splendid opportunities for extolling *el Caudillo* and could attract his active patronage.[50] Moreover, a film about the Cid could slake the public's taste for epic films and even be tied to the genre of Biblical epics which had proven to be hugely popular in the U.S. and Europe. Casting Charlton Heston, the lead in *The Ten Commandments* and *Ben Hur*, as the hero in Bronston's Spanish epic was a giant step to establishing this linkage, but it was also, more subtly, underscored in *El Cid*. As he is starting on his journey into exile, the Cid gives a drink to a leper named Lazarus. There are several messages in this scene which will be discussed later, but it has been observed that this encounter echoes scenes from Ben Hur where the hero secretly visits his mother and sister who have been stricken with leprosy and where Jesus gives the parched Ben Hur a drink of water as he is being taken to the galleys.[51]

Bronston's business operations were particularly well-adopted to financing epic films, despite the enormous expense. Rather than financing a film as it was being made from studio funds, Bronston received payment from the distributors of the film in advance. In order to do this he had to produce his films on a very tight schedule, since he needed to have impressive footage from his newest film to show to the distributors or their representatives to persuade them to invest in it.[52] Bronston also received important financial support from Pierre S. Du Pont III. The Du Pont company sold oil in Spain, but it was paid in Spanish pesetas, a soft currency. Spanish law forbade these funds from being transferred out of the country. By investing in a film in Spain, and using the pesetas to pay basic production costs, an investor could collect a share of the profits, paid in hard currencies that the film made overseas.[53] Du Pont had invested in Bronston's films to collect hard currency for his company's oil sales, but he went further and signed notes guaranteeing Bronston's payments in the sum of millions of dollars. Bronston was able to borrow yet more money on the strength of these guarantees.[54] Bronston's system was vulnerable; his film empire was effectively a tripod resting on three legs: a steady stream of films that made substantial profits, the backing of DuPont and the support of Franco's regime. Ultimately, two of these legs would fail and Bronston's studio and businesses would collapse. But until that happened he was able to spend enormous amounts of money on his films.

This money was spent lavishly on costumes, props—including armour and all manner of medieval weaponry—and sets. Key scenes in *El Cid* are set in the cathedral at Burgos. However, filming there was deemed unsatisfactory as the cathedral was rebuilt in the thirteenth century, and extensively renovated afterwards in late Gothic style, which was unknown in the Cid's time. So a massive exterior and partial interior of the Romanesque cathedral was built for the film. It took ninety days to construct and was solid enough to hold replica stained glass windows, created by twentieth-century Spanish artisans. As the production designer for the film stated, 'We didn't spare anything, we knew the money was there'.[55] The climax of the Cid's career, and also of *El Cid*, was the capture of Valencia. This was filmed in Peñíscola, a town with a thirteenth-century castle, on the seacoast north of Valencia. Unlike Valencia, or almost every other town in twentieth-century Spain,

Peñíscola was largely contained within its medieval walls. There were sections, however, where television antennas and other vestiges of modernism were visible; these were concealed by seemingly medieval walls, built for this purpose by hundreds of local workmen labouring for three months.[56]

Yet Bronston was also able, through his alliance with Franco, to command even further resources to use in filming *El Cid*. For the battles in front of 'Valencia' 1700 troops from the Spanish army were placed at Anthony Mann's disposal as well as 500 mounted policemen from Madrid. (Bronston paid two dollars a day for each of these military extras, this fee included the horses.)[57] Bronston also had carte blanche to film in Spain's historic buildings. No models or miniatures were used in the film. In addition to Bronston's sets, four of Spain's most magnificent castles were photographed in the film: Ampudia, presiding over the raided village the Cid rescues at the start of the film; Torrelobatón, as the castle at Vivar, the Cid's birthplace; Belmonte, looming over the Cid's single combat for Calahorra and, as has been noted, Peñíscola, as Valencia. And as icing on an already rich cake, the Franco regime certified that *El Cid* was a film 'in the Spanish National Interest', entitling its makers to a substantial subsidy from the Ministry of Tourism and Information.[58] As it was, the low cost of filming in Spain and Franco's assistance helped ensure that *El Cid* made an enormous profit. The cost of making the film was estimated at 6.25 million dollars (Mann estimated that it would have cost 30 million dollars to have filmed it in the US).[59] *El Cid* made over 12 million dollars in domestic rentals in the US, which made it the fourth highest grossing film released in America in 1961. Rentals represent only a fraction of what a film earns and it has been estimated that *El Cid* made over 26 million dollars in the US.[60] And these figures represent only the US earnings; the earnings in Europe and the rest of the world must have been substantial.

IV

Bronston, like Faust, made a bargain which made his dreams come true, at least for a time. But what did Mephistopheles get in return? Put more directly, we have seen that there are assertions that *El Cid* was a Francoist film. What truth is there to these accusations? Obviously *El Cid* fulfilled a number of propaganda objectives for the Franco regime: it glorified the Spanish past by portraying one of its greatest heroes and it presented vistas and historic buildings designed to entice tourists to visit Spain. But *El Cid* went beyond this, extolling Franco to an extent that no American film had ever done or would ever do again. It is possible that Franco himself played a role in shaping the script of *El Cid*; he is credited with having written the screenplay for a Spanish film, *Raza* ('Race') which was released in 1941.[61] While Franco's direct influence on *El Cid* must be speculation, there is little doubt that officials of his government did supervise, and very probably contributed to, the film. Enrique Llovet, a career diplomat and the First Secretary of the Ministry of Foreign Affairs *Instituto de Cultura Hispaníca*, also worked as a scriptwriter and consultant for Bronston from 1959 until 1964 and it is very likely that he played a role in shaping *El Cid*.[62]

Lovett definitely wrote the scripts for two out of four films that Bronston made for the Spanish government, films which demonstrate that Bronston had no qualms about making propaganda on behalf of Franco.[63] Two of these films, *El Camino Real* ('The Royal Road'), made in 1963 and *Sinfonia easpañola* ('A Spanish Symphony'), made in 1964, were relatively innocuous. The first of these, a thirty minute film about Juniperro Serra, a Spanish Franciscan who founded a string of missions in eighteenth-century California, was an attempt to remind Americans of past cultural ties to Spain. The second film was a travelogue of Spain, almost two hours in length. While this film was a part of the Franco's regime's cherished goal of promoting tourism, it also, tendentiously portrayed a prosperous country, free of censorship or repression. Nevertheless, these films were anodyne and uncontroversial compared to the other two films Bronston made for the Spanish government. One of these, also notionally designed to promote tourism, was *El Valle de los Caidos* ('The Valley of the Fallen') extolling the grandiose monument and cathedral that Franco had built to honour himself and the dead of the Spanish Civil War. What made this project bitterly controversial—and a fact not mentioned in Bronston's film—was that Franco's monumental complex was built by the forced labour of Republican prisoners.[64] The final film, *Objetivo 67* ('Objective '67'), made in 1963, was the most overtly political of these films; presenting Franco's four year plan for economic development. It also praised the advances in productivity and technology that had allegedly taken place under Franco's rule.[65]

Thanks to Bronston's acquiescence, and almost certainly, thanks to the intervention of Franco's officials, *El Cid* contains unmistakeable elements of Francoist propaganda. Scholars have pointed to some scenes which may have been intended as propaganda on behalf of *El Caudillo*: John Aberth claims that a scene of the Cid being hailed by his troops after the fall of Valencia was meant to invoke Franco being hailed by his followers, Neal Rosendorf more plausibly argues that the spectacle of churches destroyed by Moslem armies at the beginning of the film was intended to recall the Loyalist destruction of churches and persecution of priests and nuns during the Civil War.[66] However, there are two themes in *El Cid* which are unmistakeably Francoist propaganda. The first appears at the beginning of the film. After the narrator has praised the Cid as a unifier who brought Spaniards together against a common enemy that enemy is revealed. Ben Yusuf (played by Herbert Lom), the leader of the Almoravids, who invaded Spain in the eleventh century and who are portrayed in *El Cid* as a fanatical Moslem horde, berates the emirs of Spain, whom he regards as weak and lacking in zeal.

> The Prophet has commanded us to rule the world. Where in all your land of Spain is the glory of Allah? When men speak of you they speak of poets, music-makers, doctors, scientists. Where are your warriors? You dare call yourselves sons of the Prophet? You have become women! Burn your books! Make warriors of your poets! Let your doctors invent new poisons for our arrows! Let your scientists invent new war machines! And then—Kill! Burn! Infidels live on your frontiers, encourage them to kill each other. And when they are weak and torn, I will sweep up from Africa and the empire of the one God, the True God, Allah, will sweep across Spain, then across Europe, then—the whole world.[67]

To twenty-first century audiences this seems to depict militant Islamic groups such as al-Qaeda or Isis, but in the world of the early 1960s, when these groups did not exist, this rhetoric reflected American fears of Communist plans to sow internal divisions in the 'free world' and then overrun separate countries until world domination was achieved.[68] Franco had been zealously portraying himself (not without success) to the US and European powers as the unifier of Spain who prevented Communists from establishing a beachhead in the Iberian peninsula and then overrunning Europe.[69] 'Ben Yusuf' serves a necessary dramatic purpose in the film as the Cid's nemesis but his first appearance in *El Cid* is also a reminder to American audiences of Franco's claims that Spain was a bulwark against the spread of Communism.

Another feature of Franco's self-representation that is echoed in *El Cid* is the presentation of the Cid as a man of destiny, who reluctantly sacrifices, at the urgent pleas of his followers, his hopes of personal happiness in order to save Spain.[70] This theme is foreshadowed early in *El Cid* when Rodrigo captures emirs sacking a village church, an incident which eventually leads to Rodrigo's fatal duel with Count Gormas, his prospective father-in-law. Rodrigo comments to the priest of the village, 'I thought that this would be the shortest road to my bride'. The priest responds 'You did take the shortest road, my son. Not to your bride but to your destiny'. This theme culminates as the Cid, having just been reconciled with his wife, is met by an army of supporters, who demand that he lead them. With extreme reluctance and despite the pleas of Jimena, Rodrigo agrees to lead them. The separation from his family torments the Cid, who at a later point in the film, cries out 'Am I not a man? Am I not permitted to think of my wife, my children?' But for the sake of Spain, the Cid accepts his destiny.

Surveying the extensive cooperation, indeed alliance, between Bronston and other filmmakers, Neal Rosendorf concluded that 'for close to two decades the Franco regime effectively turned the US film industry into an arm of its Ministry of Information and Tourism'.[71] There is a good deal of truth in this observation, but it is an oversimplification. We have seen that a number of scholars have maintained *El Cid* is a film advocating racial equality, certainly not a message that Franco or his officials were concerned to propagate. Assuming that these scholars are correct who then was responsible for the film's progressive orientation? Ironically, in view of his later stance as a conservative icon, the film's star Charlton Heston, may have played an important part in giving the film its liberal messages. At this time, Heston was a Civil Rights activist, who in May 1961, over the objections of studio executives, marched in a picket line in Oklahoma City in a successful effort to force the city's restaurants to integrate. Two years later, at the behest of Martin Luther King and Harry Belafonte, Heston led a contingent of Hollywood celebrities in the march on Washington for Jobs and Freedom.[72]

Other people who played a prominent role also had liberal political leanings and agendas. Ben Barzman, who was the leading scriptwriter, had been blacklisted during the McCarthy era. In 1950, Anthony Mann had directed *The Devil's Doorway*, a film which denounced whites for their racial prejudice against native Americans and cautiously urged tolerance for inter-racial romance.[73] Tellingly, *The Fall of the Roman*

Empire, a later film that Bronston produced, Mann directed, and for which Barzman wrote the screenplay, contains passages that are unmistakeable endorsements of racial equality. In the film, the emperor Marcus Aurelius, portrayed as a wise and just ruler, addresses representatives from all over the Roman Empire: 'Here within our reach [are] golden centuries of peace, a true *Pax Romana*. Wherever you live, whatever the colour of your skin, when peace is achieved, it will bring to all, *all*, the supreme right of Roman citizenship'. In 1964, when this film was released, a promise of citizenship and equal rights to everyone, regardless of their skin colour, had a potent resonance. The point is reiterated later in the film, when a friend and aide to Marcus Aurelius, addresses a gathering of Germanic peoples and denizens of the Roman Empire: 'Here we meet in friendship, the blonde peoples of the north and the dark people of the south'.[74] Interestingly, John Fraser, who played Alfonso VI in *El Cid*, would write in his autobiography that the Cid was 'a passionate advocate of tolerance' and the 'prophet of integration'.[75] No historian, even Menéndez Pidal, ever went this far and it is difficult to imagine where Fraser could have read this; almost certainly he was repeating what he had been told on the set of *El Cid*.

Contemporaries also saw *El Cid* as supporting the struggle for racial equality; in a review written on the release of the film, an anonymous critic for *Time* magazine wrote that the Cid portrayed in the film was 'a champion of Civil Rights'.[76] At the beginning of the film, the narrator extolls the Cid as someone who 'called upon all Spaniards, whether Christian or Moor, to face a common enemy who threatened to destroy the land of Spain'. After seeing 'Ben Yusuf' incite his followers to destroy the Christians the film then shows Rodrigo capturing emirs who attacked and despoiled a village and its church. Rodrigo brings his prisoners back to his native village, where an enraged mob is ready to lynch the emirs. One person, seated on a horse, waves a noose, shouting 'Hang them!' Another man in the crowd demands that the prisoners be hung and asks 'What other way is there to treat the Moors?' Rodrigo counters, pointing out that if he did this the local peasants would face the threat of their villages being destroyed in reprisal. Rodrigo frees the emirs, over the objections of the crowd and the king's officials, who charge him with treason. The scene of a white man preventing a mob from lynching prisoners evokes some of the ugliest and most notorious racial crimes in American history and this allusion was strengthened by the fact that the emirs were, as was regrettably common at the time *El Cid* was made, played by English actors in black makeup. This scene in *El Cid*, which has no analogue in any literary or historical text, at once pointed to the racial violence in the American past and depicted Spain's legendary hero as opposed to it. Later, in the film, Rodrigo explains to Jimena why he did hang his prisoners, broadening his act of mercy into an endorsement of co-existence. He tells Jimena that when there was an outcry to kill the emirs 'Suddenly I felt why are we killing each other?' Jimena observes that there has always been war between Christians and Moors and Rodrigo responds thoughtfully, 'I know—always. You do not think then that we can all live in peace?'

The fullest advocacy of racial harmony in *El Cid* comes in the friendship of the Cid with Yusuf al-Mu'tamin ibn Hud, the emir of Zaragoza. In actual fact, the Cid was a mercenary who served al-Mu'tamin from 1081 until the emir's death in 1085. Undoubtedly the Cid, as a valued employee, was on good terms with the emir, but there is no evidence that their relationship was any deeper than this. It is a very different situation in *El Cid*. Al-Mu'tamin is one of the emirs captured and then released by Rodrigo. On his release, he swears eternal friendship with the Cid and he keeps his word, later saving the Cid from an ambush. (Both incidents are fictitious.) In the film, the Cid allies with al Mu'tamin. While their troops, Christian and Moor, are celebrating the alliance and feasting, the Cid and al Mu'tamin look at their men eating and drinking together, and they converse:

> Cid: How can anyone say this is wrong?
> al Mu'tamin: They will say so, on both sides.
> Cid: We have so much to give to each other and to Spain.

Clearly the filmmakers are not commenting on eleventh-century Spain in this scene, but are championing an integrated society in America. Leon Hunt has provocatively argued that the close friendship between the Cid and al-Mu'tamin has 'the dimensions of a forbidden, inter-racial romance'.[77] This may be putting the case too strongly, but there is no doubt that the friendship portrayed between the emir and the Cid in the film is a friendship between equals of different races.

At least one scholar has maintained that the film's insistent presentation of the Cid as a believer in tolerance who wished to live in peace with the Moslems undermined the Francoist interpretation of the Cid as a hero who unified Spain to lead a crusade against the Moors.[78]

These two messages are both in the film and both are contradictory, but for the most part the filmmakers skilfully sidestep conflict by depicting the Cid as the opponent of radical, militant Moslems who follow 'Ben Yusuf', but as also advocating peaceful co-existence with other Moslems. The film was thus able to present simultaneously the Francoist image of the Cid as the crusading protector of Europe and the champion of racial co-existence.

Nevertheless, tension existed between the messages and in at least one case, a pro-Civil Rights message was placed in the film in disregard of Francoist propaganda. The film's depiction of the relationship between the Cid and King Alfonso VI has received little critical attention, perhaps because it does not easily fit into many interpretations of the film. In *El Cid*, Alfonso is pictured as a selfish, insecure and callow young man when he ascends to the throne. This was admittedly Menèndez Pidal's depiction of the king and it was probably attractive to the filmmakers for the same reasons it appealed to the film's venerable historical consultant: a weak, vindictive Alfonso made the Cid look more heroic by contrast and served to place the blame for the Cid's quarrels with his sovereign lord on Alfonso himself.[79] *El Cid* goes further than this as John Fraser—who tellingly had just played Wilde's lover, Lord Alfred Douglas in *The Trials of Oscar Wilde*—portrays Alfonso as slightly effeminate and dominated by his sister, and thus in the beginning of his reign, lacking both masculinity and *gravitas*.

The makers of *El Cid* did this to tie Alfonso to their Civil Rights message. At a climactic moment in the film Alfonso refuses to do battle with Rodrigo and his Moslem allies, arrogantly declaring that he will only fight with Christians in his army.[80] He is soundly defeated. Then the king shows physical courage when a serious wound is cauterized and he endures the pain silently. This is a start but, as the film emphasizes, it is not enough. But at the end of the film, Alfonso puts aside his jealousies and injured pride and leads his troops to Valencia to aid the Cid. He meets the Cid—strikingly in this scene John Fraser is dressed identically to Charlton Heston and bears a strong physical resemblance to him, suggesting a father-son relationship—and while Alfonso asks the hero's forgiveness, the Cid renews his loyalty to his king. Alfonso is at last ready to fight alongside his Moslem allies at the same time that he has emerged as a fully masculine figure. The unmistakeable lesson is that being a good king and a good man means overcoming bigotry and prejudice. As the Cid approvingly tells Alfonso, 'You have conquered yourself'.

The Cid is also overjoyed at the reconciliation with his king. As the Cid is dying, he tells Jimena, 'I have not failed…Chimene, I want you and my children to remember me riding with my king tomorrow'. And it is this loyalty to his king and his acknowledgement of royal authority that made this element of the plot rather awkward in Franco's Spain. The idea of a national hero giving his blessing to the king, and thus securing the monarch's legitimacy, conformed perfectly both to Franco's self-image and his self-presentation. Yet in the early 1960s, Franco's successor was not a subject discussed publicly in Spain. For one thing, Franco was aware that he was only ruler of Spain for life and he did not encourage planning for what would happen when his life ended. Additionally, a choice of successor would create political problems. To many Spaniards the obvious option would be a restoration of the monarchy but a number of Franco's hardcore supporters were completely opposed to this. Eventually Franco, in 1969, would designate Prince Juan Carlos, the grandson of Alfonso XIII, the last king of Spain, as his successor. But when *El Cid* was being filmed, the future status of Juan Carlos was unclear. In fact, when Juan Carlos married Princess Sofia in 1962, Franco did not attend the wedding and ordered that it be given as little publicity as possible.[81] It is difficult to believe that the Cid's relationship with Alfonso, which raised the vexed issue of Franco's successor, was placed in the film at the behest of Franco or his officials. In this case, the desire to have the Cid teach, by example, a future king to reject bigotry and to serve his people prevailed and the propaganda for Civil Rights triumphed over propaganda for *El Caudillo*.

V

Whatever the messages of the film were, they all depended on the Cid being presented as a hero worthy of emulation. This worked against the biographical accuracy of *El Cid* on several levels. The first was that it led the filmmakers to include anecdotes of dubious authenticity because they presented the Cid in a heroic or virtuous light. One of the most striking scenes in *El Cid* has Rodrigo forcing Alfonso to swear in a public assembly that he had no involvement in the murder of his older brother—and rival for the throne—Sancho. This was not a scriptwriter's invention, the account of forcing Alfonso to take an oath attesting to his innocence first appears in a chronicle written in 1236. Although this material was not recorded until almost two and a half centuries after the Cid had died, Menéndez Pidal enthusiastically declared that this account was accurate and the incident had really taken place.[82] More recently scholars have been sceptical, with Richard Fletcher dismissing the story as 'fantastic'.[83] But the scriptwriters for *El Cid* could not have anticipated these criticisms and they were repeating what their historical consultant believed. But they went much further than Menéndez Pidal had, in depicting Alfonso ordering the Cid's exile as a reprisal by the king, for the Cid's forcing him to swear the oath. In actual fact, *El Cid* conflates two separate exiles of the Cid. Alfonso ordered the Cid into exile around the year 1081 because he had led an unauthorized, and diplomatically inconvenient, raid on the emir of Toledo, who was under Alfonso's protection. The Cid and Alfonso reconciled in 1087, on terms favourable to Rodrigo. (Alfonso needed able commanders to help him battle the Almoravids.) In 1089, the Cid failed to rendezvous with Alfonso during a campaign and the king, rightly or wrongly, suspected treachery. The Cid was exiled again and his wife and children were briefly imprisoned.[84] By revising the facts of the Cid's exile, the filmmakers were able to present the historical Cid who was a recalcitrant, ambitious vassal as an unwaveringly loyal subject persecuted by his ungrateful king.

Another scene in the film where the Cid displays remarkable loyalty to his king is where, after his conquest of Valencia, the Cid proclaims that he is ruling Valencia as a vassal of Alfonso. Here again, the filmmakers are following the lead of Menéndez Pidal, who cited the *Poema de mio Cid* and other twelfth-century sources as proof that the Cid actually proclaimed that Alfonso ruled Valencia.[85] Again modern scholars are sceptical citing the lack of contemporary corroboration and the fact that charters issued by the Cid styled him as the prince of Valencia.[86] And once again, *El Cid* goes beyond the already favourable interpretation of Menéndez Pidal. The scene in the film where the Cid's followers, including his allies, urge him to take the throne of Valencia but he selflessly declines is completely fictitious. The film also simplifies the Cid's capture of Valencia in a way that makes the city's conquest look almost humanitarian. In *El Cid*, Rodrigo besieges Valencia and reduces the inhabitants to near starvation. He then bombards the city with loaves of bread. This inspires the people of the city to rise up against al-Qadir, the emir of Valencia, who has been living in luxury while they were starving. The emir is thrown over the city wall and the gates of the city are opened for the Cid. This implausible scenario seems like an optimistic, not to say fantastic, enactment of American beliefs that massive aid, accompanied by a modicum of force would trigger popular revolts which cause Communist regimes to topple.

In reality, al-Qadir was toppled from power by the elites of Valencia, who were seeking an accommodation with the advancing Almoravid army. Al-Qadir was executed on 28 October 1092. The Cid did not begin his siege of Valencia until July 1093. He did, however, starve the city into surrender and in June 1094, Valencia surrendered even though no bread was catapulted into the city. *El Cid* then compresses the Cid's five year rule over Valencia into a period of months and two major victories over the Almoravids, as well as a protracted, successful siege of a fortress, into a single climactic battle. This compression of events simplifies the narrative and reduces confusion and tedium. But it serves other purposes as well. The Cid's rule over his Moslem subjects in Valencia was harsh. In addition to heavy taxes and forcing the Moslem population of the city to pay a staggering fine, the Cid, after an unsuccessful attempt to extort supposedly hidden treasure from Ibn Jahhaf, the *qadi* (judge) of Valencia—who had ruled the city between al-Qadir's overthrew and its capture by the Cid—had the unfortunate man burned alive.[87] The Cid's actions had been chronicled—and most unusually, condemned—by Menéndez Pidal so the filmmakers must have known of the Cid's severity towards his Moslem subjects, yet *El Cid* does not contain even an allusion to these cruelties.[88]

Yet *El Cid* does more than lionize the Cid as 'the purest knight of all' and a Spanish national hero, it presents him as Christ-like figure and a figure who also becomes, if not divine, then certainly a legend. The film's identification of the Cid with Christ is not a matter of one or two casual allusions; the identification is made persistently and, it must be said, unsubtly throughout film.[89] At the beginning of *El Cid*, when Rodrigo comes to the aid of a village whose church has been sacked by Moslems, he carries a crucifix on his back which has been riddled with arrows. Not only does this scene duplicate the fifth Station of the Cross, and associate the Cid with Christ, but the association is deepened by the arrows in the crucifix which are harbingers of the Cid's death at the end of the film.[90] The crucial scene in *El Cid* where he goes into exile he comes across not one, but three roadside crosses, erected on a hillock, side by side. In the shadow of these blatant reminders of the Crucifixion, the Cid gives water to a leper who identifies himself as Lazarus. The Cid is then joined by Jimena and they take shelter in a barn, echoing the

Holy Family's stay in a manger before they journeyed into exile. At this point, one half expects the Holy Spirit to descend on the Cid, but in this case, the filmmakers used a modicum of restraint.

Any restraint, however, was cast to the winds in a scene where Count Garcia Ordóñez, now a loyal adherent of the Cid is executed by 'Ben Yusuf'.[91] Ordóñez is being, in what is a *leitmotif* for this film, crucified, and has this exchange with 'Ben Yusuf' about the Cid:

> 'Ben Yusuf': He is a man like other men. He will die. I will kill him.
> Ordóñez: He'll never die. Never.
> 'Ben Yusuf': You dare think of him as we think of our Prophet?
> Ordóñez: We do!
> 'Ben Yusuf': Then this will be more than a battle. It will be our god against yours.

These are only particularly overt scenes in which the Cid is identified with Christ, but this identification is a theme throughout *El Cid*. When, for example, the Cid catapults loaves of bread into Valencia, he proclaims 'Citizens of Valencia, I bring you bread!' Having the Cid giving people bread instead of stones echos several verses in the gospel.[92]

The association of the Cid with the divine comes to a climax at the end of the film. 'Ben Yusuf' attacks Valencia and the Cid is struck by an arrow and mortally wounded. His soldiers are demoralized at the prospect of his death and to rally them in the next day's critical battle, he orders, on his deathbed, that his dead body be placed in armour, tied to his horse and led into battle. It underscores the importance of this 'resurrection' that it has been prophesied several times in the film, as when the Cid encounters Lazarus, who bears the name of a man who Jesus raised from the dead, and also when Ordóñez declares that the Cid will never die. The scene itself transfers the battle for Valencia into a cosmic struggle between good and evil with the body of Cid mounted on a white charger riding though fleeing enemy soldiers and, in a scene which has been compared with depictions of Michael defeating Satan, trampling 'Ben Yusuf' to death.[93] The body of Cid, still mounted on his white charger, rides alone along the beach, parallel to the ocean, into a receding azure sky, passing, as the narrator intones, out of history into legend.

The Cid's status as a hero, an exemplar and finally a deified figure validates both of the rival lessons of *El Cid*: that Spain needs a leader who, out of duty, unifies Spain against a godless threat but also that all countries need a leader who unifies his people and inspires them to live, despite racial and religious differences, in peaceful co-existence.

VI

Why does *El Cid* deserve careful study by someone interested in biographical film? Although very popular in its own day, *El Cid* is largely forgotten today except by film scholars. The Cid is not an iconic, or even particularly well-known figure outside of the Iberian peninsula. One of the messages in the film, the glorification of Franco, hasn't been relevant for over four decades. The other message that the film conveys, that of racial equality and co-existence, remains, of course, profoundly relevant. Yet the treatment of this theme in *El Cid* is, by twenty-first century standards, oblique and slightly quaint. But the co-existence of these rival messages demonstrates two important features of films. The first is that works of film propaganda may, because filmmaking is fundamentally collaborative and involves the labour of many disparate levels contain propaganda messages not intended by the sponsor, patron or producer of the film. The second is that film, as a visual medium may simultaneously convey incompatible messages that it would be difficult to do in print.

Above all, *El Cid* provides striking examples of factors that lead to a biographical film deviating from historical veracity. For example, there is the reliance on sources, not for their reliability or accuracy but because they relate stories that the filmmakers wish to relate. Then there is also the revision of the sources or even more basically the wholesale invention of events to serve exemplary, commercial, dramatic and political motives. And there are of course, messages relevant to contemporary audiences, whether educational, political or social that filmmakers wish to convey. None of these deviations should lead a historian or anyone else to regard these deviations as failures on the part of the filmmakers. They have artistic license and are not obliged to adhere strictly to fact, although they do bear aesthetic and social responsibility for the messages that they convey. It is, however, part of a historian's job to observe and correct—but not condemn—the portrayal of the past in historical films, just as they do with historical novels and historical plays. And historians should use deviations from accuracy in historical and biographical films as starting points to understanding the contexts in which these films were made and how the filmmakers used the camera lens as a mirror to reflect both their own societies and their own cultures.

Acknowledgements I am grateful to David Smith, Laila Haidarali and Andrew Priest for their helpful comments on an earlier draft of this essay.

Notes

1. The name 'el Cid' is derived from the Arabic *al-sayyid*, which means 'lord' or 'leader'. This honorific was probably used during Rodrigo's lifetime and it was certainly applied to him by the mid-twelfth century; see Fletcher, 1989, p. 3.
2. Jancovich, 2000, p. 90. Another scholar maintains that *El Cid* advocates both Cold War détente and interracial harmony in a decolonised world (Bretéque, 2004, p. 250).
3. Aberth, 2003, pp. 135–47. Neal Rosendorf, in his commentary on the 2007 DVD of *El Cid*, stresses the Francoist themes in the film. Kevin Harty emphasizes the anti-Communist and pro-Franco elements of *El Cid*, although he also states that *El Cid* 'nods in the direction of the American Civil Rights movement' (Harty, 2009, pp. 162–66, quotation on p. 166). Burt, 2008, p. 81, argues against the interpretation of *El Cid* as championing Civil Rights, observing that one of the film's villains, al-Qadir the emir of Valencia, is shown with both white and black women in his harem. Therefore, Burt argues, the film was actually critical of multi-racialism. As will be discussed below, however, there is a considerable amount of evidence against this interpretation. It might also be observed that Burt is reading a great deal of significance into a minor detail which takes up about twenty seconds of screen time.
4. Burt, 2008, p. 85. It must be said, however, that, given the known attitudes of the scriptwriter, the director and Charlton Heston (at least in the early 1960s) on racial equality, it is very difficult to believe that the film was intended to promote racial segregation.
5. For details of these accounts see Fletcher, 1989, p. 99.
6. See Fletcher, 1989, pp. 92–93, 95–99, 135–36. *Campeador* was another honorific by which Rodrigo Díaz was known. The term is the Romance language rendition of 'campi doctoris', literally, 'teacher of the [battle] field', which in the late Roman Empire designated a military instructor or drill sergeant. When the term resurfaced in eleventh-century Spain it carried the meaning of 'champion' and it was a widely used to describe the Cid. See Fletcher, 1989, p. 115.

7. For the dating of the poem see Fletcher, 1989, pp. 92–93 and *The Poem of the Cid*, pp. 14–16.
8. Jancovich, 2000, p. 86; cf. Heston, 1995, p. 242; Aberth, 2003, pp. 127–28; Elley, 2014, p. 157.
9. See Winkler, 1996, pp. 334–35. A particularly striking example of this occurs when the Cid, rather than seizing Valencia for himself, acknowledges Alfonso VI as king of Valencia. The Cid's friend and ally, the emir al-Mu'tamin exclaims 'What a noble subject—if only he had a noble king!' This is a rendering of a well-known line in the *Poema*: 'Dios, que buen vassal—si oviesse buen señor!' (Winkler, 1996, p. 334).
10. A collection of ballads, the *Romancero del Cid*, was published in Lisbon in 1605. It was a considerable success and was reprinted 26 times. The dramatic potential of these ballads was appreciated by the Spanish playwright Guillén de Castro who adapted some of them for the stage. One of these ballads, *Las moscedades de Rodrigo*, written in the fifteenth century, inspired Castro's drama, *Les mocedades del Cid* (literally, 'The young days of the Cid'), written in 1618. Castro's play, in turn, not only inspired Corneille, it supplied him with much of the plot for *Le Cid*.
11. Heston, 1995, pp. 242, 245; Barzman, 2003, pp. 285–90, 311.
12. The names of the characters in *Le Cid* are the French equivalents of their Spanish names, e.g., Rodrique for Rodrigo, Chimène for Jimena, etc. To avoid confusion, I have retained the Spanish names for the characters in the play. In *El Cid*, thanks to Barzman's use of Corneille, the Cid's wife is called Chimene (in an anglophone rendering of Chimène) not Jimena, but again, I will refer to her by her Spanish name.
13. The single combat for Calahorra—which is not in Corneille—may have some slight basis in medieval sources and, perhaps in historical fact. The Spanish scholar Ramón Menéndez Pidal (whose role as historical consultant for *El Cid* will be discussed a little further on), drawing on the *Carmen Campi Doctoris* and the *Historia Roderici*, describes a single combat in which the Cid bested a champion of the king of Navarre in single combat. At stake was the disputed town and castle of Pazuengos; see Menéndez Pidal, 1934, pp. 90–91. If, as seems likely, this episode was the basis for the single combat over Calahorra in *El Cid*, then the film's script raised the stakes of the conflict and changed the employer of the Cid's opponent from the king of Navarre. (This may be because Americans, thanks to stories taught in school about Columbus and Isabella of Castile and her husband, Ferdinand of Aragon, are aware that Aragon was a kingdom in medieval Spain. Most Americans, on the other hand, have never heard of the kingdom of Navarre.)
14. Basinger, 2007, p. 159.

15. For a balanced, but not uncritical, appraisal of Menèndez Pidal's career and work see Fletcher, 1989, pp. 4–6, 202–7.
16. Fletcher, 1989, pp. 202–3.
17. Fletcher, 1989, pp. 192–93.
18. Fletcher, 1989, p. 193.
19. Fletcher, 1989, pp. 193–96.
20. Menéndez Pidal, 1939, p. 470; cf. Menéndez Pidal, 1934, p. 445.
21. Barzman, 2003, p. 306.
22. Rózsa, 1982, p. 181.
23. Heston, 1980, p. 98.
24. Heston, 1995, p. 242.
25. Heston, 1995, pp. 245–46.
26. Fletcher, 1989, p. 5.
27. Barton and Fletcher, 2000, p. 101. The *Poema de mio Cid* relates that the Cid *killed* fifteen Moors in a single combat: Hamilton and Perry, 1984, p. 47.
28. Hamilton and Perry, 1984, p. 25.
29. Fletcher, 1989, pp. 197–98.
30. Mann, 2009, p. 133.
31. Nadel, 1993, p. 415.
32. Rosendorf, 2007, p. 79.
33. Rosendorf, 2007, pp. 49–50.
34. Rosendorf, 2007, p. 83.
35. Rosendorf, 2007, p. 80.
36. Subsidies from the British government reimbursed a significant portion of the costs. But producers had to pay the costs up front and were reimbursed depending on how many people in Britain saw the film (Rosendorf, 2001, pp. 117–20). This arrangement was unfavourable to the smaller, independent producers.
37. Rosendorf, 2001, pp. 128–34.
38. Rosendorf, 2001, pp. 124–27.
39. Rosendorf, 2001, pp. 136–41.
40. Rosendorf, 2007, pp. 79, 87–88.
41. Rosendorf, 2007, p. 87.
42. Rosendorf, 2014, pp. 76–77. *The Royal Hunt of the Sun* would eventually be made in 1969; it was produced by the much smaller production company, Cinema Center Films.
43. Rosendorf, 2014, p. 54.
44. Rosendorf, 2007, p. 85.
45. Rosendorf, 2007, p. 88.
46. Rosendorf, 2014, Chapter 1, provides an excellent discussion of the Franco regime's campaign to promote Spanish tourism.

47. Rosendorf, 2007, pp. 77–78.
48. Rosendorf, 2007, p. 86.
49. For Bronston's career in Hollywood and his departure from it, see Martin, 2007, pp. 175–77; Rosendorf, 2014, pp. 61–63.
50. For Franco's identification with the Cid see Preston, 1995, pp. xvii, 52, 329, 641–42.
51. Bretéque, 2004, p. 248.
52. Besas, 1985, p. 55.
53. Barzman, 2003, pp. 308, 321, 433, n.1; Besas, 1985, p. 54.
54. Rosendorf, 2014, pp. 63, 72–73.
55. Barzman, 2003, p. 236; cf. Martin, 2007, p. 77.
56. Barzman, 2003, p. 333; Martin, 2007, p. 79.
57. Rosendorf, 2007, p. 92; Martin, 2007, p. 79.
58. Rosendorf, 2007, p. 92.
59. The figure of 6.25 million dollars was an estimate made in *Time* magazine (22 December 1961), p. 45; it may not be accurate. This amount would be worth well over 50 million dollars today.
60. Besas, 1985, p. 62; Martin, 2007, p. 69. The figure of 26 million dollars would be worth about 210 million dollars today.
61. Preston, 1995, pp. 417–18. Besas, 1985, pp. 19–20, is sceptical of Franco's authorship of the screenplay but acknowledges that Franco may have provided ideas for *Raza* and that it was made with Franco's full approval and support.
62. Rosendorf, 2014, p. 67.
63. Rosendorf, 2014, pp. 70–71. The two films for which Llovet wrote the scripts were *Sinfonia Española* and *Objetivo 67*.
64. According to Franco's biographer, 20,000 Republican prisoners toiled on the project. See Preston, 1995, pp. 351–52.
65. Rosendorf, 2014, pp. 68–72, 111–12; Besas, 1985, pp. 60–61. For Franco's considerable personal interest in the monumental complex at the *Valle de los Caídos* see Preston, 1995, pp. 631, 679.
66. Aberth, 2003, pp. 141–42 and Rosendorf on the commentary to the 2007 DVD of *El Cid*.
67. 'Ben Yusuf' is the name in *El Cid* for Yusuf ibn Tashfin (1009–1106), the ruler of the Almoravid empire, which was centred in Morocco. Yusuf first invaded Spain in 1086, answering appeals from the Moslem emirs in Spain, who feared that Alfonso VI would soon conquer them. Yusuf was a devout Moslem who did regard the emirs as religiously lax and militarily ineffective and he deposed and exiled a number of them. However the cruel megalomaniac portrayed in the film is a caricature of a ruler respected for his prudence, sense of honour and administrative ability; see Bennison, 2016, pp. 38–48.

68. Richard Burt, 2008, p. 81, has argued that 'Ben Yusuf' and his followers could not be intended to represent Communists since they were strict monotheists while Communists are atheists. However, scriptwriters and audiences of the period did not share Burt's precision or literal-mindedness. A number of films, made in the Cold War, but set in the Middle Ages, used Moslems to represent Communists. An example is *The Black Knight* (1954), where the 'Saracens' seek to topple King Arthur through the machinations of a network of traitors in his court. Fortunately the hero, Sir John (Alan Ladd), goes undercover, joins their ranks and exposes their schemes. For further discussion of the 'Saracens' representing Communists in this film see Lupack, 1991, pp. 29–40; Aberth, 2003, pp. 13–16.
69. Preston, 1995, pp. 598–626, 680–81.
70. For an example see Preston, 1995, pp. 265–66.
71. Rosendorf, 2007, p. 79.
72. Heston, 1995, pp. 260–62, 315–17; Heston, 1980, pp. 119–20, 261; also see Ross, 2011, pp. 282–87.
73. Basinger, 2007, pp. 71–75.
74. For the liberal politics of *The Fall of the Roman Empire*, see Briggs, 2009, pp. 235–36.
75. Fraser, 2004, p. 178.
76. *Time*, 22 December 1961, p. 45.
77. Hunt, 1993, p. 75.
78. Jancovich, 2000, p. 91.
79. Menéndez Pidal, 1934, p. 475. For a sharply different assessment of Alfonso see Fletcher, 1989, p. 119.
80. The historical Alfonso was broad minded enough to have an aristocratic Moslem woman as his mistress; see Barton, 2015, pp. 125–27. More importantly, far from refusing to ally with Moslems, Alfonso VI banished the Cid in 1081, to punish him for leading a raid against Alfonso's client, the emir of Toledo.
81. Preston, 1995, pp. 701, 741–43.
82. Menéndez Pidal, 1934, pp. 116–18.
83. Fletcher, 1989, pp. 118–19.
84. Fletcher, 1989, pp. 152–53, 156–58.
85. Menéndez Pidal, 1934, p. 346.
86. Fletcher, 1989, p. 179.
87. Fletcher, 1989, pp. 180–82. Ibn Jahhaf's execution may have triggered a rebellion by Moslem inhabitants of Valencia in 1094; the details of this rising, however, remain obscure.
88. Menéndez Pidal, 1934, pp. 361–63.

89. See Burt, 2008, pp. 78–80, 85–87. Martin Winkler has pointed out the frequency of Biblical reference in the dialogue of *El Cid*; see Winkler, 1996, pp. 333–34.
90. In contrast to the film, the historical Cid died of natural causes in July 1099.
91. The historical Ordóñez was not executed in 1094 but was killed in the battle of Uclés in 1108; see Reilly, 1988, pp. 353–55.
92. Matthew 7:9 and Luke 11:11.
93. Shippey, 2009, p. 173. The historical Yusuf ibn Tashfin never encountered the Cid in battle and died of natural causes at the age of ninety-seven.

Bibliography

Aberth, J. 2003. *A Knight at the Movies*. New York and London: Routledge.

Barton, S. 2015. *Conquerors, Brides and Concubines: Interfaith Relations and Social Power in Medieval Iberia*. Philadelphia: University of Pennsylvania Press.

Barton, S., and Fletcher, R. (eds.). 2000. *The World of El Cid: Chronicles of the Spanish Reconquest*. Manchester and New York: Manchester University Press.

Barzman, N. 2003. *The Red and the Blacklist: The Intimate Memoir of a Hollywood Expatriate*. New York: Friction.

Basinger, J. 2007. *Anthony Mann*, 2nd edition. Middleton, CT: Wesleyan University Press.

Bennison, A. K. 2016. *The Almoravid and Almohad Empires*. Edinburgh: Edinburgh University Press.

Besas, P. 1985. *Behind the Spanish Lens: Spanish Cinema Under Fascism and Democracy*. Denver, CO: Arden Press.

de la Bretéque, F. A. 2004. *L'imaginaire medieval dans le cinema occidental*. Paris: Honoré Champion.

Briggs, W. 2009. 'Peace and Power in *The fall of the Roman Empire*', in M. Winkler (ed.), *The Fall of the Roman Empire: Film and History*, pp. 225–40. Malden, MA and Oxford: Wiley Blackwell.

Burt, R. 2008. *Medieval and Early Modern Films and Media*. New York: Palgrave Macmillan.

Corneille, P. 1978. *Le Cid*, ed. P. H. Nurse. London: Harrap.

Elley, D. 2014. *The Epic Film*. Abingdon: Routledge.

Fletcher, R. 1989. *The Quest for El Cid*. London: Hutchinson.

Fraser, J. 2004. *Close Up: An Actor Telling Tales*. London: Oberon Books.

Harty, J. 2009. 'Agenda Layered Upon Agenda: Anthony Mann's 1961 Film *El Cid*', in N. Haydock and E. L. Risden (eds.), *Hollywood in the Holy Land*, pp. 161–68. Jefferson, NC: McFarland.

Heston, C. 1980. *The Actor's Life: Journals 1956–1976*. Harmondsworth, Middlesex: Penguin.

Heston, C. 1995. *In the Arena*. New York: Simon and Schuster.

Hunt, L. 1993. 'What Are Big Boys Made Of? *Spartacus*, *El Cid* and the Male Epic', in P. Kirkham and J. Thumim (eds.), *You Tarzan: Masculinity, Movies and Men*, pp. 65–83. London: Lawrence and Wishart.

Jancovich, M. 2000. 'The Purest Knight of All: Nation, History and Representation in *El Cid* (1960)', *Cinema Journal* 40 (2000), pp. 79–103.

Lupack, Alan. 1991. 'An Enemy in Our Midst: *The Black Knight* and the American Dream', in Kevin J. Harty (ed.), *Cinema Arthuriana: Essays in Arthurian Film*, pp. 29–40. New York: Garland.

Mann, A. 2009. 'Empire Demolition', in M. Winkler (ed.), *The Fall of the Roman Empire: Film and History*. Malden, MA and Oxford: Wiley-Blackwell.

Martin, M. 2007. *The Magnificent Showman: The Epic Films of Samuel Bronston*. Albany, GA: Bear Manor Media.

Menéndez Pidal, R. 1934. *The Cid and His Spain*. H. Sutherland (trans.). London: John Murray.

Menéndez Pidal, R. 1939. *La España del Cid*. Buenos Aires: España-Calpe Argentina.

Nadel, A. 1993. 'God's Law and the Wide Screen: *The Ten Commandments* as Cold War "Epic"', *PMLA* 108 (1993), pp. 415–30.

Preston, P. 1995. *Franco: A Biography*. London: Fontana Press.

The Poem of the Cid. R. Hamilton and J. Perry (trans.). 1984. Harmondsworth, Middlesex: Penguin.

Reilly, B. 1988. *The Kingdom of León-Castilla Under King Alfonso VI, 1065–1109*. Princeton, NJ: Princeton University Press.

Rosendorf, N. 2001. 'The Life and Times of Samuel Bronston, Builder of "Hollywood in Madrid": A Study in International Scope and Influence of American Popular Culture' (PhD dissertation, Harvard University).

Rosendorf, N. 2007. '"Hollywood in Madrid": American Film Producers and the Franco Regime, 1957–1970', *Historical Journal of Film, Radio and Television* 27 (2007), pp. 77–109.

Rosendorf, N. 2014. *Franco Sells Spain to America: Hollywood, Tourism and Public Relations as Postwar Spanish Soft Power*. Basingstoke: Palgrave Macmillan.

Ross, S. J. 2011. *Hollywood Left and Right: How Movie Stars Shaped American Politics*. New York: Oxford University Press.

Rózsa, M. 1982. *Double Life: The Autobiography of Miklós Rózsa*. Tunbridge Wells: Midas Books.

Shippey, T. 2009. 'El Cid: Defeat of the Crescentade', in N. Haydock and E. L. Risden (eds.), *Hollywood in the Holy Land*, pp. 169–85. Jefferson, NC: McFarland.

Winkler, M. 1996. 'El Cid: Ein mittelalterlicher Heldenmythos in Film', in L. Gaebel (ed.), *Herrscher, Helden Heilige*, pp. 327–40. St Gall: UVK.

Joan of Arc Through Medieval Eyes and Modern Lenses: Dreyer 1928 and Bresson 1962

Elisabeth van Houts

Introduction

Joan of Arc (1412–1431) is an exceptionally well-known medieval woman. Born as a daughter of a well off farmer in north-eastern France during the Hundred Years War she claimed that divine messages told her to liberate her country from the English and to have the Dauphin Charles crowned king. Against all expectations the royal court accepted her as a visionary, kitted her out as a knight, and gave her an army with which she in spectacular fashion liberated Orléans. A few months later Charles was indeed crowned at Reims. But then the tide for Joan turned. Her campaign faltered and she failed to liberate Paris. Instead the French betrayed and captured her and sold her to the English, who put her on trial as a heretic. Duly convicted, she died at the stake in Rouen on 30 May 1431. Two decades later after tireless lobbying by her supporters, family and the citizens of Orléans, a second trial quashed

E. van Houts (✉)
Emmanuel College, Cambridge, UK
e-mail: emcv2@cam.ac.uk

T. S. Freeman and D. L. Smith (eds.), *Biography and History in Film*, Palgrave Studies in the History of the Media,
https://doi.org/10.1007/978-3-319-89408-9_3

the original verdict and Joan was rehabilitated. Celebrated and vilified in equal measure in her own time, her legacy throughout the ages has been similarly mixed. Was she a self-centred fraud who claimed to be divinely inspired, and crossed normative boundaries by dressing and acting as a man, or was she a charismatic visionary who with astounding courage injected fresh energy in France's recovery from war? Throughout modern French history, broadly speaking, two rival views competed with one another. On the one hand, there is Joan the martyr-saint seen by the Roman Catholic Church as a defender of her faith and fully deserving the sainthood bestowed on her in 1920. On the other hand, there is the secular female fighter of the Republic of France, adored as an inspiration for its military forces. Most recently a third view of her has dominated the French political scene with the National Front having appropriated Joan as a mascot for its ultra-right, populist policies against immigration and multiculturalism.[1]

Any historian contemplating a biography of Joan is faced with an enormous historiography that has grown up around her and her time. And added to this there is also the cultural significance of her legacy in literature and art, which includes film. It is no exaggeration to say that Joan of Arc is one of the best-known women of western Europe and certainly one of the best-documented ones of the Middle ages. That we know so much about her is due to the voluminous number of contemporary sources.[2] Among them stand out the records of her two trials: the first one in 1431 when she was convicted of heresy and sentenced to death, and the second one in 1456 when, posthumously, she was completely exonerated as a result of the nullification of the first trial. Combined the two trial records allow us to come close to her own voice and that of 160 contemporaries who had known her. They provide an unparalleled amount of information about Joan's youth, her career as a visionary and fighter, and, in the eyes of the Church, a heretic. Celebrated and vilified in writings in equal measure since her death, she was nevertheless one of the first women whose life was recreated on screen. Most were biographical in the sense that they span her whole life from peasant girl to the convicted heretic who died on the stake. Thus far, only two filmmakers, Carl Theodore Dreyer (1889–1968) and Robert Bresson (1901–1999), have famously limited her portrayal to the period at the end of her life when she was on trial and these are the films I will concentrate on in this chapter.

Dreyer and, inspired by his predecessor's work, Bresson both start their films with a historical authentication of Joan but both emphasise different aspects. In 1928 Dreyer, a protestant Danish filmmaker living in France at the time, began his film with shots of the medieval manuscript containing the trial records and a brief historical introduction of this archival record by the French historian Pierre Champion (1880–1942). In contrast, forty years later, in 1962 Bresson, a Roman Catholic French film director, opened his film not with a medieval book about Joan but with a person closely related to Joan. The opening shot focused on Isabella, mother of Joan, who together with her sons, appealed to the bishop of Paris to overthrow Joan's conviction, an appeal that resulted in the successful nullification trial. Both filmmakers persuade their audience of the meticulous attention they have paid to the historical facts they are about to present, one by stressing the written record of Joan's demise and the other by emphasising her family's determination to rescue her reputation.[3] Given the men's ideology as artists theirs were interesting introductions to Joan the record and Joan the woman of flesh and blood. Moreover, both Dreyer and Bresson at various stages in their careers claimed not to be concerned with matters of historical detail because they were interested primarily in Joan's emotional state faced with intense interrogation and death on the stake.[4] The filmmakers' explicit declaration of disinterest in historicity combined with their close adherence to the trial records, present a biographical conundrum. They used the bare outline of the trial narrative as a framework for a portrait of Joan that is an interpretation of the gaps left by the written word. Despite the huge amount of information about Joan in the form of her own replies to interrogation and the witness statements about her twenty years later, her personality remains tantalisingly elusive. This elusiveness allowed plenty of margin between the words and their context to enable artists such as Dreyer and Bresson to imagine Joan's character and emotions. Naturally, their imagined Joans were deeply influenced by their own contemporary world and both men, in different degrees as we shall see, viewed Joan very much as a young and innocent woman victimised by a male clergy. While Dreyer stressed the Christ-like suffering of an ignorant and bewildered peasant girl at the hands of vindictive clerical lawyers, for Bresson she was a composed and unfazed young woman, fully aware of the full weight of the court she was facing.[5] In their different ways, the two filmmakers draw in their audience by focussing their camera intently on Joan and her interrogators as an invitation to their viewers to absorb Joan's emotion and pain. This then is a dramatic attempt at reliving the emotional experience of Joan's last days, and one that historians know is impossible to capture in words in a conventional biographical account.

Joan's Medieval Life Story

The story of Joan of Arc played out against the background of the Hundred Years War (c. 1300–1450) in France.[6] During her lifetime France north of the Loire was occupied by the English who were allied with the Burgundians. How and why in 1429 Joan persuaded Robert de Baudricourt, leader of the garrison at Vaucouleurs, to take her to Chinon, the castle where the Dauphin resided, remains unclear. Three facts contributed to her ultimate success. First, her family was well known and trusted. Secondly, she was not the first woman to claim to have had visions, and given the propensity of the Dauphin's family to welcome female visionaries at court, Joan may have tapped into knowledge of the royal family's spiritual longings. Thirdly, Joan knew how to sell herself as she had a knack for public speaking and ceremony—she confessed in the open air before a large crowd. Robert de Baudricourt in due course was convinced enough to give her an escort of some young men. At the same time, the town of Vaucouleurs provided Joan with a sword as well as a male outfit so that she could travel unhindered.[7] On the way to Chinon they stopped at Toul for a private reason.[8] While still at home her parents had arranged for her to marry a long-standing family friend, whose name we do not know. At her 1431 trial, she said that she had always obeyed her parents except in two cases, first when she went to Vaucouleurs and secondly when she refused to get married claiming that she had vowed to remain a virgin from the moment she had first heard her voices. At Toul she appeared before an ecclesiastical court which sided with Joan as they believed her story, namely that she never had agreed to marry—as no marriage was valid without consent from both parties, the court decided in favour of Joan. From Toul she resumed her trip to Chinon, where historians have been able to reconstruct what happened when she met the Dauphin Charles.[9] On 23 February a private small gathering with the Dauphin took place at which the archbishop of Reims, Regnault de Chartres, was present as well. There the archbishop advised Charles to send her to Poitiers to have her virginity tested and to subject her to an interrogation by church officials.

As his reason, he stated that since she was a peasant girl she ought to be tested in two ordeals as 'the king had to prevent himself from making a fool of himself in the eyes of foreign lands'.[10] At Poitiers between 1 and 21 March she was indeed put to the test and interrogated by Paris doctors, under the chairmanship of the archbishop of Reims, who had fled English occupied France; they deemed her a reliable young virgin.[11] We know from the 1456 witness account of the Dominican William Seguin that on this occasion Joan was confident, articulate, persuasive and displayed a sharp wit.[12] After she passed these two ordeals (the virginity test and the interrogation) she went back to Chinon where on 27 March the royal court began to acknowledge her existence, and many pamphlets and letters were produced to publicise her claim that she was indeed the maiden who had come to make Charles king.

Once accepted as a genuine 'messenger from God', Joan spent time at Chinon being kitted out properly as a knight with full armour, a banner and sword and other arms all provided and paid for by the Dauphin, and receiving extensive instruction in military matters from John, Duke of Alençon.[13] He and a mercenary leader called La Hire both became lifelong supporters and admirers. Her most outstanding victory came by taking the city of Orléans in May 1429, which had been besieged for seven months by the English.[14] The battle of Orléans was one of the most bloody in French history, but nevertheless it was seen as a miracle then and now that the French won. As for the inhabitants of Orléans, they were so grateful that after her death they provided her widowed mother Isabelle with a monthly pension for life. The spectacular defeat of the English at Orléans goes some way to explain their determination to get rid of her sooner rather than later. After the success at Orléans, several other cities fell: Jargeau (11–12 June), Beaugency (17 June) and Patay (18 June), all cities en route to Reims which opened its gates to the Dauphin's party in July where on the 17th Charles was crowned king of France. In recognition of Joan's military achievements Charles ennobled her family and gave the town of Domremy a tax exemption.[15]

However, the very man she had helped to achieve his coronation, now crowned, began to distance himself from her. It is one of Larissa Taylor's convincing arguments that Joan of Arc at this stage simply didn't understand the politics. Instead of realising that she had been used as a visionary, whose vision had become reality in the form of the king's coronation, the royal support had only come her way as long as she had been useful.[16] The military campaigns that followed Reims were a disaster. Famously, in May 1430 at Compiègne, she was almost certainly betrayed by its citizens who captured Joan and handed over to the Burgundians.[17] She was kept in prison at various places mostly in the northwest of France occupied by the English far away from Lorraine, her homeland in the east, and the Orléans area, where her supporters lived. Her Burgundian captors ransomed her to the English, who promptly took her to English occupied Rouen where just before Christmas 1430 she was incarcerated in the city's secular prison in preparation of her trial as heretic.

The trial of 1431 was organised by the deputy Inquisitor general of France, the Dominican Jean le Maistre and the judge Pierre Cauchon, bishop of Beauvais, in whose diocese Joan had been held captive.[18] Cauchon and most of the other judges had been trained as theologians and canon lawyers at Paris. There is no doubt to the extent that the college of judges was firmly under the control of their English secular occupiers of France. Before the trial proper could begin, a pre-trial had been underway since 9 January 1431 when the prosecutor Jean d'Estivet started collecting evidence against Joan. He sent agents to Joan's home area to collect evidence about her youth, her visions and other activities. Although none of this evidence was made known publicly and was never appended to the formal report on her trial, it is clear from the very detailed questions asked by the judges that they had information about her. Also at the Nullification trial, some witnesses reported that d'Estivet's agents had questioned them in early 1431. What is crucial to understand is that the absence of the publication of the evidence in advance of the trial meant that no formal accusation was formulated against Joan justifying the trial. In Joan's case questions were asked and assembled but no official *diffamatio* was drawn up. Why not? The logical conclusion is the one that many historians have reached, namely that there simply was not enough evidence available to condemn her.[19] This foul play, going ahead on the basis of insufficient evidence, was indeed cited by various clergy at the Nullification trial in 1456 who had been present at the 1431 trial.

During the pre-trial, Joan was questioned in a total of fifteen sessions: between 21 February and 3 March six sessions were held in public in front of a large male audience of theologians and judges. Then from 10 to 17 March, nine private sessions were held behind closed doors, sometimes with three of them held on one day alone. The purpose of the fifteen sessions was to collect evidence that could be used against

Joan during the formal trial, a gruelling experience for anyone. All this time Joan dressed in male attire was guarded by men in a secular male prison and not, as would normally have been the case with a female prisoner, in an ecclesiastical prison guarded by women. Furthermore, Pierre Cauchon placed an informer with Joan as he assigned her a confessor, Nicholas Loiseleur, whom Joan trusted. And he had a window installed in her prison through which he and his English paymasters regularly witnessed Joan's discussions with her confessor.[20]

The formal trial took place on 26 March when seventy articles were formulated against her. On 27 and 28 of March, they were read out before her. One week later, on 5 April the seventy charges were reduced to Twelve Articles of accusation, mainly summaries of what she had said herself in her testimonies.[21] They were approved by two bodies of clergymen, namely the assembled clergy at the Rouen trial and the theologians at the university of Paris to whom the charges were sent. During the two months that they were waiting for an answer from the Paris theologians, the Rouen judges put enormous pressure on Joan to accept the charges. It is during these weeks on 9 May that Pierre Cauchon took her to the torture chamber and told her that, if she continued to resist, she would be tortured, proof that Dreyer's famous scene is historical even though Bresson only alluded to it, as we will see below.[22] After a two months wait the response came back from Paris that the university authorities put their approval to the conclusions reached at Rouen.[23] On 23 May, the slightly revised version of the Twelve Articles was read out to her. They were followed by the conclusions from the Paris theologians who deemed her to be schismatic and heretical. The next day, 24 May, she was taken to the churchyard of Saint-Ouen at Rouen where she was formally charged in public.[24] There for the first time she was wearing a dress. She revoked her testimony that she had heard voices, as this notion had been the basis for the Twelve Articles and the conclusions from Paris, the case against her almost collapsed. Because she was dressed as a woman, she was nevertheless found guilty and condemned to life imprisonment. However, two days later, by which time she had taken off her dress and resumed wearing male clothes, she also announced that she heard her voices again. The judges argued that this constituted a relapse, that her renunciation had been false, and in another formal trial session she was condemned to death and handed over to the secular authorities of Rouen, the English, for the execution of the death sentence. One week later, on 30 May 1431 dressed in a penitential dress with a sign reading 'Relapsed, Heretic, Idolator, Schismatic' she was paraded around Rouen escorted by 120 English soldiers.[25] She was burned on the stake on a purpose-built high platform on the market square in Rouen. Immediately afterward John, duke of Bedford, regent in the name of King Henry VI, issued a letter announcing the death of the 'false prophetess'; it was sent in multiple copies across Europe.[26]

As Larissa Taylor has pointed out, when we assess Joan's behaviour we have to bear in mind that this was the fourth time that she had been publicly questioned about her faith, her voices and her divine mission.[27] The first three times had taken place two years earlier at Vaucouleurs, Chinon and Poitiers, in circumstances that were far less hostile to her. On these three occasions she was given the benefit of doubt. Not so at Rouen, where the English were absolutely determined to remove her from the political scene once and for all. Those who attended the trial and left a record, those who witnessed her and testified in 1456, and the record of the trial of 1431 itself (for all its problems to which I return) are unanimous that she showed enormous resilience, stamina and forbearance. She spoke with intelligence, alertness and astounding recall of what had been said to her. She was eloquent, witty and confident, attributes which could be interpreted as cocky and challenging to the judges. She revealed knowledge of procedure and law, which must have been given to her by the six Dominicans present, of whom several testified at the Nullification trial.

On the downside, albeit entirely understandable, she lied, made things up and played a tactical game occasionally going on the offensive.[28] For example one day she asked to put her case to the pope himself, an entirely legitimate request. There is also evidence that the Dominicans advised her by signs and nudges during the trial. The Dominican expert advice Joan received may raise eyebrows as the Dominicans were the very order to whom the Inquisition had been entrusted. Yet, these were Norman Dominicans, who loathed the English presence in Rouen and were particularly aware of the carnage the English had caused when they occupied Rouen in 1418. Under English occupation, they had very little leeway to act openly against the English king. Many of those who witnessed her burning had been moved, especially the Normans, who thought the trial had been concocted by the English.

Yet, as said before, thanks to the efforts of her family and the inhabitants of Orléans her reputation was saved. In 1450 Charles VII instructed

William Bouillé, canon at Noyon, to conduct preliminary enquiries for a retrial.[29] It was Bouillé who turned Joan from bold charismatic military leader, talented soldier and quick-witted young woman into the Joan we know from tradition: a simple peasant girl chosen by God to humble the powerful. In 1452 Cardinal d'Estouteville, papal legal in France, reopened the dossier. He was a Norman whose father had been in English captivity and whose brother had defended Mont St. Michel. He was no friend of the English. He received support from Grand Inquisitor of France, Jean Bréhal, a Norman. As Craig Taylor has pointed out, the motivation of these men to launch a new trial may have had more to do with a strategy to reconcile Normans with the French king to remove any stain of their past collaboration with the English, rather than motivated by a wish to rehabilitate Joan of Arc.[30] Thus in his view it was the Normans who pushed for a retrial. But the ultimate impetus came from Joan's family, who campaigned relentlessly for her rehabilitation, supported by her fans in Orléans. In fact the trial was brought as an action of her family.[31] On 7 November 1455, in a scene imagined memorably in Bresson's opening shot, Joan's mother Isabelle together with her sons Jean and Pierre and several inhabitants of Orléans came to Paris where they petitioned the archbishop of Reims to open an enquiry to clear Joan's name. Isabelle asked the Grand Inquisitor to squash the 1431 verdict of Joan as a schismatic and heretic. Her petition came after an initial twenty-two people had been interviewed in May about Cauchon's conduct. With this dossier compiled D'Estouteville went to Rome to receive support from Pope Nicholas V (1447–1455). Once papal support had been granted, the local population in Domrémy agreed to provide witness statements. Thus, it is crucial to realise that the support of Joan's family and village was absolutely essential in order for the higher authorities in Normandy to set the actual appeal in motion.

Between 10 January and 28 May 1456 a total of 160 witness statements from people in Lotharingia, Orléans, Paris, Lyon and Rouen were taken. At Toul, 34 people from Domrémy were interviewed plus her cousin Durand Laxart who had escorted her to Vaucouleurs. At Orléans the interrogation of 35 witnesses took place. Then at Rouen various people including the Poitiers judge Seguin, the notaries of the 1431 trial and importantly Jean Aulon, Joan's personal squire were questioned. The Nullification trial, itself, took place on 7 July 1456 at Rouen, 25 years after Joan's death. Joan's actions, so the final sentence argued, should be seen as a source of admiration rather than deceitful behaviour.[32]

The judge then quashed the previous trial and cleared Joan and her family of any infamy. These conclusions were read out publicly in the cemetery of Saint Ouen, the very place where in May 1431 the original verdict had been publicised. On the market place, where she was executed, a permanent cross was to be erected in her memory.[33] Yet, any attempt at a cult was forbidden as no images and epitaphs should be set up in Rouen. Interestingly, no individuals were blamed nor was anything said about Joan's orthodoxy or martyrdom, and no judgement was issued on Joan's orthodoxy. Also, although Brehal promised to circulate letters about the nullification across France, the request by the family to have a nullification record included in the *Grandes Chroniques de France* was refused.[34] As Larissa Taylor has noted, by 1456 Joan had become a symbol for France and a legend had been born.[35] Dreyer and Bresson are just two of the many artists who commemorated Joan and her extraordinary story in art and it is to them that I now turn.

Martyrdom and Anticlericalism—Dreyer 1928

Dreyer's iconic 1928 film has to be understood in the context of the French struggle between state and church for the memory of Joan of Arc. In 1905 a little more than a century after the French Revolution, the republic of France declared the separation between state and church. Partly in retaliation of the demotion of the Roman Catholic church's importance, the clergy of Orléans reactivated plans for Joan's canonisation. In 1909 Pope Pius X declared Joan 'blessed' and in 1920, delayed by the First World War when Joan became a source of immense inspiration for the soldiers at the front. Joan was declared a saint. What remains interesting is the seasawing actions between the Republican state and the Roman Catholic Church for the memory of Joan. The former saw her as the fearless standard-bearer of the Republic of France, while the latter portrayed her first and foremost as a Christian martyr who had died in the face of hostile questioning of her status as God's visionary. A crucial aspect of this competition was the battle of statues, erected in Paris in the nineteenth century by both sides who fought for the best urban sites to celebrate her enduring presence.[36] These statues were, in a way, the predecessors of the films.

Inspired by the publicity surrounding her canonisation, Carl Theodore Dreyer went back to the sources to distil his own version of Joan. Dreyer stressed the truth of his narrative at the start by showing a shot of (an unidentified) manuscript purporting to be one of the trial manuscripts, and of Pierre Champion the distinguished medievalist who acted as the director's academic adviser.[37] By concentrating on the trial he seems from the outset to go for the martyr model as the film shows as no other, Joan's pain and suffering under interrogation by a very hostile Pierre Cauchon. He concentrated on faces, both of the clergy and of Joan, played by the actress Renée Falconetti, because so he later explained in an interview, 'nothing can compare to the human face'.[38] Dreyer attributed Christ-like features to her, such as Joan's making of a replica crown of thorns in prison with which her guardians subsequently mocked her. In this way he underlined his view of Joan as the simple uneducated peasant girl who was persecuted for her serious and intense belief. He also left his viewers in no doubt that the trial took place under the control of the English secular authorities—the opening scene of the trial focused on clergy and English soldiers in the courtroom. By cutting out the story of Joan as warrior, and by thus not showing scenes of her as a fighter besieging Orléans or being present at the coronation of King Charles VII, he denied his viewers the opportunity to view Joan as the liberator warrior which France's Third Republic government had worked so hard on to promote.

However, by focussing on Joan's internal pain and her struggle to defend her own faith, we should not jump too easily to the conclusion that Dreyer, after all a protestant Danish filmmaker, was an admirer of the Roman Catholic Church. On the contrary, Dreyer took the opportunity to literally put the spotlight on the clergy both as a collective and as individuals to present them to his audience as a conspiratorial group of bullies. His famous shots of individual culpability of the assembled priests, nakedly portrayed with warts and all, in the unseemly pursuit of an innocent peasant girl, could not fail to throw negative light on the very Church that so recently had declared Joan a saint. Dreyer's filming method of 'abstraction' was suited precisely to highlight personal suffering in an environment shorn of all superfluous clutter.[39] The stark black and white setting of the film allows no distraction from the actions of the main protagonists. Above all, as a silent film, Dreyer's portrayal of Joan was a 'biography' of image and not as its etymology implies, one of words. The absence of words underlined the viewers' focus on the visual, both in the portrayal of the actors, the words of the interrogation and Joan's answers displayed in vignettes in between shots, and finally the use of close-ups, though some (e.g. Susan Sontag) have condemned Dreyer's 'male gaze' as too intrusive.[40]

The contemporary reaction to the film was hostile. The Archbishop of Paris demanded cuts to the film to remove too violent scenes, a demand with which the distributor concurred without consulting the filmmaker. At least this is what the *New York Times* of 20 January 1929 reported.[41] According to Finke and Shichtman the film was banned for a while in England (due to its anti-English stance), though I have not found evidence for this statement. Otherwise, film critics noted that sensitive viewers might find the film too real and too nearly physically torturous. Little could they anticipate the influence Dreyer had on film-making in general and on film history.

The film critics' point about the film being too physically torturous raises the important question of violence in the film. Any viewer would agree that the realistic filming of Joan of Arc's final moments on the stake is not only reasonably accurate (except that the environment in a castle is untrue—Joan was put on the stake in public on Rouen market place, and Dreyer's shot of the people's riots and protests afterwards never happened), but the lingering of the camera on Joan's body allows the viewer time to digest the appalling truth of her death. There is, however, another aspect of the film that is responsible for its reputation not to shrink away from violence and that concerns the representation of the historically accurate scene in the torture chamber of Rouen castle. As this was an ecclesiastical trial of heresy, under canon law torture was permitted albeit under carefully prescribed circumstances, even though in many countries secular law (including the English Common Law) forbade torture.[42] Though while most modern historians agree that it seems highly unlikely under the politically charged circumstances that the ecclesiastical judges seriously contemplated torturing Joan during the trial, it was nevertheless shocking at the time—and ever after—that Pierre Cauchon took her to the torture chamber and under threat put pressure on her to confess, and, as we know from the Nullification trial, had a torturer selected for her.[43] There is no doubt that the clergy meant to frighten her in the hope that she would confess to the charges laid before her. Dreyer's lingering shots on the various instruments of torture (the whipping tools, the wheel, the quartering machine) leave the viewer in no doubt about the potential use of them on the judges' victim. In contrast, as we shall see, Robert Bresson, for very good reasons avoided the subject of torture.

A Modern Young Woman—Robert Bresson 1962

Robert Bresson had been trained as a sculptor but turned to film in the 1950s. He pioneered the so-called 'camera-stylo' style pioneered by the film critic André Bazin.[44] Both Bresson and Bazin advocated the total control exercised by a director at the expense of any input by the actor; in Bresson's words: 'the film actor should content himself with saying his lines. He should not allow himself to show that he already understands them. Play nothing, explain nothing'.[45] The crux of the caméra-stylo style was that the director creates, not the actor. If we hazard a guess as to what this means for a biographical approach to a historical figure (rather than a fictional one) we can only surmise that Bresson considered himself firmly in charge of the portrayal of Joan through the actress Florence Carrez. This attitude explains the stillness and spare performance of the actors in the *Procès de Jeanne d'Arc*. From Pierre Cauchon to Joan of Arc the protagonists almost seem like puppets in the hands of a puppet master who dictates their movements. Another reason for the often mechanical behaviour and expressionless faces is Bresson's penchant for using untrained actors. Not surprisingly given his dictatorial behaviour, he could afford such directing style much more easily with unknown characters. As Florence Carrez explained in an interview thirty years later, she was picked out by Bresson as he saw her for the first time, even though she had no acting experience whatsoever.[46] In the interview, she is unfailingly positive about Bresson as director though confesses that he was deeply demanding. Another of his actors was more forthright. For Bresson's earlier film *Journal d'un curé de campagne* (1950) about a young priest who is dying of a fatal illness, the film director used a young inexperienced actor who was, like Bresson, a practicing Catholic. For a year before filming began, Bresson met him every Sunday to impress upon him the conception of his character. True to his earlier profession he worked on his actors as a sculptor works on clay![47]

But whereas Dreyer is famous for his short shots and close-ups, Bresson used only medium to long-distance shots. Dreyer's dramatic characterisation of the individual clergymen provides excitement and an element of surprise for the viewer. In contrast, Bresson's accent lies on monotony and a certain boredom to hammer home the point that Joan was relentlessly questioned and persecuted by unsympathetic clergy. In the film, Pierre Cauchon is not the uncompromising and threatening judge as he is in Dreyer's film. In fact Bresson, as Tony Pipolo has argued, disagreed strongly with Dreyer's almost perverse lingering shots on the judges, whose caricature behaviour distracted and distorted rather than illuminated Joan as the protagonist.[48] The restrained style of acting imposed upon Pierre Cauchon by Bresson emphasises his position as the Church's puppet in the hands of his English paymasters. Joan, as in Dreyer's film, is portrayed as a simple relatively unsophisticated, though determined young woman unprepared to give into the Church. For Bresson, too, Joan was first and foremost a martyr, sacrificed on the altar of the Anglo-Burgundian-Church alliance in Rouen. Though unlike the mastery of Dreyer's film there are no suspenseful or playful scenes to break the monotony of the filming. What is emphasised is the relentless dreariness and awfulness of Joan's situation. At the end of the film when Joan is led to the scaffold the camera, famously, is focussed on her hands and feet while she scuffles forward. On the stake, we are spared Dreyer's graphic scenes and instead the viewer is placed behind Joan and shares her view of the cross, held in front of her by one of the Dominican priests who had supported her during the trial. For Bresson too, Joan died a martyr, though as a result of the contemporary political environment in France he dared not remind his audience too explicitly of the issue of torture. This needs an explanation.

Bresson's 'Le procès de Jeanne d'Arc' has to be studied against the backdrop of selective state censorship during the period leading up to Algiers' independence. For it was the state's censorship that precluded Robert Bresson in 1962 to include more than a very oblique reference to the historically accurate report that Pierre Cauchon threatened Joan with torture: in a shot of no more than three or four seconds Joan is seen strapped to a wooden bed or chair surrounded by clergy. In my opinion this almost imperceptible allusion to torture is the most striking difference between Bresson and Dreyer, and not as Finke and Shichtman assert, the use of sound and (bizarrely) colour.[49] Despite his conscious choice not to copy Dreyer's torture chamber scene, Bresson equals Dreyer in the choice for simplicity of setting and filming. Whereas Dreyer's graphic scene of the torture chamber was a means to emphasise the duplicity of the Church and his own anticlericalism, Bresson's stance was influenced by a different context, namely the Algerian War of independence.

The Algerian War was fought between 1954 and 1962.[50] In 1962 under huge pressure by the United Nations, France withdrew its troops and Algeria declared its independence. The war is still a highly contentious and sensitive subject in France with debate raging on the merits of post-colonialism, the state's treatment of French Algerians many of whom live in overcrowded impoverished suburbs. No one has done more for the debate on the memorialisation of the war than the Algerian-French historian Benjamin Stora, professor at the university of Paris VII. Though as late as 2004–2005 he too admitted that 'the phase of memorial reconciliation between the two sides of the sea [the Mediterranean] is still a long way off'.[51] Acknowledgements that the war took place have taken long to surface. Only in 1999, thirty-seven years after the independence of Algiers, the National Assembly acknowledged that a war had been fought and only two years later did the government take responsibility for the many dead that fell during the massacre in Paris in 1961.[52]

One of the most sensitive and contested aspects of the Algerian War is the use of torture by both parties, which for years was denied. Only in 2001 did one general of the French army, Paul Ausseress, in his autobiography admit that during his regime in Algiers in 1957, torture had been a necessary evil, though he denied having himself committed acts of torture.[53] The fascist leader Jean le Pen, who recently has done so much to promote Joan of Arc as the symbol of his National Front party, has also been accused of torture though a general amnesty has prevented the state from taking him to court.[54] Already during the war itself, French intellectuals such as Jean Paul Sartre publicised and denounced the use of torture by the French government, an accusation that was consistently denied by the army and political leaders.[55] State censorship kicked in, too, to suppress the flood of allegations which were not restricted to newspaper articles but found their way into fiction and film. In 1958 Henri Alleg was told that his book *La Question* ('The Question') could not be published due to its allegations that the French state had been actively involved in torture.[56] Two years later in 1960 the filmmaker Jean-Luc Godard had his film 'Le petit soldier', set in Algiers, taken out of circulation because the film contained graphic scenes of torture committed by French soldiers. It was not until 1963 that the film was allowed back in the cinemas.[57] Seen against the background of heightened sensitivity on the issue of torture it is no surprise that Bresson did not follow in Dreyer's footsteps in this respect.

Finally, a significant contribution to the biography of Joan is Robert Bresson's place reserved for Joan of Arc's mother, another divergence from Dreyer's film, as noted by Pipolo.[58] It is highly significant,

I think, that the film opens with a scene showing the mother and her two sons petitioning Church authorities to have the case reopened. Historians are in no doubt about the crucial role she played in having her daughter's conviction of heresy quashed. If it had not been for her, and indeed other members of Joan's family, the Nullification trial would never have happened. Why did Robert Bresson foreground Joan's mother? According to Pipolo, Bresson's Roman Catholic faith was an important source of artistic inspiration with the Virgin Mary as Christ's mother a role model for several strong maternal figures in his films.[59] Mary as intercessor between God and Man is the most obvious example for Joan's mother interceding on her daughter's behalf with the pope, through the archbishop of Reims. No other film, as far as I am aware, stresses the actions of Joan's mother as her ultimate saviour.

Conclusion

Both filmmakers do on the whole faithfully follow the narrative of the trial records. Inevitably, there is a teleological compression of the daily minutiae of the trial witness accounts. Nevertheless, they both lay bare the stark biographical detail of the last days of Joan's life as it is concealed in the court records of her trial. This contemporary 'hidden' biography of Joan is not unusual in the Middle Ages. The life story details we find in trial records, most exceptionally detailed in the records of Bishop Jacques Fournier, the source for Le Roy Ladurie's *Montaillou*, were purposefully gathered with one aim only to convict the accused of heresy.[60] From the late twelfth century onwards church authorities became masters of the veiled and fragmented biographical record of those whom they suspected of unorthodoxy. These biased versions of medieval people's lives were a stark contrast to the equally biased, if thoroughly positive, pen portraits that frequently led to sainthood. Medieval saints' lives, of men and women, were the most frequent form of biographical writing, strongly shaped by tradition and composed according to hagiographical templates.[61] Only very rarely did it happen that someone convicted of heresy at a church trial was subsequently remembered (or rehabilitated) in a biography. In fact, heresy trials ended with the burning of the convicted heretics at the stake precisely in order to literally reduce the body to ashes and to obliterate all remnants that might otherwise be used as relics. The heretic's ashes symbolised the *damnatio memoriae* (the damning of the person's memory), and no biography was supposed to remind contemporaries of the person's life. This explains the absence of a contemporary biography of Joan of Arc. As for secular pen portraits, they were written mostly of men, who were emperors, kings or other rulers. This tradition too explains why biographies of women, let alone those of modest backgrounds such as Joan, were relatively rare. Paradoxically, the lack of a medieval biography of Joan has allowed later biographers, artists and filmmakers a free hand to mould the rich trial material into a biographical shape according to the norms and ideas of their own time.

In a pre-feminist world of the late 1920s and early 1960s, Dreyer and Bresson stress most of all Joan's young age and powerlessness. Yet, the viewer of Bresson's Joan can imagine her career as a charismatic and intelligent leader and fighter, something that cannot be said of Dreyer's Joan, who—in our eyes—seems simply too pathetic. Bresson's Joan also prepares us for the Joan of our own time, even though the modern academic view of Joan's biographers could not be more different. Craig Taylor (2006), Larissa Taylor (2009) and Helen Castor (2014), all in their own way, reveal a young woman of astounding self-confidence, intelligence and bravery, on the battlefield and in court. These scholarly biographers see extensive autonomy and agency in their Joan. At the same time, they acknowledge compellingly that Joan could act as she did only as long as her contemporaries believed that her behaviour was inspired by God.

Notes

1. Finke and Shichtman, 2010, pp. 145–46.
2. The historiography on Joan of Arc is enormous. Readers may find it helpful to know that a collection of translated sources with an excellent commentary is Taylor, 2006. The original trial record in Latin of 1431 can be found in Tisset and Lanhers, 1960–71, and that of the nullification trial of 1456 in Duparc, 1977–89. A brief but very helpful discussion of all sources can be found in Taylor, 2009, pp. 192–97. Amongst the scholarly biographies I recommend Taylor, 2009; Castor, 2014.
3. In fact, Dreyer condensed the trial to one day (Airlie 2001, p. 167), while Bresson gives more a sense of development over a length of time, though his screenplay is mostly a composite of both trials (Pipolo 2010, pp. 160–61).
4. Dreyer explicitly said that 'I did not study the clothes of the time and things like that...The year of the event seemed as inessential to me as the

distance to the past. All these pictures express the character of the person they show and the spirit of the time.' quoted in Natalie Zemon Davies, 'Any resemblance to persons living or dead; film and the challenge of authenticity', *American Historical Review* 1988, pp. 1173–85; Margolis, 1997, pp. 470–74.

5. In an interview Bresson argued that he saw Joan of Arc not as Dreyer's simple peasant girl but as 'very elegant… as a modern young woman' (cited by Pipolo 2010, p. 163).
6. Good introductions on the Hundred Years War can be found in Curry, 1993; Castor, 2014, pp. 19–86.
7. Taylor, 2009, pp. 20–31.
8. Taylor, 2009, pp. 32–34.
9. For a reconstruction, see Taylor, 2009, pp. 40–43.
10. Quoted in Taylor, 2009, p. 42.
11. Taylor, 2009, pp. 42–49.
12. Taylor, 2006, no. 3, pp. 72–73.
13. Taylor, 2009, pp. 47–49.
14. Taylor, 2009, pp. 51–72.
15. Taylor, 2009, pp. 92–95.
16. Taylor, 2009, pp. 96–97, 102–3.
17. Taylor, 2009, pp. 117–29.
18. Taylor, 2006, nos. 34–56, pp. 137–224; Taylor, 2009, pp. 130–52.
19. Taylor, 2009, p. 132.
20. Taylor, 2009, p. 134.
21. Taylor, 2006, no. 58, pp. 207–12.
22. Taylor, 2009, pp. 153–54.
23. Taylor, 2009, pp. 154–57.
24. Taylor, 2009, pp. 157–60.
25. Taylor, 2009, pp. 163–69.
26. Taylor, 2006, no. 57, pp. 225–28.
27. Taylor, 2009, p. 130.
28. Taylor, 2009, pp. 135–36.
29. Taylor, 2006, nos. 71–102, pp. 262–49; Taylor, 2009, pp. 172–89.
30. Taylor, 2006, p. 42.
31. Taylor, 2006, p. 44; Taylor, 2009, p. 179.
32. Taylor, 2006, no. 102, p. 348.
33. Taylor, 2006, no. 102, p. 349.
34. Taylor, 2006, p. 45.
35. Taylor, 2009, p. 182.
36. Gildea, 1994, pp. 154–62; McWilliam, 2004, pp. 386–96.
37. Margolis, 1997, pp. 470–72.
38. Quoted in Aberth, 2003, p. 282.

39. Aberth, 2003, p. 279.
40. Finke and Shichtman, 2010, p. 120.
41. Aberth, 2003, pp. 279–80; Finke and Shichtman, 2010, p. 113.
42. The classic study is Langbein, 1976 rev. 2006; see also Tracy, 2012. Countries that allowed torture as in Roman law were Germany, France and all mediterranean countries; it was not allowed as proof of evidence in Scotland, England, Scandinavia and the Low Countries.
43. Taylor, 2009, p. 154.
44. Drazin, 2011, pp. 272–73.
45. Quoted in Drazin, 2011, p. 279.
46. In extra section added to the DVD version of the film in the series World Cinema Classics part of the Artificial Eye series.
47. Drazin, 2011, p. 278.
48. Pipolo, 2010, p. 166.
49. Incidentally, Finke and Shichtman, pp. 119–20 allege erroneously that Bresson used colour where Dreyer's film was black and white.
50. Stora, 2004; Evans, 2012.
51. Quoted from an interview with Benjamin Stora on the INA website 2005 (http://ina.fr/voir_revoir/algerie/itv_stora.light.en.html) accessed 13 February 2012; see also Stora, 2004, p. 100.
52. Stora, 2004, p. 97; Evans, 2012, pp. 335–39.
53. Stora, 2004, pp. 26–27, 97; Evans, 2012, pp. 210–15.
54. For the various phases of the amnesty process, see Stora, 2004, pp. 92–93.
55. Evans, 2012, pp. 224, 286.
56. Evans, 2012, pp. 223–25.
57. Stora, 2004, p. 118.
58. Pipolo, 2010, pp. 160–61.
59. Pipolo, 2010, pp. 359–61.
60. Le Roy Ladurie, 1980; Arnold and Biller, 2016. For its exceptional detail of 'the texture of human life', see Arnold, 2013, p. 508.
61. Bates, Crick and Hamilton, 2006, pp. 1–13.

Bibliography

Sources

Duparc, Pierre. 1977–89. *Procès en nullité de la condemnation de Jeanne d'Arc*, 5 Vols. Paris: Klincksieck.

Taylor, Craig, trans. and annot. 2006. *Joan of Arc: La Pucelle*. Manchester Medieval Sources series. Manchester: Manchester University Press.

Tisset, P., and Lanhers, Y. 1960–71. *Procès de condemnation de Jeanne d'Arc*, 3 Vols. Paris: Klincksieck.

Literature

Aberth, J. 2003. *A Knight at the Movies: Medieval History on Film*, Chapter 6, pp. 257–98. New York: Routledge.

Airlie, Stuart. 2001. 'Strange Eventful Histories: The Middle Ages in the Cinema', in P. Linehan and J. L. Nelson (ed.), *The Medieval World*, pp. 163–83. London: Routledge.

Arnold, J. 2013. 'Heresy and Gender in the Middle Ages', in Judith M. Bennett and Ruth MazoKarras (eds.), *The Oxford Handbook of Women and Gender in Medieval Europe*, pp. 496–510. Oxford: Oxford University Press.

Arnold, J. H., and Biller, P. (eds.). 2016. *Heresy and Inquisition in France, 1200–1300.* Manchester: Manchester University Press.

Bates, David, Crick, Julia, and Hamilton, Sarah (eds.). 2006. *Writing Medieval Biography 750–1250: Essays in Honour of Professor Frank Barlow*. Woodbridge: Boydell and Brewer.

Blaetz, R. 2001. *Visions of the Maid: Joan of Arc in American Film and Culture.* Charlottesville: University of Virginia Press.

Castor, Helen. 2014. *Joan of Arc, a History.* London: Faber and Faber.

Curry, A. 1993. *The Hundred Years War*. Basingstoke: Macmillan.

Drazin, Charles. 2011. *The Faber Book of French Cinema*. London: Faber and Faber.

Evans, Martin. 2012. *Algeria: France's Undeclared War.* Oxford: Oxford University Press.

Finke, Laurie A., and Shichtman, Martin B. 2010. *Cinematic Illuminations.* Baltimore: The John Hopkins University Press.

Gildea, Robert. 1994. *The Past in French History.* New Haven: Yale University Press.

Langbein, J. H. 1976 rev. 2006. *Torture and the Law of Proof: Europe and England in the Ancien Régime*. Chicago: University of Chicago Press.

Le Roy Ladurie, E. 1980. *Montaillou: The World-Famous Portrait of Life in a Medieval Village*. London: Penguin.

Margolis, Nadia. 1997. 'Trial by Passion: Philology, Film and Ideology in the Portrayal of Joan of Arc (1900–1930)', *The Journal of Medieval and Early Modern Studies* 27, pp. 446–93.

McWilliam, Neil. 2004. 'Conflicting Manifestations: Parisian Commemoration of Joan of Arc and Etienne Dolet in the Early Third Republic', *French Historical Studies* 27, pp. 381–418.

Pernoud, Régine, Clin, Marie Véronique, and trans. J. duQuesnay Adams. 1999. *Joan of Arc: Her Story.* New York: St. Martin's.

Pipolo, Tony. 2010. *Robert Bresson: A Passion for Film*, Chapter 4, pp. 153–81. Oxford: Oxford University Press.

Stora, Benjamin. 2004. *Histoire de la guerre d'Algérie, 1954–1962*, 4th edition. Paris: La Découverte.

Sullivan, Karin. 1999. *The Interrogation of Joan of Arc*. Minneapolis and London: University of Minnesota Press.

Taylor, Larissa Juliet. 2009. *The Virgin Warrior: The Life and Death of Joan of Arc*. New Haven and London: Yale University Press.

Tracy, Larissa. 2012. *Torture and Brutality in Medieval Literature*. Cambridge: Brewer.

Vauchez, A., and trans. J. Birell. 1997. *Sainthood in the Later Middle Ages*. Cambridge: Cambridge University Press.

Wheeler, B., and Wood, Charles T. (eds.). 1996. *Fresh Verdicts on Joan of Arc*. New York: Garland.

Blood, Lust, and the Virgin Queen: Helen Mirren's *Elizabeth I*

William B. Robison

> *Brass shines as fair to the ignorant as gold to the goldsmiths.* Elizabeth I (1581)

Among the many actresses who have played Elizabeth I on film and television,[1] a handful have achieved iconic status in that role, notably Flora Robson in *Fire Over England* (1937) and *The Sea Hawk* (1940), Bette Davis in *The Private Lives of Elizabeth and Essex* (1939) and *The Virgin Queen* (1955), Glenda Jackson in *Elizabeth R* (1970) and *Mary Queen of Scots* (1971), Cate Blanchett in *Elizabeth* (1998), and *Elizabeth: The Golden Age* (2007). Others, if not quite iconic, are well known to students of Tudor historical films, i.e., Sarah Bernhardt in *Les Amours de la reine Élisabeth* (1912), Diana Manners in *The Virgin Queen* (1923), Florence Eldridge in *Mary of Scotland* (1936), Jean Simmons in *Young Bess* (1953), even Miranda Richardson in *Blackadder II* (1986), and Quentin Crisp in *Orlando* (1992). In 2005 the brilliant Helen Mirren bid fair to join the iconic elite with the Channel 4/HBO miniseries *Elizabeth I*, part of

W. B. Robison (✉)
Southeastern Louisiana University, Hammond, LA, USA
e-mail: wrobison@selu.edu

T. S. Freeman and D. L. Smith (eds.), *Biography and History in Film*, Palgrave Studies in the History of the Media,
https://doi.org/10.1007/978-3-319-89408-9_4

a new 'twenty-first century' wave of Tudor cinema and television that began in 1998 and continues unabated. For that period Mirren gives the most compelling performance among a group that includes Blanchett, Judi Dench in *Shakespeare in Love* (1998), Catherine McCormack in *Gunpowder, Treason and Plot* (BBC 2004), Anne-Marie Duff in *Elizabeth I: The Virgin Queen* (PBS 2005, BBC 2006), Vanessa Redgrave and Joely Richardson in *Anonymous* (2011), Margot Robbie in *Mary Queen of Scots* (2018)[2] and a host of lesser-known onscreen Elizabeths.[3]

Part One of *Elizabeth I* opens at Whitehall in 1579 with intertitles stating: 'Elizabeth has been on the throne for twenty years and so far refused to marry. Without a husband there can be no direct heir and as a consequence there is danger of civil war between those competing for the succession. England is a small and vulnerable Protestant country and the Catholic powers, led by Spain, are waiting to seize the heretic Queen's throne.' This is rather misleading. Elizabeth had not flatly rejected marriage and continued to take courtship seriously.[4] With the queen alive, there was no immediate danger of civil war per se among competing claimants to the throne, though Elizabeth had faced an armed rebellion in 1569 and remained the target of Catholic plots intended to replace her with Mary, Queen of Scots.[5] England was a small country relative to France, Spain, and the Holy Roman Empire, and its navy in 1579 was less formidable than legend claims; however, just how vulnerable it was is debatable. It was, after all, an island protected by the sea and frequently bad weather, as well as the fleet.[6] It had not been invaded successfully since Elizabeth's grandfather Henry VII did so in 1485 and would not be again until William III did it in 1688. Spain failed in four invasion attempts in 1588, 1596, 1597, and 1601.[7] The 'Catholic powers' were hardly monolithic, for—as the film reminds us—France and Spain were enemies, and the French were eager for a marriage alliance between Anjou and Elizabeth. Philip and the papacy were often at odds, the Spanish king disliked the Queen of Scots, and German Catholics had other concerns, notably the Turks.[8]

The story proceeds with Elizabeth's servants undressing her, reversing the way *Elizabeth and Essex* begins.[9] The queen undergoes a gynecological exam to insure she is still *virgo intacta* and capable of bearing children if she agrees to wed the French Duke of Anjou. Her councilors William Cecil, Lord Burghley (Ian McDiarmid), and Sir Francis Walsingham (Patrick Malahide) support the proposed marriage, as does parliament, but Robert Dudley, Earl of Leicester (Jeremy Irons)—amid considerable wistful flirtation—argues against it. Gilbert Gifford (Simon Woods) makes a fictional attempt to assassinate Elizabeth, Leicester rescues her, and Walsingham extracts Gifford's confession that he acted on behalf of Spain. When the latter reports in council that Mary, Queen of Scots was involved, Elizabeth angrily declares that she will not execute a fellow monarch. Anjou (Jérémie Covillault) arrives with his servant Jean de Simier (Erick Deshors), and the queen is smitten. Leicester shows her a book opposing the marriage, and she orders that the author, Protestant pamphleteer John Stubbs (Martin Savage), have his hand cut off. Simier reveals that Leicester is married to Lady Essex (Diane Kent), and Elizabeth banishes him. Her councilors hesitate to endorse the marriage, she weeps, and Anjou departs.[10]

The action skips to 'seven years later,' Walsingham tells Elizabeth the pope has excommunicated her (which happened in 1570), Burghley warns that Philip II of Spain may attempt to seize the throne, and Walsingham adds that he may work through Mary, but Elizabeth remains unmoved. At Walsingham's behest, Gifford—turned informer—meets with Sir Anthony Babington (Gregory Streatfeild) and an unidentified priest, presumably John Ballard, about a plot against the queen. Elizabeth summons Leicester back to court after an imaginary seven-year absence, and he declares that his romantic feelings are unchanged. At her request, he arranges a secret—and entirely fictional—meeting between her and Mary (Barbara Flynn), which resolves nothing. After initially refusing, she allows Leicester to command English troops supporting the Dutch rebels against Spain, and he departs along with his young stepson Robert Devereux, 2nd Earl of Essex (Hugh Dancy). Burghley and Walsingham show Elizabeth a letter implicating Mary in the Babington Plot, and she has the male conspirators hanged, drawn, and quartered and agrees to have Mary brought to trial. Leicester returns, admitting failure, and joins those urging her to put Mary to death. She signs the necessary warrant and orders William Davison (Mykolas Dorofejus) not to give it to the council, but he does so anyway. Walsingham witnesses Mary's beheading at Fotheringay and reports it to Elizabeth, who gives way to hysteria.[11]

Later, she reconciles with Leicester, observing, 'What is the crown when love's voice speaks to us?' But she notes that war with Spain is imminent and that they cannot be lovers. As the Spanish ambassador Don Bernardino de Mendoza (Martin Marquez) leaves court, he warns that Spain will burn Elizabeth, Essex draws his dagger to attack him, but Leicester stops him. Leicester advises Essex that the queen's 'favor changes with her moods,' tells him to 'love her constantly,' and presents him to the queen, who flirts with the younger man. With the Spanish Armada approaching, she refuses Burghley's request to go to safety and determines to speak to her troops. In a rather contrived bit, Leicester advises her to wear armor and feeds her a line of dialogue, 'I could swear your majesty has the heart and soul of a king.' She delivers the famous Tilbury Speech to the usual cheers. News arrives that the English have defeated the Armada, but the celebration is spoiled when Leicester collapses. The scene shifts to Elizabeth nursing him as he dies, another bit of fiction. Part One concludes with a strangely older-looking Elizabeth standing among captured banners and urging the crowd to remain humble before God, noting that they are her 'only solace,' and—borrowing lines from her Golden Speech of 1601—adding that they 'may have yet a greater prince but they shall never have a more loving one.'

Part Two opens with more misleading intertitles: 'By 1589 Elizabeth I was the heroine and savior of her country. The defeat of the Spanish Armada had secured the English nation and the English Protestant Church. There was no more talk of her need to take a husband and produce an heir. But who would succeed her? Who would take her extraordinary power for themselves [sic]?' Elizabeth was momentarily lauded after the Armada, though less so than by Protestant providentialist historians in the next century. But she lost her heroic status among the sailors and soldiers whom she failed to pay and was soon facing severe economic problems. In addition, the Anglo-Spanish War continued until 1604, when James VI and I finally made peace with Philip III.[12] The Scottish Borders remained problematic[13] and Ireland rebellious.[14] Furthermore, threats to the English Protestant Church were not at an end. English Protestants continued to fear Catholic plots, real and imagined, particularly until the Glorious Revolution in 1688 but even down to the Gordon Riots in 1780. Complicating matters is that English 'Protestants'—moderate 'Anglicans,' Puritans, Presbyterians, Separatists, etc.—did not agree about what the English Church was or should be and often saw one another as dangerous.[15] The succession, however, was a very real issue.[16]

Action ensues with Elizabeth having white make-up applied and a wig placed on her head, after which she banishes mirrors from the palace—a trope that dates to Ben Jonson, often appeared in the nineteenth century, and is featured in *The Private Lives of Elizabeth and*

Essex.[17] The queen watches Essex riding in the courtyard on a gigantic artificial horse and laughs while Burghley, his son Robert Cecil (Toby Jones), and Walsingham grumble. Essex jousts with Sir Walter Raleigh (Ben Pullen), who unhorses him. When Elizabeth gives Raleigh a token, Essex insults him, the latter demands satisfaction, they duel, and Essex is wounded. Meanwhile, Elizabeth is angry that Walsingham's daughter Lady Frances (Charlotte Asprey) is Essex's admirer. The queen insists on dressing Essex's wounds in Leicester's old rooms, which she gives to him. They flirt and then engage in some heavy petting, but she stops and leaves. Later she agrees to a council proposal to send a naval expedition against Philip to restore the deposed Dom Antonio to the throne of Portugal but orders them not to tell Essex about it. However, he finds out, departs in secret, and comes back covered with glory. Meanwhile, Burghley persuades her to put Robert on the council, which makes Essex jealous. While asking parliament for subsidies to pay for the war and harvest failures, she collapses, and Essex accuses Dr. Rodrigo Lopez (Toby Salaman) of poisoning her. Cecil objects, but Lopez is executed for treason. When it emerges that Essex obtained evidence against Lopez under torture, the queen is initially angry but forgives him.[18]

Cecil shows Elizabeth a pamphlet suggesting that Essex should be her successor. Making matters worse is that Lady Frances is pregnant with Essex's child (in reality, they were secretly married at the time). Later, the queen informs Cecil about rumors that someone at court has been writing to James VI about the succession. By this time Walsingham is dead, so she has Cecil arrange a fictional meeting with James (Ewan Bremner), who asks how he likes being ruled by a woman and declares that when he is king, 'I shall have handsome young men around me, and we shall use woman as dogs do bitches, for our pleasure and our profit.' When Elizabeth returns to court, Essex denies writing to James, and Elizabeth offers him command of an expedition to Cadiz. The action then skips to a celebration of his success, which makes Elizabeth unhappy. Bad news arrives from Ireland, and debate erupts in council about whom Elizabeth should send there as Lord Deputy. This leads to the famous incident in which Essex draws his sword in anger against the queen, who then decides to send him. Burghley dies, and after his funeral, Elizabeth and Essex reconcile. She gives him a ring as a token of her goodwill, an old myth that first appears onscreen in *Les Amours de la reine Élisabeth*. Next, after time has passed, Robert Cecil informs Elizabeth that Essex has not engaged the rebellious Earl of Tyrone and suggests the latter is in a league with Spain. No action in Ireland occurs onscreen.[19]

Essex returns from Ireland without permission. After the privy council charges him with various offenses, Elizabeth has him confined to Essex House. She then tricks Lady Frances into revealing that he has been corresponding with James. When she sends Francis Bacon (Will Keen) to bring Essex to court, the earl imprisons him. Essex and the Earl of Southampton (Eddie Redmayne) then attempt to raise a rebellion, which fails miserably. Essex defends himself before parliament (the trial was actually in Star Chamber), where he and Southampton are condemned for treason. Elizabeth spares the latter, but Essex goes to the block in the Tower. The remainder of Part Two is essentially a dénouement. Elizabeth broods, discusses taxes and monopolies with Cecil, and delivers the Golden Speech before parliament in 1601. She next appears in bed in 1603, her finger in her mouth. Her doctors can find no reason for her illness. She demands a mirror to look at herself and says, 'There was a man once …' When Cecil asks whether she means Leicester or Essex, she says only, 'The hardest thing to govern is the heart.' Later, her ladies tell Cecil she has been standing for fifteen hours and has not eaten for three weeks. She refuses his request to go to bed, saying, 'If you saw such things in your bed as I see in mine, you would not go there.' Cecil leaves, and she walks toward her bed, saying, 'That man, whoever he was …' After lying down, she tells her ladies, 'Fetch me a priest, girl, I'm minded to die.'[20]

Though none of this century's films is particularly accurate—that is, based on reliable contemporary sources and current scholarship—the script for *Elizabeth I* is more plausible, more coherent, and less burdened with presentism than most. Its main weakness as filmic biography is in focusing too much on the queen's largely imaginary love affairs with Leicester and Essex, though that hardly makes it unique. At the same time, its attempt at realism in depicting executions makes it one of the bloodiest Elizabethan films, with the deaths of the Babington plotters, the Queen of Scots, Dr. Rodrigo Lopez, and Essex shown in gruesome detail. Overall, if visually less flashy than *Elizabeth* and *Elizabeth: The Golden Age*, it is also less bombastic and bigoted—both of Shekhar Kapur's films with Blanchett are stridently anti-Catholic.[21] Not the least of advantages Mirren's film has over Duff's *Elizabeth I: The Virgin Queen* is that it allows characters to look and act their age. Mirren, Blanchett, and Duff aside, the most notable twenty-first-century Elizabeths are just supporting characters. Dench appears briefly in a film that makes no pretense to historicity, Redgrave and Richardson are wasted in a movie about the discredited theory that the 17th Earl of Oxford wrote Shakespeare's works, and McCormack is in a production that squanders acting talent on a weird account of Mary, Queen of Scots and James VI and I.

Mirren's most obvious contribution to *Elizabeth I* is her performance. As director Tom Hooper notes, 'One of her gifts as an actress is when you are watching her, you believe in her, you believe in what she is doing. When she acts, it feels incredibly real and truthful and natural.' However, she was central to the film's making in more ways than one. Hooper and writer Nigel Williams conceived the project with her in mind, had no interest in casting anyone else as the queen, and did not begin writing the script until she agreed to take the role. They initially planned a two-hour show beginning in 1589 and focusing on Elizabeth and Essex, but after reading the first draft of the script Mirren convinced them to include more politics and historical detail and begin the story a decade earlier in 1579, thereby incorporating Elizabeth's relationship with the aging Leicester,[22] enhancing the roles of Burghley[23] and Walsingham,[24] and extending the program to two parts with a total running time of nearly four hours. Mirren also sought to emphasize not only Elizabeth's personal life—in which the two earls figured prominently—but also her political role and status as an icon.[25] Thus, Part One also includes Anjou's courtship from 1579 to 1581, the intrigues leading to the Queen of Scots' execution in 1587,[26] and the Armada in 1588, while Part Two depicts not only her fanciful romance with Essex,[27] but also influence passing from older courtiers to a new generation riven by faction, the struggle over the succession, and the queen's decline. Both parts feature interaction with the privy council and parliament[28] and emphasize the queen's concern for her image. Mirren helped to attract a particularly strong cast, many sharing her experience on stage, cinema, and television. Irons and Dancy acknowledge taking roles as Leicester and Essex specifically in order to work with her.[29]

Though Elizabeth, like her father Henry VIII and cousin Mary, Queen of Scots, has been popular with filmmakers and audiences throughout the history of cinema and television, no filmic depiction covers her life from birth to death except for documentaries. Only *The Six Wives of Henry VIII* (1970), *The Tudors* (2007–2010), and some versions of *The Prince and the Pauper* deal with her childhood. *Young Bess* technically covers the years 1533–1558 but concentrates on the period 1543–1549. Blanchett's *Elizabeth* crams the period 1555–1572 into what seems like a much shorter time. Davis' *The Virgin Queen* begins in 1581 and ends with Sir Walter Raleigh married to Bess Throckmorton, which occurred in 1591 but happens more quickly in the film. *Elizabeth: The Golden Age* is set c. 1585–1590, while *Fire Over England* and *The Sea Hawk* focus on the year of the Armada, 1588. *Les Amours de la reine Élisabeth* covers the years 1588–1601, while *Elizabeth and Essex* and Judith Anderson's *Elizabeth the Queen* (1968) begin in 1596 and end in 1601. Only two productions address Elizabeth's entire reign—*Elizabeth R* begins in 1549 with the Privy Council's investigation of Elizabeth's relationship with Sir Thomas Seymour, and *Elizabeth I: The Virgin Queen* opens in 1554 with her arrest for suspected complicity in Wyatt's Rebellion.[30]

Mirren's *Elizabeth I*, which spans the last twenty-four of the queen's forty-five years on the throne, covers more of her reign than any except *Elizabeth R* and *Elizabeth I: The Virgin Queen* unless one counts films about Mary, Queen of Scots that begin before or at Elizabeth's accession in 1558 and end with Mary's execution in 1587, i.e., *The Loves of Mary, Queen of Scots* (1923), *Mary of Scotland*, *Das Herz de Königin* (*The Heart of a Queen*, 1940), *Mary Queen of Scots*, *Gunpowder, Treason, and Plot*, and *Mary Queen of Scots* (2018). However, Elizabeth is not the 'star' in those productions. Other films about Mary concentrate on a short time span culminating with her execution, i.e., film versions of Friedrich Schiller's play *Maria Stuart* and Gaetano Donizetti's opera *Maria Stuarda*, as well as *You Are There: The Execution of Mary Queen of Scots* (1954), *The Queen's Traitor* (1967), and *La dernière nuit* (1981). The ludicrous television series *Reign* (2013–2017) deals with the period 1557–1567, though the final episode jumps ahead to Mary's execution. Elizabeth also has lesser roles in such older films as *Dorothy Vernon of Haddon Hall* (1924) and *Pearls of the Crown* (1937), and cameos in others.[31]

Casting for first-billed characters in *Elizabeth I* was more age-appropriate than is often the case. Mirren was fifty-nine while shooting a film in which Elizabeth ages from forty-six to sixty-nine (1579–1603), though the queen was losing her looks by 1579 and the actress always has appeared younger than she is.[32] By comparison, in major films that overlap with *Elizabeth I* chronologically, Duff was twenty-five in *Elizabeth I: The Virgin Queen* and aged little, McCormack thirty-one in *Gunpowder, Treason and Plot*, Davis thirty-one in *Elizabeth and Essex* and forty-seven in *The Virgin Queen*, Jackson thirty-four in *Elizabeth R* and thirty-five in *Mary, Queen of Scots*, Robson thirty-five in *Fire Over England* and thirty-eight in *The Sea Hawk*, Blanchett thirty-eight in *Elizabeth: The Golden Age*, Richardson forty-six and Redgrave seventy-four in *Anonymous*; Bernhardt sixty-eight in *Les Amours de la reine Élisabeth*, Anderson seventy-one in *Elizabeth The Queen*. Among other first-billed actors, Irons was fifty-six as Leicester from forty-six to fifty-five (1579–1588),[33] Dancy thirty as Essex from twenty to thirty-five (1585–1601),[34] McDiarmid sixty-seven as Burghley from fifty-nine to seventy-seven (1579–1598),[35] Malahide sixty as Walsingham from forty-seven to fifty-eight (1579–1590),[36] Jones thirty-eight as Robert Cecil from twenty-six to thirty-nine (1579–1603),[37] Flynn fifty-six as Mary, Queen of Scots from thirty-six to forty-four (1579–1587),[38] and Bremner thirty-three as James VI.

Mirren researched her look with costume designer Mike O'Neill and hair and make-up artist Fae Hammond, and the costuming is excellent. O'Neill created a wardrobe that went from 'a very informal sense of clothing' to a 'semi-iconic state' for the court to the iconic dresses from paintings, though he resisted duplicating them exactly. Mirren opined, and the scholarship of Susan Doran, John Guy, and Anna Whitelock confirms, that Elizabeth did not always dress as formally as in her portraits, for which she rarely posed.[39] However, the queen's formal apparel in the film is sumptuous and magnificent. Hammond gave Mirren numerous different looks in the film by using the queen's own propensity for a variety of wigs and jewelry. Hooper often framed Elizabeth, dressed in red or other bright colors, with other characters costumed in black or framed by dark scenery, which makes her stand out, as she chose to do in reality.[40] Reviewing the 2015 docu-drama *Armada* for *The Guardian*, Kate Maltby asked why Elizabeth is 'always depicted as a grotesque.'[41] Indeed, she often is, perhaps most blatantly in *Elizabeth R*, and there is no getting around the fact that she lost her hair, had bad teeth, and wore copious amounts of white make-up. However, the makers of Elizabeth I literally resisted the temptation to lay it on quite so thick.

Mirren felt it important to humanize Elizabeth, recognizing that the 'story is about how the personal and the political come together and split apart and come together.' Thus, for her, 'Costumes are marvelous because obviously they make the statement for you, but then you have to start fighting your way out of the costume and the make-up, so it's both a tool and a liability because you want to make this person a living, breathing person and not just a painting.' Hooper likewise sought to bring the queen down to earth, sometimes quite literally. For example, Mirren does not deliver the famous Tilbury Speech from horseback like Robson, Jackson, Duff, and Blanchett. Rather, she walks among her troops, almost awkwardly at times. Though strikingly less grandiose than Blanchett—who looks more like Galadriel than Gloriana in *Elizabeth: The Golden Age*—she gives a much more accurate version of the speech.[42] Also 'down-to earth,' though perhaps not deliberate, is the execution of the Babington plotters. Admittedly most viewers may find the blood and gore quite realistic enough. But public executions were theater as well as punishment, conducted not at ground level but on a platform that served as a kind of stage (later in the show, Dr. Lopez does die on an elevated platform).

Hooper shot the whole program in Lithuania, most of it on sets built entirely inside an old Soviet-era sports stadium in Vilnius and including a scale model of Whitehall Palace based on the original plans and built with advice from architectural historian Simon Thurley. The sets are very good, but there is little footage that goes beyond them.[43] This is rather limiting at times, and there is a noticeable scarcity of outdoor scenes. The Spanish Armada makes no appearance. The closest viewers get is a ghostly ship sailing up the Thames that turns out to be English and reports the 'invincible' Armada's defeat.[44] This low-key approach to one of the greatest naval battles in history is similar to that in *Elizabeth R* and *Elizabeth I: The Virgin Queen*, but is in stark contrast to *Fire Over England* and especially *Elizabeth: The Golden Age*, though the spectacular staging of the battle in the latter is highly inaccurate. Viewers do not see either of the spectacular raids on Cadiz, by Drake in 1587 and Essex in 1596. Neither is there any footage of Essex in Ireland despite the role of his Irish ventures in his eventual fate, nor are there scenes at the courts of Elizabeth's fellow rulers.

There are some curious omissions from the cast and plot. Philip II of Spain, who was Elizabeth's principal enemy from 1585 until his death in 1598, does not appear at all, though he is a prominent character in *Fire Over England*, *The Sea Hawk*, *Elizabeth R*, *Elizabeth I: The Virgin Queen*, and *Elizabeth: The Golden Age*, as well as in films about Sir Francis Drake like *Seven Seas to Calais* (1962) and the television series *Sir Francis Drake* (1961–1962). Also missing is the formidable Spanish general Alessandro Farnese, Duke of Parma, a persistent threat to Elizabeth while Governor-General of the Netherlands from 1578 to 1592 and a key player in plans for the Armada invasion in 1588. The only Spanish character in the cast is Mendoza.[45] There is no deep consideration of foreign policy, colonization, or privateering. Sir Francis Drake (David Delve) and Howard of Effingham (Rimantas Magdzevicius) are barely noticeable, and John Hawkins does not appear at all. Raleigh features in quarrels with Essex but (perhaps mercifully) gets less screen time than in *Elizabeth and Essex*, Davis' *The Virgin Queen*, and *Elizabeth: The Golden Age*.[46] Aside from Anjou and his servant Jean de Simier, there are no French characters, not even Elizabeth's occasional nemesis Catherine de Medici, and there is no consideration of the bitter religious wars in France that so profoundly influenced Elizabethan diplomacy.[47] Though Leicester and Essex are seen departing for war in the Netherlands in 1585, there is little explanation of the Dutch Revolt against Spain and none of the assassination of William of Orange in 1584 and the fiasco wherein Leicester accepted the title of Governor-General of the Calvinist United Provinces in 1586, incurring the queen's wrath. Elizabeth twice dismisses the Dutch offhandedly, once telling Anjou, 'I never cared for the Dutch. I find them common,' and later saying to Leicester, 'The Dutch have no religion. They have cheese.'[48]

With or without cheese, the film's handling of religion is a problem. To its credit, *Elizabeth I* does focus on the dilemma Anjou's Catholicism posed, and it features realistic debate among privy councilors about the implications of a possible marriage. However it has Leicester oppose the match for personal rather than religious reasons, which shows just how far the emphasis on Leicester warps the film's perspective. Anjou is largely a foil for the English earl. The scene with Stubbs functions primarily to allow Leicester to needle Anjou and Simier to reveal to Elizabeth that the earl is secretly married to Lady Essex. There is no mention of the Catholic Throckmorton Plot of 1583, for which the script substitutes Gifford's fictitious attempt to assassinate the queen. There is no reference to William Allen, Robert Parsons, or other Catholic missionaries, and the credits identify the two Catholic clergymen in the film only as 'Jesuit Priest' (John McEnery) and 'Priest (Charles Millham).' Elizabeth has a 'Chaplain (Malcolm Terris),' but there are no named Protestant clerics. Neither is there any indication that Archbishop of Canterbury Edmund Grindal was suspended from office in 1577 for failing to suppress sectarian 'prophesyings' or that John Whitgift replaced him in 1583 and began a crackdown on both

Catholic recusants and Puritans. Nor is there any reference to the Martin Marprelate tracts, the Archpriest Controversy, or the Wisbech Stirs.[49]

As Alessandra Stanley notes, 'There is a lot of Elizabeth, but not much of the Elizabethan Age.'[50] Rob Lane's score is quite beautiful, but there is little period music except for Elizabeth playing the virginals when Walsingham comes to deliver the news that the Queen of Scots is dead. The influential politician and towering intellect Francis Bacon is little more than a flunky for Essex, whom he subsequently betrays. Christopher Hatton (Geoffrey Bersey) is a mere cipher. A number of privy councilors who appear in other films are missing, notably Thomas Radcliffe, 3rd Earl of Sussex. One of the most glaring omissions is William Shakespeare, not only because of his stature as a playwright and poet but also because of his ties to Essex and narrow escape from arrest following the earl's failed rebellion for having staged the controversial play *Richard II*.[51] This is all the stranger because Southampton figures prominently in Part Two. Also absent are Ben Jonson, Christopher Marlowe, Philip Sidney, and Edmund Spenser. Mirren, however, is frank about the inaccuracies: 'I find that historical detail is so much more interesting than anything we can invent nowadays … my only sadness was that we couldn't get more historical detail into it … and if there are a couple of things that we got deliberately wrong historically, that was a very deliberate, and very thought about and argued over issue.'[52]

In the end, *Elizabeth I* is a complex film that defies easy analysis. It is arguably the most genuinely feminist Elizabeth film, and it accomplishes that without the ridiculously anachronistic rhetoric one hears from Anne Boleyn in *The Other Boleyn Girl* (2008). Mirren's Elizabeth is a strong woman but believably human in dealing with extraordinarily challenging circumstances. This is particularly apparent when it comes to the queen's sexuality.[53] The greatest twentieth-century Elizabeth, Glenda Jackson, is aloof even when flirting with suitors, while Blanchett's queen succumbs rather easily and unbelievably to temptation with Leicester, only to later reconstitute her virginity by cutting her hair, painting her face, and emulating the Virgin Mary. Eldridge, McCormack, and Robson have no occasion for romance, while Duff is unconvincing and Davis jittery, neurotic, and repressed in *The Private Lives of Elizabeth and Essex* and downright silly in *The Virgin Queen*. Mirren's Elizabeth desperately wants more than she can have from Leicester, Anjou, or Essex, and she exhibits both intense desire and great strength of will in resisting what would have been disastrous politically. Mirren's performance at Tilbury is not quite as good as Jackson's but is more animated than Robson's dry delivery, more powerful than Duff's lame declamation, and more convincing than the outright fantasy that has Blanchett suddenly younger-looking with flowing red hair, tight-fitting armor, a horse straining at the bit, and a speech that bears almost no resemblance to the original.

Yet Mirren's Elizabeth is preoccupied by the same trumped-up romances with Leicester and Essex that appear in old-fashioned Elizabethan historiography, popular biographies, and novels, and in all previous filmic portrayals. Given the recent burst of publications on Elizabeth's reign,[54] such a scenario is even less tenable now than in 2005, but it was already discredited then. Of course historical films are seldom much informed by the latest historical scholarship. But focusing so much on the two earls leaves Mirren's Elizabeth with one foot in political reality and the other in imaginary romance. Even though she was one of the most interesting figures in history, it seems as though filmmakers continue to doubt whether the real Elizabeth can carry a dramatic production without the help of fabricated love stories. Apparently surviving her mother's judicial murder, disinheritance, legislated bastardy, arrest and imprisonment, smallpox, rebellion, excommunication, assassination attempts, usurpation plots, military threats, religious dissent, financial instability, cantankerous councilors, unruly parliaments, and general misogyny while growing up in constant danger and ruling for forty-five years over one of the most brilliant eras in English history is not enough to keep audiences in their seats without, as Geoffrey Rush's Philip Henslowe might put it, 'love and a bit with a dog' (also, perhaps, a dragon).[55]

Yet, for whatever flaws it may have, Mirren's *Elizabeth I* is, in aesthetic terms, the best film about the queen since Jackson's *Elizabeth R* and the only one close to being in the same league. Because it is compelling despite its imperfections, it poses real difficulties for historians. There are three fundamental questions for a historian to ask about a historical film: (1) Does it have aesthetic value? (2) Is it historically accurate? (3) Is it too burdened with presentism? These questions are linked, for the better a film is and the more it addresses issues that matter to viewers, the more likely it is to convince audiences that it is accurate. Artistically, *Elizabeth I* is a triumph, winning reviewers' accolades and numerous awards.[56] Moreover, it gets a lot of the period detail—the 'look' and the 'feel'—right, and it tells a gripping tale. Unfortunately, this makes it hard for historians to point out errors without seeming like grumpy, know-it-all, pedantic philistines and spoilsports, yet the inaccuracies are significant, and scholars have a responsibility to address them.

Herein, however, lies opportunity. History students are often remarkably good at reading serious history, watching historical films, comparing the two, and identifying the problems with the latter. That can be as useful a learning experience as reviewing and discussing a book with a flawed or overstated thesis, and students take to it with enthusiasm and at times a certain malicious glee. With a film that is artistically strong and thematically complex, the challenge for students is greater and the rewards more substantial.[57] Of course many viewers will approach *Elizabeth I* with the same giddy delight as Hooper, who described Mirren's work as 'the performance of a lifetime,' or producer Barry Reisz, who declared, 'If I never work again in this industry, I'll be able to say I worked with Helen Mirren,' or of Mirren herself, who opined—in a decade friendlier to historical statuary—'There should be a beautiful statue to Elizabeth I. I think it would be quite nice to have one of Elizabeth I and one of Elizabeth II sort of looking at each other.'[58] But with all due respect for Mirren's many achievements, no one should confuse image with reality, a statue with the flesh-and-blood human it represents, Elizabeth's self-fashioning with her true self, or her portrayal by any actress, even Mirren or Jackson, with the actual queen.[59]

Notes

1. 'Film' as used here includes television. Works that explicitly address Mirren's *Elizabeth I* include Latham, 2011; Parrill and Robison, 2013; on other Elizabeth films, Betteridge, 2003; Dobson and Watson, 2002; Doran and Freeman, 2009; Ford, 2009; Semenza, 2010. Recent biographies include Doran, 2003; Guy, 2016; Levin, 2003; Loades, 2006; Richards, 2012; Starkey, 2000; older but still essential are MacCaffrey, 1993; Neale, 1934.
2. Latham, *passim*; Parrill and Robison, pp. 20–22, 29–33, 46–82, 86–87, 93–97, 144–7, 159–60, 182–86, 197–99, 218–21, 292–94, 301–03.
3. Lesser known twenty-first century Elizabeths include Josephine Barstow, *Gloriana* (2000); Imogen Slaughter, *Elizabeth* (2000); Margot Kidder, *Mentors* 2:2: *Her Grace Under Pressure* (2000); Heather May in *Map Makers—Religion* (2004); Diana Aquila, *Elizabeth Rex* (2004); Mary Kababik, *Sword of Hearts* (2005); Tallulah Bond, *The Gunpowder Plot: Exploding the Legend* (2005); Michelle Connolly in *Revealed* 4:10: *The Secret Life of Elizabeth I* (2006); Lindsay Kemp, *La Mandrágora* (12 July

2006); Gay Linn Kirkpatrick. *The Secret History of America's Beginnings* (2006–2007) and *The Girls Next Door* 3:13: *Surely You Joust* (2007); Angie Pleasence, *Doctor Who* 3.2: *The Shakespeare Code* (2007); Simona Cuciurianu, *Imperium* 3:1 *Duell zwischen Kreuz und Krone* (2008); Mimi Forrester, *Tudor Rose* (2008); Julie Kavner, *The Simpsons* 20:20: *Four Great Women and a Manicure* (2009); Jürgen Holz, *Shakespeare's Sonnette* (2009); Mary Waters, *Elizabeth* (2010); Julie Porter, *The Pirate Queen* (2011); Maria Skountzou, *Maria Stiouart* (2011); Yuka Keicho, *JoJo's Bizarre Adventure* 1:5: *Ankoko no kishi-tachi* (2012); Joanne Page, *Doctor Who: The Day of the Doctor* (2013); Marleen Lohse, *Frauen, die Geschichte machten* 1.5: *Elisabeth von England* (2013); Deb Pickman, *Blank Verse* (2013); Frances Barber, *Psychobitches* (2.1, 2014); Anita Dobson, *Armada* (2015); Joany Schild, *H VIII The Male Heir* (2015); Sophia Lund, *The Last Days of Mary, Queen of Scots* (2015); Rachel Butler, *Doing Something About Gandhi* (2015); Sarah Louise Woods, *Zombies in Hertford* (2015); Helen McCrory, *Bill* (2015); Charlotte Sieglin, *Terra X—Von Francis Drake zu den Arabischen Korsaren* (2015); Rachel Skarsten, *Reign* (2015–2017); Helen Bradbury, *Bloody Queens: Elizabeth and Mary* (2016); Lucy Montgomery, *The Windsors* (2016); Isla Bliss and Madeleine Power, *Six Wives with Lucy Worsley* (2016); Michelle Keegan, Sarah Alexander, and Katy Brand, *Drunk History* 2.1, 2.6 (2016), 3.2 (2017); Lily Cole, *Elizabeth I* (2017); Rebecca Scott, *Reinas Virgen Y Martir* (2016–2017); Emilia Ufir in *Graine Uaile—The Movie* (2017). For the many twentieth-century Elizabeths, see Betteridge, 2003; Latham 2011; Parrill and Robison, 2013.

4. This is the argument of Doran, 2015b; see also Robison, 2017.
5. See Bossy, 1991, 2001; Childs, 2014, on the plots; Kesselring, 2007, on the rebellion.
6. On the Elizabethan navy, see Loades, 1992, Chapters 7–9; Rodger, 1997, Chapters 17–23.
7. On Spain's failed invasions, see Wernham, 1984, 1994.
8. On Elizabethan foreign policy, see Doran, 2000; Wernham, 1980; for Philip II's grand strategy, Parker, 1998.
9. For a fuller summary of the plot, see Parrill and Robison, 2013, pp. 49–56; on the relationship of the beginning to *The Private Lives of Elizabeth and Essex*, see Latham, 2011, p. 239.
10. For the historical Gifford, see Plowden, 2004; on Stubbs, Mears, 2004; on Lady Essex (Lettice Knollys), Adams, 2004b.
11. On Babington, see P. Williams, 2004; on Ballard, Edwards, 2004; on Davison, Adams, 2004a.
12. On the Anglo-Spanish War, see Hammer, 2004, especially Chapters 4–6; Younger, 2012.

13. On the Scottish Borders, see Sadler, 2006, Chapters 20–21.
14. On Elizabethan Ireland 1579–1603, see Ellis, 1998, Chapter 12; on Tyrone's Rebellion, Morgan, 1993.
15. See Robison, 2014, pp. 145–78; the recent literature on Elizabethan religion is voluminous, but particularly informative in this regard are Collinson, 1979, 1983, 1990, 2013; Lake, 1988, 2002, 2004, 2016a.
16. The essays in Doran and Paulina Kewes, eds., 2016, make this abundantly clear.
17. On the mirrors, see Dobson and Watson, 2002, pp. 159–65, 177–78, 273–74, 315 n. 42; Parrill and Robison, 2013, p. 184.
18. On Lopez, see Samuel, 2004.
19. By comparison, *The Private Lives of Elizabeth and Essex* and *Elizabeth R* devote considerable attention to events in Ireland, even if the former plays the conflict there much like a Western.
20. On Elizabeth's death and problematic lying in state, seeLoomis, 2010.
21. Haigh, 'Kapur's Elizabeth,' 2009, pp. 122–35; Vivienne Westbrook, 2009, pp. 164–77.
22. On Leicester, see Adams, 2002; Goldring, 2014.
23. On Burghley, see especially Alford, 2008; Graves, 1998; Jones, 2015; Loades, 2008; Usher, 2016; all supersede Read, 1955, 1960.
24. On Walsingham, see Alford, 2012; Cooper, 2013; all supersede Read, 1925.
25. Mirren, quoted in 'Making *Elizabeth I*,' 2006; MacCaffrey, 1993.
26. For context, see Guy, 2004, Chapters 22–30; 2016, Chapters 1–5.
27. On the reality of the Earl of Essex's relationship with the queen, see Guy, 2016, Chapters 6–20; Hammer, 1999.
28. On Parliament, see Dean, 1996; Elton, 1989; Loades, 1997; these largely supersede Neale, 1949, 1953, 1957.
29. Irons, quoted in 'Making *Elizabeth I*,' 2006.
30. Parrill and Robison, pp. 82–84, 164–79, 232–34, 247–90.
31. *Mary, Queen of Scots* (2018) had not been released at the time this chapter was completed; *Reign* (2013–2017) had not begun at the time the following book was published, Parrill and Robison, pp. 40, 42, 107, 135, 141–43, 159, 163–64, 187, 301.
32. In 2011 Mirren, at age sixty-six, finished first in a 'Body-of-the-Year' sponsored by the L.A. Fitness gym chain.
33. Tom Hardy was twenty-eight in *Elizabeth I: The Virgin Queen*, Daniel Massey thirty-eight in *Mary, Queen of Scots*, Robert Hardy forty-five in *Elizabeth R*, Leslie Banks forty-six in *Fire Over England*, Herbert Marshall sixty-five in *The Virgin Queen*. Irons' earl is more mature in years and behavior than both Tom Hardy and the best-known Leicester of recent years, Joseph Fiennes, aged twenty-eight when playing Leicester

from twenty-five to thirty-seven in Blanchett's *Elizabeth*, though that film ends seven years before Mirren's *Elizabeth I* begins, and neither Leicester nor Burghley appears in *Elizabeth: The Golden Age*.

34. Sam Reid was twenty-four in *Anonymous*, Lou Tellegen in Bernhardt's *Queen Elizabeth*, Errol Flynn in *Elizabeth and Essex*, and Hans Matheson in *Elizabeth I: The Virgin Queen* were all thirty, Robin Ellis twenty-nine in *Elizabeth R*, Charlton Heston fifty-four in *Elizabeth the Queen*.
35. Ian Hart was forty-one in *Elizabeth I: The Virgin Queen*, Ronald Hines forty-two in *Elizabeth R*, Henry Stephenson forty-seven in *Elizabeth and Essex*, David Thewlis forty-eight inn *Anonymous*, Trevor Howard fifty-eight in *Mary, Queen of Scots*; Richard Attenborough seventy-five in *Elizabeth*, Morton Selten seventy-seven in *Fire Over England*.
36. Ben Daniels was forty-one in *Elizabeth I: The Virgin Queen*, Geoffrey Rush fifty-six in *Elizabeth: The Golden Age*, Stephen Murray fifty-nine in *Elizabeth R*, Richard Warner sixty in *Mary, Queen of Scots*.
37. Daniel Evans in *Elizabeth I: The Virgin Queen* and Edward Hogg were thirty-two in *Anonymous*, Henry Daniell forty-five in *Elizabeth and Essex*, Tim McInnerny forty-nine in *Gunpowder, Treason and Plot*; Hugh Dickson in *Elizabeth R* unknown; Charlotte Winner in *Elizabeth I: The Virgin Queen* unknown.
38. Clémence Poésy was twenty-three in *Gunpowder, Treason and Plot*; Samantha Morton thirty in *Elizabeth: The Golden Age*; Vanessa Redgrave thirty-four in *Mary, Queen of Scots*; Vivian Pickles forty in *Elizabeth R*.
39. On Elizabeth's day-to-day life, see Doran, 2015a; Guy, 2016; Whitelock, 2014.
40. 'Making *Elizabeth I*,' 2006.
41. Maltby, 2015.
42. See Frye, 1992, pp. 95–114; Green, 1997, pp. 421–45; my forthcoming article, 'Gloriana or Galadriel? Elizabeth I's Tilbury Speech on Film and Television.'
43. Hooper, 2006.
44. For an accurate account of the Armada campaign, which never seems to make it onscreen, see Martin and Parker, 2002.
45. Just how much is missing about Spain is evident from Parker, 1998, especially Chapters 6–10; 2014, Chapters 15–19; on the persistence of the Black Legend in films about Philip, see Robison, 2016, pp. 233–54.
46. See, for example, MacCaffrey, 1981, 1992; Ronald, 2009.
47. The best account of the French Wars of Religion is Holt, 2005.
48. Arnade, 2008, demonstrates that the Dutch were doing considerably more than making cheese.
49. On just how much this omits, see, for example, Houliston, 2007; Questier, 2008.

50. Stanley, 2006.
51. See Lake, 2016b.
52. Mirren, quoted in 'Making *Elizabeth I*,' 2006.
53. On this complex subject, see Levin, 2013.
54. The works cited here represent only a portion of the massive recent output.
55. From *Shakespeare in Love*.
56. The show won nine Emmy Awards, three Golden Globes, two Screen Actors Guild Awards, a British Academy of Film and Television Arts award, a Broadcast Film Critics Association Award, a Costume Designer's Guild Award, a Monte Carlo Festival Award, a Producers Guild of America Award, a Peabody Award, and a Visual Effects Society Award, '*Elizabeth I*,' IMDB (http://www.imdb.com/title/tt0465326/awards), accessed 26 September 2017. Among reviewers, Lowry, 2006, described it as 'the kind of towering … performance from Helen Mirren that almost defies conventional superlatives'; Stanley, 2006, as 'a richly drawn portrait of a powerful woman who is both ruthless and sentimental, formidable and mercurial, vain and likable'; Shales, 2006, as 'a lusty and lavish historical spectacular' in which 'Mirren makes the first Elizabeth an even more fascinating and anguished enigma than Bette Davis did on the big screen,' and other reviews are similarly favorable, e.g., Cohen, 2006; O'Hare, 2006.
57. This is based on my own extensive in-class experience, but see also Carlson, 2007, pp. 419–28.
58. Mirren, quoted in 'Making *Elizabeth I*,' 2006.
59. For a less starry-eyed assessment of Elizabeth, see Walker, 1998.

Bibliography

Adams, Simon. 2002. *Leicester and the Court: Essays on Elizabethan Politics*. Manchester: Manchester University Press.

Adams, Simon. 2004a. 'Davison, William (d. 1608)', in *Oxford Dictionary of National Biography*. Oxford: Oxford University Press.

Adams, Simon. 2004b. 'Dudley [*née* Knollys; *Other Married Name* Devereux], Lettice, Countess of Essex and Countess of Leicester (1543–1634)', in *Oxford Dictionary of National Biography*. Oxford: Oxford University Press.

Alford, Stephen. 2008. *Burghley: William Cecil at the Court of Elizabeth I*. New Haven: Yale University Press.

Alford, Stephen. 2012. *The Watchers: A Secret History of the Reign of Elizabeth I*. London: Bloomsbury Press.

Arnade, Peter. 2008. *Beggars, Iconoclasts, and Civil Patriots: The Political Culture of the Dutch Revolt*. Ithaca: Cornell University Press.

Betteridge, Thomas. 2003. 'A Queen for All Seasons: Elizabeth I on Film', in Doran and Freeman (ed.), *The Myth of Elizabeth*, pp. 242–59. New York: Palgrave Macmillan.

Bossy, John. 1991. *Giordano Bruno and the Embassy Affair*. New Haven: Yale University Press.

Bossy, John. 2001. *Under the Molehill: An Elizabethan Spy Story*. New Haven: Yale University Press.

Carlson, Eric Josef. 2007. 'Teaching Elizabeth Tudor with Movies', *Sixteenth Century Journal* 38, no. 2, pp. 419–28.

Childs, Jessie. 2014. *God's Traitors: Terror and Faith in Elizabethan England*. Oxford: Oxford University Press.

Cohen, David S. 2006. 'Movie Review: "Leading Ladies Split HBO Love"', *Variety*, 11 June.

Collinson, Patrick. 1979. *Archbishop Grindal 1519–1583: The Struggle for a Reformed Church*. Berkeley: University of California Press.

Collinson, Patrick. 1983. *The Religion of Protestants: The Church in English Society 1559–1625*. Oxford: Oxford University Press.

Collinson, Patrick. 1990. *The Elizabethan Puritan Movement*, rprt. Oxford: Clarendon Press.

Collinson, Patrick. 2013. *Richard Bancroft and Elizabethan Anti-Puritanism*. Cambridge: Cambridge University Press.

Cooper, John. 2013. *The Queen's Agent: Sir Francis Walsingham and the Rise of Espionage in Elizabethan England*. New York: Pegasus.

Dean, David. 1996. *Law-Making and Society in Late Elizabethan England: The Parliament of England 1584–1601*. Cambridge: Cambridge University Press.

Dobson, Michael, and Watson, Nicola J. 2002. *England's Elizabeth: An Afterlife in Fame and Fantasy*. Oxford: Oxford University Press.

Doran, Susan. 2000. *Elizabeth I and Foreign Policy 1558–1603*. London: Routledge.

Doran, Susan. 2003. *Queen Elizabeth I*. New York: New York University Press.

Doran, Susan. 2015a. *Elizabeth I and Her Circle*. Oxford: Oxford University Press.

Doran, Susan. 2015b. *Monarchy and Matrimony: The Courtships of Elizabeth I*. London: Routledge.

Doran, Susan, and Freeman, Thomas S. (eds.) 2009. *Tudors and Stuart on Film: Historical Perspectives*. New York: Palgrave Macmillan.

Doran, Susan, and Kewes, Paula (eds.). 2016. *Doubtful and Dangerous: The Question of Succession in Late Elizabethan England*. Manchester: Manchester University Press.

Edwards, Francis. 2004. 'Ballard, John (d. 1586)', in *Oxford Dictionary of National Biography*. Oxford: Oxford University Press.

Ellis, Steven G. 1998. *Ireland in the Age of the Tudors: English Expansion and the End of Gaelic Rule*, 2nd edition. London: Routledge.

Elton, G. R. 1989. *The Parliament of England 1559–1581*. Cambridge: Cambridge University Press.

Ford, Elizabeth A. 2009. *Royal Portraits in Hollywood: Filming the Lives of Queen*. Lexington: University Press of Kentucky.

Frye, Susan. 1992. 'The Myth of Elizabeth of Tilbury', *Sixteenth Century Journal* 23, pp. 95–114.

Frye, Susan. 1993. *Elizabeth I: The Competition for Representation*. Oxford: Oxford University Press.

Goldring, Elizabeth. 2014. *Robert Dudley, Earl of Leicester and the World of Elizabethan Art: Painting and Patronage at the Court of Elizabeth I*. London: Paul Mellon Centre.

Graves, Michael A. R. 1998. *Burghley: William Cecil, Lord Burghley*. London: Longman.

Green, Janet M. 1997. '"I My Self": Queen Elizabeth I's Oration at Tilbury Camp', *The Sixteenth Century Journal* 28, pp. 421–445.

Guy, John. 2004. *Queen of Scots: The True Life of Mary Stuart*. Boston: Houghton Mifflin Harcourt.

Guy, John. 2016. *Elizabeth: The Forgotten Years*. New York: Viking.

Haigh, Christopher. 2009. 'Kapur's Elizabeth', in Doran and Freeman (ed.), *Tudors and Stuart on Film: Historical Perspectives*, pp. 122–35. New York: Palgrave Macmillan.

Hammer, Paul E. J. 1999. *The Polarisation of Elizabethan Politics: The Political Career of Robert Devereux, 2nd Earl of Essex 1585–1597*. Cambridge: Cambridge University Press.

Hammer, Paul E. J. 2004. *Elizabeth's Wars: War, Government, and Society in Tudor England, 1544–1604*. New York: Palgrave Macmillan.

Holt, Mack. 2005. *The French Wars of Religion, 1562–1629*, 2nd edition. Cambridge: Cambridge University Press.

Hooper, Tom. 2006. 'Interview: HBO "Elizabeth I"'. http://www.hbo.com/movies/elizabeth-i/inside/interviews/interview/helen-mirren.html. Accessed 26 September 2017.

Houliston, Victor. 2007. *Catholic Resistance in Elizabethan England: Robert Persons's Jesuit Polemic 1580–1620*. London: Routledge.

Irons, Jeremy. 2006. 'Interview: HBO "Elizabeth I"'. http://www.hbo.com/movies/elizabeth-i/inside/interviews/interview/helen-mirren.html. Accessed 26 September 2017.

Jones, Norman. 2015. *Governing by Virtue: Lord Burghley and the Management of Elizabethan England*. Oxford: Oxford University Press.

Kesselring, Krista. 2007. *The Northern Rebellion of 1569: Faith, Politics and Protest in Elizabethan England*. New York: Palgrave Macmillan.

Lake, Peter. 1988. *Anglicans and Puritans? Presbyterianism and English Conformist Thought—Whitgift to Hooker.* London: HarperCollins.

Lake, Peter. 2002. *The Antichrist's Lewd Hat: Protestants, Papists, and Players in Post-Reformation England.* New Haven: Yale University Press.

Lake, Peter. 2004. *Moderate Puritans and the Elizabethan Church*, rprt. Cambridge: Cambridge University Press.

Lake, Peter. 2016a. *Bad Queen Bess? Libels, Secret Histories and the Politics of Publicity in the Reign of Queen Elizabeth.* Oxford: Oxford University Press.

Lake, Peter. 2016b. *How Shakespeare Put Politics on the Stage: Power and Succession in the History Plays.* New Haven: Yale University Press.

Latham, Bethany. 2011. *Elizabeth I in Film and Television: A Study of the Major Portrayals.* Jefferson, NC: McFarland.

Leonard, John. 2006. 'Movie Review: "Virgin Territory: God Save Helen Mirren, Who Delivers One of the Great—Though Not the Greatest—Elizabeths Ever"'. *New York Magazine*, 24 April.

Levin, Carole. 2003. *The Reign of Elizabeth I.* New York: Palgrave Macmillan.

Levin, Carole. 2013. *The Heart and Stomach of a Queen: Elizabeth I and the Politics of Sex and Power*, 2nd edition. Philadelphia: University of Pennsylvania Press.

Loades, David. 1992. *The Tudor Navy: An Administrative, Political and Military History.* London: Routledge.

Loades, David. 1997. *Tudor Government: Structures of Authority in the Sixteenth Century.* Oxford: Wiley-Blackwell.

Loades, David. 2006. *Elizabeth I: A Life.* London: Bloomsbury.

Loades, David. 2008. *The Cecils: Privilege and Power Behind the Throne.* London: National Archives.

Loomis, Catherine. 2010. *The Death of Elizabeth I: Remembering and Reconstructing the Virgin Queen.* New York: Palgrave Macmillan.

Lowry, Brian. 2006. 'Movie Review: "Elizabeth I"', *Variety*, 15 April.

MacCaffrey, Wallace. 1981. *Queen Elizabeth and the Making of Policy 1572–1588.* Princeton: Princeton University Press.

MacCaffrey, Wallace. 1992. *Elizabeth I, War and Politics 1588–1603.* Princeton: Princeton University Press.

MacCaffrey, Wallace. 1993. *Elizabeth I.* London: Edward Arnold.

'Making *Elizabeth I.*' 2006. *Elizabeth I*, DVD, Bonus Features (HBO Home Video).

Maltby, Kate. 2015. 'Movie Review: "Why Is Elizabeth I, the Most Powerful Woman in Our History, Always Depicted as a Grotesque"', *The Guardian*, 25 May.

Martin, Colin, and Parker, Geoffrey. 2002 *The Spanish Armada*, revised edition. Manchester: Manchester University Press.

Mears, Natalie. 2004. 'Stubbe [Stubbs], John (c. 1541–1590)', in *Oxford Dictionary of National Biography*. Oxford: Oxford University Press.

Mirren, Helen. 2005. 'Interview: HBO "Elizabeth I"'. http://www.hbo.com/movies/elizabeth-i/inside/interviews/interview/helen-mirren.html. Accessed 26 September 2017.

Morgan, Hiram. 1993. *Tyrone's Rebellion: The Outbreak of the Nine Years War in Tudor Ireland*. Woodbridge: Boydell and Brewer.

Neale, J. E. 1934. *Queen Elizabeth I*. London: Jonathan Cape.

Neale, J. E. 1949. *The Elizabethan House of Commons*. London: Jonathan Cape.

Neale, J. E. 1953. *Elizabeth and Her Parliaments 1559–1581*. London: Jonathan Cape.

Neale, J. E. 1957. *Elizabeth and Her Parliaments 1584–1601*. London: Jonathan Cape.

O'Hare, Kate. 2006. 'Movie Review: "Elizabeth I" Tells Tale of One Queen and Two Robins', *Zap2It*, 21 April.

Parker, Geoffrey. 1998. *The Grand Strategy of Philip II*. New Haven: Yale University Press.

Parker, Geoffrey. 2014. *Imprudent King: A New Life of Philip II*. New Haven: Yale University Press.

Parrill, Sue, and Robison, William B. 2013. *The Tudors on Film and Television*. Jefferson, NC: McFarland.

Plowden, Alison. 2004. 'Gifford, Gilbert (1560–1590)', in *Oxford Dictionary of National Biography*. Oxford: Oxford University Press.

Pritchard, Arnold. 2017. *Catholic Loyalism in Elizabethan England*, rprt. Chapel Hill: University of North Carolina Press.

Questier, Michael. 2008. *Catholicism and Community in Early Modern England: Politics, Aristocratic Patronage and Religion c. 1550–1640*. Cambridge: Cambridge University Press.

Read, Conyers. 1925. *Mr. Secretary Walsingham and the Policy of Queen Elizabeth*, 3 Vols. Cambridge: Cambridge University Press.

Read, Conyers. 1955. *Mr. Secretary Cecil and Queen Elizabeth*. London: Jonathan Cape.

Read, Conyers. 1960. *Lord Burghley and Queen Elizabeth*. London: Jonathan Cape.

Richards, Judith M. 2012. *Elizabeth I*. London: Routledge.

Robison, William B. 2014. 'Stripped of Their Altars: Film, Faith, and Tudor Royal Women from the Silent Era to the Twenty-First Century, 1895–2014', in Julie A. Chappell and Kathy A. Kramer (eds.), *Women During the English Reformations: Renegotiating Gender and Religious Identity*, pp. 145–78. New York: Palgrave Macmillan.

Robison, William B. 2016. 'Marrying Mary to the Black Legend: Anti-Catholicism and Anti-Marian Messages in Anglo-American Films About

Philip II of Spain', in Sarah Duncan and Valerie Schutte (eds.), *The Birth of a Queen: Essays on the Quincentenary of Mary I*, pp. 233–54. New York: Palgrave Macmillan.

Robison, William B. 2017. 'The Unexpected Virgin: The Perpetual Succession Crisis of Elizabeth I', in Valerie Schutte (ed.), *Unexpected Heirs in Early Modern Europe*. New York: Palgrave Macmillan.

Robison, William B. 'Gloriana or Galadriel? Elizabeth I's Tilbury Speech on Film and Television', forthcoming.

Rodger, N. A. M. 1997. *The Safeguard of the Sea: A Naval History of Britain 660–1649*. New York: W. W. Norton.

Ronald, Susan. 2009. *The Pirate Queen: Queen Elizabeth I, Her Pirate Adventurers, and the Dawn of Empire*. Stroud: The History Press.

Sadler, John. 2006. *Border Fury: England and Scotland at War 1296–1568*. London: Routledge.

Samuel, Edgar. 2004. 'Lopez [Lopes], Roderigo [Ruy, Roger] (c. 1517–1594)', in *Oxford Dictionary of National Biography*. Oxford: Oxford University Press.

Semenza, Greg Colon. (ed.). 2010. *The English Renaissance in Popular Culture*. New York: Palgrave Macmillan.

Shales, Tom. 2006. 'Movie Review: "HBO's 'Elizabeth I': Her Royal Majesty Helen Mirren"', *The Washington Post*, 22 April.

Stanley, Alessandra. 2006. '"Elizabeth I": The Flirty Monarch with an Iron Fist', *The New York Times*, 21 April.

Starkey, David. 2000. *Elizabeth: The Struggle for the Throne*. London: Chatto and Windus.

Usher, Brett. 2016. *Lord Burghley and Episcopacy 1577–1603*. London: Routledge.

Wernham, R. B. 1980. *The Making of Elizabethan Foreign Policy 1558–1603*. Berkeley: University of California Press.

Wernham, R. B. 1984. *After the Armada: Elizabethan England and the Struggle for Western Europe 1588–1595*. Oxford: Oxford University Press.

Wernham, R. B. 1994. *The Return of the Armadas: The Last Years of the Elizabethan War Against Spain 1595–1603*. Oxford: Oxford University Press.

Walker, Julia M. (ed.). 1998. *Dissing Elizabeth: Negative Representations of Gloriana*. Durham: Duke University Press.

Westbrook, Vivienne. 2009. 'Elizabeth: The Golden Age: A Sign of the Times?', in Doran and Freeman (eds.), *Tudors and Stuart on Film: Historical Perspectives*, pp. 164–77. New York: Palgrave Macmillan.

Whitelock, Anna. 2014. *The Queen's Bed: An Intimate History of Elizabeth's Court*. New York: Sarah Crichton Books.

Wiegand, David 2006. 'Bloody Good Drama as Helen Mirren Strips Up Passions in "Elizabeth I" Movie', *SF Gate*, 21 April.

Williams, Penry. 1984. 'The Crown and the Counties', in Christopher Haigh (ed.), *The Reign of Elizabeth I*. London: Macmillan.
Williams, Penry. 2004. 'Babington, Anthony (1561–1586)', in *Dictionary of National Biography*. Oxford: Oxford University Press.
Williams, Sally. 2005. 'Movie Review: "Monarch of the Moment"', *The Telegraph*, 10 September 2005.
Younger, Neil. 2012. *War and Politics in the Elizabethan Counties*. Manchester: Manchester University Press.

Shakespeare in Love and *Anonymous*: Two Films More or Less About Shakespeare

David Bevington

Shakespeare in Love (1998) and *Anonymous* (2011) make a lively pair for comparison under the topic of film biographies. Neither one is a biopic in the usual sense of offering a film account of a person's life and accomplishments, such as we find in many studies of this present collection. Neither film offers an overview like that of assessing how Lincoln came to be president of the United States and how he handled the delicate political problems of the Emancipation Proclamation, for instance. These two films are, in part at least, deliberately fictional. Not for a minute, we can well suppose, did Marc Norman and Tom Stoppard, the script-writers for *Shakespeare in Love*, actually believe that the historical William Shakespeare fell in love with a young woman named Viola de Lesseps, whose arriviste parents insisted on marrying her off to the Earl of Wessex. There was no Earl of Wessex then (the house had died off in 1066 as a consequence of the Norman invasion), and no daughter named Viola whose burning passion was to be on stage in an Elizabethan play. De Lesseps is the name of the Frenchman who developed the Suez Canal,

D. Bevington (✉)
University of Chicago, Chicago, IL, USA

T. S. Freeman and D. L. Smith (eds.), *Biography and History in Film*, Palgrave Studies in the History of the Media,
https://doi.org/10.1007/978-3-319-89408-9_5

failed in an attempt to build a Panama Canal, and presented the Statue of Liberty to the United States, whatever one wants to make of that.

Similarly, one can easily imagine (although one never knows) that Roland Emmerich as director and John Orloff as script-writer for *Anonymous* did not really expect us to believe that Queen Elizabeth gave birth to so many bastard sons as are alleged in this film, one of them Robert Devereux the second Earl of Essex and another Edward de Vere, destined to be the seventeenth Earl of Oxford. De Vere, according to this film, unaware that he was sleeping with his mother, sired Henry Wriothesley, the third Earl of Southampton, and who, as the love child of De Vere and the Queen, would have been both Oxford's son and his half-brother. The related revelation of these incestuous circumstances in *Anonymous* make for a rollicking and sensational plot, all cleverly woven into a fictionalized biography of Oxford, but these pieces of misinformation are so over the top that the viewer is apt to be thoroughly confused as to what is historically plausible and what is not.

Although both films employ fiction in a highly imaginative and often entertaining way, I wish to make the case for a profound difference. *Shakespeare in Love* is a jeu d'esprit that wears its remarkable learning lightly. No, Shakespeare did not learn from his love affair with Viola de Lesseps how to finish writing *Romeo and Juliet*, with which he had been having such trouble with writer's block, but it is possible to wonder if Shakespeare, having left his wife and children back in Stratford, had a love affair in London from which he drew artistic inspiration. No, the playwright John Webster did not, as a ragamuffin youngster, take delight in torturing rats and in dropping one of them down the cleavage of a young woman masquerading as an actor, but Webster was a young man when Shakespeare wrote *Romeo and Juliet* and must have been hugely impressed by Shakespeare as an older colleague in the profession, especially in the writing of bloody revenge tragedies. No, Queen Elizabeth did not go to see this play in a public theatre and then oblige the fictional Earl of Wessex to give Shakespeare the money he needed to buy a share in London's leading theatrical company, but she must have admired Shakespeare; the rumor is that after she had seen *Henry IV* she expressed a wish to see Falstaff in love, whereupon Shakespeare obliged with his *The Merry Wives of Windsor*. This film displays numerous instances of bouncing off historical fact with piquant fictional drolleries of this sort, a number of which will be explored further in the essay that follows.

Anonymous, conversely, has a not-so-secret agenda in virtually everything it does, which is to make a case for the Earl of Oxford as the covert author of Shakespeare's writings. This is not only a frayed topic to which not a single Shakespearean critic and scholar to my knowledge offer the slightest allegiance, it is also the cause in this film of special pleading. Reviewers of this film have, for the most part, given it high marks for clever plotting, for skillful performances by many of the actors, and for visual splendor, but have objected to the film's 'pile-up of factual errors' and 'wild conjectures', and above all to the film's unabashed endorsement of the Oxfordian theory as to who wrote the plays and poems.[1] Advertisements for the film in 2011 trumpeted the question: 'Was Shakespeare a Fraud?' Images borrowed from *Shakespeare in Love* depicted a brainless Shakespeare, as acted by Joseph Fiennes, muttering to himself, 'This writing stuff is hard. At least I don't have to be funny'. Road signs reading 'Welcome to Warwickshire Shakespeare's County' were altered with the word 'Shakespeare's' crossed out at the behest of the county council in protest to *Anonymous*. Distinguished actors like Derek Jacobi and Vanessa Redgrave offered explicit or implicit endorsements of the Oxfordian theory by appearing in the film and, in the case of Jacobi, taking the role of prologue and master of ceremonies. Jacobi is well known to be an anti-Stratfordian, as are a number of other talented actors, including Mark Rylands. That of course is their privilege, but the film does not play fair. From start to finish, the case is stacked against Shakespeare's own authorship.

'Looney', was the verdict of some viewers; 'Absurd', said others.[2] Gregory Doran, director of the Royal Shakespeare Company, compared the Oxfordian theory to the idea that Shakespeare caused an air crash in 1960 because a Shakespeare enthusiast in 1890 campaigned for the introduction of starlings into New York's Central Park (since starlings are mentioned by Shakespeare), whereupon starlings multiplied in the United States and eventually choked the jet engines of an airliner attempting to take off from Logan Airport in Boston in 1960.[3] Was Shakespeare to blame for the stigma associated with disfiguring skin conditions? asked a writer facetiously, since Shakespeare seems to be so obsessed with flawless pale complexions.[4] Critics have pointed out, in refutation of the notion that Shakespeare's lack of a university education militates against his candidacy for authorship, that John Keats and Charles Dickens didn't attend a university either. The fact that the Earl of Oxford died in 1604, well before the writing and staging of plays like

King Lear, Macbeth, and *The Tempest*, has been raised repeatedly as a stumbling block for the Oxfordian theory. And so it goes. Others, to be sure, like Rhys Ifans, who took the role of Oxford, saw the film not as an attack on Shakespeare but as a celebration of his work that explores seriously the question of authorship.[5] And of course the Oxfordians have their answers to the objections raised by their opponents. (The dates assigned to the late plays are suspect, or someone could have doctored the texts after Oxford's death to make them appear later than 1604, etc.)

If I should show my own partisanship in this controversy, I'm glad to do so. Here is a limerick I wrote on the subject:

> Will Shakespeare to Oxford once said
> My lord, you've an excellent head
> For a tragical line.
> *King Lear* is quite fine
> For a chap who for years has been dead.

Let me now examine a number of the fictions in *Shakespeare in Love*, with a view to showing how I believe them to be inventive and playful in an artistically clever and appropriate way. Time and time again they transform something that is known about Shakespeare into something quite improbable that is nonetheless expressive of a significant truth about the London stage in the 1590s and Shakespeare's place in it. Take, for example, the writing block that is preventing Shakespeare (Joseph Fiennes) from getting on with writing 'Romeo and Ethel the Pirate's Daughter,' his ill-fated first attempt at *Romeo and Juliet*. Doubtful it is that Shakespeare ever suffered writer's block; he produced about two plays a year over the nearly two decades of his professional career, as regular as clockwork, and wrote substantial lyric poems when the theatres were temporarily closed because of the plague. He was active on stage as a member of his professional company for many of these years. He had a reputation for being, if anything, too free-flowing in his writing; Ben Jonson once complained of him, 'I remember the players have often mentioned it as an honour to Shakespeare, that in his writing, whatsoever he penned, he never blotted outline. My answer hath been, "would he had blotted a thousand"'.[6] More positively, the co-editors of the First Folio, John Heminges and Henry Condell, wrote of their fellow actor and playwright that 'His mind and hand went together, and what he thought he uttered with that easiness that we have scarce received from him a blot in his papers'.[7] Why then does the film bring up this fictional and manifestly untruthful account?

Well, for one thing a lot of viewers will realize that this portrayal of writer's block is so ridiculous as to be funny for that very reason. Tom Stoppard is a formidably witty and well-informed playwright who takes delight as an intellectual in writing for intellectuals. The film succeeds in a widely popular way, but it also contains rewards for the *cognoscenti*. The charge of writer's block is quite harmless as an accusation against Shakespeare, if only because it is so patently untrue. Joseph Fiennes is wonderfully entertaining as Shakespeare nibbling nervously at his pen, crumpling up one sheet of foolscap after another, and throwing them in the wastebasket. That little acting business is itself another joke that runs against historical probability: handmade paper was so expensive that no writer, especially a needy one like Shakespeare in this film, could afford such prodigality. The exercise produces still another erudite jest when Shakespeare narcissistically tries out a series of misspellings of his name to see what logo will suit him best: Shakspere, Shakspeare, etc. These are the variant spellings that turn up in the few extant samples we have of Shakespeare's own signing of his name, some of them on his last will and testament when he was evidently in terminal ill health.[8] They are often used by Oxfordians as evidence of his presumed marginal literacy, though in fact the variations are minor. Tom Stoppard disposes grandly of this theory by turning the variations of spelling into an identity crisis. (I say 'Tom Stoppard' because I imagine these witticisms, and so much of what is brilliant about the film's script, to be the very kind of thing for which he was drafted to help salvage a project that appears to have been in disarray. Evidently the person who was originally to have been the film's director, Edward Zwick, was not comfortable with Marc Norman's playscript, and hired Stoppard to introduce major improvements. When Julia Roberts, cast originally as Viola, refused to take the part unless Daniel Day-Lewis would play Shakespeare, Day-Lewis was not interested and Universal Pictures got cold feet about the project. Miramax ultimately took on the film, with John Madden as director and Harvey Weinstein as producer.)

Shakespeare's writer's block in this film also sets up a comically imagined relationship between Shakespeare and Philip Henslowe (Geoffrey Bush), who has the unenviable task of prying loose from Shakespeare the as-yet-unwritten play script that the hapless dramatist has sold in advance to Henslowe and Richard Burbage for much-needed cash. Henslowe in turn is in debt to a loan shark named Hugh Fennyman (Tom Wilkinson), whose henchmen put Henslowe's feet to the fire, in a hilarious literalization of that cliché, as their way of strong-arming Henslowe to pay up. All Henslowe can do is to wheedle and beg Shakespeare to get on with his play so that Henslowe can get the money he owes Fennyman. This has no historical basis at all, of course. Henslowe, builder of the Rose Theatre on the Bankside and business partner with the great actor Edward Alleyn, his son-in-law, kept a deliciously misspelled Diary detailing the affairs of their acting company, the Admiral's Men; he had no dealings with the rival acting company that Shakespeare joined in 1594 with Richard Burbage and others, the Lord Chamberlain's Men. Stoppard mixes up historical identities and invents nonhistorical persons like Fennyman (and, later, Viola de Lesseps, the Earl of Wessex, etc.) in a way that *Anonymous*, interestingly, does not. My contention is that *Anonymous*, with its vast array of characters drawn from Elizabethan history, is a travesty of historical truth while *Shakespeare in Love*, knee-deep in non-historical characters and events that never took place, offers a compelling and even verisimilar portrait of London's theatrical world circa 1594–1595.

In the present instance, *Shakespeare in Love* is true to the entrepreneurial spirit of dog-eat-dog that must have been a part of Shakespeare's daily theatrical life. The streets bustle with activity; deals between aspiring playwrights and producers demand quickness of wit and creative energy. London at this time attracted many new writers, drawn by a dream of quick success that was denied to most citizens. The acting companies, forming and reforming unpredictably in such a competitive world, had newly discovered in the late 1580s and early 1590s that touring the provinces was dreary and unprofitable compared with offering plays to London's potentially vast theatre audience. The money was to be found in the big city, and the companies that succeeded in this enterprise needed new plays, lots of them. On tour they could make do with a handful of scripts, acted again and again in Bristol, Manchester, or wherever; in London a company needed a new play every week or oftener.[9] Writers were in demand, but they had to be good and had to move quickly. *Shakespeare in Love* captures brilliantly this frenetic world of striving for success.

Writer's block is also a key ingredient in *Shakespeare in Love*'s story of—well, Shakespeare in love. When Shakespeare, at his wit's end with 'Romeo and Ethel the Pirate's Daughter', attends a seemingly endless parade of auditions conducted by his acting company to find the right actors for a play, he has to put up with one recitation after another of lines from the playwright-du-jour of the London theatrical scene, Christopher Marlowe, Shakespeare's exact contemporary (both born in 1564) and at this point in the early 1590s a huge *succès de scandale* with his *Tamburlaine* plays and *Doctor Faustus* and all. The young hopefuls trying out for actor's parts all seem to know Marlowe's plays by heart. This audition business, by the way, is another deliciously anachronistic reinvention of history in this film: Shakespeare's company did not need or want to conduct auditions of this sort, since Shakespeare and his fellows were an ensemble company ready to divide up acting roles among themselves without the cost and expense of time involved in drafting new talent. But never mind, in this film we have auditions. The magical moment occurs when Shakespeare, bored out of his skull, suddenly hears a hopeful thespian reciting some lines from Shakespeare's own *The Two Gentlemen of Verona*. Good heavens! This is of course Viola de Lesseps, magnificently played by Gwyneth Paltrow in the best role she ever undertook, dressed up as a young man named Thomas Kent, with her hair tied into a knot beneath her cap, delivering quite persuasively a speech in which Proteus expresses his longing for Sylvia. It turns out that Viola has learned to admire the dramatic work of the relatively unknown Shakespeare, and has come to this particular acting company since he is in it. Her avid wish is to be an actor on the Elizabethan stage, where women were not included. Herewith is another topsy-turvy view of historical reality: women were excluded from the stage, to be sure, but the idea that a clever and cultivated young person like Viola could pass herself off as a young male suitable for the role of Romeo stretches credulity to the breaking point.

Viola is present, in another scene, when this same *The Two Gentlemen of Verona* is taken to court for a private showing before Queen Elizabeth (Judi Dench; marvelous). Some of Shakespeare's plays were indeed shown at court, mainly after King James I had succeeded to the throne in 1603. *The Two Gentlemen* is perhaps the least likely choice to imagine having earned this accolade. Despite Viola's attachment to it, the play is very early and hardly vintage Shakespeare. The Queen did occasionally enjoy a play, but we know of none by Shakespeare other than, according to a rumor reported above, *Henry IV* and then, one hopes, *The Merry Wives of Windsor*. But *Two Gentlemen* does have a really funny monologue of Lance and his dog. That alone is worth the price of admission.

Undoubtedly a dog did appear on stage when this play was publicly performed. The dog is there in the filming of this episode, and it does what animals invariably do on stage, which is to steal the scene. The Queen, greatly amused, recognizes dramatic potential in Shakespeare and remembers him later on. Perhaps too we are to imagine that Viola's infatuation with Shakespeare first springs from her delight with a dog that entangles itself in its leash, refuses to answer its master's questions, threatens (in another part of the play) to urinate on a lady's farthingale, and ends up being the star of the show. Love can have many strange beginnings.

At any rate, once Shakespeare has bathed his wounded ego—still reeling from the assaults on it from importunate creditors—with the reassuring discovery of a genuine fan, he wants to meet and get to know this person. Does he subliminally sense that beneath the male disguise there lies feminine beauty? He soon discovers, at any rate, that 'Thomas Kent' is in fact a beautiful young woman. I need hardly point out that Stoppard is here playing inventive games with that staple of Shakespearean comedy, the young woman (acted by a young male) disguising herself as a male, as in *The Merchant of Venice*, *As You Like It*, *Twelfth Night*, *All's Well That Ends Well*, *Cymbeline*, and, to be sure, *The Two Gentlemen of Verona*. Perhaps it is Julia's role in that play as the rejected inamorata of Proteus, disguising herself as a page in order to be able to follow the faithless Proteus to Milan, that prompts Viola to become so deeply invested in this particular play: it was Shakespeare's first venture into cross-dressing. Viola's own name points forward to *Twelfth Night*, where Viola is the heroine disguising herself in order to be a part of Orsino's household and to serve him. Here we encounter still another of Stoppard's creative fantasies, at the end of the film, when Shakespeare, deeply sorrowful at losing Viola de Lesseps to the hated Earl of Wessex, resolves to write a play about a Viola that will turn out to be his *Twelfth Night*. Historically this is impossible as explaining why Shakespeare wrote that play, since Viola de Lesseps is a fiction, but it may suggest another way in which the writing of *Twelfth Night* was deeply personal for Shakespeare: the plot of twin brother and sister, in which the brother appears to drown but is at last reunited with her beloved sibling, could well be providing Shakespeare a way of dealing with the death of his only son, Hamnet, twin brother of Shakespeare's younger daughter Judith. The boy died in 1596, never again to be Shakespeare's son and heir; in *Twelfth Night*, as if magically, the lost son is recovered.[10] *Cymbeline, The Winter's Tale*, and *The Tempest* all pursue a similar fantasy.

After repeated attempts, and after chasing after the mysterious would-be actor in a water taxi manned by a Thames boatman who annoyingly wants to know whether he knows Christopher Marlowe and whether he would be willing to read the boatman's own attempt at play-writing (a fictional vignette that offers a fine glimpse of what travel by water was like in the 1590s), Shakespeare finally manages to track down 'Thomas Kent' at an impressive mansion belonging to a wealthy merchant named de Lesseps. The young person he has been chasing quickly disappears into the house, but Shakespeare learns that he has arrived in time for a splendid evening masqued entertainment that de Lesseps and his wife are putting on to honor their daughter's betrothal to Lord Wessex (Colin Firth). Though uninvited, Shakespeare manages to sneak in with some minstrels and dance with the lovely young person he now knows to be Viola. After they have touched hands and have exchanged glances in their brief encounter, Shakespeare is evicted from the dance by order of Wessex, who clearly views him as an unwanted intruder and potential rival. Shakespeare, deliriously happy and excited, makes his way to a garden in the back of the de Lesseps mansion, where, lo and behold! he sees Viola at a window. Viola, startled, becomes aware of his presence. He climbs up to her precariously with the aid of vines. The two young people are interrupted by the voice of the Nurse (Imelda Staunton). Shakespeare, losing his grip, falls back into the pool and then escapes before Wessex's thugs can detain him. He makes his way back to his digs, a new man, ready to write *con brio* and *con amore*.

What Stoppard has done here is brilliant in its audacity. The sequence is of course a mirror image of Romeo's first encounter with Juliet: the evening feast put on by the wealthy bourgeois Capulet family, Romeo's uninvited arrival in a masque, his dancing briefly with Juliet, his being challenged by the furious Tybalt who cannot bear to see Montagues in the Capulet house, his unwillingness to leave until he can speak again with Juliet, her appearance at her window, their exchange of vows, his need to retire from the scene before the Capulets find out he is there. The film provides a balcony, following stage tradition; in the text of *Romeo and Juliet*, no balcony is mentioned, nor does the word appear elsewhere in Shakespeare's works. A much larger fiction is that, in *Shakespeare in Love*, this brief encounter gives Shakespeare the story he needs for his impoverished script about Romeo and Ethel the pirate's daughter. Writer's block is a thing of the past. The famous love scene in *Romeo and Juliet* is cribbed right out of Shakespeare's own night-time adventure. Juliet is a version of Viola. The very things that Viola says to Shakespeare, when they become lovers the next night in Viola's own bedroom behind a door guarded by the vigilant and agitated Nurse, are words that turn up more or less verbatim in Shakespeare's play. 'Wilt thou be gone?' Viola protests to Romeo when he prepares to leave. 'It is the nightingale, and not the lark, / That pierced the fearful hollow of thine ear'. Stoppard is again playing with a familiar legend about Shakespeare, that he was what Robert Greene (or perhaps Henry Chettle) called a copycat, almost a plagiarist, an 'upstart crow beautified with our feathers' who stole beauties of language from his fellow dramatists, including Greene himself.[11]

The fiction here is even larger than that. *Shakespeare in Love* plays with the idea that the love affair with Viola de Lesseps was Shakespeare's direct source for *Romeo and Juliet.* The actual source, as is widely known, was a long and at times lugubrious poem by Arthur Brooke entitled *The Tragical History of Romeus and Juliet, written first in Italian and now in English by Ar. Br.*, 1562. As Brooke freely acknowledged, his version was in turn indebted to Matteo Bandello's *Novelle*, 1554, based in turn on Luidi da Porto's *Historianovellamenteretrivata di due Nobile Amanti*, c. 1530, which had taken the story from Macuccio of Salerno's *Il Novellino*, 1476. The story went back even further than that, at least to Xenophon's *Ephaesiaca* in the fifth century. It was a story with nearly as rich and varied a tradition as in legends of King Arthur or the fall of Troy. Tom Stoppard knows this, and assumes that at least a sizable portion of his audience knows something about the play's sources. The fiction of an original story inspired by a romantic encounter is a wonderful joke. This fiction has a tradition of its own: Alexandre Duval's one-act comedy called *Shakespeare amoureux, ou la pièce à l'étude*, 1803, fancifully depicts Shakespeare as falling in love with an actress playing Richard III.[12]

In the film, Shakespeare also profits from the sage advice of Christopher Marlowe (Rupert Everett), who offers his opinion that the title 'Romeo and Ethel the Pirate's Daughter' will never sell tickets. What about *Romeo and Juliet*? he suggests. Even this world-famous phrase, it seems, is not Shakespeare's own invention. The hapless Shakespeare of this film is a classic illustration of that phrase from a Beatles' song, 'With a little help from my friends'. Well, Shakespeare did indeed know, quite superbly, how to assemble his incomparable works from all sorts of other writers.[13] He went to Italian short stories mainly for his plots in the romantic comedies: all the interwoven stories of *The Merchant of Venice*, for example, about Shylock, the wooing of Portia, the three caskets, the elopement of Jessica, the episode of the rings, etc., came to him conveniently in one package in an Italian short story in Ser Giovanni Fiorentino's *Il Pecorone*, 1558. He seems to have written his history plays with a copy of the second edition of Raphael Holinshed's *The Chronicles of England, Scotland, and Ireland*, 1587, on the desk in front of him, even if he freely altered historical information and used other sources as well. His plays about the ancient classical world, *Julius Caesar, Coriolanus, Antony and Cleopatra*, etc., were heavily indebted to Thomas North's translation of Plutarch's *The Lives of the Noble Grecians and Romans*, 1579 and 1595, to the point on one occasion at least of virtually plagiarizing Plutarch's magnificent description of Cleopatra as she meets Mark Antony on the Nile (where Shakespeare deftly transforms his near-verbatim copy into a wholly new dramatic context by giving the speech to the sardonic though admiring Enobarbus).[14] Another passage of nearly literal borrowing is to be found in *The Tempest*, when kindly old Gonzalo, cast ashore on an unknown island with his companions, reflects on what kind of ideal Utopian commonwealth he would create if he could begin life anew in this strange spot (2.1.150–71). His language is nearly word for word out of John Florio's 1603 translation of Michel de Montaigne's essay 'Of the Cannibals'. Another speech, that of Prospero when he bids farewell to 'Ye elves of hills, brooks, standing lakes, and groves' (5.1.33–57), is taken from an invocation of Medea in Ovid's *Metamorphoses*, book 7, as translated by William Golding, 1567. Robert Greene (or Chettle) was right, in a sense, to describe Shakespeare as an 'upstart crow beautified with our feathers', even if that remark was offered as an undeserved and jealously inspired insult. Once again, the script writers of *Shakespeare in Love*, prominently Stoppard, have presented viewers of the film with what appears to be an outlandish fiction behind of which lies a profound truth about Shakespeare.

Christopher Marlowe is an important figure in *Shakespeare in Love*, and the subject of one of the film's most comically outrageous untruths: the suggestion that Shakespeare was unintentionally responsible for the notorious murder of Marlowe. Historically, that brilliant dramatist and poet, at the age of 29, was killed on May 23, 1593 in Deptford, in a brawl, by one Ingram Frizer. Evidently Marlowe began the violence by drawing Frizer's dagger and giving him a couple of cuts on the head. Frizer responded by stabbing Marlowe above the right eye. Frizer was the personal servant and business agent of Sir Thomas Walsingham, cousin of Sir Francis Walsingham, dead by this time but formerly Secretary of State and a zealous protector of the Queen against the Babington conspiracy and other numerous assassination plots in the 1580s. Marlowe enjoyed the patronage of Sir Thomas, to the point of staying at Sir Thomas's estate of Scadbury in Kent at the time of Marlowe's arrest on order of the Privy Council to answer charges of 'atheism'. He died before he could answer the accusations against him. Marlowe had been involved as a courier and spy by Elizabeth's government, and he had a reputation for being confrontational, flippant, and heterodox in every imaginable way.[15]

In *Shakespeare in Love*, what happens instead is Lord Wessex, outraged by Shakespeare's intrusion at the de Lessops's masked ball and intent on revenge, demands that Viola reveals to him the name of the hated visitor, to which she replies that his name is Christopher Marlowe. When Shakespeare learns of Marlowe's death, he blames himself for this because, in an effort to protect his own life, he has let Wessex persist in his misunderstanding that Marlowe was the unwanted wooer of Viola. The clear implication is that Wessex's henchmen then did away with Marlowe, even if a rumor goes about that the death was by accident. Sid Smith, in *The Chicago Tribune*, January 6, 1999, characterizes this as 'pure conjecture' on Stoppard's part, but that is surely wrong. It is not a conjecture at all, which would imply putting forth a hypothetical explanation of Marlowe's death, but another of the film's balmy fibs. Of course Shakespeare had nothing to do with the death of Marlowe, but the film's flight of fancy offers a delicious twist to the mundane truth of the matter, which is that Shakespeare and Marlowe were rivals, and that Marlowe was the more precocious and notoriously successful of the two in the early 1590s. We can imagine Shakespeare experiencing some of what Harold Bloom has famously called 'the anxiety of influence' (1973).[16] Shakespeare's *Richard II* (1595–1596) was surely written with Marlowe's *Edward II* (1591–1593) in mind, and *The Merchant of Venice* (1596–1597) is in part a re-visiting of Marlowe's controversial depiction of Barabas the villainous Jew in Marlowe's *The Jew of Malta* (c. 1589–1590). *As You Like It* (1599) quotes familiarly from Marlowe's amorous poem, *Hero and Leander*: 'Who ever loved that loved not at first sight?' (3.5.82). It is also true, of course, that Shakespeare would go on to tower over Marlowe in reputation, so that the depiction of Shakespeare as quavering before the literary might of his rival is another of the film's comic ironies. (*Anonymous*, I will argue below, also presents the viewer with a wholly fictional account of the death of Marlowe. But, whereas *Shakespeare in Love* imagines this to be a comically hilarious mixup, *Anonymous* uses its account to denigrate Shakespeare as despicable and to suggest how the murder of Marlowe can be seen as helping to explain how Shakespeare came to be chosen as the frontman for the writings of the Earl of Oxford.)

Allusions to *Romeo and Juliet* abound in *Shakespeare in Love*, understandably so, since that is the play that finally, after many perils and uncertainties, goes into production. When a Puritan fulminates in the street outside the Rose Theatre against the libertinism and profanity of stage plays, he calls down 'a plague on both their houses!', paraphrasing Mercutio's invective against the feud of the two families as he is about to die in a street brawl.[17] The famous 'balcony' scene, which in Shakespeare's original lacked a balcony, is transformed, as we have seen, into Shakespeare's brief and exquisite encounter with Viola in the garden behind her family's mansion. We see the lovers in bed after Shakespeare and Viola learn that they must part. The reason for the bitter–sweet end to their romance is very different from that of the play: we are shown the scene in which Romeo kills Tybalt in revenge for the death of Mercutio, but that is because the acting company is rehearsing the show for full production. Romeo must leave Verona because a price is on his head for homicide. In the film, the lovers must part because Shakespeare is already married and because Viola must become the unwilling bride of Wessex. This is a fine variation on the play's characterization of them as 'star-crossed lovers'.[18] The difficulty is not a family feud but a more recognizably modern story of a truly passionate love affair that flowers briefly only after both the lovers are doomed to other destinies. Their last moment together in bed is also deliberately anachronistic: *Romeo and Juliet* invites us to assume that their marriage is indeed briefly consummated, but decorously so in an Elizabethan theatre where a boy actor played the part of Juliet. Modern film allows us to glimpse briefly the beauty of two naked bodies.

The film wonderfully allows us to see how great art can transform a poignant human situation into something truly exquisite. Shakespeare and Viola's love affair ends painfully, in a separation that neither partner can prevent. In *Romeo and Juliet*, the lovers' saga ends in mutual suicide, profoundly ironized by how nearly they have come to a happy resolution: Romeo might have learned that the sleeping Juliet is only in a deep trance, and Juliet might have awakened in time to prevent Romeo from swallowing poison. Friar Laurence and the Watch might have arrived before it was too late. The lovers have only the briefest time to kiss each other farewell, and then Juliet takes her own life by stabbing herself with Romeo's dagger. The film shows us how this business could actually have been staged at an Elizabethan theatre, aiming the camera at the lovers from the side or rear so that we can observe the distraught emotions of the audience. When Gwyneth Paltrow as Juliet awakens and says to Friar Laurence, 'Where is my Romeo?', her Nurse, standing in the yard of the theatre and drenched with tears, calls out 'There!' in a futile attempt to stop Juliet from taking her own life. When Paltrow stabs herself, she pulls a red band of cloth from her bodice to signify her blood. Not even stage blood, just a red cloth. Why does this film choose to lay bare the artifices of theatre and film so brazenly? Somehow, the effect is transcendent. The theatre audience is stunned into horrified silence, and so are we. As Philip Henslowe keeps saying, in a kind of mantra for the entire show, 'It's a mystery'. He offers this piety in the hope that when things are going badly with the production of *Romeo and Juliet* they will eventually work out. It stands also as a larger affirmation about theatre at its best. *Shakespeare in Love* is essentially about the magic of theatre. To achieve that end it dramatizes the improbable, incessantly teasing the audience with loopy lies. How do these lies work to tell important truths that cannot be expressed as effectively in any other way? It's a mystery.

Details of the film are part of its overall vision. Shakespeare's desire to consult about his sex life with a quack astrologer named Doctor Moth (deliciously played by Antony Sher) is of course unhistorical, but it affords us an instructive glimpse into the life and career of Simon Forman, an astrologer, occultist, and quack doctor in the Elizabeth age who was widely suspected of being in league with the devil and of having a gargantuan sexual appetite aimed indiscriminately at the women under his care. He was an inveterate playgoer who has left us his account of four of Shakespeare's plays. The acting company's tribulations with the Master of the Revels, Edmund Tilney (Simon Callow), become wildly improbable when that unsmiling functionary marches with his troops to close down *Romeo and Juliet* for having the effrontery to employ an actress in its cast, but the threat of censorship was undeniably a factor with which the players had continually to contend. When it turns out that Shakespeare and Richard Burbage are sharing the sexual favors of a certain Rosaline, some members of the film audience will recall what may be just a dirty story about actors but which was nonetheless current in London in the 1590s, that Shakespeare one day overheard his acting colleague Burbage arrange an assignation with a female theatre groupie, whereupon Shakespeare decided to go pluck the sweet fruit of this dalliance for himself before Burbage could get there. He was 'at his game', as John Manningham reports in his commonplace book in 1602, when word came to their bedchamber that 'Richard the Third' was at the door. 'Shakespeare caused return to be made that William the Conqueror was before Richard the Third', wrote Manningham. 'Shakespeare's name William'. [19] The references to growing tobacco in Virginia are off historically by a considerable number of years. The actor employed to recite *Romeo and Juliet*'s prologue about 'Two households' that are 'alike in dignity' surely did not have a massive problem with stuttering. Shakespeare's company surely was never driven to the expedient of offering the seemingly minor role of the Apothecary to a financial angel, the obstreperous Hugh Fennyman, as a way to keep the needed money coming. Tom Wilkinson is marvelous as the tyro Fennyman, who sees the entire play as revolving around his role of the Apothecary, and who keeps cutting into Romeo in his eagerness to deliver his few lines with gusto and conviction.

This business of casting a minor role out of financial desperation is a favorite theatrical joke. It plays a major part, for example, in what I think is Woody Allen's funniest film, *Bullets over Broadway* (1994), when a hapless would-be scriptwriter and director (played by John Cusack), looking about for actors for a show he hopes to stage called *God of Our Fathers*, finds that he has to give a major female role to Olive Neal (Jennifer Tilly), the moll of the gangster who has reluctantly agreed to bankroll the production but will do so only if Olive, who can't act her way out of a paper bag, is cast for the part.

The ending of *Shakespeare in Love*, with Shakespeare coming to the realization that his parting from Viola could inspire his next play, was apparently Stoppard's idea, introduced when several shoots of the final scene seemed not to work. As in every other instance of his intervention, this one deals fast and loose with the facts: *Twelfth Night* (1600–1602) was to come not as an immediate sequel but some five years after *Romeo and Juliet*, during which time Shakespeare had written *Much Ado About Nothing*, *The Merry Wives of Windsor*, *As You Like It*, and his finest English history plays. It is true that Viola is the leading female part in *Twelfth Night*, but then there never was a Viola in Shakespeare's life to commemorate in this way. The name 'Viola' does not appear in the earlier plays and writings from which Shakespeare drew ideas for *Twelfth Night*, including Nicolò Secchi's *Gl'Inganni* (1562) and Curzio Gonzaga's similarly-titled play of 1592, or Barnabe Rich's story 'Of Apollonius and Silla' based on a story by Matteo Bandello, or even Shakespeare's own *The Comedy of Errors* and Plautus's *Menechmi* to which *The Comedy of Errors* was indebted. 'Viola' could have been suggested instead by the name of the violet-like flower called viola, by the sweetness of the stringed instrument, or perhaps because 'Viola' is a kind of anagram for 'Olivia', with whom Viola is paired and contrasted throughout the play. Most of the names in *Twelfth Night* appear to be Shakespeare's fictional choices: Sir Toby Belch, Sir Andrew Aguecheek, Maria, Sebastian. There was an Orsino Orsini Migliorati in fifteenth-century Rome whose wife was the mistress of Pope Alexander VI, but we have no way of knowing if Shakespeare knew that or even cared. The name 'Orsino' in Italian means 'little bear'. How would that fit? Viola then may simply be one of the dramatist's many fictional choices. Shakespeare tends to be inventive this way in his romantic comedies.[20]

I have less to say about *Anonymous* in this essay, but I do want to point out some ways in which I think its use of fiction and improbability is strikingly unlike that in *Shakespeare in Love*. The source materials out of which this film's narrative lines emerge are essentially the often-repeated hypotheses of the Oxfordians: that the Earl of Oxford wrote Shakespeare's plays, employing this actor as a frontman because writing plays for public audiences was regarded by England's elites as beneath their social dignity, that Shakespeare himself was a barely literate actor who never attended a university, that a university education was the *sine qua non* of literary accomplishment, that Oxford was a gifted writer whose intimate acquaintance with England's ruling class gave him first-hand knowledge of how persons at court (like Polonius) would converse, that Oxford was under great pressure to conceal his identity as playwright, and still more. Thus, in the film, we see Edward de Vere (later the Earl of Oxford) as a child prodigy at the age of eight or nine writing *A Midsummer Night's Dream* and enacting the part of Puck in his own play before the young Elizabeth. As a young man, he is obliged to live in the repressively puritanical household of William Cecil, where he kills a spying servant hiding behind an arras and thereby gains an experience that he will turn into fiction when he writes the death of Polonius in *Hamlet*. When Cecil finds out about this homicide, he uses this information to blackmail de Vere into marrying Cecil's daughter, Anne, who compels him to renounce literary ambition.

Nearly every part of the story thus far is based on Oxfordian theory. De Vere did indeed marry Anne Cecil, but historically he was an abusive and ungrateful wretch as her husband, not a victim of her and her family's supposedly puritanical horror of writing for the sin-soaked public theatres. He wrote a handful of sonnets and other verse as courtiers were expected to do, poems that are graceful enough in their way but hardly exceptional, hardly displaying the genius needed to write *A Midsummer Night's Dream*. Even the hypothesis of eight- or nine-year authorship is preposterous; English letters can point to John Keats's great poems written shortly before his death at the age of twenty-five and to Thomas Chatterton who died when he was eighteen, but child prodigies in literature mature far more slowly than do music composers like Mozart and Schubert. Oxford's purported fascination with theatre is fictional. Apart from Francis Meres's listing (*Palladis Tamia*, 1598), of Oxford as among the greatest contemporary writers of comedies (Meres does not mention Oxford in his list of writers of great tragedies), no historical evidence supports the notion that he wrote plays. The notion that William Cecil, Lord Burghley, was the model for Polonius in *Hamlet* is one of the most enduring claims of the Oxfordian thesis; after all, as Burghley's son-in-law, Oxford would have had numerous occasions to study Burghley's mannerisms and his penchant for political meddling. But the thought that the author of Shakespeare's great plays could create a character like that without modeling it on a real-life courtier is demeaning to the very idea of creativity.

In short, the authors of *Anonymous* seem wedded to the indefensible notion that the author of the works assigned to Shakespeare wrote directly out of his own experience, just as some critics have assumed that since 'Shakespeare' wrote so well about war he must have been a soldier himself, etc. No allowance is made for literary imagination. 'Shakespeare', when viewed in this light, must surely have been Oxford. And although *Shakespeare in Love* might seem at first glance to adopt the same autobiographical fallacy, my contention is that the very opposite is true. That film is so entertainingly witty in the fictions it playfully puts to use that we catch the superb irony. *Shakespeare in Love* is the very embodiment of literary and theatrical imagination.

Of course, the Oxfordian program has an answer for the biographical problems enumerated here. Oxford, in this hypothesis, did write plays, but felt compelled to conceal his having done so. Thus it is in *Anonymous* that Oxford decides to write plays secretly that would be helpful to the Earl of Essex (presented in this film as one of Queen Elizabeth's illegitimate sons) when that dashing young man ventures on a treasonous conspiracy to overthrow the Queen's ministers. *Henry V*, and later *Richard III*, we are told, were Oxford's propagandistic oeuvres endorsing the cause of revolution. Historically, to be sure, Essex did mount an abortive revolt in 1601 against the Queen, whereupon Shakespeare and his company, the Lord Chamberlain's Men, were called on the carpet for having staged a revival of *Richard II* (not *Richard III*) on the very eve of the rebellion. In *Richard II,* a coup d'etat against King Richard is led by his ambitious cousin, Henry Bolingbroke, Duke of Hereford and Lancaster, who thereby attains the throne as Henry IV. The scene of Richard's deposition was especially troublesome to the authorities and indeed to the Queen herself, who was heard to remark some months after the play's January 1601 revival, 'I am Richard II; know you not that?'[21] The deposition scene was so politically sensitive that it was censored when the play was printed in quarto in 1597 and 1598, even though this publication occurred well before the Essex rebellion. Shakespeare scholars generally agree that the acting company was not at fault, and indeed they were exonerated by the authorities in 1601. Doing revivals was part of their stock in trade. Perhaps Shakespeare and his fellows did sympathize to an extent with Essex; he was something of a darling with the players and with public theatre audiences. But that is a far cry from the film's representing Oxford as the author of *Richard III*, writing it and other history plays as propaganda for the Tudor throne and for Oxford's role as defender of the Queen.

To be sure, the film does not implicitly claim that all its fictions are fact. Surely we are not expected to believe that all the Queen's amours represented here were historical: that she was the lover of Oxford, by whom she gave birth to Henry Wriothesley, the third Earl of Southampton, and was earlier the lover of the Earl of Leicester, with whom she fathered none other than Edward de Vere, destined to become the Earl of Oxford. The trouble is that many details of this series of incestuous affairs are put forward ultimately to support the view that Oxford wrote Shakespeare's plays. The film characterizes *Richard III* as Oxford's thinly veiled attack on Robert Cecil, William Cecil's allegedly hunchbacked son, who became the chief minister of state after his father's death in 1598. Here the dating of the plays seems all wrong: the film contends that *Richard III* was written after *Henry V*, 1599, doing so in order to update a play from 1592 to 1594 in such a way as to make it seem relevant to Robert Cecil's unrelenting opposition to Essex. The film also updates the long amorous poem called *Venus and Adonis* that had been published in 1593 over Shakespeare's name, with a warm dedication to the Earl of Southampton. The film's contention is that Oxford wrote it in the late 1590s as a way of reminding Queen Elizabeth of their affair. Presumably Oxford then had Shakespeare's name put on the title page because the poem was too frank in its depiction of amorous feeling for Oxford to allow his name to be used as author.

The death of Christopher Marlowe offers a useful way of comparing *Shakespeare in Love* and *Anonymous*, since that homicide figures in both films. *Shakespeare in Love* plays with what is plainly a joke of mistaken identities, when Shakespeare allows Lord Wessex to persist in his mistaken belief that the intruder at the de Lessops's masked ball, namely Shakespeare himself, was Marlowe, toward whom the jealous Wessex vows revenge. *Anonymous* frames the matter as one more demonstration of the validity of the Oxfordian claim to authorship of Shakespeare's plays. De Vere makes an attempt to bring the dramatist Ben Jonson into his orbit as the presumed author of *Henry V*, but this Jonson refuses to let his name be associated with a play he regards as beneath his own standard and proposes William Shakespeare instead. When Shakespeare discovers that the real author is de Vere himself, Shakespeare agrees to serve as the nominal writer, but extracts enough money in return from de Vere to build the Globe Theatre. Christopher Marlowe has the misfortune to learn the real truth of authorship also, at which point he is found with his throat slit. Whether Shakespeare is directly responsible for this murder is not made explicit in the film, but Ben Jonson certainly thinks so, and confronts Shakespeare with this accusation.

Shakespeare is thus a loathsome creature in this film, inexperienced as a minor actor, unscrupulous to the point of being responsible for the murder of the brilliant rival Marlowe, guilty also of extortion, a drunken lout ready to sell his soul for money. One can see how the thesis of this film, in extolling the genius of Oxford, has a plausible motive in demoting Shakespeare to the ranks of the unworthy, but this surely is hitting beneath the belt. History memorializes Shakespeare as a man and a writer who was deeply loved and admired by many, including

Ben Jonson, who wrote of Shakespeare in his poem 'To the memory of my beloved, the author Mr William Shakespeare', that he stood with Aeschylus, Euripides, and Sophocles among the greatest tragedians in literary history; and as for comedy, 'Leave thee alone, for the comparison / Of all that insolent Greece or haughty Rome / Sent forth'.[22] In his *Discoveries*, Jonson wrote, 'I loved the man, and do honor his memory (on this side idolatry) as much as any'.[23] This despite the fact that Jonson had many critical things to say about Shakespeare as well, as quoted above at note 6. The film attempts to explain how a writer of such massive integrity and unbribable pugnacity as Jonson could have become involved in a scheme to draft Shakespeare as frontman for Oxford, but it won't wash. Too many other distinguished persons of that era testify to Shakespeare as deserving the epithet 'gentle'. Henry Chettle, apologizing for the unseemly attack by Robert Greene (or perhaps Chettle himself) on Shakespeare as 'an upstart crow, beautified with our feathers', wrote of Shakespeare that he was 'civil' and 'excellent in the quality he professes'. 'Besides', continued Chettle, 'divers of worship have reported his uprightness of dealing, which argues his honesty and his facetious grace in writing that approves his art'.[24] The film does not overcome a major difficulty of the Oxfordian hypothesis in positing a conspiracy of lying about authorship to which persons of great literary and cultural standing (including Jonson's teacher, the historian William Camden)[25] either consented in secret or were bamboozled into believing. The Oxford theory rests on conspiracy. So does the film. That is a part of its entertaining nature. We all love conspiracies.

Another prevailing thesis of many Oxfordians is that the Earl of Oxford, before he died in 1604, left instructions to his devoted followers to guard his writings carefully and release them from time to time for performances, and to authorize publication in quarto volumes and eventually in large folio publication in 1623, with alternations as necessary to account for any allusions that would indicate a date after 1604. Many great plays follow that date, after all, including *King Lear, Macbeth, The Winter's Tale*, and *The Tempest*, containing references to events like Guy Fawkes's Gunpowder Plot of late 1605 and January 1606, as alluded to in *Macbeth*.[26] The thesis of posthumous revision seems extraordinarily unnecessary: why posit a secret agreement to rewrite these plays when Shakespeare was still alive and receiving accolades for his work? But then, why posit a university education as quintessential for serious authorship when Oxford and Cambridge both conducted their education of the young largely through Latin, Greek, and Hebrew texts appropriate for the training of an Anglican clergy? *Anonymous* intrepidly takes on all these challenges to common sense. It does so with hypotheses that have been repeated again and again in Oxfordian writings since the time of J. Thomas Looney's *'Shakespeare' Identified in Edward de Vere, the Seventeenth Earl of Oxford*, 1920,[27] as well as in arguments advanced earlier on behalf of some other putative authors, including Sir Francis Bacon, Sir Walter Ralegh, and Edmund Spenser, all of whom were proposed as joint authors of the Shakespeare canon by Delia Bacon in 1857,[28] and Christopher Marlowe, whose death (in a scenario first formulated by Wilbur G. Zeigler in 1895) was staged in 1593 so that Marlowe could live on as the secret author of Shakespeare's plays without being detected.[29] The number of claimants to this throne cause one to wonder about the validity of any particular claim.

Perhaps the most outrageous notions put forth in *Anonymous* concern Queen Elizabeth's various amorous affairs and her giving birth to a number of illegitimate children, including Oxford. These ideas may well be proffered tongue in cheek; Elizabeth is today widely suspected of having slept with Robert Dudley, soon to become the Earl of Leicester, early in her life, and thus no 'Virgin Queen' in that technical sense, but a promiscuous woman she was not. A film is of course entitled to whatever license it pleases in such matters, but in terms of the film's overriding Oxfordian thesis this portrayal of royal debauchery strikes me as dishonest. It is there to underpin the claim that Oxford wrote Shakespeare's plays. When Oxford learns from Robert Cecil that he, Oxford, is said to be one of the Queen's bastard offspring, he confronts her about the allegation. Their conversation takes place after the Essex rebellion has run its disastrous course. The Queen agrees to save Southampton (who is after all supposedly their son) from execution on a charge of having claimed the throne for himself during the upheaval of the Essex rebellion, but she exacts a price: Oxford must remain anonymous as the true author of the plays attributed to Shakespeare, who is to be allowed to retire to Stratford-upon-Avon with his dishonestly acquired wealth. The Oxford thesis thus has the imprimatur of no less a figure of authority than Queen Elizabeth I, arguably England's greatest ruler of all time. In the film Oxford dies in 1604 (a true fact), leaving his manuscripts in the hands of Ben Jonson, who is sorry to have given the Earl such trouble (something that is not true). Robert Cecil determines to destroy these manuscripts as the work of the hated Oxford, rejoices when he learns that the Rose

Theatre has burnt to the ground with the manuscripts inside, but they did survive and ultimately come into the hands of Ben Jonson. They are published under the name of William Shakespeare, an authorship Ben Jonson knows to be false. But, says the film, we can understand today who the real author was. Long Live the Earl of Oxford!

Anonymous is wittily put together, displaying a lot of dexterity in inventing so complex a story in which so many famous Elizabethans are imagined to contribute to the fictional narrative of the Earl of Oxford as the author of the Shakespeare canon. Still, I find myself wondering if the film is an embarrassment to some Oxfordians, being as it is so full of poppycock. But then so is the whole Oxfordian enterprise. Poppycock.

Notes

1. See Douglas Lanier, referred to in Sawyer, 2013.
2. See, for example, Massie, 2011.
3. Doran, 2014.
4. *The Telegraph*, 30 June 2014.
5. Rhys Ifans quoted online, 'Anonymous (film)', Wikipedia.
6. Ben Jonson, *Discoveries*, in Bevington, Butler, and Donaldson, 2012, 7.521–2, lines 468–70.
7. Heminge and Condell, 1623, A3.
8. For photographic images of Shakespeare's signatures, see Schoenbaum, 1981, pp. 93–97.
9. McMillin and Maclean, 1998.
10. Wheeler, 2000.
11. *Greene's Groatsworth of Wit, Bought with a Million of Repentance* (1592), sometimes attributed to Henry Chettle. Quotations from Shakespeare in this essay are from Bevington, 2014.
12. See Pujante and Hoenselaars, 2003.
13. On Shakespeare's sources, see Bullough, 1966.
14. *Antony and Cleopatra*, 2.2.201–50.
15. See, for example, Hutchinson, 2006; Nicholl, 1992; Downie and Parnell, 2000; and Honan, 2005.
16. Bloom, 1973.
17. See *Romeo and Juliet*, 3.1.105–7.
18. *Romeo and Juliet*, Prologue, 6.
19. Bruce, 1868, entry for 13 March 1601 (1602 in modern calendar reckoning).
20. A stage version of 'Shakespeare in Love', entitled 'Shakespeare in Love: The Play', opened in the summer of 2014 in London's Noel Coward

Theatre, as written by Lee Hall, directed by Declan Donnellan of 'Cheek by Jowl' and designed by Nick Ormerod, with Lucy Briggs-Owen as Viola and Tom Bateman as Shakespeare. The script offered a faithful adaptation, with something like ninety percent of the film script intact. It proved to be less a love story and more about the young hero becoming Shakespeare and Viola becoming a great actress. Marlowe's role was enlarged, as he whispered theatrical ideas into Shakespeare's ear until the latter truly found his own voice. The dog, Spot, became the source of a running joke throughout the play ('Out, damned spot! Out, I say', cribbed from *Macbeth*). Tom Stoppard, whose first response was that he 'didn't want the gig', allowed himself to be briefly engaged in the enterprise but then withdrew. The play got standing ovations in previews (see Healey 2014). Brantley, 2014, was less enthusiastic, characterizing the play as 'Shakespeare flavored' like some fuzzy beverage, inventively staged but raising questions as to the wisdom of transporting this film to the stage as if it were another 'Singing in the Rain'. Quite unfairly, in my view, Brantley found it necessary to dump on the original film as 'more annoyingly precious' than one might expect, plagued with 'a sense of the ersatz' and a 'twee factor that was always lurking in the movie'. Its flaws were magnified in the play to the extent of a 'disproportionate cuteness', in Bradley's view, with too much time in its leisurely pace 'for the hoary this'll-make-you-feel-smart references to register'. Bradley may be right about the dubiousness of turning the film into a play, but I was disappointed to have him brush off his Shakespeare this way by labeling the original film 'Shakespeare for Sophomores'. For me, it holds up well indeed, as I hope the present essay demonstrates.

21. See Bate, 2009, pp. 256–86.
22. Jonson, 1623, A4-A4v.
23. Ben Jonson, *Discoveries*, in Bevington, Butler, and Donaldson, 2012, 7.522, lines 473–74.
24. Chettle, 1592–1593.
25. William Camden, author of Camden, 1577, 1605.
26. *Macbeth*, 2.3.8–11.
27. Looney, 1920.
28. Bacon, 1857.
29. Ziegler, 1895.

Bibliography

Bacon, Delia. 1857. *The Philosophy of the Plays of Shakespere Unfolded*. Boston: Ticknor and Fields.

Bate, Jonathan. 2009. *Soul of the Age: A Biography of the Mind of William Shakespeare*. New York: Random House.

Bevington, David (ed.). 2014. *The Complete Works of Shakespeare*, 7th edition. New York: Pearson/Longman.

Bevington, David, Butler, Martin, and Donaldson, Ian (gen. eds.). 2012. *The Cambridge Edition of the Works of Ben Jonson*. Cambridge: Cambridge University Press.

Bloom, Harold. 1973. *The Anxiety of Influence: A Theory of Poetry*. New York: Oxford University Press.

Brantley, Ben. 2014. Review in *The New York Times*, 24 July.

Bruce, John (ed.). 1868. *Diary of John Manningham, of the Middle Temple*. Westminster: Camden Society.

Bullough, Geoffrey (ed.). 1966. *Narrative and Dramatic Sources of Shakespeare*. 7 Vols. London and New York: Routledge and Kegan Paul.

Camden, William. 1577. *Britannia*. London.

Camden, William. 1605. *Remains Concerning Britain*. London.

Chettle, Henry (Sometimes Attributed). 1592. *Greene's Groatsworth of Wit, Bought with a Million of Repentance*. London.

Chettle, Henry. 1592–1593. *Kind-Heart's Dream*. London.

Doran, Gregory D. 2014. Review in *The Telegraph*, 22 April.

Downie, J. A., and Parnell, J. T. (eds.). 2000. *Constructing Christopher Marlowe*. Cambridge: Cambridge University Press.

Healey, Patrick. 2014. Review in *The New York Times*, 22 July.

Heminge, John, and Condell, Henrie. 1623. 'To the Great Variety of Readers', *Mr. William Shakespeare's Comedies, Histories, and Tragedies*. London.

Honan, Park. 2005. *Christopher Marlowe: Poet and Spy*. Oxford: Oxford University Press.

Hutchinson, Robert. 2006. *Elizabeth's Spy Master: Francis Walsingham and the Secret War That Save England*. London: Weidenfeld & Nicolson.

Jonson, Ben. 1623. 'To the Memory of My Beloved, the Author Mr. William Shakespeare', *Mr. William Shakespeare's Comedies, Histories, and Tragedies*. London.

Looney, J. Thomas. 1920. *'Shakespeare' Identified in Edward de Vere, the Seventeenth Earl of Oxford*. New York: Frederick A. Stokes.

Massie, Allan. 2011. Review in *The Telegraph*, 25 October.

McMillin, Scott, and Maclean, Sally-Beth. 1998. *The Queen's Men and Their Plays*. Cambridge: Cambridge University Press.

Nicholl, Charles. 1992. *The Reckoning: The Murder of Christopher Marlowe*. London: Jonathan Cape.

Pujante, A. Luis, and Hoenselaars, Ton (eds.). 2003. *Four Hundred Years of Shakespeare in Europe*. Newark, London, Cranbury, NJ: University of Delaware Press, Associated University Presses.

Sawyer, Robert. 2013. 'Biographical Aftershocks: Shakespeare and Marlowe in the Wake of 9/11', *Critical Survey* 25 (2013), pp. 19–32.

Schoenbaum, S. 1981. *William Shakespeare: Records and Images*. Oxford: Oxford University Press.

Wheeler, Richard. 2000. 'Death in the Family: The Loss of a Son and the Rise of Shakespearean Comedy', *Shakespeare Quarterly* 51 (2000), pp. 127–53.

Ziegler, Wilbur Gleason. 1895. *It Was Marlowe: A Story of the Secret of Three Centuries*. Chicago: Donohue, Henneberry.

That Hamilton Woman (1941)

Samantha A. Cavell

The film opens on a tavern-filled street in Calais in the winter of 1814. An old woman, drunk and destitute, enters a shop observed by police. She steals a bottle of wine and is promptly arrested and imprisoned. In a dank cell, she recounts her story to a fellow inmate; a tale of her life as the most beautiful, celebrated, and scandalous woman of the French Revolutionary and Napoleonic Wars. It is a tragedy told with high drama and selective attention to historical detail in Alexander Korda's production of *That Hamilton Woman*. A dual allegory about the dangers of reinvention and the price of illicit love, the film follows the story of Amy Lyon, a poor girl from a Cheshire coal town, who is transformed into Emma, Lady Hamilton, wife of Sir William Hamilton, the British ambassador to Naples and the mistress of Britain's greatest naval hero, Admiral Lord Nelson. Emma's fall bookends the film with the heroine, not yet fifty and at the end of her life, returned to the gutter and haunted by lost love. With Vivien Leigh as Emma and Laurence Olivier as Nelson, the film sought to capitalize on the parallels between the historical romance and the actors' real-life adulterous love affair. It also sought to make a powerful political statement.

S. A. Cavell (✉)
Southeastern Louisiana University, Hammond, LA, USA
e-mail: samantha.cavell@selu.edu

T. S. Freeman and D. L. Smith (eds.), *Biography and History in Film*, Palgrave Studies in the History of the Media,
https://doi.org/10.1007/978-3-319-89408-9_6

Despite being a British production, the film was made in Hollywood during the autumn of 1940, partly out of wartime necessity and partly owing to the Ministry of Information's (MOI) desire to make a star-filled blockbuster that would appeal to American audiences and would not *look* like the wartime propaganda vehicle it was intended to be. Korda, who served as producer and director, maintained that Winston Churchill himself had insisted that *Lady Hamilton* (as the film was known in Britain) be made. Its purpose was to galvanize war-ravaged Britons in their efforts against Nazi Germany and, most importantly, to help prod the United States out of its isolationism. Churchill's possible involvement in pre-production reflected the personal and professional relationship between the Prime Minister and the director, which was formalized in April 1934 when Churchill signed on as an 'editor, associate producer and advisor' to Korda's production company, London Films, at a salary of £4000 per month.[1] Years later Churchill, via the MOI, used Korda and his connections in Hollywood and New York as a means of gathering and disseminating intelligence about potential US intervention in the war, and as a way to make and distribute high-gloss propaganda.[2] Rumours that the Prime Minister had been involved in writing the script are also credible as Churchill had previously worked on a treatment for another London Films script to celebrate the silver jubilee of George V. Churchill was apt to weigh in on any film project that could further the war effort, and encouraged Laurence Olivier to make *Henry V* (released in 1944) about an intrepid English army invading Normandy.[3] It is certain that Churchill commented on at least one aspect of *That Hamilton Woman*—its title. In a telegram to Korda on July 4, 1941, he suggested that 'Emma' would be preferable on the marquee. The recommendation came too late for the publicity machine which had already gone to press. Despite this, Churchill nonetheless claimed *That Hamilton Woman* as his favourite film, one he saw five times in 1941, with the ending bringing him to tears each time.[4]

Korda braved considerable danger to ensure that the film was made to his specifications as he crossed the Atlantic multiple times in 1939 and 1940, during the height of the U-boat threat. The film, however, was not Korda's only priority. He was also involved in 'supplying cover to MI-5 agents gathering intelligence on both German activities in the United States and isolationist sentiments among makers of American foreign policy'.[5] Korda acted as an *agent provocateur*, with his chief goal being 'to get Hollywood to talk America into the war'.[6] It was a service which earned him a knighthood in 1942.[7] Such high-level involvement in the war effort was, necessarily, unknown to most. During pre-production and filming of *That Hamilton Woman*, Korda drew criticism in London for his apparent abandonment of his adoptive country which was deep into the Battle of Britain and had begun to feel the effects of the Blitz. Laurence Olivier also received his share of censure for remaining in the United States when it was clear that the 'Phoney War' was over.[8] Despite requests from Lord Lothian, ambassador to the United States, that British actors remain stateside until further notice, the press in England and America were brutal in their treatment of both director and star.[9]

Korda would, however, receive even harsher criticism from some factions of the American government for producing a film that was too heavy-handed with its pro-war message. His support for Churchill's anti-appeasement policies was visible in earlier films like *The Private Life of Henry VIII* (1933), although the timing of *That Hamilton Woman* made its message all the more potent. Much of the criticism, and conversely the film's appeal to the MOI, lay in the story of Britain's timeless hero, Horatio Nelson, and his determination to defend the nation against an existential threat. Parallels between Napoleon and Hitler were easy to draw, and the script made good use of the fact that when Britain was threatened with invasion in 1804, the nation also stood alone and yet managed to rally a spirited defence. Moreover, the story allowed the truly terrifying aspects of the present reality to be framed in the more comforting and easily digestible guise of a love story. The oblique title placed the focus on Emma Hamilton rather than Lord Nelson, and allowed the producers plausible deniability when it came to the issue of their intention to disseminate propaganda in the United States. It helped that Korda had the cooperation of a *bona fide* star in Vivien Leigh who was willing to portray a character whose fortunes and foibles echoed those of Scarlett in *Gone with the Wind* (1939), allowing the production to capitalize on the actress' popularity and her Oscar-winning success.

Some artistic license was taken with the historical narrative in order to make a political statement against appeasement and abstinence from war as unsubtly as possible. In the most famous scene Olivier's Nelson argues against the proposed Peace of Amiens with the Board of Admiralty:

> Gentlemen you will never make peace with Napoleon. He doesn't mean peace today. He just wants to gain a little time to rearm himself at sea and make new alliances with Italy and Spain, all to one purpose – to destroy our empire! Years ago, I said the same thing at Naples ... but now it is England, our own land. Napoleon can never be master of the world until he has smashed us up and believe me gentlemen, he means to be master of the world. You cannot make peace with dictators – you have to destroy them, - wipe them out!

This cinematic call to arms saw Korda targeted by the non-interventionist, America First Committee, whose most famous spokesman was Charles Lindbergh. He also became the focus of Senator Gerald Nye's Committee on Interstate Commerce, which accused the director of being part of a 'British Army of Occupation' and of 'pushing and hauling at America to drag us into war'.[10] Korda was called to testify at Nye's committee hearing on December 12, 1941, but after the Japanese attack on Pearl Harbor on December 7, the hearing was cancelled.[11] Korda did submit a written statement on the matter which argued 'with effortless dissimulation, that the film had no propaganda intention whatsoever', and cited the eminent American historian, Alfred Thayer Mahan as his source for the offending Nelson speech.[12]

In Hollywood, Korda also faced judgement from Joseph Breen, the Motion Picture Production Code chairman, who objected to the portrayal of adultery, no matter how historically accurate the story. The code, established in 1930, dictated the rules of 'moral decency' for the film industry and stipulated what could and could not be shown to audiences in matters of sex, violence, profanity, nudity, drug use, criminal activity, sedition, and other social, political, and religious issues.[13] Whether by neglect or design, Korda failed to submit the script for approval to Breen's office until principal filming was well underway. Breen refused to green light the project on the grounds that it glorified adultery and that neither of the participants, Emma nor Nelson, were in the slightest bit contrite or considerate of the moral implications of their actions. Korda was forced to add a scene in which Nelson's wheelchair-bound father, Edmund, a Norfolk parson, chastises his son about the relationship. Edmund emphasizes how damaging the situation was to Fanny, Nelson's wife, and demands that he break off the affair. In the final version of the film another scene shows Nelson and Emma admitting their wrongdoing to each other. When faced with meeting Fanny and Edmund, they are undone. Emma laments: 'Now for the first time I begin to understand what William meant, what we're doing is so dreadfully wrong, of course I should have realized it before. Because it is wrong it cannot bring happiness', before collapsing in tears. In the following scene, such misgivings are forgotten and the affair reaches a new level of intensity as Nelson separates from Fanny in order to continue his relationship with the still-married Emma.

Love scenes were also chastened according to the demands of the Motion Picture Production Code. Images of Nelson in Emma's bed, within her cavernous boudoir at Sir William's Neapolitan palazzo, show the hero convalescing from battle while Emma hovers and feeds him tenderly. Innuendo triumphs over logic, and the likelihood that a palazzo would have sufficient guest accommodations to house the ailing admiral in his own quarters. Korda overtly emphasized romance in other ways and took full advantage of the marriage of Leigh and Olivier, which took place during filming, with publicity posters touting 'The Year's Most Exciting Team of Screen Lovers!'[14] While *That Hamilton Woman* benefited from an abundance of factual detail when it came to romance, the film, in fact, presented a far tamer version of the affair than the historical truth.

These two overarching themes: the consequences of marital infidelity; and the politics of war against a dictator, provide a framework for understanding the film's effectiveness as both propaganda and a paean to love. These themes, woven into the plot and character development of the film, are visible in a chronological assessment of the script. The circumstances of Emma and Nelson's affair are central to the narrative and provide the emotional heart of the film. The '*tria juncta in uno*' of Nelson, Emma, and Sir William Hamilton was a scandal that simultaneously titillated and appalled the British public, although the film spends little time on their three-way cohabitation, on the Continent and in England, or on the complexities of the real relationship.[15]

The story of Emma's rise begins at the Palazzo Secca, Sir William Hamilton's Neapolitan home, in 1786. Although he is introduced to viewers as the British Ambassador to Naples, twenty-nine years of service in the Kingdom of the Two Sicilies saw the real Sir William invested only as 'minister plenipotentiary', not a full ambassador. It was a pointed reflection of his limitations in the eyes of the Foreign Office.[16] Actor Alan Mowbray's portrayal of Sir William, who was then fifty-seven years old, as a pragmatic and placid observer is accurate by contemporary accounts. He was notable for an 'ironic detachment, never expecting too much of either his nearest and dearest or himself, and certainly not the world at large whose opinions and behaviour he viewed on the whole with amiable contempt'.[17] A passion for antiquities and the study of volcanoes, of which he wrote extensively, seldom transferred to his personal relationships after the sudden death of his first wife in 1782.

Into this emotional void stepped a twenty-two-year-old Emma. In the film, we learn of her scandalous early life through a conversation between Sir William and the French ambassador. Mowbray's Hamilton accurately chronicles her chequered past; from her role as a singing, dancing, nearly naked 'nymph' at Dr. Graham's 'Temple of Health', to her position as the mistress of Sir Harry Fetherstonhaugh (the writers abbreviate his name to 'Fetherstone') and subsequently that of Charles Greville, Sir William's nephew. The film does not address the fact that the relationship with Fetherstonhaugh produced a daughter, also named 'Emma' (Carew), who was farmed out to be raised by a family in the country. Although brought up in comfortable circumstances she would, for many years, know her mother only through newspapers and fashion plates which tabloided her glamorous life on the Continent—one in which the child could never participate.[18] At the age of eighteen Emma Carew was, at last, able to live with her mother, although the true nature of their relationship could never be admitted in public. As Emma Hamilton's financial situation worsened in later years, her daughter, whose health was far from robust, was sent to Italy to work as a governess. She would never see her mother again.

Our cinematic introduction to Leigh's youthful Emma comes via a famous George Romney portrait, as Sir William's servants unpack it from a crate shipped from London along with other specimens of classical art. He looks on and muses over the parallel between Emma's 'past' and a priceless Greek sculpture that had been cast down into the mud, then resurrected. Greville has sold the items to his uncle in order to pay off debts. Among the sale items is Emma herself. The script is well-crafted to tell Emma's sad tale, her love for Greville, and her belief in his desire for them to be married. When Sir William breaks the news that Greville has cast her aside, Emma's shock is palpable. Leigh evokes the innocence, pathos, and ambition of the historical Emma and effectively conveys her resignation and acceptance of a situation which, she confesses, 'offered all a young woman could want from life'. In reality, Greville's betrayal revealed itself over the course of several months and ended with his blunt instruction that she should 'go to bed with him, Sir Wm'. Emma responded with an impassioned letter: 'Greville, you cannot you must not give up on me. You have not the heart to do it … You love me I am sure … And I only say this is the last time I will beg or pray … Pray write for nothing will make me so angry [as silence] … . If you affront me I will make him marry me'.[19] Sir William did indeed marry Emma five years later in 1791. While it is undeniable that Hamilton admired his beautiful bride, contemporary letters suggest that the marriage was one of convenience for them both.

The historical Sir William was, however, deeply impressed with Emma's intellect, creativity, and her graciousness as a hostess. As one observer noted, Emma was 'a great natural genius … a singular mixture of right and wrong'.[20] She became fluent in French and Italian, and singing lessons honed her talent into a fine soprano. She also embraced Sir William's love of classical art and drew on her experience as an artist's model to some of the greatest portraitists of day, including Sir Joshua Reynolds and Romney, to invent 'The Attitudes'. These were ground-breaking performance art presentations of classical virtues and emotions that combined her flair for dance, movement, and drama. The film mentions Emma's performances only in passing and the dialogue is dismissive of her gift. In reality, Emma's 'Attitudes' were the toast of cultured Europe. Johann Wolfgang Goethe, a notorious curmudgeon, was entranced by her performance and requested an encore the following evening. He later wrote of her 'beautiful face and perfect figure' and of the performance itself: 'She lets down her hair, and, with a few shawls give so much variety to her poses, gesture, expressions etc., that the spectator can hardly believe his eyes. He [the viewer] sees what thousands of artists would have liked to express realized before him'.[21] Such an artistic achievement was all the more spectacular in light of Emma's lack of formal education. Her ability to absorb the fundamentals of visual classicism and translate her understanding into an entirely new art form demonstrated the depth of her intelligence and the skill of her artistry. Engravings were made of 'The Attitudes' and circulated to a wide audience, from middle-class enthusiasts to discerning patrons of the arts throughout Europe. They also made her a household name in London, well before she began her scandalous relationship with Lord Nelson.

Emma's quick wits and charm are also conveyed in the film's portrayal of her favoured position at the court of Queen Maria Carolina of Naples. The daughter of Maria Teresa of Austria and sister of Marie

Antoinette of France, Maria Carolina served as the de facto political ruler of Naples. Described as 'charismatic and ruthless' she was a skilled leader without whom, as Sir William noted in a letter to Greville, 'the whole state would fall into confusion'.[22] Although the details of the queen's relationship with King Ferdinand are played for comic effect in the film, the spirit of the matriarchal relationship is faithfully presented. Ferdinand preferred to concern himself with hunting rather than affairs of state, leaving his wife to manage politics and international relations which she pursued aggressively, with the aim of drawing Austria into the war to 'overthrow the French Republicans and avenge her murdered sister'.[23] The film addresses the point that Emma's unmarried circumstances prevented her from being presented at court, an impediment she vaulted by becoming Lady Hamilton. In life, Emma worked her way into the highest circles of the court even before her marriage. She made herself indispensable to Maria Carolina and helped the queen to entertain (and manipulate) scores of English dignitaries from whom she sought assurances for the protection of her tiny nation. Emma's influence was substantial, although the scene in which she first meets Nelson and uses her royal sway to secure him 10,000 Neapolitan troops for the assault on Toulon, is a simplification of the facts. In 1793 Nelson dealt directly with Sir John Acton, Ferdinand's acting prime minister, to obtain 2000 soldiers to reinforce Lord Hood's action on the French coast.[24] Acton worked closely with Maria Carolina, and while it is likely that the queen approved the troops, there is no evidence of Emma's direct involvement in the deal.

Emma and Nelson's second meeting took place five years later, in 1798, after his victory at the Battle of the Nile on August 1, which saw the destruction of the French Fleet and left Napoleon and his army stranded in North Africa. The film shows Emma's dismay over Nelson's wartime injuries which rendered him sightless in one eye and without his right arm. Olivier frequently wears an eye patch to hide the effect of his deformity, a measure not taken by the real Nelson. The make-up used to create the appearance of a non-responsive eye is impressive for the time, as is the appearance of his empty right sleeve which produces the quintessential Nelson silhouette. In life, the Admiral's failing health after the Nile campaign, a combination of many months of stress and a concussion suffered during the battle, roused even greater sympathy from Emma who guarded him jealously, then flaunted his heroism with parades and balls, in equal measure.[25] From this point, their relationship blossomed. Emma's adulation fed the ego of a man obsessed with fame and glory. While Fanny's letters were fraught with worry and pleas for him to return home to the quiet and safety of Norfolk, Emma's offered breathless praise for his gallant heroism. She was exciting, glamorous, and possessed a lust for life that was impossible for Nelson to resist. She also spent thousands of pounds on a September 29 party, festooned with columns inscribed '*veni, vidi, vici*' and favours of ribbons and buttons featuring his likeness, an honour that overwhelmed him with its scale and generosity.[26]

Nelson's deteriorating relationship with his step-son from Fanny's first marriage, Josiah Nisbet, is reflected in the film although, in 1799, the real Josiah was no pubescent midshipman. He was nineteen and already in command of the frigate HMS *Thalia*, thanks to Nelson's influence.[27] The cinematic Josiah's denigration of Nelson's relationship with Lady Hamilton emphasizes the public nature of the affair and the social backlash it generated, although the boy's drunken and temperamental behaviour are drawn from fact. Nelson worked hard to bolster Josiah's career, despite his lack of promise, and even requested help from fellow captains to control the young man's drinking and brutality, all to no avail. Both factors ended Josiah's career at sea in 1800.[28]

Considering the film's purpose, it is understandable that the script ignores Nelson's own professional censure which took place in 1799. As Napoleon tightened his grip on the Italian States, Nelson openly disobeyed orders from the Admiralty in order to remain in Naples to protect both the queen and Emma from the threat of a domestic political coup.[29] The queen's artful handling of Nelson, who was awed by her royal position and her attentions, developed in him a 'naïve attachment, to the point of sycophancy'.[30] Nelson threw his allegiances, and the naval forces at his disposal, behind a grateful Maria Carolina. It was a decision fueled by sentiment and by outrage at the snub he received from George III's government, who bestowed on him a mere barony rather than the viscountcy he expected after the Nile victory. Nelson not only saw to the royal family's evacuation from Naples after the coup, but to their subsequent return, an event that was accompanied by a brutal retribution on several thousand Neapolitan 'rebels'. Nelson and Emma supported the queen in her trials and executions which lasted for many months. His loyalty would be rewarded with a Sicilian dukedom as he became the Duke of Brontë, a title he prized, but which many powerful Britons mocked as a worthless foreign honour.[31] Sir William too, would be censured and recalled for allowing Nelson and the ships of the Royal Navy to become embroiled in the civil wars of another state. According to one British reporter of the diplomatic situation, 'Our ships have been frequently employed to serve as prisons to Sicilian and Neapolitan Gentry which to seriously reflecting men appears rather extraordinary should be permitted [*sic*]'.[32]

Despite the gravity of the situation, Nelson was given the benefit of the doubt, as a victim of manipulations by both the queen and Emma Hamilton: 'His natural inclination operates with what he conceives it is his duty to grant. This good disposition, however, may produce inconveniences'.[33] The scale of Nelson's victories, and his skillful management of his own publicity, did much to absolve him of wrongdoing in professional circles and in the public mind. This was never more evident than when Nelson and the Hamiltons returned to England in November 1800 after Sir William's recall by the Foreign Office. Nelson's request to bring the couple back to England in his HMS *Foudroyant*, a large and prestigious eighty-gun ship of the line, was summarily denied. Instead they were offered a frigate for the voyage, although Emma declined to take passage on such a small ship, possibly due to the onset of morning sickness.[34] At this time she was almost certainly pregnant with Nelson's child. Nelson refused to leave her and used the excuse of his poor health to take time off from naval duties and accompany the Hamiltons on the dangerous overland trek back to England.[35] Between Sir William's own health problems during the voyage and the huge celebrations that greeted Nelson in every city they visited, passage across the Continent was slow. Lord Minto, ambassador to the Court of Vienna, wrote of his concern for the state of Nelson's personal and professional situation: 'I who am a lover of naval merit & indeed a sincere friend of the man, hope we shall again hear of him in his proper element'.[36] His wife, Lady Minto, was less tactful and suggested the reason for his predicament was that Emma '[led] him about like a bear'. Others opinioned without sympathy: 'Lady Hamilton is without exception the most coarse, ill-mannered, disagreeable woman I ever met with' and '[I] joined in the general abuse of her'.[37] This blend of sympathy and outrage was a taste of things to come.

Nelson's return to England was a time of celebration for the nation and the end of an era for the *tria*. Now under the scrutiny of the British press, the government, and the Admiralty, their domestic arrangement became problematic and demanded at least minimal efforts at concealment. Nelson's arrival in London on November 8, 1800, with the Hamiltons in tow reunited him, unhappily, with his wife. It was the first time they had seen each other in seven years. The film portrays the scene with some accuracy as a moment for both fêting and awkwardness. *The Naval Chronicle* reported on the scene: 'The noble Admiral dressed in full uniform, with three stars on his breast and two gold medals was welcomed by repeated huzzas from the crowd while the illustrious tar returned with a low bow'. It went on to comment on the state of the party, 'Lord Nelson looked extremely well, but in his person is very thin; so is Sir William Hamilton; but Lady Hamilton looked charmingly, and is a very fine woman'.[38] Fanny, Lady Nelson's, appearance did not rate a mention. The dinner that took place at Nerot's Hotel that evening can only be imagined as agonizing for all those present. In the following weeks, the four spent evenings at the theatre together in an unsuccessful attempt to diffuse gossip. They even included Nelson's father for wholesome good measure.

The triumphant return of the hero on film does not portray the vicious gossip that, in life, permeated every tier of society. London patricians and even fellow servicemen criticized Nelson's ostentatious display of medals and honours which filled his breast and topped his hat and were worn at every public appearance.[39] Emma's flamboyant past was rehashed and subjected to new scorn and speculation. Her weight gain in particular, became the subject of much derision and cartoonists like Gillray and Rowlandson were merciless. Gillray's 'Dido in Despair' (1801) depicted an obese Emma lamenting her lover's return to sea, this time for the Battle of Copenhagen which would yield Nelson yet another victory.[40] Her aged husband lay sleeping, oblivious. Antiques strewn at her feet were complemented by a book featuring naked versions of 'The Attitudes' which lay open on the settee. When this cartoon was produced, Emma would have been heavily pregnant. Newspapers like the *Morning Herald* and *Morning Chronicle* discussed her weight and 'rosy' condition with little delicacy.[41] Her adoption of French empire-line fashion with its high waist and flowing skirts may have begun a London fashion sensation, but was necessary to help hide her condition. While the sharpest barbs were aimed at Emma, Nelson, Fanny, and Sir William were not immune to the slings and arrows of the press.[42]

The real Sir William became a cipher in London; shunned in diplomatic circles and even cast aside by Emma and Nelson who became more intently focused on each other. Age, gout, and debilitating stomach ailments were compounded by depression over the loss of his most treasured vases when the ship transporting them from Naples sank in a storm. In years past his cuckolded state inspired few histrionics. In fact, in a letter to Greville from Naples, he suggested that he was grateful to Nelson for taking his young, energetic wife off his hands.[43] The mood changed somewhat when Nelson purchased Merton Place, a run-down cottage on the outskirts of London near Wimbledon. He had formally separated from Fanny and taken up residence there with Emma and her husband. Sir William, who was obliged, for appearance's sake, to keep an official residence in Piccadilly found life at Merton frustrating. The cost of maintaining two households was a further burden on his already indebted state. When the Foreign Office refused to grant him a pension for his nearly four decades of service, he was forced to sell what little remained of his antique collection. Other factors also weighed on his mind. Sir William wrote to Greville of his mounting irritation: 'Nothing at present disturbs me but my debt, and the nonsense I am obliged to submit to here to avoid coming to an explosion which wou'd be attended with many disagreeable effects, and would totally destroy the comfort of the best man and the best friend I have in the world'.[44] Despite the situation, his respect and love for Nelson remained undiminished.

Such respect meant that he allowed Emma to give birth to Nelson's daughter, Horatia 'Thompson', at the Piccadilly house. 'Thompson' was the code name the couple had invented in order to discuss their romance and the baby in correspondence. Caution was hardly necessary, the entire nation knew their secret, although the need to maintain appearances was essential to Emma's social survival. Immediately after the birth, the child was sent to a wet nurse who would bribe a fortune out of the *tria* in order to keep mum. Horatia's birthday was backdated by three months and was recorded as having taken place in Naples. She would be known as the godchild of Emma and Nelson. Later, Nelson adopted her formally.

Other strains on the household of three were visible in the wake of Horatia's birth. The Prince of Wales, a serial philanderer, had long coveted Emma's sexually charged beauty. In Nelson's absence, he made bold romantic overtures towards her, and in doing so ignited the admiral's most virulent jealousies. The most extraordinary aspect of this threat to the affair was Sir William's intervention to quiet Nelson's concerns. In a letter to Nelson he wrote justifying his planned dinner party for the prince:

> I am well aware of the danger that would attend the prince's frequenting the house, not that I fear that Emma could ever be induced to act contrary to the prudent conduct she has hitherto pursued … I have been thus explicit as I know well your Lordship's way of thinking.[45]

Sir William's active role in the maintenance of their relationship was indicative of his depth of feeling for them both. Indeed, his death in 1803 (at the age of 73) was a devastating moment for Emma and Nelson, a family tragedy which elicited genuine mourning from them both.[46]

Korda's film omits such details to better focus on the love story and the political message. Accordingly, much screen time is given to explaining the true story of Nelson's desire to keep fighting at Copenhagen, despite orders to withdraw. Emma describes the event to her mother, Mrs. Cadogan:

> When his commander in chief saw that the enemy outnumbered us more than two to one he sent a signal to Nelson telling him to give up the fight and withdraw … when the signal was pointed out to him [Nelson], he picked up a telescope, put it to his blind eye and said: 'I'm darned if I can see any signal', and went on fighting.

It was a clear example of how a man should respond to apparently overwhelming odds in wartime.

The parallel between moral bankruptcy and financial insolvency is handled thoughtfully in the film's script. While in Naples, Emma's proclivity for gambling is on display while Nelson hovers over the card table and begs caution. Debt becomes a more pressing issue after the death of Sir William. Leigh's Emma makes clear to her mother that she refused to press her husband for a financial settlement, offering that she was 'never his wife' and renouncing any claim on his estate. Upon Nelson's return from Copenhagen, his jealousies are reignited as she hides correspondence. He soon learns that the missives are bills, not love letters from secret admirers. The real Emma Hamilton faced considerable financial challenges in the years after her husband's death. His estate went to Greville leaving Emma's outrageous spending, greedy relatives (both hers and Nelson's), and household staff whose generous compensations represented tacit hush-money, to compound the burden. Emma remained mindful of the wishes of others and of her need to maintain the illusion of wealth. With half of Nelson's income going to Fanny, there was never enough money to go around. It was a burden Emma faced with her usual optimism and disregard for reality, qualities well-conveyed in Leigh's performance.

Barely two years of domestic bliss ended with Nelson's appointment as commander in chief of the Mediterranean Fleet in May 1803. After hoisting his flag in HMS *Victory*, he received news that Emma was pregnant with their second child. The baby, whom they named 'Emma', would not live past her sixth week, a tragedy that compounded Emma's grief at having lost Nelson to the demands of 'honor and duty'.[47] The film suggests that Emma was instrumental in sending Nelson back to sea to defend England in its time of need. In reality, there was little that could have kept him from the glory of battle.[48]

The script suggests that Emma received a vision of Nelson's death at the moment of his departure from Merton: 'We will never see him again'. According to popular belief, however, it was Nelson who predicted his own death before the Trafalgar campaign. Years earlier, after the Battle of the Nile, one of Nelson's captains, Benjamin Hallowell, fished a piece of the mainmast from the French flagship *L'Orient* out of the water after her magazine ignited and blew the vessel to pieces. As a token of the battle, Hallowell had the mast made into a coffin and presented it to his admiral with the words 'when you are tired of this life you may be buried in one of your trophies'.[49] Nelson had been delighted with the gift and kept it safely stored after his return to England. Before departing for the Mediterranean, legend maintained that Nelson had the coffin removed from storage and prepared for his use.[50] Such morbidity is absent from Korda's film, although the death of Nelson in the Battle of Trafalgar is reverently reconstructed.

Scenes of British ships in line of battle are accompanied by a rousing chorus of 'Heart of Oak', the eighteenth-century anthem of the Royal Navy that was still relevant and popular in 1940. While the soundtrack would appear to take cinematic license, the real ships' crews sang this and the popular, 'Britons Strike Home' as they approached the enemy. The provenance of the order for the immortal signal, 'England expects that every man will do his duty', including Lieutenant Pasco's suggestion to substitute 'confides' for 'expects' (which did not have to be spelled out in signal flags) is recreated on film. The fateful warning offered by Nelson's flag captain, Thomas Masterman Hardy, that the decorations on the admiral's chest would make targets for sharpshooters is also included although, in truth, Nelson wore a simple undress uniform with fabric replicas of his honours which would have been difficult to spot from a distance. Nelson's instruction that 'no captain can do very wrong if he places his ship alongside that of the enemy', is packed into the dialogue to ensure that the time-honored narrative is faithfully rendered on film.

The division of the fleet into two columns, which would pierce the line of the combined Franco-Spanish fleet, breaking it into three parts which could then be destroyed in detail, is reenacted using a number of large-scale models. The tactics are further explained in the film by Hardy in a subsequent meeting with Emma. The daring of Nelson's innovative attack, and the danger it posed to the leading ships of the two columns, Nelson's *Victory* and Admiral Cuthbert Collingwood's *Royal Sovereign*, which both received the full fury of the enemy's guns during the approach, are offered as a prelude to the news of Nelson's death. The historical battle saw enormous damage inflicted upon the ships of the British van as they suffered a withering fire for nearly twenty minutes before being able to effectively return fire. On board *Victory* fifty men were killed and wounded before she fired her first shot.[51] The film conveys the fact that Nelson remained on deck throughout the first two hours of the battle until 1:15 p.m. when a sharpshooter stationed in the mizzen top of the French ship *Redoubtable* fired a musket ball that penetrated Nelson's left shoulder, continued through the lung, and severed his spine. The film shows the assassin taking aim at the exposed Nelson, although recent research argues that between the smoke from the guns, which would have blanketed the deck in the light conditions, and the movement of the two ships involved, it was unlikely that aim had anything to do with Nelson being struck. The admiral, like so many of his men, was killed by a random shot.[52]

Every move and utterance made during the nearly three hours of Nelson's painful death in the dark cockpit was later recorded by those present. The film painstakingly recreates these scenes, and does credit to the composition of Benjamin West's iconic painting 'The Death of Nelson'. His parting kiss from Hardy, final request that his hair and everything else that was his go to Lady Hamilton, and his words, 'Thank God, I have done my duty', required no dramatic embellishment for the sake of the film.

According to Hardy, Dr. Scott, Dr. Beatty, and others who were present, Nelson's last thoughts were of Emma. The film wastes no time on mundane details, like the fact that Hardy and Captain Blackwood had, before the battle, witnessed a codicil to Nelson's will which implored: 'I leave Emma Lady Hamilton therefore a legacy to my King and country and that they will give her an ample provision to maintain her rank in life'.[53] It was not to be. The veneration of Nelson after Trafalgar did not extend to fulfilling his dying wish regarding Emma and his daughter.

The public and many of Nelson's relatives believed that Emma was set to inherit a vast fortune from Nelson and the state. She was once again hounded for money from friends and family and tried her best to keep up appearances and preserve Nelson's memory at Merton. While purveyors of 'Nelsonia', which often featured her image on trinkets, souvenirs, and prints made fortunes from the death of the hero, Emma waited in vain for a pension or lump sum award. The pension instead went to Fanny. Others, including Nelson's brother, William, benefitted financially from the admiral's demise. Despite Emma having helped William with monetary gifts over the years, he offered no return of the favour in her time of need. Many friends and admirers, including the Prince of Wales, vanished from Emma's life. Sir Harry Fetherstonhaugh provided £500, although it was understood as a payment to keep Emma quiet and maintain his anonymity as Emma Carew's father.[54] Emma would be pursued by creditors for the rest of her life. She lost Merton and all the possessions she and Nelson had collected, effectively wiping out the last tangible reminders of their relationship. In 1810 Emma's mother, Mrs. Cadogan, her most constant friend and supporter, died. Now on her own, Emma struggled to remain relevant in high society. She courted potential suitors. She did her best to avoid harassing creditors. The humiliation of an arrest for debt 1813 paled in comparison to the shame that accompanied the unauthorized publication of *The Letters of Lord Nelson and Lady Hamilton* in April 1814. It was a scandal more damaging than anything that had come before. These deeply personal letters brought the character flaws of both parties into stark relief with the sympathetic image of pure, idyllic love. Any chance of a pension from the state evaporated and Emma's health began to fail.

In July 1814 Emma and Horatia boarded a ship for Calais to escape arrest and a return to debtors' prison. In Calais Emma spent money she did not have in an attempt to regain her social standing and increase her daughter's chances of a profitable marriage. The façade would not last long. Amoebic dysentery, likely contracted years earlier in Naples, contributed to Emma's painful and untimely death in January 1815.

Horatia, aged fourteen, was now an orphan. She returned to England on the good graces of an Englishman at Calais, and after spending years as a servant to wealthier relations, she married a clergyman at age twenty-one and escaped to a new life. Despite a troubled start, Horatia's marriage was happy and blessed with many children. While the spectre of her famous adoptive father loomed large, she would forever deny that Emma Hamilton was her mother, and in doing so attempted to shed the taint of her parents' adultery.

The film eschews the details of Emma's decline. Hardy's delivery of the terrible news is received by Leigh's Emma in desperate silence. Her collapse in the darkened room at Merton is followed by an all-too-brief return to Emma, the old woman, languishing in prison. When asked by her cellmate, 'And then? What happened after?' she replies, 'There is no then. There is no after'. Such sentiments speak to an utter loss of optimism and faith in her abilities to rise again. The real Emma's behaviour in Calais suggested that she maintained a hopefulness until the end, although the final judgement weighed on the film's heroine was a necessary compromise to satisfy the Motion Picture Production Code which determined that 'the adulterous parties must be punished'.[55]

The box office success of *That Hamilton Woman*, meant that the film's message reached a wide audience. A classical tragedy of love and loss cloaked in the glamour of Hollywood and the beauty of its two leading actors captivated movie-goers worldwide. Even Hardy's cinematic condemnation of nations 'neutral against England' who were 'so scared of Bonaparte they daren't lift a finger to help the people who fight him' was cushioned by period costumes and lavish sets, enough to distance the film from the here-and-now of 1941 and world war. Korda understood the film's mission perfectly. In a letter to Olivier he summed up their achievement: 'Propaganda can be a bitter medicine. It needs sugar coating – and *Lady Hamilton* is a very thick sugar-coating indeed'.[56]

Notes

1. Drazin, 2002, p. 109.
2. Drazin, 2002, pp. 237–38.
3. Robison in Schutte and Finn, 2018.
4. Gilbert, 2000, pp. 807, 882; Manchester and Reid, 2013, p. 392.
5. Olster, 1995, p. 122.
6. Drazin, 2002, p. 229.

7. Korda received the first OBE to be given to a person in the film industry. *London Gazette*, 1942, Issue 35719, p. 4175.
8. Korda, born Sándor László Kellner in Hungary in 1893, began making films in the small town of Kolozsvár before moving to Budapest. In 1919 he was arrested for having supported the short-lived Communist government. After his release from prison he left Hungary never to return. Korda went on to make films throughout Europe before establishing himself in Hollywood as a director/producer of large-scale historical dramas. Korda successfully navigated the transition to 'talkies' and remained in the United States until a conflict with studio executives at Fox saw him immigrate to Britain in 1931. There he founded London Films and began a career as one of Britain's premier directors. In 1933 he earned an Academy Awards Best Picture nomination for *The Private Life of Henry VIII*. Over the course of his career Korda directed sixty-eight films and produced many more. He became a subject of Great Britain in 1936 and cemented his patriotism with films that supported the war effort and British national pride. He died in London in 1956 at the age of sixty-two. Kulik, 1975, pp. 14, 26–28, 54.
9. Holden, 2007, pp. 157–62.
10. Olson, 2014, pp. 224–77; Gerald P. Nye quoted in Drazin, 2002, p. 238.
11. Drazin, 2002, p. 239.
12. Korda to Wendell Willkie, 11 September 1941, ibid.
13. Leff and Simmons, 2001, pp. 270–71, 286–87.
14. IMDb, 'That Hamilton Woman'.
15. The motto of the Order of the Bath was adopted by the threesome to reference their relationship. Nelson was made a Knight Companion of the Bath after the Battle of Cape St. Vincent in 1797.
16. R. Knight, 2005, p. 157.
17. Constantine, 2001, p. 290.
18. The last correspondence from Emma Carew (a.k.a. Hart/Hartley) to her mother was a plea for information about the identity of her father and possible financial assistance.
19. Morrison, 1893–94, Vol. 1, Ms 153, 1 August 1786.
20. C. Knight, 1861, p. 144.
21. Goethe, 1970, p. 208.
22. Williams, 2006, p. 170. For Sir William's quote see Sir William to Carmarthen, 20 November 1786, TNA FO 70/3, f. 306.
23. Rodger, 2005, p. 461.
24. R. Knight, 2005, p. 157.
25. Rodger, 2005, p. 461.
26. Williams, 2006, p. 212.
27. Winfield, 2005, p. 136.

28. R. Knight, 2005, p. 330.
29. Maria Carolina and Ferdinand were despised by many Neapolitans. Nelson was ignorant of the situation and unwisely 'backed an aggressive policy which provoked the French conquest of Naples and wrecked Britain's nascent coalition against Napoleon', Rodger in Cannadine, 2005, pp. 17–18.
30. Ibid., p. 327.
31. See complaints from Lord Minto, Lord Spencer, and Capt. Alexander Ball in R. Knight, 2005, p. 338.
32. William Daniels to Lady Minto, 9 August 1799, BL Add. MS 37852.
33. Ibid.
34. R. Knight, 2005, pp. 339–40.
35. Cornelia Knight to Capt. Berry 2 July 1800 in Nicolas, 2003, Vol. iv, p. 263.
36. Minto to Lord Keith, 30 August 1800, NMM KEI/18/5.
37. Lady Minto to her sister, n.d. 1800 and James Harris, Lord Minto's nephew on Lady Hamilton in R. Knight, 2005, p. 342.
38. Tracy, 1998, Vol. 2, p. 118.
39. R. Knight, 2005, p. 347; Vincent, 2003, pp. 384–85.
40. Gillray, NMM, PAF 3874.
41. Williams, 2006, p. 254.
42. See Isaac Cruikshank's 'Smoking Attitudes' which alludes to Sir William's sexual impotence and Nelson's virility. For attacks on Fanny see Williams, 2006, p. 259.
43. Hamilton to Greville, 6 March 1799, TNA FO 70/12, f. 74.
44. Hamilton to Charles Greville, 24 January 1802 in Morrison, 1893–94, Vol. 2, p. 182.
45. Hamilton to Nelson, 19 September 1801 quoted in Fraser, 2004, p. 272.
46. Constantine, 2001, p. 282; R. Knight, 2005, pp. 434–35; Williams, 2006, pp. 297–98.
47. The baby born in late January–early February 1803 was Emma's second daughter to be named 'Emma'.
48. R. Knight, 2005, p. 350.
49. Hallowell to Nelson, 23 May 1799 in Nicolas, 2003, Vol. 3, p. 89.
50. Nelson's prescience about his own death may be apocryphal but the strange coffin was not. R. Knight, 2005, pp. 530–31; Fairburn, 1805, p. 33; Noble, 1849, p. 509; Tracy, 1998, Vol. 3, p. 243.
51. R. Knight, 2005, p. 515.
52. Davey, 2015, p. 101; Rodger in Cannadine, 2005, p. 26.
53. Nicolas, 2003, Vol. 2, pp. 140–41.
54. Williams, 2006, p. 334.
55. Motion Picture Production Code quoted in Drazin, 2002, p. 234.
56. Olivier, 1982, p. 91.

Bibliography

Manuscript and Archive Sources

British Library (BL). William Daniels to Lady Minto, 9 August 1799, Add. Mss. 37852.

Internet Movie Database (IMDb). 'That Hamilton Woman'. http://www.imdb.com/title/tt0034272/combined.

National Maritime Museum (NMM), Greenwich, UK. KEI/18/5; 'Dido in Despair', PAF 3874.

The Gazette Online. The London Gazette, 25 Sep 1942, Issue 35719. https://www.thegazette.co.uk/London/issue/35719/page/4175.

The National Archives (TNA), Kew, UK. Foreign Office (FO) 70/3, f. 306; 70/12, f. 74.

Printed Sources

Constantine, David. 2001. *Fields of Fire: A Life of Sir William Hamilton*. London: Weidenfeld & Nicolson.

Davey, James. 2015. *In Nelson's Wake: How the Royal Navy Ruled the Waves After Trafalgar*. New Haven, NJ: Yale University Press.

Drazin, Charles. 2002. *Korda: Britain's Only Movie Mogul*. London: Sidgwick & Jackson.

Fairburn. 1805. *The Life, Memoirs and Anecdotes of the Late Lord Nelson*, 5th edition. London.

Fraser, Flora. 2004. *Beloved Emma: The Life of Emma Lady Hamilton*. London: Anchor Publishing.

Gilbert, Martin. 2000. *The Churchill War Papers: The Ever Widening War 1941*, Vol. 3. London: W. W. Norton.

Goethe, Johann Wolfgang. 1970 reprint. *Italian Journey, 1786–1788*. London: Penguin Classics.

Holden, Anthony. 2007. *Olivier*. London: Max Press.

Knight, Cornelia. 1861. *Autobiography of Miss Cornelia Knight*, 2 Vols. London.

Knight, Roger. 2005. *The Pursuit of Victory: The Life and Achievements of Horatio Nelson*. New York: Basic Books.

Kulik, Karol. 1975. *Alexander Korda: The Man Who Could Work Miracles*. London: W.H. Allen.

Leff, Leonard, and Jerold Simmons. 2001. *The Dame in the Kimono: Hollywood, Censorship, and the Production Code*. Lexington: University Press of Kentucky.

Manchester, William, and Paul Reid. 2013. *The Last Lion: Winston Spencer Churchill, Defender of the Realm, 1940–1965*. New York: Bantam.

Morrison, Alfred. 1893–1894. *The Collection of Autograph Letters and Historical Documents Formed by Alfred Morrison: The Hamilton and Nelson Papers*, 2 Vols. London: Privately Printed.

Nicolas, Nicholas H. 1864, 2003 reprint. *The Dispatches and Letters of Vice Admiral Lord Viscount Nelson*, 7 Vols. London: Elebron Classics.

Noble, T. 1849. *The Life of Nelson*. London.

Olivier, Laurence. 1982. *Confessions of an Actor: Laurence Olivier an Autobiography*. New York: Simon & Schuster.

Olson, Lynne. 2014. *Those Angry Days: Roosevelt, Lindbergh and America's Fight Over World War II, 1939–1941*. New York: Random House.

Olster, Susan Michele. 1995. 'Remakes, Outtakes, and Updates in Susan Sontag's "The Volcano Lover"', *Modern Fiction Studies* 41 (1), pp. 117–139.

Robison, William B. 2018. 'The Bard, the Bride, and the Muse Bemused: Katherine of Valois on Film in Shakespeare's *Henry V*', in Kavita Mudan Finn and Valerie Schutte (eds.), *The Palgrave Handbook of Shakespeare's Queens*. London: Palgrave Macmillan.

Rodger, N. A. M. 2005. *The Command of the Ocean: A Naval History of Britain, 1649–1815*. New York: W. W. Norton.

Rodger, N. A. M. 2005. 'Nelson and the British Navy: Seamanship, Leadership, Originality', in David Cannadine (ed.), *Admiral Lord Nelson, Context and Legacy*. Hampshire, UK: Palgrave Macmillan.

Tracy, Nicholas. 1998. *The Naval Chronicle, 1799–1804*, Vol. 2. London: Chatham Publishing.

Tracy, Nicholas. 1998. *The Naval Chronicle, 1804–1806*, Vol. 3. London: Chatham Publishing.

Vincent, Edgar. 2003. *Nelson: Love and Fame*. New Haven, CT: Yale University Press.

Williams, Kate. 2006. *England's Mistress: The Infamous Life of Emma Hamilton*. New York: Ballantine Books.

Winfield, Rif. 2005. *British Warships in the Age of Sail, 1793–1817: Design, Constriction, Careers, and Fates*. London: Seaforth Publishing.

Twelve Years a Slave and the 'Unthinkability' of Enslaved Autobiography

Sean M. Kelley

When Barack Obama was elected president in 2008, some pundits argued that it heralded a new 'post-racial' era. To say that was wishful thinking would be a gross understatement. But it is quite clear that in the late 2000s and early 2010s popular interest in the history of slavery and race in the United States was on the rise. In the eighteen months preceding the release of director Steve McQueen's *Twelve Years a Slave*, the *New York Times* ran over two hundred articles focused on American and New World slavery, on topics ranging from First Lady Michelle Obama's genealogy to Walmart's plan to build a superstore on a slave burial ground in Alabama. Scholarly interest was also on the rise, invigorated by a new generation of historians concerned with the role of slavery in the making of American capitalism. But perhaps most importantly, McQueen's film was released eighteen months after the shooting of the unarmed seventeen-year-old Trayvon Martin attracted international attention to the issue of white violence towards African Americans. The anti-racist organization Black Lives Matter was founded only weeks

S. M. Kelley (✉)
University of Essex, Colchester, UK
e-mail: skelley@essex.ac.uk

T. S. Freeman and D. L. Smith (eds.), *Biography and History in Film*, Palgrave Studies in the History of the Media,
https://doi.org/10.1007/978-3-319-89408-9_7

before the film appeared. The release of McQueen's film in August 2013 was therefore quite timely, its tone and content very much in step with both popular interests and academic trends. *Twelve Years a Slave* went on to win three Academy Awards, including Best Picture, and a host of other honours, including Best Picture at the Golden Globes and Best Film from BAFTA.

Based on Solomon Northup's classic 1853 slave narrative of the same name, the film almost took a radically different form. As Steve McQueen tells it, the idea for filming a story about a free northern man being kidnapped into slavery in the Deep South emerged before he became acquainted with Northup's narrative. He actually worked on the concept for some time with screenwriter John Ridley but reached a dead end. It was only then that McQueen's wife suggested working from historical documents, which led to his discovery of Northup. 'I was pretty upset with myself that I didn't know this book', he later said, 'and slowly but surely I realized that most people, in fact all the people I knew, did not know this book' (Chiwetel Ejiofor and Steve McQueen, interview by Terry Gross, Fresh Air, NPR, October 24, 2013).

McQueen can certainly be forgiven for not knowing of Northup's narrative—relatively few non-academics did prior to the making of the film. But his confessed inability to conceive of finding an actual autobiography on which to base his film calls to mind Michel Rolph Trouillot's observation on the Haitian Revolution as an event that was 'unthinkable even as it happened'.[1] After all, autobiography and biography presume personhood, while slavery, in its abstract logic if not in actual practice, denied the personhood of its subjects. This assumption has led to what some historians have called a 'chain of silence' regarding slavery, or the invisibility of enslaved people as historical subjects, worsened by the persistence of racism. McQueen's admission speaks to a host of interrelated issues concerning black autobiography and biography from the era of slavery, issues that in many respects carried over to the film. These include the reliability and veracity of the slave testimony and the related question of authorial voice. So while McQueen's version of *Twelve Years a Slave* is a mostly faithful adaptation of Northup's original narrative, it does not grapple with some of the more difficult issues surrounding slave autobiography. McQueen is not to be faulted for this. Commercial cinema should not be judged by academic criteria, and addressing these issues would have resulted in a very different film. But that is actually the point: it is difficult to reconcile the divergent imperatives of commercial feature film and the complex politics of slave autobiography. McQueen did about as well as can be expected given the system in which he worked.

Twelve Years a Slave was only the latest in a long tradition of cinematic representations of slavery dating back to the dawn of filmed storytelling, with the earliest known depiction being a 1903 adaptation of Harriet Beecher Stowe's *Uncle Tom's Cabin*. This film established a pattern in which many cinematic depictions of slavery were taken from fiction. Indeed, some of these rank among the most popular films of all time, not coincidentally because they often played to the worst racial stereotypes. Thomas Dixon's novel *The Clansman* (1903) became D. W. Griffith's *Birth of a Nation* (1915), while Margaret Mitchell's *Gone with the Wind* (1935) became Victor Fleming's 1939 cinematic spectacular of the same title.[2]

But apart from obvious differences of tone and interpretation, *Twelve Years a Slave* was distinguished from most of its predecessors in that it was drawn not only from historical sources, but also that it was based on an autobiographical narrative. This reluctance to take a biographical approach to slavery has not been limited to filmmakers. African American biography has always been a politically fraught topic. Slave narratives in particular were hotly contested texts prior to emancipation, since they highlighted individuality and personhood in the face of a dehumanizing institution. Slavery's defenders often sowed doubts regarding their authenticity, which as we will see carried over into modern scholarship. In fact, until relatively recently, even most historians believed that recovering the life stories of enslaved individuals was largely impossible due to the lack of authentic sources written from the point of view of the enslaved. The 'true' story of slavery, it was thought, could only be told in the aggregate; individual experiences were unrecoverable. This is surely one reason why so many earlier cinematic treatments turned to fiction for inspiration. The historical record, it was believed, simply did not permit access to the kind of interiority that makes for compelling film. Even *Roots*, the 1977 blockbuster television miniseries, which at the time was presented as the fruit of heroic genealogical research by Alex Haley, was later admitted to be 'faction', a combination of 'fact' and 'fiction'. Even for Haley, it seems, the possibility of doing African biography was unthinkable.[3]

Contrary to popular perception, much more auto- and biographical testimony survives than most people realize, in court depositions, missionary records, and other diverse sources. And of course, a significant body of autobiographical material survives in what are usually called the 'slave narratives', which blossomed as a literary genre in the late eighteenth and early nineteenth centuries. In the larger context of Atlantic slavery, these canonical slave narratives are almost unique, limited for the most part to the Anglo-American sphere. Almost no such texts were produced in Latin America or in the many other locales where Atlantic slavery flourished, though a great deal of autobiographical testimony survives for these in forms other than the classic 'slave narrative'. Adopting the strictest definition of 'slave narrative', there are anywhere between about 110 and 120 canonical narratives, a figure that does not include the 2500 of the narratives collected by the Federal Writers' Project in the 1930s or the thousands of incidental, fragmentary testimonies embedded within other types of records scattered in archives around the Atlantic, from Britain to Brazil.[4]

Most scholars of the canonical slave narrative suggest that it emerged in the Anglo-American world during the eighteenth century with the publication of Briton Hammon's *A Narrative of the Uncommon Sufferings* (1760), Ottobah Cugoano's *Thoughts and Sentiments* (1787), and Gustavus Vassa's *Interesting Narrative* (1789).[5] Other autobiographical and biographical texts by Africans and African Americans predate these, but did not embrace what would eventually become the defining features of the genre. Above all, slave narratives were part of the anti-slavery movement, condemning slavery and asserting black equality. The authors were quite open about their politics. Both Vassa and Cugoano were active in the early effort to abolish the transatlantic slave trade, and their narratives were deliberately crafted as a rebuttal to proslavery arguments. The texts themselves, of course, countered the suggestion that economic self-interest led slave traders and slave owners to treat enslaved people with kindness by offering examples of brutality and corruption. But in addition to the images of slavery offered in the texts, the very existence of books like Vassa's, written in elegant English prose and salted with Biblical and classical references, stood as an implicit refutation of African savagery. It was no coincidence that both Cugoano and Vassa proudly listed themselves as the author, with the title of Vassa's *Interesting Narrative* adding emphasis by including the epigram 'by himself'. The act of producing black autobiography was therefore always political, an affirmation of the author's humanity in the face of slavery's dehumanizing tendencies, and a powerful refutation of black cultural and intellectual inferiority.

While the early focus of the anti-slavery movement (and consequently, of many narratives) had been the transatlantic slave trade, abolition (by Britain in 1807 and by the United States in 1808) brought a shift in the narratives' focus to the institution of slavery itself. In contrast with eighteenth-century authors, most nineteenth-century authors had been born in the New World. This brought an Americanization of a different sort, a shift away from a concern with the British colonial world and towards a focus on the United States. Despite the fact that slavery persisted in the British Empire until 1833 (replaced by 'Apprenticeship' until 1838), fewer than a half-dozen British narratives were published. In contrast, in the United States, some 55 or so narratives were published between 1800 and the end of slavery in 1865.[6] This 'golden' age saw the maturation of the slave narrative as a genre, with its many themes fully elaborated. These included the 'kind' slave owner whose paternalism was eventually exposed as illusory through financial trouble or other means; slaves who had been damaged by slavery, rendered ignorant or emotionally stunted; the vulnerability of enslaved women, particularly young and attractive ones, to the master's sexual predations; the hollowness and hypocrisy of the master's Christianity; and the narrator's discovery of freedom, which often arrived with and through literacy. There was a gendered dimension to the narratives as well, with most being written by men. Several of these included an episode of violent resistance to a slave owner or an overseer, a moment when the protagonist asserts his personhood by fighting back, demonstrating, in the words of Frederick Douglass, 'how a slave was made a man'.[7]

What made the slave narratives so powerful was their perceived authenticity. It was one thing to hear about the horrors of slavery from white abolitionists, some of whom had never witnessed Southern slavery, but another thing entirely to hear from those who had experienced it first-hand. It was the narratives' 'true' quality that led northerners to buy the books by the thousands and to turn out to hear some of the more famous authors recount their experiences in theatres and athenaeums. Slave owners and their apologists understood that the narratives' power lay in their veracity and consequently made it a target of attack. This usually took one of two forms. The first was to charge that the narrator simply lied. Some narratives were picked apart by proslavery activists and revealed to contain errors. In at least one instance, this led to an embarrassing retraction by the narrative's editor. Authors and publishers guarded against charges of this kind by including as much specific detail as possible—names, places, distinctive events—as well as third party testimony to the truth of the narrator's claims, and sometimes even legal documentation. Revealing so much detail was always a difficult decision, however, since naming names, especially those of collaborators, could easily put people in legal or physical danger. All of this back and forth, and the decision to include many or few details, in the end speaks to the importance of the perceived veracity and truth of the slave narratives as one of the main battlegrounds in the fight over slavery.

The second line of the proslavery attack also spoke to veracity but focused specifically on authorship, charging that the narratives were the product of interactions between abolitionist editors and illiterate, ignorant former slaves, scarcely capable of understanding what was being written in their name. This was in many respects a more viable attack than simply denouncing the author as a liar. Most (though hardly all) enslaved people were illiterate, so editors and interlocutors of some kind often were involved in crafting the narratives. They are, as modern scholars emphasize, hybrid, multi-vocal texts. Some editors, moreover, rendered former slaves' experiences in florid Victorian prose, which tended to highlight the narratives' collaborative nature. Authors attempted to head such charges off by stressing that the narrative was a true rendering of events as presented by the narrator. The preface to Charles Ball's (composed by Isaac Fisher, who actually referred to himself as 'the author') was typical in asserting that 'The narrative is taken from the mouth of the adventurer himself; and if the copy does not retain the identical words of the original, the sense and import, at least, are faithfully preserved'. A strict adherence to 'the facts' was the coin of the realm. Once more, Isaac Fisher on Charles Ball: 'Many of his opinions have been cautiously omitted, or carefully suppressed, as being of no value to the reader….The design of the writer, who is no more than the recorder of the facts detailed to him by another, has been to render the narrative as simple, and the style of the story as plain, as the laws of the language would permit'.[8] Questions of authorship and voice, then, were also contested terrain in the politics of black autobiography, and modern scholars agree that they are highly complex texts that require extensive criticism whether for literary or historical purposes.

The coming of the Civil War in 1861 did not spell the end of the slave narrative. Harriet Jacobs's *Incidents in the Life of a Slave Girl* (published under the pseudonym 'Linda Brent'), for example, appeared in 1862. Hers, however, was one of the last to strike familiar abolitionist themes. Northern victory in the war and the abolition of slavery by constitutional amendment in 1865 relegated slavery (if perhaps not other forms of oppression) to the past. The abolitionist leader William Lloyd Garrison famously declared victory in the war against slavery, resigned from the American Anti-slavery Society (AAS), and ceased publication of his newspaper, the *Liberator*. Surprisingly, especially given their strong links to the abolitionist movement, slave narratives continued to appear in print well into the twentieth century. However, absent the urgency to bring about an end to slavery, these narratives never attracted the same notice as their antebellum predecessors and did not sound abolitionist themes as consistently or insistently. Instead postbellum narrators saw themselves as the keepers of a collective historical memory. Though few said so explicitly, this was a particularly important project in the late nineteenth century, as Northern and Southern whites forged a political reconciliation on the basis of white supremacy. Louis Hughes, author of one of the more compelling postbellum narratives, rhetorically asked what the value of one man's reminiscences might be. In answer to his own question, he asserted that 'the enlightenment of each generation depends upon the thoughtful study of the history of those that have gone before, everything which tends to fullness and accuracy in that history is of value'. Hughes's narrative was intended to bring about an end to slavery but to bear witness to injustice for posterity. Truth, however, was still central to the slave narrative, even after emancipation.[9]

Solomon Northup's narrative conformed in many respects to the basic conventions of the genre, but added several unusual twists. His story first reached the public in 1852 in a lengthy newspaper account of his ordeal. At the invitation of David Wilson, a writer known more for his travelogues than for his abolitionist sympathies, Northup expanded on his story in a book-length memoir, which was released in 1853. It sold well. Unlike most narrators, who were born into slavery, Northup was born free in the Saratoga-Glens Falls area of upstate New York. His status as a free man lent his narrative an element not to be found in most others. New to slavery himself, Northup in effect served as a guide for the uninitiated into the plantation world with the reader discovering slavery along with him in a series of steps, beginning with his being lured to Washington, DC to play the violin for a circus, to his kidnapping and imprisonment in one of the city's infamous slave pens, to the sea journey to the New Orleans slave market, and finally to a remote plantation on Bayou Boeuf in Louisiana.

Northup's story unfolds in a series of episodes and character studies calculated to reveal the various facets of antebellum slavery. His sketches of the enslaved are quite varied. Overall they emphasize the psychological damage inflicted by unpredictable outbursts of slave owner violence, while simultaneously highlighting perseverance and even opposition to slavery. We meet Lew Chaney, who hatches a plot with several others to fight his way to freedom in Mexico, only to betray his companions when he became convinced it would fail. There is Eliza, the one-time concubine to a Washington-area planter, who is separated from her mixed-race children and dies of despair in Louisiana. And then there is Patsey, for whom slavery, in Northup's words, 'had shrouded her intellect in utter and everlasting darkness'. Patsey had the added misfortune to have been very beautiful—Northup described her as 'a splendid animal'…'slim and straight'. In a drama played out countless times in Southern households, she attracted the sexual attention of Mr. Epps and the bitter jealousy of Mrs. Epps.[10]

Northup's sketches of whites invoke the theme of corruption even more strongly. His first master, William Ford, embodied the paternalist ideal, or as Northup wrote, 'there never was a more kind, noble, Christian man'.[11] Ford, however, soon ran into financial difficulties and was forced to sell Northup (while still holding the mortgage) to his plantation carpenter, Tibeats (Tibaut). In Northup's narrative, as in others, master class paternalism is exposed as a fraud. Northup rendered Tibeats and his final master, Edwin Epps, with less subtlety. In different ways, the two come off as craven, brutal, and (in Epps's case) dissipated. Other whites were similarly corrupted by slavery, if perhaps less prone to violence. Armsby, the poor white man married to a free black woman, betrays Northup's trust and informs Epps of Northup's plot to get him to mail a letter for him. Again, the message is not particularly subtle: slavery corrupts whites as well as blacks. The exception was the carpenter, Bass, a Canadian who was presumably uncorrupted by slavery. While doing itinerant work in Louisiana he crossed paths with Northup, who prevailed upon him to carry a letter to government officials and friends in New York. Word eventually reached his former patron, Henry Northup, who then initiated the legal process that resulted in Solomon's release, rendered in *deus ex machina* fashion in the memoir. The narrative concludes with a brief epilogue about the failed prosecutions of the men who had kidnapped him, as well as that of James Birch, his jailer in Washington, DC.

Twelve Years a Slave was quite successful. Northup became nationally famous and made a series of public appearances with prominent abolitionists, such as Frederick Douglass and Gerrit Smith. He starred in two different stage productions, and appears to have had a strong hand in the adaptations (both, however, were critical and commercial failures).[12] The dramatic nature of Northup's story, along with its happy ending, undoubtedly appealed to Victorian narrative tastes. But other factors added to the book's commercial success. Most slave narratives were written by people who had experienced slavery in the Upper South. This is hardly surprising since to write and publish a narrative one needed to be free, and it was far easier to escape from slavery in the Upper South than it was in the Lower South. Not coincidentally, most slave narratives concluded with a harrowing tale of escape. These were usually heart-pounding scenes, which lent an air of suspense and usually functioned as the narrative's climax. They often served as a demonstration of the author's ingenuity, an implicit refutation of the notion of black cognitive inferiority. Henry Box Brown, for example, shipped himself from Richmond to Philadelphia in a crate. Ellen Craft disguised herself as a white, male planter accompanied by a slave (in reality her husband, William) on a trip to the North. That they escaped from the Lower South state of Georgia (their narrative was titled *Running a Thousand Miles for Freedom*) is the exception that proves the rule that most narrators came from the Upper South. One narrative that did not feature such a climax was *Narrative of the Life of Frederick Douglass* (1845). Worried that revealing his means of escape would prevent others from repeating it, he withheld details. In subsequent autobiographies, however, he revealed that he passed himself off as a free black sailor.[13]

Northup's narrative lacked such a climax—if anything, it was anticlimactic—but it compensated for this with several unique elements. First and foremost, audiences responded to the storyline of the free man kidnapped into slavery, and with the narrative appearing less than three years after the passage of the Fugitive Slave Act of 1850, which made it far easier to return escapees to the South, northern audiences were receptive to charges that this led to a spate of kidnappings for profit. Northup's narrative also differed in its setting. He had experienced slavery in the deepest South, in Louisiana. Although 61% of all slaves lived in the Lower South, a large majority of antebellum narratives were written by people who had experienced slavery in the Upper South. Northup was able to detail many things that other former-slave narrators could not, such as the domestic maritime slave trade and life on a cotton plantation. And, since he was hired out for several harvests, his is the only antebellum narrative to provide a detailed description of life on a sugar plantation, the most brutal and deadly of enterprises. It is for these reasons that historians have found Northup's narrative to be so valuable. His descriptions of plantation life in the Deep South are without parallel.

As often happened, proslavery authors questioned Northup's veracity. The line of attack was borrowed from the trial of James Birch, his jailer in Washington, DC, whose defence argued that Northup had conspired with his kidnappers to allow himself to be abducted. As the plan allegedly ran, Northup would then be rescued from slavery and receive a share of his own sale price from the kidnappers. This, maintained Birch's lawyers, explained why Northup agreed to travel to Washington against advice, as well as why he and his abductors were so careful to have him secure free papers. The argument was subsequently circulated in the Democratic and Southern press. Modern historians have not given credence to these charges. Why, they ask, would Northup participate in the prosecution of his kidnappers given that a public trial might draw attention to the alleged plot? Why provide such accurate descriptions of his abductors, when it would have been safer for him if they had not been apprehended? Few even at the time apparently believed these charges, but they do highlight the importance of truth as a feature of the slave narrative.[14]

Northup's narrative lost its appeal as slavery receded into history. After being reprinted at least seven times between 1853 and 1900, *Twelve Years a Slave* went out of print for the next sixty-nine years. This lapse coincided with the appearance of the first professional academic treatments of slavery. Not surprisingly, few of these made use of the slave narratives. The most famous and influential of these early treatments was Ulrich B. Phillips's *American Negro Slavery* (1918), followed by his *Life and Labor in the Old South* (1929). Phillips, a descendant of Georgia planters who wrote at the height of the Jim Crow order, produced works that reflected the views of the Southern elite, with its 'moonlight-and-magnolias' plantation mythology. Slave owners, he famously argued, treated their human property with kindness and he likened slavery to a school for uncivilized Africans and their children. Phillips's work drew heavily on master class sources, such as plantation records. But though aware of the existence of the slave narratives, he dismissed their validity out of hand. His reasons echoed those of the proslavery critics, charging that they 'were issued with so much abolitionist editing that as a class their authenticity is doubtful'. Interestingly, he seems to have viewed Northup's as an exception, calling his narrative 'a vivid account of plantation life from the underside'. Tellingly, however, Phillips never used Northup's narrative as a source on slave life, but rather to illustrate a discussion of the kidnapping of free blacks into slavery.[15]

Phillips's white supremacist interpretation dominated American scholarship on slavery into the Civil Rights Era. The ground finally shifted in 1956 with the publication of Kenneth Stampp's *The Peculiar Institution*. Stampp provided an interpretation suitable to the times, in effect turning Phillips's on its head: slave owners were cruel, profit-minded, and exploitative. And where Phillips had excluded slave testimony from his work, Stampp's work contained many references to the narratives, though to little fanfare. Northup received brief mention in Stampp's discussion of labour routines, but even Stampp felt the need to qualify his acceptance of the narrative by reminding readers that it was written with the help of 'a Northerner'.[16]

As the Civil Rights and Black Power Movements gained momentum in the 1960s, slave narratives moved to the centre of most scholarship. John Blassingame used them extensively in his landmark 1972 book, *The Slave Community*, which argued for the validity of 'black autobiographies which pass the tests commonly applied to historical sources', by which he meant the published narratives of the nineteenth century. Blassingame, however, was more circumspect regarding the narratives produced by the Federal Writers' Project in the 1930s, in part because he questioned whether elderly black Southerners spoke frankly to the project's mostly-white interviewers.[17] With the appearance of Eugene D. Genovese's monumental *Roll, Jordan, Roll* (1972) and the simultaneous publication of a multivolume collection of WPA narratives under the title *The American Slave: A Composite Autobiography*, the vast majority of works on American slavery made extensive use of them. Most of these works did not attempt biography, but a few, such as those by Terry Alford, Allan D. Austin, and Melton McLaurin did.[18]

Though stressing that testimonies should never be read uncritically, it was clear that academic historians had conquered their earlier reticence regarding the veracity of both the canonical and the WPA narratives. Outside the academy, however, awareness of autobiographies written by former slaves was slim. Even today, most history undergraduates are exposed to no more than one or two of them (usually Douglass and part of Vassa), and many historians in the field are unaware of the vast amount of incidental autobiographical testimony that survives in Africa, Latin America, and the Caribbean. McQueen's initial belief that he could only tell the story he wanted through fiction is entirely understandable.

In adapting the narrative, McQueen made a series of bold and at times counter-intuitive decisions. One of these was to translate the narrative's rather spare, matter-of-fact prose to the screen. The script, for example, calls for many long periods of time without dialogue. But perhaps the most striking decision was to endow Northup with a stoic, almost opaque quality. Chiwetel Ejiofor's portrayal is powerful, but Northup's interior thoughts rarely come through. The effect is to replicate the narrative's just-the-facts prose style, which was adopted deliberately as a way to underscore the notion, as editor David Wilson expressed it, that Northup 'has strictly adhered to the truth'.[19] McQueen's decision not to exercise licence and invest Northup's character with thoughts and emotions not expressed in the text signals its authenticity to viewers.

Many of McQueen's decisions resulted in a kind of tension or dissonance. Much of the film was shot on surviving plantations across Louisiana, which provided a stunningly beautiful backdrop to the exploitation and violence depicted in the screenplay. According to McQueen, he did not set out to emphasize the visual and aural beauty of Louisiana but rather went into the project without any particular aesthetic vision. Location scouting in Louisiana gave him one. 'It [the environment] was just so rich', he said, adding that 'the most horrible things happen in the most beautiful places' (Chiwetel Ejiofor and Steve McQueen, interview by Terry Gross, Fresh Air, NPR, October 24, 2013). Though he did not say so, in emphasizing the beauty of the setting, the film invokes, almost literally, the 'moonlight-and-magnolias' mythology, a jarring contrast to the events of the story. The film's dialogue is similarly unsettling. Much of it was lifted straight from Northup's and retains what to modern ears is a rather stilted and formal Victorian tone. As with the location, the fussy formality of the dialogue contrasts with the base inhumanity depicted in the story. The Victorian dialogue also signals fidelity to the narrative, underscoring its truth by establishing a chain of evidence that runs from the film, to the narrative, and back to Wilson's guarantee of faithfulness to Northup's original story.

The film's sound editing and music are equally arresting, if perhaps not as deliberately incongruous. In the very first scene we hear an overseer instructing enslaved labours in the use of a large machete-like cane knife in a sugar field. 'Make it sing', he says as he demonstrates, and it almost does. Northup's skill as a fiddler plays a prominent role in both the narrative and the film. McQueen (and sound editor Ryan Collins) gave Northup's violin a deeply textured, at times raw and slightly scratchy sound, suitable to the backwoods setting. Northup's lively fiddle playing creates a sense of disjuncture for several scenes, including the separation of a mother and children at a New Orleans slave sale and a late-night forced square dance for the drunken and volatile Epps.

But McQueen's most striking aesthetic decision was to allow the camera to linger on a scene for a longer time than usual for a feature film. It is particularly noticeable in three of the film's most violent scenes, which all but command the audience to bear witness to slavery's brutality. The first of these takes place in the slave pen in Washington, where the jailers beat Northup repeatedly for asserting his status as a free man. For one minute and twenty-four seconds the camera does not move as we watch Birch and his henchmen lay on twenty-eight lashes. The scene late in the film where Northup and then Epps whip Patsey featured a single shot lasting four minutes, forty-six seconds. In contrast to the slave pen scene, the tension in this scene was broken by dialogue and the continual movement of the camera. But in perhaps the most shocking and memorable scene, one in which the carpenter Tibeats nearly kills Northup by hanging him from a tree, McQueen raised the tension to almost unbearable levels by allowing the camera to linger motionless on Northup's figure for 90 seconds. Shot from a medium-long distance without dialogue, we watch (and hear) Northup dying of strangulation. Together, these three shots last for nine minutes, ten seconds, or almost 7% of the film's total running time.

While the film is overall quite faithful to the narrative, there are departures from it, as well as some historical improbabilities. Most of these are likely due to McQueen's larger aesthetic and political vision for the film rather than to a cavalier attitude towards history. The plantations, for example, invariably feature white-colonnaded Greek Revival mansions that would not have been out of place in *Gone With the Wind*. In reality, plantation agriculture was relatively new to Louisiana's Red River parishes in the 1840s, so the area would have had a much rougher look in Northup's time, with fewer mansions and more cabins. A few planters of Ford's status might have owned such showcases, but many of them still lived in much more modest dwellings. Smaller slaveholders like

Epps could only dream of owning one. It is no accident that most of the plantation houses that appear in the film were actually located in the more established parishes along the Mississippi River. Backwoods plantations were also famously ill-kept. Many planters were so eager to make their fortunes that they never bothered to remove the stumps of felled trees and planted cotton around them. Of course, shooting the film against this kind of backdrop would have given it a very different feel and would not have set up the same ironic engagement with the moonlight-and-magnolias myth.

The portrayal of Northup's life in New York was similarly inaccurate, but probably also the result of conscious political and aesthetic choices. His life in the film is portrayed as thoroughly bourgeois. He lives in a comfortable house, shops with his family, and tucks his children into bed at night. New York comes off as a colour-blind utopia, where shopkeepers address black men as 'Mister'. It hardly needs pointing out that in reality black New Yorkers did not enjoy equal standing, that most lived a precarious existence in the employ of whites, and that racial prejudice was as strong in New York as anywhere. Solomon Northup spent much of his pre-abduction life in vain pursuit of the propertied 'competence' idealized by Americans of the era. Relegated like most African Americans to manual labour, he rafted lumber on Lake Champlain, dug canals, performed agricultural work for local whites, and farmed barren tracts of rented land. Work often took him away from his family for weeks at a time. Like many working men of the era, Northup drank, and at one point saw a log-rafting contract voided for allegedly being drunk on the job (Northup later won a lawsuit against his employer).[20] As with the dewy plantation settings, McQueen's vision of Northup's earlier life was likely calculated to set up a contrast with his life in slavery. Stressing his struggles would have made the contrast less sharp, and at worst might even have suggested a false equivalence between the racism and poverty suffered by black Northerners and enslavement in the South, a staple theme of proslavery propaganda.

More difficult is the pivotal scene in which Northup and Epps flog Patsey. The scene itself is mostly faithful to the narrative: Epps orders Northup to whip Patsey, and with no choice but to obey, he complies (in the narrative Epps threatens to flog Northup, but in the book Epps puts a gun to Northup's head). After many lashes, Northup refuses to continue, so Epps takes over. The scene is one of the most disturbing in both the book and film, with the only significant difference being that Patsey was tied to a tree for the whipping in the film but staked to the ground in the narrative. What the film does not reveal, is that Northup spent eight of his twelve years as a driver, that is, as a plantation foreman whose responsibility it was to maintain the pace of work. The driver's principal tool was the whip, and Northup tells us that he wore one around his neck every day and used it frequently. Drivers occupied a problematic place in the plantation hierarchy, and historians have long found it difficult to position them. The driver was, in Blassingame's words, 'the classic man caught in the middle', threatened with demotion and flogging if he failed to satisfy the master, but despised and mistrusted by the enslaved community at large.[21]

Northup therefore needed to explain his service as a driver without opening himself to charges of collaboration. In his narrative, Northup maintained that he mastered the art of appearing to strike without actually doing so. His fellow slaves, he claimed, would 'squirm and screech in agony, although not one of them had in fact been even grazed'. It is impossible to know whether Northup was telling the truth or whether he was trying to explain away active complicity in the slave system. Of course, even complicity must be viewed within the context of a violent coerced labour system, where refusal of an order was not an option. Indeed, for McQueen the scene is the culmination of several on the theme of Northup's will to survive. And to the extent that we see Northup making moral trade-offs for survival, the film probes some very difficult issues. But within limits, for exploring these issues too deeply—to insinuate that Northup acted as a driver to secure additional privileges, for example—might have blunted the film's larger message and inadvertently fuelled right-wing backlash and denial, in the same way that apologists for police brutality like to highlight the 'problem' of black-on-black violence.

Interestingly, one scene that apparently struck audiences as inauthentic (one online critic referred to it as a 'WTF moment') seems to have been based on truth. It involves the character of Mistress Shaw, played wonderfully by Alfre Woodard. The enslaved concubine of a neighbouring planter, Mistress Shaw was the de facto plantation mistress. We see her hosting Patsey to a formal tea on the veranda and explaining that tolerance of Mr. Shaw's philandering was a 'small but reasonable price' to pay for the chance to escape the worst of slavery. The scene is a startling one, but it does appear in the narrative, though almost as an aside. In fact, however, publically open 'husband-and-wife' relationships between white male slaveholders and enslaved women, while always scandalous, were not uncommon, and many were tolerated locally despite their illegality.[22]

But more important than these rather minor issues, the film never addresses the slave narrative's long, contested history, with Northup's story taken entirely at face value. One might argue that this is a necessary corrective to a long history of discounting slave testimony as either fabrication or ventriloquism, that enslaved narrators must be believed. And since the 1970s, academic historians would certainly agree. But something about this runs counter to one of the principal articles of the historian's faith, that no source can reveal objective historical truth, and that all must be critically analysed. Is it possible to convey such a criticism in a commercial feature film? Almost surely not, but this is an idle quibble, a symptom of what the Germans call *Berufskrankheit*, or the compulsion to let professional concerns infect other areas of life. For now, *Twelve Years a Slave* stands as the best cinematic interpretation of American slavery.

The film's true impact will take time to evaluate, but one legacy appears to have been to help dispel the 'unthinkability' of autobiographical testimony by enslaved people. In the few short years since the film's release, a host of slavery-themed films have come out, and several of these have taken a biographical approach of some description. Nate Parker's *Birth of a Nation* (2016) examined the famous 1831 revolt led by Nat Turner in Virginia, and the same year saw a remake of the classic television miniseries *Roots*. The latter, of course, was still 'faction', but this time the producers employed historians as consultants. Another legacy, however, seems to be a sense among at least some African Americans that too many films about slavery have been made recently. The films' focus on past oppression, they charge, distracts from present-day action. The future of enslaved biography on film is unclear, but the debate does serve as a reminder that, to paraphrase Faulkner, the past is never past.[23]

Notes

1. Trouillot, 1995, p. 73.
2. For discussions of slavery in film, see Davis, 2000; Woolfork, 2009.
3. Wright, 1981.
4. Blight, 2007, pp. 11–12; Escott, 1985, p. 40.
5. Hammon, 1760; Carretta (ed.), 1995; Carretta, 2004. On Hammon's as the 'first' slave narrative, see Davis and Gates, 1985, p. xix. The best

survey of slave narratives as literary and historical sources is Davis and Gates (eds.), 1985. See also Andrews, 1988; Blassingame (ed.), 1977; Philip D. Curtin (ed.), 1967; Ernest (ed.), 2014; Fisch (ed.), 2007.

6. Ajoe, 2014, p. 362; Blight, 2007, pp. 11–12.
7. Douglass, 1845, pp. 65–66.
8. Ball, 1970, pp. iii, xi.
9. Hughes, 1897, p. 3.
10. Northup, 2017, p. 108.
11. Northup, 2017, p. 56.
12. Fiske, Brown, and Seligman, 2013, pp. 117–23.
13. Brown, 1849; Craft, 1860; Douglass, 1845.
14. Fiske, Brown, and Seligman, 2013, p. 139.
15. On the publishing history of *Twelve Years a Slave*, see Fiske, Brown, and Seligman, 2013, pp. 167–69; Phillips, 1929, p. 219; Phillips, 1918, p. 444.
16. Stampp, 1956, p. 74.
17. Blassingame, 1979, p. xii; Blassingame, 1985, pp. 84–88.
18. Genovese, 1972; Rawick (ed.), 1971–1979; Alford, 1977; Austin, 1984; McLaurin, 1991.
19. Northup, 2017, p. 13.
20. Fiske, Brown, and Seligman, 2013, pp. 27–41.
21. Blassingame, 1972, p. 258.
22. Buchanan, 2013. On interracial relationships, see Rothman, 2003.
23. *New York Times*, 6 June 2016.

Bibliography

Ajoe, Nicole N. 2014. 'Caribbean Slave Narratives', in John Ernest (ed.), *The Oxford Handbook of the African American Slave Narrative*, pp. 362–70. New York: Oxford University Press.

Alford, Terry. 1977. *Prince Among Slaves: The True Story of an African Prince Sold into Slavery in the American South*. New York: Harcourt, Brace, Jovanovich.

Andrews, William L. 1988. *To Tell a Free Story: The First Century of Afro-American Autobiography, 1760–1865*. Urbana: University of Illinois Press.

Austin, Allan D. 1984. *African Muslims in Antebellum America: A Sourcebook*. New York: Garland.

Ball, Charles. 1970. *Fifty Years in Chains*, reprint edition. New York: Dover Publications.

Blassingame, John W. 1972. *The Slave Community: Plantation Life in the Antebellum South*. New York: Oxford University Press.

Blassingame, John W. 1979. *The Slave Community: Plantation Life in the Antebellum South*, revised and enlarged edition. New York: Oxford University Press.

Blassingame, John W. (ed.). 1977. *Slave Testimony: Two Centuries of Letters, Speeches, Interviews, and Autobiographies.* Baton Rouge: Louisiana State University Press.

Blassingame, John W. 1985. 'Using the Testimony of Ex-Slaves: Approaches and Problems', in Charles T. Davis and Henry Louis Gates Jr. (eds.), *The Slave's Narrative.* New York: Oxford University Press.

Blight, David W. 2007. *A Slave No More: Two Men Who Escaped to Freedom, Including Their Own Narratives of Emancipation.* Orlando: Harcourt.

Brown, Henry Box. 1849. *Narrative of Henry Box Brown...* Boston: Brown & Stearns.

Buchanan, Kyle. 2013. 'The Toughest Scene I Ever Wrote', online at http://www.vulture.com/2013/12/john-ridley-12-years-a-slave-toughest-scene-i-wrote.html. Accessed 25 September 2017.

Carretta, Vincent (ed.). 1995. *Olaudah Equiano: The Interesting Narrative and Other Writings.* New York: Penguin.

Carretta, Vincent (ed.). 2004. *Unchained Voices: An Anthology of Black Authors in the English-Speaking World of the 18th Century*, expanded edition. Lexington: University Press of Kentucky.

Craft, William. 1860. *Running a Thousand Miles for Freedom; Or, the Escape of William and Ellen Craft from Slavery.* London: William Tweedie.

Cugoano, Ottobah. 1825. 'Narrative of the Enslavement of Ottobah Cugoano, a Native of Africa; Published by Himself, in the Year 1787', in Thomas Fisher (ed.), *The Negro's Memorial; or, Abolitionist's Catechism; by an Abolitionist*, pp. 120–27. London: Hatchard.

Curtin, Philip D. (ed.). 1967. *Africa Remembered: Narratives by West Africans from the Era of the Slave Trade.* Madison: University of Wisconsin Press.

Davis, Charles T., and Gates, Henry Louis, Jr. (eds.). 1985. *The Slave's Narrative.* New York: Oxford University Press.

Davis, Natalie Zemon. 2000. *Slaves on Screen: Film and Historical Vision.* Cambridge: Harvard University Press.

Douglass, Frederick. 1845. *Narrative of the Life of Frederick Douglass.* Boston: Anti-Slavery Office.

Ernest, John (ed.). 2014. *The Oxford Handbook of the African American Slave Narrative.* New York: Oxford University Press.

Escott, Paul D. 1985. 'The Art and Science of Reading WPA Slave Narratives', in Charles T. Davis and Henry Louis Gates Jr. (eds.), *The Slave's Narrative*, pp. 40–47. New York: Oxford University Press.

Fisch, Audrey (ed.). 2007. *The Cambridge Companion to the African American Slave Narrative.* Cambridge: Cambridge University Press.

Fiske, David, Brown, Clifford W., and Seligman, Rachel. 2013. *Solomon Northup: The Complete Story of the Author of Twelve Years a Slave.* Santa Barbara: Praeger.

Genovese, Eugene D. 1972. *Roll, Jordan, Roll: The World the Slaves Made*, Vintage edition. New York: Random House.

Hammon, Briton. 1760. *A Narrative of Uncommon Sufferings, and Surprizing Deliverance of Briton Hammon, a Negro Man….* Boston: Green & Russell.

Hughes, Louis. 1897. *Thirty Years a Slave: From Bondage to Freedom.* Milwaukee: South Side Printing Co.

McLaurin, Melton A. 1991. *Celia, a Slave: A True Story.* Athens: University of Georgia Press.

Northup, Solomon. 2017. *Twelve Years a Slave: Authoritative Text.* Norton Critical Editions. New York: W.W. Norton.

Phillips, Ulrich B. 1918. *American Negro Slavery.* Baton Rouge: Louisiana University Press.

Phillips, Ulrich B. 1929. *Life and Labor in the Old South.* Boston: Little, Brown, and Company.

Rawick, George P. (ed.). 1971–1979. *The American Slave: A Composite Autobiography*, 41 Vols. Westport, CT: Greenwood Press.

'Room for Opinion: Do Dramas About Slavery Stifle Tales of Black Lives Now?', *New York Times*, online edition, June 6, 2016.

Rothman, Joshua D. 2003. *Notorious in the Neighborhood: Sex and Families Across the Color Line in Virginia, 1787–1861.* Chapel Hill: University of North Carolina Press.

Stampp, Kenneth M. 1956. *The Peculiar Institution: Slavery in the Antebellum North.* New York: Vintage.

Trouillot, Michel-Rolph. 1995. *Silencing the Past: Power and the Production of History.* Boston: Beacon.

Woolfork, Lisa. 2009. *Embodying American Slavery in Contemporary Culture.* Urbana: University of Illinois Press.

Wright, Donald R. 1981. 'Uprooting Kunta Kinte: On the Perils of Relying on Encyclopedic Informants', *History in Africa* 8 (1), pp. 205–17.

Lincoln Biography and National Reconciliation in the Films *Birth of a Nation* and *Lincoln*

Kate Masur

It was about the best advance publicity a filmmaking team could hope for.[1] The newly reelected American president, Barack Obama, invited director Stephen Spielberg, writer Tony Kushner, and the cast and crew of *Lincoln* to the White House for a private screening on the eve of the film's national release. This was the first major movie about Abraham Lincoln in more than seventy years, and it promised relevant lessons about moral leadership and political process. One month later, with the film in wide distribution, Republican and Democratic leaders of the U.S. Senate proclaimed a recess so that senators could attend a special screening at the Capitol. President Obama publicly praised *Lincoln*, telling *Time* magazine it made him think about the 'trade-offs' and 'compromises' required to get things done. Spielberg's *Lincoln*, an epic about bare-knuckled politics in the service of moral righteousness, had caught the attention of official Washington.[2]

K. Masur (✉)
Northwestern University, Evanston, IL, USA
e-mail: kmasur@northwestern.edu

T. S. Freeman and D. L. Smith (eds.), *Biography and History in Film*, Palgrave Studies in the History of the Media,
https://doi.org/10.1007/978-3-319-89408-9_8

Almost one hundred years earlier, D.W. Griffith's *Birth of a Nation* was the first Hollywood film to receive such a reception in Washington. As with *Lincoln, Birth of a Nation*'s publicity team had the clout and connections to bring the film to Washington, DC. Both films treated the Civil War, and both were released as the nation celebrated important anniversaries: *Birth of a Nation* came out fifty years after the war's end; *Lincoln* at the sesquicentennial. As with *Lincoln*, *Birth of a Nation's* publicists sought approbation from Washington dignitaries and arranged special screenings for them. Hollywood's first 'blockbuster', *Birth of a Nation* has long been considered one of the most significant films ever made. It is no surprise, then, that in creating and marketing *Lincoln*, Spielberg and his associates might have sought to engage with Griffith's film.[3]

This essay explores how the 2012 *Lincoln* invoked, argued with, and sometimes paid homage to *Birth of a Nation*, focusing particularly on the link between *Lincoln's* portrayal of Abraham Lincoln as a figure of national unity and its retrograde vision of the Reconstruction era.[4] Spielberg and Kushner's representation of Lincoln drew heavily on *Birth of a Nation* and other early-twentieth-century sources that characterized Lincoln as empathic and as a hero to northerners and white southerners alike. That vision of Lincoln as a national hero, this essay argues, was inseparable from the fantasy that if Lincoln had not been assassinated, the nation would have come together peacefully after the war and been spared decades of racial conflicts. *Birth of a Nation* exemplified and helped popularize that narrative, which portrayed Republicans in Congress as villains and white southerners as heroes for resisting federal laws that promised equality for African Americans. Historians have long since discredited that version of history. It lives on, however, in fantasies about Abraham Lincoln and his tragic death, and the film *Lincoln* unfortunately perpetuates and extends it.

In this essay, I approach historical film as a type of narrative art. Many historians choose to look at films' historical accuracy, comparing how the film tells a particular story with what we know about what actually happened. I do see film as an important purveyor of history, and I believe that getting the story right matters. But I find it more interesting to investigate how historical films adopt familiar tropes and plot lines—purposely or inadvertently or both—and how they convey messages through characters and the evocation of emotion. I therefore read historical films similarly to how one might read a novel, essentially as creative narratives that are embedded in the historical moment in which they are created and structured by conventions of genre, and whose creators seek to convey messages about large-scale human dilemmas. Historical films, particularly of the Hollywood blockbuster variety, are containers for historical memory, that is, for the stories that a society or a nation tells itself about its pivotal conflicts, who its proper protagonists are, who is a savior and who is saved, and what a happy ending might look like.[5]

The analysis begins with the question of how Lincoln came to appear as a national hero in the first place. Lincoln guided the United States to victory in a war whose consequences for many inhabitants of the Confederacy were disastrous. The war killed a much greater percentage of white men of fighting age in the Confederacy than in the Union. The movement of armies and battles themselves brought immiseration and destruction to many regions of the U.S. South. Moreover, the Confederacy's defeat and the abolition of slavery were deeply felt humiliations for many white southerners, who had hoped to form their own separate nation founded on the inviolability of human bondage. President Abraham Lincoln led the effort to conquer the Confederacy, and he went to great lengths in the process, stretching the limits of the president's powers by declaring the suspension of habeas corpus, encouraging his generals to move aggressively against the enemy and, above all, issuing the Emancipation Proclamation and making the U.S. armed forces agents of abolition. For all these reasons, immediately after the war, many white southerners saw Lincoln as an enemy and a tyrant, and some even sympathized with his assassin, John Wilkes Booth, a Confederate partisan and avowed white supremacist.[6]

Yet Lincoln's reputation among white southerners rose dramatically over time, abetted in no small measure by white southern outrage at what transpired in Washington, DC, after the president's assassination in April 1865. The new president, Andrew Johnson, was a former slaveholder from east Tennessee who had built his political career as an opponent of the planter aristocracy. Johnson was unexpectedly sympathetic to white southerners seeking full restoration of their political and civil privileges. But he also proved incapable of working with the Republican majority in Congress and a poor advocate for his own policies. By spring 1866, congressional Republicans had united against him and were able to pass legislation over his vetoes. The following year, against Johnson's wishes, Congress placed the former Confederate states (except Tennessee) under military rule, demanded that black men be permitted to vote, and mandated that the states rewrite their constitutions to include protections for African Americans' civil and political rights. Those policies, commonly known as 'radical Reconstruction', were a horror and a humiliation to white people across the South. Many believed that Congress had acted unconstitutionally, and they reacted viscerally against the demand that they treat African Americans as full citizens. The Republican-controlled Congress was the target of their greatest wrath, and among Republicans, Congressman Thaddeus Stevens of Pennsylvania stood out for his skillful political maneuvering and for his advocacy of equal rights for African Americans and support for land redistribution in the former Confederacy. Believing the new federal policies illegitimate, white southerners took extraordinary measures to undermine them, resorting to political corruption and terrorism to disfranchise black voters, drive out federal officials, and reclaim what they called 'home rule'.

White southerners' reaction against radical Reconstruction helped fuel Lincoln's rise as a symbol of reconciliation. Reflecting on the upheavals through which they had lived, white southerners increasingly allowed themselves to imagine that if Lincoln had survived, the supposed horrors of Reconstruction would have been avoided—that somehow Lincoln would have kept the congressional Republicans in check and that Lincoln himself would have been solicitous of white southerners, not vindictive as the congressional Republicans supposedly were. It was a convenient idea, of course, because it could not be disproven. By the time Woodrow Wilson, then a professor at Princeton, wrote about Reconstruction for the *Atlantic* in 1901, growing numbers of white southerners felt good about Lincoln. Acknowledging the challenges the nation faced at the end of the Civil War, Wilson thought 'perhaps' Lincoln could have carried out Reconstruction 'with dignity, good temper, and simplicity of method'. Before Lincoln died, Wilson wrote, his goal was to 'bring the people of the southern states' back into the Union, 'defeated, but not conquered and degraded'.[7] Yet that generous policy was abandoned, Wilson explained, as radical Republicans overtook President Johnson and imposed on the South policies that were unconstitutional and dictatorial. The period in which black men voted was a disaster. 'At last', he glossed, 'the whites who were real citizens got control again'.[8] Wilson's account, though comparatively measured, had all the hallmarks of the growing narrative that mingled admiration for

Lincoln with a stern critique of congressional Reconstruction policy and a fantasy that Lincoln would have done better—by which they generally meant would have given white southerners control over affairs in their region.

White southerners' public approval of Lincoln grew as the centennial of Lincoln's birth arrived in 1909. That year, J.G. de Roulhac Hamilton, a prominent North Carolina historian, published an article in *Sewanee Review* that linked white southerners' increasingly positive apprehension of Lincoln to their negative views of federal Reconstruction policy. Hamilton had studied Reconstruction at Columbia University under direction of William Archibald Dunning, the leading Reconstruction historian of his era, and Hamilton's book on Reconstruction in North Carolina was published in 1906. In his 1909 article on Lincoln, Hamilton wrote that white southerners had once despised and feared Lincoln as an opponent of slavery and leader of the Union war effort. After the assassination, however, as white southerners watched President Andrew Johnson's struggle with Congress, 'the belief grew and extended that Lincoln's death was the greatest loss that the South could have suffered. He would have been able, as no other man, to check the radicals in Congress and, failing in that, he could have carried the country against them'. Moreover, according to Hamilton, white southerners had increasingly learned of 'Lincoln's belief in the natural inferiority of the negro', which 'was also not without its effect upon Southern opinion of him during this period'.[9] The post-Civil War South was characterized by great 'bitterness', Hamilton wrote, 'but it was and is directed against the authors of Reconstruction'. By contrast, 'Everything has tended to implant in the minds of this generation of Southerners, reverence for [Lincoln's] memory as part of their heritage'.[10]

Hamilton highlighted Lincoln's capacities for empathy and mercy and argued that those qualities drew white southerners' admiration. White southerners had come to believe, Hamilton wrote, that Lincoln 'could be depended on to be fair and kind' and that 'in his heart was infinite sympathy for human distress and genuine feeling for his Southern countrymen'.[11] That argument about Lincoln's personality had a direct corollary in politics: If Lincoln had lived, he would never have permitted the vindictive radical Republicans to impose their unjust Reconstruction policies on white southerners. White southerners now emphasized that the Kentucky-born Lincoln was *one of them*, Hamilton wrote. They took pride in his 'Southern birth and blood, gladly acknowledging the debt that the South, not only as a part of the nation, but individually, owes him, and placing him in the same category with Washington as a maker of the nation'.[12] For the white southerners represented by Hamilton's article, Lincoln no longer represented sectionalism, slave emancipation, or military defeat; instead he stood for sectional reconciliation among whites, skepticism about racial equality, and even white southern identity.

Lincoln's hundredth birthday in 1909 roughly coincided with the birth of Hollywood film and the fiftieth anniversary of the Civil War itself (1911–1915). These were years when Americans were thinking deeply about the meaning and character of the American nation. Narratives of post-Civil War sectional reconciliation that had percolated for years intensified during and after the Spanish-American War, when white northerners and southerners fought alongside one another against a shared enemy. Lincoln was a popular subject in early film, and early short films often emphasized his capacities for empathy, showing him granting pardons to undisciplined northern soldiers and even to Confederates. In film as in the broader culture, many people believed that what made Lincoln a great leader and a national hero was his capacity for mercy and his deep understanding of all Americans. As Hamilton summarized the view: 'Regardless of war with the Southern States, to him at least, all Americans, North, South, East, and West, were his kindred and fellow-countrymen. His heart held room for all and felt with all'.[13]

This broader context helps explain how Griffith's 1915 *Birth of a Nation*, a film that lauds the Ku Klux Klan and white supremacy, could also have cast Lincoln in a positive, even loving light.[14] Griffith made his blockbuster at a moment when Lincoln's greatness was associated with his empathic character and, in particular, his capacity for sympathy for the white South. The film drew on popular representations of Lincoln, including his portrayal in Thomas Dixon's *The Clansman*, the novel on which *Birth of a Nation* was based. In keeping with the tenor of the era, Dixon's famous and popular work cast Lincoln as 'The Friend of the South'. Griffith also drew on the historical scholarship of Woodrow Wilson, who was by then president of the United States. Some of the film's title cards quoted directly from Wilson's *A History of the American People*.[15] Drawing on such sources, *Birth* portrayed Lincoln as beleaguered by the war and empathic toward constituents, including white southerners. In one crucial set of scenes, Elsie Stoneman, the daughter of a northern congressman, urges Mrs. Cameron, the mother of Confederate soldier Ben Cameron, to 'ask mercy from the Great

Heart' when they learn that Ben has been sentenced to death for a war crime. The two women meet with Lincoln, who is persuaded to take pity on Mrs. Cameron and grant Ben a pardon. The women are emotional as Lincoln reveals his merciful character, which extends even to a Confederate soldier and his mother.

The film advances the narrative that Lincoln's Reconstruction policies would have pleased the white South in a scene in which the southern Cameron family learns of the president's assassination. Reading the newspaper, family members react with horror. They are shown conversing, and the title card reads, 'Our best friend is gone. What is to become of us now!' As in Lincoln's pardon of Ben Cameron, the scene suggests that Lincoln loved white southerners and that his assassination foretold disaster for them. And sure enough, Lincoln's murder opens the door to more power for Congressman Austin Stoneman, who—driven by the influence of conniving 'mulatto' characters—inflicts on white southerners all the traditional horrors of Reconstruction. The film's portrayal of Lincoln, including the lengthy assassination scene and the immediate shift to the Cameron family's distress at news of his death, sets the stage for ghastly 'Negro rule' in the South and the mandate that white southerners reassert control, resorting to terrorist violence if necessary.

The character in the film who authors the Reconstruction policies that are so anathema to the Camerons and other white southerners is Congressman Austin Stoneman, who is portrayed as Lincoln's foil. The Stoneman character was a thinly veiled caricature of Thaddeus Stevens of Pennsylvania, and the film represents him as a dangerous tyrant, drawing a stark contrast with the calm and reasonable President Lincoln. Stoneman and Lincoln meet in a crucial wartime scene that foreshadows Reconstruction. A title card reads, 'The Radical leader's protest against Lincoln's policy of clemency for the South.' Stoneman acts agitated and impassioned, and he proposes to Lincoln, 'Their leaders must be hanged, and their states treated as conquered provinces', a reference to the radical Republican idea that for a period of time, the sovereignty of the ex-Confederate states should be suspended while the federal government took charge. Lincoln, looking troubled, is unmoved. He replies, 'I shall deal with them as though they had never been away'. As Stoneman departs, frustrated, the soundtrack plays 'My Country 'Tis of Thee', reinforcing the correlation between the nation's ideals and Lincoln's generosity toward white southerners.[16]

In keeping with the tenor of its era, *Birth of a Nation* thus gave Abraham Lincoln a prominent place in a vision of national reconciliation between white southerners and white northerners. The film deemphasized Lincoln's role in abolishing slavery; indeed it did not mention the Emancipation Proclamation. Instead, like the white southerners described by Hamilton, Griffith elevated Lincoln by emphasizing his capacity for empathy and by contrasting him with radical Republicans in Congress. The film asked viewers to stand alongside the Cameron family and imagine what would have happened if Lincoln had lived, and it implied that the Camerons' 'best friend' would have kept the radical Republicans at bay and allowed the former Confederate states back into the Union on easy terms, without demanding protection of African Americans' rights or black men's enfranchisement as voters. In the face of a dangerous and empowered Congress and a leadership vacuum in the White House, the film suggested, the Ku Klux Klan and racial terrorism had been necessary to reestablish proper order and make the nation whole.

It is worth underscoring that the idea that Lincoln's second term in office would have been characterized by extreme leniency toward the white South is not based on a balanced assessment of existing evidence. It is of course impossible to know how Lincoln would have contended with the immense challenges the nation faced as the Civil War ended. But it is also implausible to imagine, as Griffith and others did, that he would have readily abandoned newly emancipated black southerners to the tender mercies of white southerners. Lincoln likely would have worked better with congressional Republicans than Johnson; few could have done worse. And it is improbable that the result would have been policies that more readily capitulated to the will of the white South, or more quickly. To the contrary, Lincoln, tested by war, might well have had more desire to see Union victory secured and more patience for military occupation than his successor in the presidency. His adaptability as a politician might have led him gradually to embrace positions taken by radical Republicans in Congress, something he had done many times during the war. On 11 April 1865, Lincoln publicly expressed support for limited voting rights for African American men. This was not the sort of policy white southerners welcomed. Three days later, Lincoln would pay with his life for his prosecution of the war and emancipation, gunned down by the white supremacist and Confederate sympathizer John Wilkes Booth. In short, Lincoln was more than willing to fight white southerners while he lived, and there is no reason to assume that he would have been more solicitous of them after the war, particularly of those who essentially wanted to return to the status quo ante.[17] Nevertheless, the *idea* that Lincoln would have been kind to white southerners after the war was important to his construction as a national hero in an era of increasingly entrenched white supremacy. As *Birth of a Nation* makes clear, that portrayal of Lincoln was well suited to in a nation in which the rights and dignity of African Americans were subordinate or even sacrificed completely.

A new palette of Lincoln imagery came into public prominence in the Depression Era, influenced by the publication of Carl Sandburg's monumental biography whose first volume, *The Prairie Years*, was released in 1926. *Birth of a Nation* had portrayed Abraham Lincoln as stooped and increasingly haggard. He wore a shawl, implying physical vulnerability and perhaps suggesting ostensibly feminine qualities of patience and empathy. Sandburg, by contrast, represented Lincoln as a vibrant man from the West, a teller of tall-tales and a folk hero in the model of Davy Crockett.[18] This was a vision of Lincoln well-suited to the Depression, for it emphasized Lincoln as a boot-strapper, a young man from the rural West who worked his way up, demonstrating physical strength and admirable morality along the way. Sandburg's popular books significantly shaped the boom in Lincoln imagery that characterized the 1930s. Soon after *The Prairie Years* was released, D.W. Griffith himself consulted with Sandburg about making a Lincoln biopic. Sandburg did not end up working with Griffith, but Griffith's *Lincoln* (1930) was one of many New Deal-era films featuring Lincoln, the two most acclaimed of which were *Young Mister Lincoln* (1939) and *Abe Lincoln in Illinois* (1940). As historian Nina Silber has argued, during the New Deal people increasingly invoked the 'emancipator' part of Lincoln's story, touching on both the particular history of African Americans and slavery and, more generally, on the broader theme of human emancipation from oppression.[19]

The Lincoln boom soon ended, however, and when Spielberg and Kushner joined forces in the early twenty-first century, it had been decades since anyone made a major Hollywood film about Lincoln. After World War II, popular interest in the sixteenth president had subsided. David Donald's 1947 essay, 'The Folklore Lincoln', which catalogued several strands of popular thought about Lincoln, was perhaps the apex of a certain kind of fascination with Lincoln's meanings in American culture, and Donald had called Lincoln 'the central symbol in American democratic thought.'[20] But Lincoln's popularity as a subject for popular film was waning, a process hastened by the civil rights era, when some challenged Lincoln's reputation as the 'Great Emancipator' by emphasizing his reluctance to issue the Emancipation Proclamation, his support for 'colonizationist' projects to remove black people from the United States, and his skepticism that black and white people could ever coexist as equals in one nation.[21]

As Spielberg and Kushner set out to return Lincoln to the big screen, then, they had at their disposal a wide array of popular and cinematic imaginings of Lincoln, most of which dated to the first several decades of the twentieth century. Among those earlier representations of Lincoln, the one in *Birth of a Nation* was particularly important. From the moment of *Birth of a Nation*'s release in 1915, filmmakers and critics had debated the relationship between its racist imagery and Griffith's brilliance as a director and promotor. The film had generated immense controversy for its degrading representations of black people and its glorification of anti-black violence. To many it seemed an aggressive attempt to demean and intimidate black Americans and to legitimate white supremacy throughout the nation. Black communities mobilized against the film, the newly founded N.A.A.C.P. called for boycotts, and courts ultimately determined that its content fell within the realm of protected speech.[22] Because of its prominence and its complexity, *Birth of a Nation* continues to demand a reckoning from anyone who cares about the history of American film, and especially from those interested in making movies about the Civil War and the abolition of slavery, events at the heart of *Birth of a Nation*.

Several aspects of *Lincoln* suggest that Spielberg and his associates had *Birth of a Nation* in mind as they worked.[23] Spielberg and his colleagues echoed Griffith in their grandiose hope that people would see the film as a work of real history. Griffith had famously speculated that soon 'the children in the public schools will be taught practically everything by moving pictures. Certainly they will never be obliged to read history again'.[24] *Birth of a Nation* had included title cards labeled 'historical facsimile', to suggest that the ensuing scene represented an actual historical event. Spielberg made similar gestures in *Lincoln*, in which textual titles occasionally set viewers down in a particular historical time and place. Like Griffith, Spielberg and his publicists sought to promote the historical authenticity of the film. They publicly explained the lengths to which they had gone to ensure that the sounds in the film were authentic.

And, convinced that the film had serious educational value, the filmmakers arranged to distribute *Lincoln* for free—with lesson plans and an 'Educator's Guide'—to any U.S. middle or high school that wished to show it.[25]

In more formal ways, too, Spielberg riffed on and borrowed from *Birth of a Nation*. As film historian Melvyn Stokes has pointed out, the scene of Lincoln surveying the battlefield at Petersburg, Virginia, evokes the closing Petersburg scenes in *Birth of a Nation*.[26] But it is the final images of *Lincoln* that make Spielberg's formal engagement with Griffith most clear. *Birth of a Nation* ended not just with white northern and southern families unified through marriage, but also with Jesus Christ, labeled by a title card the 'gentle Prince in the Hall of Brotherly Love in the City of Peace'. The audience first sees a scene in which a warlike god presides over a tableau of death and chaos. The spectral figure of Christ appears, superimposed on a harmonious crowd of people, and raises his hands in a gesture of blessing. The last scenes of *Lincoln* are stunningly similar, with Lincoln fading onto the screen in front of a crowd. As he finishes delivering his legendary second inaugural address, he raises his hands as Christ does at the end of *Birth of a Nation*. Lincoln quotes Scripture, stating that 'the judgments of the Lord are true and righteous altogether', a candle flickers, and the film ends. Given the parallels, it is difficult to imagine that *Lincoln's* ending is not a direct reference to *Birth of a Nation*, proposing Lincoln as a secular Savior and suggesting that we in the audience can look to his words and actions for guidance in the present.

Beyond such formal gestures, Spielberg's film engaged with the content itself of *Birth of a Nation*. Notably, the filmmakers followed *Birth of a Nation* in making Thaddeus Stevens Lincoln's central foil. Stevens was not a significant character in Doris Kearns Goodwin's *Team of Rivals*, the book on which the film was originally based.[27] Yet Stevens's important role in *Lincoln* seems almost inevitable in light of the filmmakers' broader dialogue with *Birth of a Nation*. The 2012 Stevens is not the malevolent authoritarian of the 1915 Stoneman character, but Spielberg did use the two men to create a contrast. From the beginning of the film, Stevens's idealism is portrayed as a threat to the president's agenda. Viewers see that if Stevens continues to insist on his uncompromising vision of racial equality, the 13th Amendment, which Lincoln is pushing, will not pass. Stevens's evolution during the course of the film—and his final vote in favor of the amendment, which permanently abolished slavery—is crucial to one of the film's central messages: that powerful people need to make tough compromises in order to accomplish good things.

By making Thaddeus Stevens a central figure in the film, Spielberg and Kushner created another way of engaging with *Birth of a Nation:* the portrayal of Lydia Hamilton Smith. In real life, Smith, an African American woman, was Stevens's housekeeper and probably (though it has never been proven) his common-law wife. During their lifetimes, rumors swirled that they were in a domestic partnership, and Stevens's political opponents used such insinuations in attempts to discredit him. *Birth of a Nation* wholeheartedly embraced such rumors by featuring a character based on Smith and making her the source of Congressman Stoneman's ostensibly misguided racial egalitarianism. In *Birth of a Nation* her name is Lydia Brown, and the film makes her mixed-race, sexual relationship with Stoneman the centerpiece of all that is wrong with radical Republicanism. For instance, when the film introduces the idea that Stoneman cares about Brown's feelings, a title card describes her as, 'The great leader's weakness, that is to blight a nation'. Brown herself is shown as a manipulative and volatile character desperately seeking power and glory for herself and her lover.

Spielberg and Kushner embraced the opportunity to rewrite this relationship on screen. The film shows Stevens grabbing a printed version of the 13th Amendment and hurrying to his Washington, DC, home. Viewers see an elegant woman of color open the door for him; they realize only gradually that the two are romantically involved and that Stevens has brought the document to her in particular. The film represents Smith as a gentle, literate woman and the couple as loving and respectful toward one another. Spielberg and Kushner echo *Birth of a Nation* in suggesting that Stevens's racial egalitarianism draws directly on his intimate relationship with Smith. But *Lincoln* bestows dignity on their relationship, representing Smith as a sympathetic character quite unlike her counterpart in *Birth of a Nation*. By choosing to feature their interracial partnership in the film but reversing its moral valences, Spielberg and Kushner condemned one of the most abhorrent aspects of *Birth of a Nation* while demonstrating and reinforcing the idea that today's America is tolerant and respectful toward interracial relationships.

In this and other ways Spielberg and Kushner sought explicitly to challenge *Birth of a Nation's* egregious white supremacy and its sympathy for the Confederate cause. Unlike *Birth of a Nation* and other creative works of the early twentieth century, Spielberg and Kushner represented Lincoln as an unstinting believer in the abolition of slavery, placing his decision to push the House of Representatives to pass the 13th Amendment at the center of the action. The film begins with two African American soldiers reciting the Gettysburg Address, a much-criticized scene but one that foregrounds the voices and agency of black men. And whereas *Birth of a Nation* implies that African Americans were content to be enslaved, Spielberg's *Lincoln* offers several dignified free black characters who despise slavery. One of them is Elizabeth Keckly, a sympathetic character in the film who, in real life, was a high-fashion seamstress who became a confidante of Mary Todd Lincoln. In fact, some of the stories related in *Lincoln*, particularly those involving Mary, come directly from Keckly's 1868 memoir, *Behind the Scenes, or, Thirty Years a Slave and Four Years in the White House.*[28]

Yet if *Lincoln* offered a full-throated condemnation of slavery and certain forms of racism, it floundered when it came to contending with the inevitable questions that would follow wartime abolition—questions of race, nation, and reconciliation. On such matters, Spielberg and Kushner largely accepted earlier narratives that linked Lincoln's greatness to his sympathy for the white South, to his opposition to radical Republicans in Congress, and—somewhat more implicitly—to his capacity for unifying white Americans across the formerly warring sections. Daniel Day-Lewis's 2012 Lincoln did tell ribald jokes and homespun stories typical of the 1930s Lincoln. Yet in the main, the personality and affect of this Lincoln was closer to those of a century earlier. Day-Lewis's Lincoln is haggard and stooped, and he dons a shawl as Griffith's 1915 Lincoln did just before he was assassinated. The 2012 Lincoln is tormented by the war, shown brooding about his decisions and about the future of the nation. He is also, like Lincolns of the early twentieth century, a man of great solicitude and mercy. As in *Birth of a Nation*, Spielberg's Lincoln is shown interacting patiently with constituents. A scene in which he agonizes about pardoning a deserter also evokes the trope of the merciful Lincoln so common in Griffith's era. The audience's sense of his capacity for empathy is heighted by his interactions with Mary Lincoln, in which he is portrayed as steady and understanding in the face of her emotional distress. In all these ways, the film suggests that Lincoln understood the human condition and was capable of looking beyond people's mortal flaws. Spielberg and Kushner seemed to agree heartily with J.G. de Roulhac Hamilton, that Lincoln's 'heart held room for all and felt with all'.

The film's characterization of Thaddeus Stevens as Lincoln's foil helped bolster *Lincoln's* narrative that if President Lincoln had lived, and therefore if congressional Republicans like Stevens had not taken charge of Reconstruction policy, then white southerners would have been happier and the nation would have been more easily reunited. To be sure, Stevens ultimately makes the 'right' choice by subordinating his indignation at the 13th Amendment's shortcomings to his desire to get it passed. But throughout the film he appears on the cusp of rigid moral extremism, a stark contrast to the pragmatic Lincoln, for whom the audience is meant to have greater admiration. A crucial moment occurs when the two men meet in the kitchen in the basement of the White House to discuss the amendment and what should happen after the war. The scene echoes the one in *Birth of a Nation* described above, in which Stoneman and Lincoln meet to discuss Reconstruction. In the 1915 film, Stoneman pushes Lincoln to take vindictive action against the South, and Lincoln refuses. In *Lincoln*, the confrontation unfolds in a similar manner. Stevens declares,

> When the war ends, I intend to push for full equality, the Negro vote, and much more. Congress shall mandate the seizure of every foot of Rebel land and every dollar of their property. We'll use their confiscated wealth to establish hundreds of thousands of free Negro farmers and at their sides soldiers armed to occupy to transform the heritage of traitors. We'll build up a land down there of free men and free woman and free children and freedom. The nation needs to know that we have such plans.

Lincoln counters, 'That's the untempered version of Reconstruction. It's not, it's not quite exactly what I intend'.[29]

But it is not simply that the two men disagree about what should happen next. Rather, those lines are followed by an exchange that portrays Stevens as a power-hungry tyrant who has no respect for the American ideal of popular self-government, while Lincoln comes across as a leader who will stand up for American democracy and its institutions. After their divergent views on Reconstruction are made clear, Lincoln asks Stevens to patiently help 'the people' overcome their differences. Stevens responds emphatically, 'I shit on the people and what they want and what they're ready for. I don't give a goddamn about the people and what they want. This is the face of someone who has fought long and hard for the good of the people without caring much for any of them … . The people elected me to represent them, to lead them, and I lead.

You ought to try it'. Lincoln objects, saying that he admires Stevens but that Stevens's extremism and inflexibility are counterproductive. Stevens then insults 'the people' again, telling Lincoln: 'You claim you trust them, but you know what the people are. You know that the inner compass that should direct the soul toward justice has ossified in white men and women, North and South, unto utter uselessness through tolerating the evil of slavery. White people cannot bear the thought of sharing this country's infinite abundance with Negroes'.[30] Lincoln quickly moves on, explaining that they must confront the world as it is, not as they wish it to be.

The scene delineates two visions for the nation's future, but the filmmakers are by no means neutral. Stevens, with his startling lines dismissing 'the people', appears positively un-American, a man of demagogic tendencies who shuns compromise and rejects the vaunted notion that elected officials are accountable to their constituents. By contrast, Lincoln stands up for 'the people' and for American institutions, rejecting Stevens's view that white Americans are incorrigibly racist. Just as in *Birth of a Nation*, when a patriotic song plays after Lincoln rejects Stoneman's vision for Reconstruction, in the 2012 scene, Lincoln is clearly meant to represent true American values, while Stevens is portrayed as a dangerous radical. The scene therefore also discredits Stevens's vision for Reconstruction. His impassioned speech about building a more democratic South is brought under scrutiny as he becomes the archetypal 'radical Republican' of the *Birth of a Nation* era, a misguided politician driven by lust for power, whose policies are alien to American institutions and will wreak havoc on the white South at a time when, the film implies, understanding and empathy are required.[31]

A later scene goes well beyond implication, explicitly portraying Lincoln as generous toward white southerners. As the war ends, an exhausted Lincoln talks with General Ulysses S. Grant about the future. Speaking of Confederate General Robert E. Lee, Lincoln instructs: 'Once he surrenders, send his boys back to their homes, their farms, their shops … . Liberality all around, not punishment. I don't want that. The leaders, Jeff and the rest of them, if they escape, leave the country while my back's turned, that won't upset me none'. Here is a vision of Lincoln shaped by the crucial early twentieth-century idea that Lincoln's greatness lay in his capacity for empathy in general and, in particular, empathy for the white South. The audience has heard Stevens's impatient, vindictive plan for remaking the South and his disregard for white Americans, even including his own constituents. Audiences know that Lincoln will die and Stevens will live. The film forecasts a dismal future; it implies that with Lincoln's death the nation would lose the chance for a peaceful reconciliation between the sections and be left at the mercy of extremists like Stevens.

In accepting and reiterating the traditional view that Lincoln could have saved the nation from the enmities and violence of Reconstruction, the film places white citizens at the center of its vision of the nation and African Americans at its periphery. The idea of Lincoln as a national healer had always been tied to his supposed sympathy for others, even his former foes. In this framework, where did newly freed black southerners stand? *Birth of a Nation* makes its position clear. They are unassimilable and dangerous outsiders, and the film imagines that Lincoln would have seen that, for he was white southerners' 'best friend'. Spielberg's *Lincoln* does not answer the question directly. Yet its structure, with white characters at the center and black characters at the margins, suggests its outlook.[32] The African American characters in the film, even William Slade and Elizabeth Keckly, who were based on real historical figures, have few spoken lines. And when the filmmakers give Keckly the chance to look ahead to the future—when Lincoln asks her what she thinks will happen to African Americans 'once slavery's day is done'—Keckly responds that she 'can't say'. Black people had always struggled to get free, she says, but she had never heard them 'ask what freedom would bring'. In the end, this is a movie about politics among white people that ignores the fact, well established by historians, that African Americans helped author their own freedom and gave voice to some of the era's most expansive and egalitarian visions of what freedom and equality could look like. Meanwhile the film maligns the one person in the film who does express an expansive idea of black freedom, Thaddeus Stevens. From its center to its peripheries, this is a movie that imagines white people as the creative forces in American history and as the constituents of American politics. The sectional reconciliation that is made impossible by Lincoln's murder is implicitly a reconciliation among whites; the film does not recognize that black people's safety and well-being would be the cost. It disregards what Frederick Douglass understood in 1875, when he asked ominously, 'If war among the whites brought peace and liberty to the blacks, what will peace among the whites bring'?[33]

Historians have devoted much attention to the ways that reconciliationist narratives of the Civil War required 'forgetting' that an irresolvable conflict over slavery had brought about the war and that abolition had been the war's preeminent result. Spielberg's *Lincoln* engages in no such forgetting. The movie tells us that slavery was at the heart of the conflict and that Lincoln struggled mightily for its abolition. And yet when it comes to imagining the future, the film reverts to early twentieth-century narratives about Reconstruction's heroes, villains, and lost opportunities. *Lincoln* surely did not glorify the Ku Klux Klan or obsess about the sexual purity of white women as *Birth of a Nation* had. But it is possible to reject those aspects of *Birth of a Nation's* Reconstruction narrative while still embracing its underlying premises about the post-Civil War era. Indeed, until the 1960s most historians did precisely that, and Spielberg's *Lincoln* does too, reiterating a familiar set of stories about Reconstruction that white southerners originally told themselves in order to justify their resistance to federal policy and creation of the Jim Crow order. These include the now-discredited arguments that congressional Republicans were motivated mainly by vindictiveness and an ignoble quest for power; that Reconstruction policy was driven by radical Republicans rather than by moderates in the party; and that Reconstruction policies, not white southerners themselves, were responsible for continuing divisiveness and violence.

To be sure, the historical narrative contained within the film does not extend temporally beyond Lincoln's assassination. But *Lincoln* projects ideas about the impact of Lincoln's death that screenwriter Tony Kushner himself articulated in a 2012 interview with National Public Radio. Speaking with a certain awkwardness and euphemism, Kushner said that 'the inability to forgive and to reconcile with the South in a really decent and humane way … was one of the causes of the … resentment and perpetuation of alienation and bitterness that led to the quote-unquote "noble cause", and the rise of the Klan'. He continued: 'The abuse of the South after they were defeated was a catastrophe, and helped lead to just unimaginable, untellable human suffering'.[34] Kushner thus affirmed the fantasy, implicit in the film, that Lincoln would have been forgiving, 'decent', and 'humane' toward the white South and that those who actually wielded power—the congressional Republicans—had 'abused' white Southerners, pushing them into 'alienation' and 'bitterness'. He stopped short of saying their turn to violence was justified, but he implied that if Lincoln had lived, the government would have more readily accepted white southerners back into the nation, their bitterness stanched by his forgiveness.

If it is not already clear that popular understandings of Lincoln's greatness rest in part on discredited ideas about Reconstruction, we may also turn to the words of Hillary Clinton, who as a candidate for the Democratic presidential nomination was asked in January 2016 to name her favorite U.S. president. She responded: 'I don't know what our country might have been like had [Abraham Lincoln] not been murdered, but I bet that it might have been a little less rancorous, a little more forgiving and tolerant. ... But instead, you know, we had Reconstruction, we had the re-instigation of segregation and Jim Crow. We had people in the South feeling totally discouraged and defiant. So, I really do believe he could have very well put us on a different path'. As the writer Ta-Nahesi Coates responded at the time, 'Clinton, whether she knows it or not, is retelling a racist—though popular—version of American history'.[35] That version maligns America's first major effort to create a biracial democracy, blames Washington politicians while exonerating white southerners who were never brought to justice, and implicitly accepts white southerners' argument that they should have been left alone to determine the status of the southern black population. That the acclaimed and liberal team that created *Lincoln* accepted and rearticulated that version of history suggests how difficult it has been to come to grips with its many falsities.

Lincoln's creators made choices at every turn about what to remember and what to forget, and about which aspects of cinematic history they would echo and which they would reject or even seek to overturn. They accomplished a great deal in this complex and gracefully wrought film. But by echoing the traditional idea that Lincoln could have saved the United States from the violence and discord of radical Reconstruction, they left out and otherwise 'forgot' the fate of black southerners. The film's logic and its imagined future requires ignoring the violence white southerners meted out against black people during the war and immediately after it (well before radical Reconstruction began), and it means sidestepping the question of what would have become of black southerners had the U.S. government done what white southerners most wanted, which was stay out of their business. Indeed it means forgetting that most white southerners rejected even a modest amount of federal involvement in securing basic rights for African Americans and that without such oversight, white southerners would have attempted to restore slavery in all but name.

Lincoln is an intriguing example of a seasoned filmmaker self-consciously addressing the tortured American history of race and film while making a biopic about the man who was arguably the nation's greatest president. It is a shame, however, that for all their professed interest in historical accuracy, the filmmakers accepted a mythic vision of Lincoln as national conciliator that is inextricably tied to discredited narratives about the history and meaning of Reconstruction. The film suggests to audiences that Lincoln might have effected a quick and somehow painless resolution to the challenges posed by the abolition of slavery; that if Lincoln had lived there would have been no Jim Crow, no need for a civil rights movement, and no unfinished business in the present. But the problem here is greater than simply a tendency to endow our heroes with superhuman powers. The suggestion that Lincoln would have presided over a smooth and speedy sectional reconciliation imagines a nation in which the well-being of white people is given priority, ignoring the reality that if the U.S. government had let white southerners have their way, they would have trampled the rights of African Americans with impunity. It is time to stop trafficking in the fantasy that Lincoln could have rescued the United States from having to face the consequences of two and a half centuries of race-based slavery.

Notes

1. The author thanks Laura McCoy for research assistance and Mariah Hepworth, Amanda Kleintop, Adam Rothman, and editors Tom Freeman and David Smith for helpful readings of earlier drafts.
2. Wickman, 2012; Pesta, 2012; Goodin, 2012.
3. For a good article on *Birth of a Nation's* initial reception in Washington, see Benbow, 2010.
4. Several other historians and film critics have suggested that *Lincoln* should be understood as an effort to overturn or supplant *Birth of a Nation's* extreme racism. See, for example, Wilentz, 2012; Scott, 2012; Palmer, 2016, p. 295. In an interview, Kushner mentioned *Birth of a Nation* and *Gone with the Wind* as films that had significant negative impact. See Hornaday, 2012. Wilentz dismisses *Birth of a Nation's* admiration for Lincoln as 'bizarre' and Kushner's Dunning School version of Reconstruction as 'odd.' The present essay attempts to explain both phenomena. Wilentz, 2012, p. 21.
5. One especially important influence has been Morrison, 1992. In a telling interview with historian Eric Foner, filmmaker John Sayles called history 'a story bin to be plundered'. Carnes 1995, p. 16.

6. In addition to evidence cited below, see Schwartz, 2000, pp. 79–82; Blight, 2011, pp. 274–75, 278; Barr, 2014, pp. 77–95, 98–99.
7. Wilson, 1901, p. 3.
8. Wilson, 1901, p. 11.
9. Hamilton, 1909, p. 136. For Hamilton's career and his anti-black views, see Rober, 2013.
10. Hamilton, 1909, p. 136.
11. Hamilton, 1909, p. 135.
12. Hamilton, 1909, p. 134.
13. Hamilton, 1909, p. 132. For Lincoln's popularity as a subject of film in the early twentieth century, see Stokes, 2011, p. 223. For another overview of Lincoln in early film, see Spears, 1977, pp. 65–82.
14. Stokes sees Lincoln in *Birth of a Nation* as a 'symbol of reconciliation.' Stokes, 2007, pp. 187–90. For the reconciliationist tenor of Civil War films of that era, see also Browne and Kreiser, 2003, pp. 58–68.
15. Dixon, 1905, front matter; Wilson, 1902.
16. This is a much-shortened version of a similar tete-a-tete in a chapter of *The Clansman* called 'A Clash of Giants.'
17. For a sensitive discussion of the ambiguity of Lincoln's ideas about Reconstruction at the end of his life, see Simpson, 1998, pp. 60–64. For speculation on how Lincoln might have managed the challenges, see for example Foner, 2010, pp. 334–36.
18. For Sandburg's influence on portrayals of Lincoln in the New Deal era, see Silber, 2015, pp. 350–54, 63. As many historians have pointed out, Sandburg drew on existing traditions in Lincoln biography—most significantly the work of Lincoln's legal partner, William Herndon. See, for example, Donald, 1956. For the early Lincoln's androgynous qualities see Stokes, 2007, p. 188.
19. Film historian Melvyn Stokes found that 1939–1940 was the 'zenith' of Lincoln's popularity for filmmakers. Stokes, 2011, p. 221; Silber, 2015. For Lincoln imagery of the 1930s and how it built on themes of Lincoln as divinely ordained savior and as western folk-hero, see also Turley, 1993, pp. 53–66. For Griffith's *Lincoln*, see Lenning, 2010.
20. Donald, 1956, p. 165.
21. As Kushner told *Smithsonian* magazine, 'This is the first serious movie about Lincoln in seventy-odd years.' It is not clear from the article whether this is an exact quotation from Kushner or a paraphrase. See Blount, 2012. See also Reinhart, 1999, pp. 7–15.
22. For a well-researched treatment of the film and its reception, see Stokes, 2007. For a newer treatment, focused on the dynamics of the protest, see Caddo, 2014, pp. 140–70. See also Litwack, 1995, pp. 36–41; Sklar, 1975, esp. p. 60.

23. To my knowledge neither Spielberg nor Kushner has spoken specifically about the impact of *Birth of a Nation* on their thinking about *Lincoln*.
24. Griffith quoted in Stokes, 2007, p. 172.
25. Brown, 2012; Peterson, 2013; Robelen, 2013.
26. Stokes, 2013, p. 85.
27. This point has been made by historian Matthew Pinsker and others. 'Film Roundtable', 2013, p. 367.
28. In an interview Kushner called *Behind the Scenes* 'a wonderful book.' Dodes, 2012.
29. The quotations I've used are from the film itself. Lincoln's second sentence is slightly different in the published screenplay. Kushner, 2012, p. 76.
30. I have transcribed the line as 'I shit on the people,' because that is how I've perceived it over multiple viewings of that scene. However, the screenplay reads, 'Ah, shit on the people.' Kushner, 2012, p. 77.
31. Stokes inexplicably says that in *Lincoln*, Stevens and Lincoln 'are allies on the same side rather than opponents arguing for different approaches to Reconstruction.' Stokes, 2013, p. 85.
32. I have written at some length about this larger issue in Masur, 2012a, 2012b.
33. Quoted in Blight, 2001, p. 132.
34. 'Kushner's "Lincoln",' 2012.
35. Coates, 2016.

Bibliography

Barr, J. M. 2014. *Loathing Lincoln: An American Tradition from the Civil War to the Present*. Baton Rouge: Louisiana State University Press.

Benbow, M. E. 2010. 'Birth of a Quotation: Woodrow Wilson and "Like Writing History with Lightening"', *Journal of the Gilded Age and Progressive Era* 9 (2010), pp. 509–33.

Blight, D. W. 2001. *Race and Reunion: The Civil War in American Memory*. Cambridge, MA: Harvard University Press.

Blight, D. W. 2011. 'Hating and Loving the "Real" Abe Lincolns: Lincoln and the American South', in R. Carwardine and J. Sexton (eds.), *The Global Lincoln*. New York: Oxford University Press.

Blount, R., Jr. 2012. 'Mr Lincoln Goes to Hollywood', *Smithsonian Magazine*, November.

Brown, D. L. 2012. 'Historical Sound Effects Captured in Spielberg's "Lincoln"', *Washington Post*, 13 November.

Browne, A. R. and L. A. Kreiser, Jr. 2003. 'The Civil War and Reconstruction', in Peter C. Rollins (ed.), *The Columbia Companion to American History on Film*. New York: Columbia University Press.

Caddo, C. 2014. *Envisioning Freedom: Cinema and the Building of Modern Black Life*. Cambridge, MA: Harvard University Press.

Carnes, M. C. (ed.). 1995. *Past Imperfect: History According to the Movies*. New York: Henry Holt.

Coates, T. 2016. 'Hillary Clinton Goes Back to the Dunning School', *The Atlantic*, 26 January.

Dixon, T. 1905. *The Clansman: A Historical Romance of the Ku Klux Klan*. New York: Doubleday.

Dodes, R. 2012. 'A Month in the Life of Lincoln' (Interview with Tony Kushner), *Wall Street Journal*, 1 November.

Donald, D. 1956. 'The Folklore Lincoln', *Lincoln Reconsidered*, 2nd edition. New York: Vintage.

'Film Roundtable: *Lincoln*'. 2013. *Civil War History* 59 (2013), pp. 358–75.

Foner, E. 2010. *The Fiery Trial: Abraham Lincoln and American Slavery*. New York: Norton.

Goodin, Emily. 2012. 'Spielberg, Day-Lewis at Capitol for Screening of "Lincoln" for Senators', *The Hill*, 19 December.

Hamilton, J. G. 1909. 'Lincoln and the South', *The Sewanee Review* 17 (1909), pp. 129–38.

Hornaday, A. 2012. 'Steven Spielberg Talks About "Lincoln" and Finding the Man Inside the Monument', *Washington Post*, 8 November.

Kushner, T. 2012. *Lincoln: The Screenplay*. New York: Theatre Communications Group.

'Kushner's "Lincoln" Is Strange, but also Savvy'. 2012. Transcript of *Fresh Air*, National Public Radio, 15 November.

Lenning, Arthur. 2010. '"There Is a Tragedy Going on Here Which I Will Tell You Later": D. W. Griffith and *Abraham Lincoln*', *Film History* 22 (2010), pp. 41–72.

Litwack, L. F. 1995. 'The Birth of a Nation', in Carnes (ed.), *Past Imperfect: History According to the Movies*. New York: Henry Holt.

Masur, K. 2012a. 'A Filmmaker's Imagination, and a Historian's, *Chronicle of Higher Education* online, 30 November.

Masur, K. 2012b. 'In Spielberg's "Lincoln," Passive Black Characters', *New York Times*, 12 November.

Morrison, T. 1992. *Playing in the Dark: Whiteness and the Literary Imagination*. New York: Random House.

Palmer, R. B. 2016. 'Spielberg's *Lincoln:* Memorializing Emancipation', in Palmer and W. H. Epstein (eds.), *Invented Lives, Imagined Communities: The Biopic and American National Identity*. Albany: State University of New York Press.

Pesta, A. 2012. 'Tony Kushner at Hero Summit: Obama Likes New "Lincoln" Movie', *Daily Beast*, 16 November.

Peterson, K. M. 2013. 'Participant Media to Give Spielberg's "Lincoln" DVDs to All U.S. Middle and High Schools', *School Library Journal*, 12 February.

Reinhart, M. S. 1999. *Abraham Lincoln on Screen: A Filmography of Dramas and Documentaries Including Television, 1903–1998*. Jefferson, NC: McFarland & Co.

Robelen, E. 2013. '"Lincoln" Is Coming to a School Near You', *Education Week*, 15 February.

Rober, J. H., Sr. 2013. 'Ransack Roulhac and Racism: Joseph Grégoire de Roulhac Hamilton and Dunning's Questions of Institution Building and Jim Crow', in J. D. Smith and J. V. Lowery (eds.), *The Dunning School: Historians, Race, and the Meaning of Reconstruction*. Lexington: University Press of Kentucky.

Schwartz, B. 2000. *Abraham Lincoln and the Forge of National Memory*. Chicago: University of Chicago Press.

Scott, A. O. 2012. 'The Underrated Radicalism of "Lincoln"', *Atlantic Online*, 4 December.

'Setting the Stage of a Second Term'. 2012. *Time Magazine*, 19 December.

Silber, N. 2015. 'Abraham Lincoln and the Political Culture of New Deal America', *Journal of the Civil War Era* 5 (2015), pp. 348–71.

Simpson, B. D. 1998. *The Reconstruction Presidents*. Lawrence: University of Kansas Press.

Sklar, R. 1975. *Movie-Made America: A Social History of American Movies*. New York: Random House.

Spears, J. 1977. *The Civil War on the Screen and Other Essays*. New York, NJ: A. S. Barnes and Co.

Stokes, M. 2007. *D. W. Griffith's Birth of a Nation*. New York: Oxford University Press.

Stokes, M. 2011. 'Abraham Lincoln and the Movies', *American Nineteenth-Century History* 12 (2011), pp. 203–31.

Stokes, M. 2013. *American History Through Hollywood Film*. New York: Bloomsbury.

Turley, D. 1993. 'A Usable Life: Representations of Abraham Lincoln', in David Ellis (ed.), *Imitating Art: Essays in Bibliography*. Boulder, CO: Pluto Press.

Wickman, F. 2012. 'What Obama Learned from *Lincoln*', *Slate*, 20 December.

Wilentz, S. 2012. 'The Lost Cause and the Won Cause', *The New Republic*, 31 December.

Wilson, W. 1901. 'The Reconstruction of the Southern States', *The Atlantic*, January.

Wilson, W. 1902. *A History of the American People*, 5 Vols. New York: Harper & Bros.

The Trials of Oscar Wilde (1960)

David L. Smith

Sixty years elapsed between Oscar Wilde's death in November 1900 and the first depiction of him on the cinema screen. But when this finally happened in 1960 he may be said to have made up for lost time, for that year saw the release of not one but two films about him. In this case, to paraphrase Wilde's own Lady Bracknell, the release of two films in the same year reflected not so much carelessness as an important moment in the history of British attitudes towards male homosexuality. Of the two films, the more successful was *The Trials of Oscar Wilde*, starring Peter Finch in the title role. It received better reviews at the time and it has remained much the more well known ever since. Unlike its rival, *Oscar Wilde*, in which Robert Morley played Wilde, *The Trials of Oscar Wilde* was made in colour and had a much bigger budget (£270,000).[1] It also addressed the issue of homosexuality in ways that, although they might seem dated today, ensured that in 1960 this film appeared more progressive and enlightened than the other. To achieve this, the film adopted a particular approach to Wilde's biography, confining itself to the years from 1892 to 1897, and concentrating on his relationship with

---

D. L. Smith (✉)
Selwyn College, Cambridge, Cambridge, UK
e-mail: dls10@cam.ac.uk

T. S. Freeman and D. L. Smith (eds.), *Biography and History in Film*, Palgrave Studies in the History of the Media,
https://doi.org/10.1007/978-3-319-89408-9_9

Lord Alfred Douglas and how this led to Wilde's trial and imprisonment for 'gross indecency'. The film did not attempt to cover the whole of Wilde's life, but it did dramatise the period which saw both his greatest literary success and the tragedy of his downfall.

It is significant that 1960 saw not only two films about Wilde but also the first production of a one-man play, *The Importance of being Oscar*, written and performed by Micheál Mac Liammóir. That year marked a key stage in changing social perceptions of male homosexuality in Britain. At that time, the so-called Labouchère Amendment to the Criminal Law Amendment Act of 1885 that created the offence of 'gross indecency' between males for which Wilde had been convicted still remained in force. In 1954, however, the Home Secretary had appointed a committee chaired by Sir John Wolfenden, the Vice-Chancellor of Reading University, to review the existing legislation relating to 'homosexual offences' and to prostitution. Three years later, in September 1957, the committee published its report, generally known as the 'Wolfenden Report', which recommended that 'homosexual activity between consenting adults over the age of twenty-one in private be no longer a criminal offence'. The Report argued that it was not 'proper for the law to concern itself with what a man does in private unless it can be shown to be contrary to the public good'. Yet it was to take nearly ten years, until the Sexual Offences Act of 1967, for legislation to be passed that decriminalised homosexual acts between consenting adults in private.[2]

This ten-year delay owed much to conservatism not only within the political establishment but also in public opinion more widely. A Gallup poll revealed that in the late 1950s only 38% of Britons supported decriminalisation whereas 47% opposed it. When, in 1954, a blue plaque had been placed on Wilde's former home at 16 (now 34) Tite Street, Chelsea, it was vandalised within a few days.[3] The Macmillan government endorsed the Wolfenden Report's recommendations on prostitution, which were embodied in the Street Offences Act of 1959, but it shelved those relating to homosexuality on the grounds that more time was needed to take account of 'public opinion'. Early in 1958, the Homosexual Law Reform Society was founded, and although this proved to be relatively weak as a lobby group it nonetheless held public meetings, of which one of the largest, at Caxton Hall in London, took place on 12 May 1960, shortly before the two films about Wilde were released. The following month, the Labour MP Kenneth Robinson tabled a motion in the House of Commons asking the government to implement the Wolfenden Report's recommendations on homosexuality. The motion was defeated by 215 votes to 101.[4]

In such a climate, 'those who favoured a change of law realized immediately that if the Tories' justification for inaction was to be "public opinion", then public opinion would have to be made to shift'.[5] It was therefore no coincidence that these years 'saw a flood of new works from the arts community that made the case for decriminalisation, sometimes in subtle and sometimes in more overt fashion'.[6] One of the most famous examples was Basil Dearden's film *Victim* (1961) which starred Dirk Bogarde as a homosexual barrister who finds himself forced to admit his own sexuality in order to break the activities of a blackmail gang. This was the first mainstream British film to treat the subject of homosexuality sympathetically and within a contemporary setting. Yet the two biopics about Wilde had addressed the same theme the previous year, and it is surely significant that films set in the 1890s allowed the cinematic treatment of homosexuality at a distance of over sixty years. Historical depictions paved the way to the contemporary realism of *Victim*, and Margaret D. Stetz has argued convincingly that 'Basil Dearden's seemingly groundbreaking film was made possible – and was made a success – by the cultural and political work accomplished by the two Oscar Wilde biopics that came shortly before it'.[7]

In addition to this highly significant historical context, the fact that two films were made on the same subject within the same year was also in part the result of a legal dispute over who possessed the rights to the surviving accounts of Wilde's trials. Warwick Films which made *The Trials of Oscar Wilde*, and Vantage Films, which made *Oscar Wilde*, both claimed to be able to use the extended quotations from the trials contained in H. Montgomery Hyde's 1948 book *The Trials of Oscar Wilde*.[8] The upshot was that the two films were made in direct competition, at considerable speed, and were released within five days of each other in the last week of May 1960.

There can be little doubt that, as Robert Tanitch has written, '*The Trials of Oscar Wilde* was the better film, more authentic in its recreation of the period, more money having been spent on it'.[9] When the two films appeared, critics were unanimous in preferring *The Trials of Oscar Wilde* to *Oscar Wilde*. In *Films and Filming*, for example, Peter Baker described the former as 'a magnificent achievement' whereas he regarded the latter as 'a bad, bad film'.[10] Margaret Hinxman in the

Daily Herald spoke for many with the headline 'Finch wins hands down'.[11] This was partly because the casting was much more believable than in the Robert Morley film. At the time of his trials, Wilde was aged 40 and Douglas was 24, and the casting of Finch (then 43) and John Fraser (29 but looking younger) was thus entirely plausible. By contrast, in *Oscar Wilde*, Robert Morley was 51 and John Neville appeared older than his 35 years, and as a result the force of the age discrepancy between Wilde and Douglas, and of the latter's youth, is largely lost.[12]

Another way in which *The Trials of Oscar Wilde* scored over its rival was in its scholarly credentials which were flagged prominently in the opening credits. It bears the same title—with its pun on legal proceedings and emotional sufferings—as Montgomery Hyde's 1948 book. The film is based on that book and John Furnell's play *The Stringed Lute*, although the screenplay by Ken Hughes is much more obviously indebted to the former than to the latter. The 'advisors' for the film are announced as the Marquis of Queensberry (David Douglas, twelfth Marquis, b. 1929) who was Douglas's great-nephew; Lord Cecil Douglas (1898–1981) who was Douglas's nephew; and Vyvyan Holland (1886–1967) who was Wilde's second and only surviving son. The latter published *Oscar Wilde: A Pictorial Biography* with Thames and Hudson, also in 1960, and in the same year Furnell's play was republished under the title *The Trials of Oscar Wilde*.[13]

The film's chronological coverage is interesting. It begins with the opening night of *Lady Windermere's Fan* on 20 February 1892 and ends with Wilde's release from prison and departure for the continent on 19 May 1897. The film thus covers the period of Wilde's greatest success and his downfall and imprisonment, and much of its dramatic power rests on the extreme contrast between these triumphant heights and tragic depths in a way that might have been diminished had it spanned a longer period of time. Wilde followed *Lady Windermere's Fan* with three more hugely successful society comedies: *A Woman of No Importance* (first performed 19 April 1893), *An Ideal Husband* (3 January 1895), and *The Importance of Being Earnest* (14 February 1895).[14] After the opening of the last of these plays, his triumph appeared total, prompting the *New York Times* to announce that 'Oscar Wilde may be said to have at last, and by a single stroke, put his enemies under his feet'.[15] Yet, just over three months later, on 25 May 1895, Wilde was sentenced to two years' imprisonment with hard labour for acts of 'gross indecency'. It was a fall of spectacular proportions, and the root of it lay in a relationship that Wilde had begun nearly four years earlier with Lord Alfred Douglas (1870–1945), the third son of the Marquis of Queensberry.

The film does not depict the first meeting between Wilde and Douglas, which apparently took place in late June 1891 when Douglas's friend the poet Lionel Johnson introduced them at Wilde's home in Tite Street.[16] Instead, the film moves straight from the opening of *Lady Windermere's Fan* into a scene at the Café Royal, with Wilde surrounded by a group of admiring journalists and friends, including Douglas. During the conversation, Douglas announces that he has 'been sent down' from Oxford and disowned by his father. Although Douglas was hardly the most diligent of students, the reality was somewhat less dramatic: he was ill at the time of his Final Honour School, declined the offer of a private examination, and left Oxford in June 1893 without taking a degree.[17]

In this scene, and indeed throughout the film, the sexual nature of Wilde's relationship with Douglas is played down, and the emphasis instead is placed on 'friendship'. In a later scene, Wilde toasts Douglas with the words 'to the importance of friendship'. The critic Bosley Crowther noted perceptively in the *New York Times* that in this film Wilde's 'relations with the young Lord Alfred Douglas were on a high spiritual plane, and his friendships with other young fellows were inspired by his middle-aged love of youth. If there was anything carnal about them, it might be better overlooked or, at least, put down to his heroic and poetic lust for life'. As a result, Crowther wondered 'if this is a fairly true account, if Mr Wilde was as noble and heroic as he is made to appear. And if he was, what was he doing with those cheap and shady young men?' This led Crowther to conclude: 'It looks to us as if they are trying to whitewash a most unpleasant case, which is one of the more notorious and less ennobling in literary history'.[18]

This delicate approach to homosexuality is especially marked in the film's handling of Wilde's relationships with working-class rent-boys and blackmailers, what he himself referred to as 'feasting with panthers'.[19] The film's next major episode concerns Alfred Wood who in 1893 had sexual relations with Wilde and attempted to extract money from him as the price for returning one of the letters that Wilde had written to Douglas. The emphasis, as in *Victim*, is on the evils of blackmail,[20] but the episode is depicted in such a way as to conceal one of its most important dimensions. Wood is played by an actor, James Booth, who was 32 when the film was made. In actual fact, Wood was aged seventeen in

1893.[21] Hyde's book says little about Wilde's sexual activities with males aged under eighteen and the film glosses over this issue with no more than a fleeting reference to 'stable boys' in a short scene where Wilde's friend Robbie Ross warns him of the rumours that are circulating about his lifestyle. This omission was no doubt partly because of sensitivity to audience reaction in 1960, but also because this aspect of Wilde's life was not reconstructed in detail until Richard Ellmann's 1987 biography and especially the more recent studies by Neil McKenna (2003), Antony Edmonds (2014), and Matthew Sturgis (2018).[22]

The film then turns to concentrate on two central and closely connected themes: Wilde's relationship with Douglas; and Queensberry's increasingly aggressive attempts to destroy that relationship and ultimately to ruin Wilde. Douglas has proved an exceptionally difficult figure to get into perspective. The received image of him as unstable, greedy, and selfish owes much to Wilde's account of him in *De Profundis*, the lengthy autobiographical 'letter' to Douglas that Wilde wrote towards the end of his imprisonment (January–March 1897).[23] The screenplay incorporates some of Wilde's aphorisms in that work, such as 'You demanded without grace and received without thanks'.[24] One of the most dramatic scenes in the film is set in a Brighton boarding house when a spoilt and volatile Douglas threatens an ailing Wilde. This is based on an actual quarrel, which Wilde dated to 10–13 October 1894 in *De Profundis*.[25] But to judge Douglas on the basis of this evidence would be to reconstruct the relationship from the perspective of only one of its protagonists. In recent years, a number of biographies, especially those by Douglas Murray and Caspar Wintermans, have offered a more sympathetic picture of Douglas and helped to rescue him from Wilde's later reproaches.[26] This process of rehabilitation began with Montgomery Hyde's own biography of Douglas, published in 1984.[27] By contrast, his account of him in 1948 had been much more two-dimensional and coloured by *De Profundis*, and this heavily influences the depiction of Douglas in *The Trials of Oscar Wilde*.[28]

The problem by the summer and autumn of 1894 appears to have been not so much that Wilde's relationship with Douglas was deteriorating, but that its ups and downs were becoming more extreme. There can be no doubt about the upset that their quarrels caused Wilde. In March 1893, he had written to Douglas: 'You must not make scenes with me – they kill me – they wreck the loveliness of life – I cannot see *you*, so Greek and gracious, distorted by passion; I cannot listen to *your* curved lips saying hideous things to me – don't do it – you break my heart – I'd sooner be rented all day, than have you bitter, unjust, and horrid – horrid'.[29] The relationship was increasingly like a roller coaster of ever more dizzying highs and lows. In July 1894, Wilde wrote:

> I want to see you. It is really absurd. *I can't live without you.* You are so dear, so wonderful. I think of you all day long, and miss your grace, your boyish beauty, the bright sword-play of your wit, the delicate fancy of your genius, so surprising always in its sudden swallow-flights towards north or south, towards sun or moon – and above all, you yourself. … London is a desert without your dainty feet … Write me a line, and take all my love – now and for ever. Always, and with devotion – but I have no words for how I love you.[30]

Again, in a similar vein, probably on 10 September 1894, Wilde declared: 'Dear, dear boy, you are more to me than any one of them has any idea; you are the atmosphere of beauty through which I see life; you are the incarnation of all lovely things. When we are out of tune, all colour goes from things for me, but we are never really out of tune. I think of you day and night. Write to me soon, you honey-haired boy!'[31] The publication of Wilde's *Complete Letters* in 2000[32] allows for a much better appraisal of his relationship with Douglas than was possible in 1960.

In dramatic terms, Queensberry fulfils the role of the villain of the film. Aged 50 at the time of the trials, the Marquis is played by Lionel Jeffries who was only 33 in 1960. Jeffries' capacity to play characters older than himself was seen most graphically a few years later in *Chitty Chitty Bang Bang* (1968) in which he played Dick Van Dyke's father despite being six months his junior. In *The Trials of Oscar Wilde*, Jeffries portrays Queensberry as a violent, almost unhinged homophobe. This is especially apparent in two scenes. The first depicts an actual visit that Queensberry paid to Wilde's home on 30 June 1894.[33] The script sticks quite closely to Wilde's later account of the visit, given at his first trial.[34] In particular, Wilde's question, 'do you seriously accuse your son and me of sodomy?' and Queensberry's response—'I don't say you are it, but you look it, and you pose as it, which is just as bad. If I catch you and my son together in any public restaurant, I will thrash you'—are reproduced almost verbatim, as are Wilde's words to his servant: 'this is the Marquis of Queensberry, the most infamous brute in London. You are never to allow him to enter my house again'.[35] This was an encounter so intrinsically dramatic that it needed little embellishment, except that the screenplay followed Hyde's book in delicately replacing the word 'sodomy' (which appears in the court transcript) with 'improper conduct'.

This quite faithful reconstruction contrasts with another, fictional scene that is designed to show the hatred that had grown up between Douglas and his father. On 18 October 1894, Douglas's elder brother, Lord Drumlanrig, died of a gunshot wound in circumstances that remain mysterious. The verdict at the time was 'accidental death', but it is possible that he took his own life in fear of a homosexual scandal in which the Liberal Prime Minister Lord Rosebery was also implicated. This tragedy had two important consequences. Firstly, it prompted an immediate reconciliation between Wilde and Douglas in the wake of their quarrel in Brighton a few days earlier (discussed above). Secondly, it made the Marquis even more deeply homophobic—he referred to 'the Snob Queers like Rosebery'—and determined to end his third son's relationship with Wilde.[36] These two consequences thus worked directly against each other.

In the film, following Drumlanrig's funeral, there is a bitter exchange which culminates in Queensberry striking Douglas and the latter threatening to shoot him. John Fraser relates in his autobiography how he urged Jeffries to hit him hard. Jeffries obliged with a blow so forceful that Fraser's head spun and he saw stars. This enabled him to deliver his next line—'Leave me alone. Or I will buy a gun. And before God I swear I will kill you without compunction'—with remarkable intensity.[37] As a scene it is very powerful, but it never took place. In fact, the Marquis did not attend Drumlanrig's funeral and Douglas made his threat several weeks earlier in a postcard warning his father that if he assaulted either Wilde or himself 'I shall try to defend myself with a loaded revolver which I always carry; and if I shoot you, or if he shoots you, we should be completely justified as we should be acting in self-defence against a violent and dangerous rough, and I think if you were dead not many people would miss you'.[38] The scene thus depicts a threat that was actually made, but not in the way that it is portrayed, face to face after Drumlanrig's funeral.

Then follows one of the dramatic highlights of the film: the scene at St. James's Theatre on the opening night of *The Importance of Being Earnest* (14 February 1895). The climax of this scene comes when a furious Queensberry, having been denied access to the theatre, storms into the foyer and presents a bouquet of rotten vegetables to Wilde, who responds with the splendid line: 'Every time I smell them I shall think of you, Lord Queensberry'. Sadly, this remark appears to be apocryphal. We have Wilde's own account of the incident, in a letter written to Douglas shortly afterwards:

> The Scarlet Marquis made a plot to address the audience on the first night of my play! ... He left a grotesque bouquet of vegetables for me! This of course makes his conduct idiotic, robs it of dignity. He arrived with a prize-fighter!! I had all Scotland Yard – twenty police – to guard the theatre. He prowled about for three hours, then left chattering like a monstrous ape.[39]

Douglas was abroad at the time and not, as in the film, present at the opening night. In a further departure from the historical record, the film has Wilde making a speech on-stage after the curtain-calls that he actually gave after the first performance of *Lady Windermere's Fan* on 20 February 1892.[40] This transposition appears to have been derived from *The Stringed Lute*, and the influence of Furnell's play is at its most visible throughout this scene.[41]

Queensberry is then shown immediately storming off to the Albemarle Club to leave the famous calling card, inscribed 'For Oscar Wilde posing [as a] somdomite'. In the film, Wilde collects the card the next day. In fact, Queensberry did not leave the card until 18 February, and Wilde only collected it ten days later.[42] This is a good example of the kind of chronological compression of events—designed to maintain the momentum of the plot and to enhance dramatic effect—that is perhaps permissible in a film of this kind. It is not entirely authentic as a reconstruction of events, but it may still be a valid biographical tool: a biopic, after all, is not a documentary, and the film does at least depict the nature and sequence of the particular events relating to the calling card accurately enough.

Queensberry later referred to his calling card as 'the booby-trap',[43] and it precisely achieved his 'intention of bringing matters to a head'.[44] This brings us, at almost exactly one hour into the film, to Wilde's actual trials in April–May 1895. He later wrote that 'all trials are trials for one's life, ... and three times have I been tried'.[45] The first trial (3–5 April) was Wilde's prosecution of Queensberry for criminal libel. This case was withdrawn and Queensberry acquitted following the production of evidence of Wilde's 'gross indecency'. That evidence was then made the basis for the second trial (26 April–1 May) in which the Crown prosecuted Wilde under the Criminal Law Amendment Act. The jury proved unable to agree upon a verdict, whereupon a retrial was ordered (22–25 May) which resulted in Wilde being sentenced to two years' imprisonment with hard labour. The film covers these events in detail, taking nearly an hour from the opening of the first trial on 3 April to the passing of sentence at the third trial on 25 May, and they thus constitute almost the entire second half of the film.

In its depiction of the trials we see not only the film's debt to Montgomery Hyde's book but also a selective approach that enables Wilde's predicament to be portrayed sympathetically. The cross-examinations of Wilde by Sir Edward Carson (James Mason) in the first trial and by Charles Gill in the second trial are quoted at length in the screenplay, as are the final words of Mr. Justice Wills passing sentence.[46] The third trial is not depicted, except for the judgement, although the closing speech by Wilde's counsel, Sir Edward Clarke (Nigel Patrick), is folded into the portrayal of the second trial.[47] Wilde's eloquent speech in defence of 'the love that dare not speak its name' is reproduced in full as a set piece which Finch delivers with great feeling:

> [it] is such a great affection of an elder for a younger man as there was between David and Jonathan, such as Plato made the very basis of his philosophy, and such as you find in the sonnets of Michelangelo and Shakespeare. It is that deep, spiritual affection that is as pure as it is perfect. ... It is beautiful, it is fine, it is the noblest form of affection. There is nothing unnatural about it. It is intellectual, and it repeatedly exists between an elder and a younger man, when the elder has intellect, and the younger man has all the joy, hope and glamour of life before him. That it should be so, the world does not understand. The world mocks at it, and sometimes puts one in the pillory for it.[48]

By contrast, the film almost entirely omits the extensive cross-examinations of the various individuals who claimed that Wilde had either 'committed indecent acts' with them, or solicited them to do so.[49] Apart from the blackmailer Alfred Wood, who is seen entering the witness box, the individuals in question are only mentioned by name—including Charles Parker, Fred Atkins, and Edward Shelley—and they are described as 'young men of about twenty'. Although Atkins was subsequently convicted of perjury, the testimonies of these witnesses were crucial in securing Wilde's conviction, but they are left out of the film, probably because of their explicitly sexual nature.

A further reason for this omission almost certainly lay in the age of some of these 'young men'. Perhaps the turning point in the first trial comes when Carson asks Wilde if he had ever kissed a former servant of Douglas's called Walter Grainger, to which Wilde replies 'oh dear no, he was extremely ugly'. By referring to him as a 'young man', the film conceals the fact that he was aged sixteen at the time of the alleged incident.[50] The extent of Wilde's sexual relations with males aged below eighteen has only become fully apparent in the recent books by Neil McKenna (2003), Antony Edmonds (2014), and Matthew Sturgis (2018).[51] Their work reveals a more sinister side to Wilde's claim that he was 'a lover of youth' and to his quip, on the eve of the first trial, that 'the working classes are with me – to a boy'.[52] Edmonds writes that 'today men who have sexual relations with boys under sixteen can be sentenced to up to fourteen years in prison, and paying for sex with a boy of sixteen or seventeen carries a sentence of up to seven years. Wilde probably committed the first of these offences, and he was certainly guilty of the second'.[53] It is a sobering thought that although the 1967 Sexual Offences Act decriminalised some of Wilde's actions, for others he might still be regarded as guilty under today's laws.

Wilde's trials also present significant evidential problems for his biographers. The extensive quotations in Montgomery Hyde's book were derived from contemporary press reports rather than from actual transcripts of the trials. Much of his book also rested in turn on Christopher Millard's *Oscar Wilde: Three Times Tried* (1912).[54] In 2000 Wilde's grandson, Merlin Holland, discovered a complete transcript of the first trial which he published three years later under the title *Irish Peacock and Scarlet Marquess*.[55] This contains 85,000 words as opposed to Hyde's 30,000 and reveals, for example, the full extent of Carson's cross-examination of Wilde about his relationships with Edward Shelley and Walter Grainger.[56] Comparable transcripts do not appear to have survived for the second and third trials, however, and it is possible that they were deliberately destroyed.[57] Certain other relevant material has also come to light. In *The Secret Life of Oscar Wilde* (2003), Neil McKenna draws on previously unused witness statements from the various individuals listed in Queensberry's 'plea of justification'.[58] These statements remain in copyright and are not available for general inspection.[59] As a biographical treatment, the film thus offers a double challenge: the fact that—despite the gaps in the surviving sources—much more is known about Wilde now than in 1960; and the film's selective use of such material as was then available in order to communicate a particular message.

To underline that point, it is worth noting two short but telling scenes from this part of the film which take on a particular resonance in the context of the years immediately after the Wolfenden Report. First, several members of Wilde's club are shown discussing the first trial. Most express disgust until one accuses them of taking it all too seriously: 'live and let live, that's what I say; anyway, I don't care what they do so long as they don't do it in the street and frighten the horses'. This was apparently a contemporary remark that has been attributed to the actress Mrs Patrick Campbell.[60] A few minutes later, shortly after the beginning of the second trial, Wilde's counsel Sir Edward Clarke is depicted talking privately with his junior counsel. Clarke refers to 'Wilde's perversion', calling it 'loathsome, degenerate, and unnatural', but he then goes on: 'and yet I feel so sorry for him … it's a terrible thing for a man of Wilde's talents and genius to be slowly crucified by a lot of blackmailers and common criminals'. He adds, in a clear message to the audience: 'the most we can hope for is that out of this hysteria of prejudice and hatred there might shine a glimmer of Christian charity and forgiveness'. In the circumstances of 1960, these scenes constitute very plain—and highly topical—support for the implementation of the Wolfenden Report's recommendations.

The film highlights the drama of Wilde's fall by fabricating a painful scene in which he and Robbie Ross arrive at Tite Street after the second trial to witness his belongings being sold off in a bankruptcy sale. In fact, the sale of Wilde's effects had already taken place before the second trial, on 24 April.[61] Ross was by then in France and Wilde was not present, but the scene adds dramatic effect by bringing the latter face to face with the loss of many of his most cherished possessions, and with a vengeful Queensberry. More significantly, the film implies that Douglas went to France, at Wilde's request, straight after the latter's arrest on 5 April. In fact, unlike Ross—who went immediately to France—Douglas stayed until 24 April, two days before the second trial opened, and he visited Wilde in custody daily.[62] In late April and May, Wilde sent him several passionate letters the last of which, written on 20 May, concluded thus: 'O my love, you whom I cherish above all things, … I love you, I love you … Love me always, love me always. You have been the supreme, the perfect love of my life; there can be no other. … O sweetest of all boys, most loved of all loves, my soul clings to your soul, my life is your life, and in all the worlds of pain and pleasure you are my ideal of admiration and joy'.[63] Like Hyde's book, the film does not do full justice to Douglas's loyalty or to the intensity of Wilde's feelings for him.

Wilde's time in prison is covered very briefly and the main scene depicts the visit of his wife Constance which took place on 19 February 1896.[64] She tells him of his mother's recent death (Lady Wilde had died on 3 February) and also informs him of her decision that he cannot see their two sons again. This proved to be their last meeting, and in May 1897 Wilde signed a Deed of Separation accepting a yearly allowance of £150 and acknowledging that this would be withdrawn if he visited Constance or the children without her permission, or 'notoriously consort[ed] with evil or disreputable companions'.[65] In the film, the scene where Constance and Ross meet Wilde on his release from prison is entirely fictional, as is the final scene at the railway station. Just before he boards the train, Wilde tells her that he has 'always loved her, and always will'. This is consistent with the treatment of Wilde's marriage throughout the film. Constance is played by Yvonne Mitchell who receives second billing even though this is a relatively small part. Mitchell plays Constance as a stoical and long-suffering wife who copes with Wilde's relationship with Douglas much as a spouse might with a heterosexual 'mistress'. This kind of role was something of a speciality of Mitchell's, as in *Woman in a Dressing Gown* (1957) three years earlier. Margaret Stetz has argued that in this respect the film 'follows precisely the guidelines of conventional, heterosexual domestic melodramas with plots based upon adultery'.[66] Wilde's final words to his wife together with Constance's comment to Ada Leverson that she 'just never understood it' were probably intended to send a reassuring message to audiences about the underlying strength of heterosexual marriage. This is reinforced when Douglas appears and Wilde cuts him and boards the train without speaking to him. Constance, Ross, and Ada Leverson then depart, ignoring Douglas, and the film ends with a voice-over of Finch reading the final lines from *The Ballad of Reading Gaol* (1898).[67]

What actually happened when Wilde was released was very different, more complex, and in some ways more interesting.[68] He was released from Pentonville early on the morning of 19 May 1897, having been brought there from Reading the previous day. He was greeted by two friends, More Adey and Stewart Headlam; later that day he went to

Newhaven and took the night boat to Dieppe where Ross and another friend Reggie Turner met him at about 4.30 a.m. on 20 May. He settled briefly at Berneval and in late August was reunited with Douglas at Rouen. He and Douglas then lived together for over two months at the Villa Giudice in Posillipo outside Naples from late September to early December 1897. However, Wilde's wife and Douglas's mother both threatened to cut off their respective allowances if they persisted with this arrangement, and so they separated. Wilde never saw Constance or his sons again, and she died at Genoa in April 1898. Wilde thereafter lived mainly in Paris until his death there, probably from cerebral meningitis, on 30 November 1900. He continued to see Douglas regularly and Douglas paid his funeral expenses.

When the film was released it proved to be a box office disaster and almost bankrupted its producers, Irving Allen and Albert R. Broccoli, who had funded the project themselves.[69] In the United States, the film was denied approval under the Motion Picture Production Code then in force, and it was only released on a states rights basis and with a different title, *The Man with the Green Carnation*.[70] The film was nevertheless a critical success. Finch's performance, in particular, attracted widespread praise and won him not only a BAFTA award as Best Actor in a Leading Role (John Fraser was also nominated) but also the Moscow Film Festival Award for the Best Actor of 1961.[71] Some critics thought this was Finch's best film performance to date: one called it 'a wholly thought-out performance' while another praised his 'definably solid understanding of any public figure who is privately sick, vulnerable and tormented'. In *Films and Filming*, Peter Baker wrote that Finch portrayed Wilde as a man 'of dignity' who was 'at peace with himself' and became 'a martyr'.[72] Finch, who loved Wilde's works, took the part very seriously and put on weight especially for it. Wilde was the first of two homosexual characters that the vigorously heterosexual Finch played on film, the second being Dr. Daniel Hirsch in *Sunday, Bloody Sunday* (1971).[73] That film showed how far attitudes towards male homosexuality and its portrayal in films had changed since *The Trials of Oscar Wilde*. The two films were both milestones in different ways, falling before and after the passing of the Sexual Offences Act in 1967.[74] Wilde himself had foreseen that the journey towards this legislation would not be easy. As he wrote to George Ives in March 1898: 'I have no doubt we shall win, but the road is long, and red with monstrous martyrdoms. Nothing but the repeal of the Criminal Law Amendment

Act would do any good. That is the essential. It is not so much public opinion as public officials that need educating'.[75]

The time since *The Trials of Oscar Wilde* was released is now almost as long (59 years) as that between the film and Wilde's death (60 years). Since 1960, there has been a huge wave of interest in his life and work. In October 2018, the on-line Bibliography of British and Irish History listed 181 items with titles containing 'Oscar Wilde', 134 of them published since 1981 and 78 of these since 2005. The major biography by Richard Ellmann (1987), subsequently corrected by Horst Schroeder (2002), has been followed by more detailed biographical studies, including those by McKenna (2003), Edmonds (2014), Frankel (2017), and Sturgis (2018).[76] One effect of some more recent works has been to draw out Wilde's Irishness and how this shaped both his personality and reactions to him. In *The Trials of Oscar Wilde*, this aspect of him is almost entirely omitted except for the moment when he gives Clarke his word 'as an Irish gentleman' that Queensberry's libel is without foundation. When Clarke later summed up in defence of Wilde, he called him 'a distinguished man of letters and a brilliant Irishman', but the film left out the latter phrase.[77] Wilde's Irish identity is now celebrated more openly than ever before, a development epitomised by David Coakley's 1994 biography and Owen Dudley Edwards's articles in the *Oxford Dictionary of National Biography* (2004) and the *Dictionary of Irish Biography* (2010).[78] Controversy nevertheless persists over the extent to which Wilde can be regarded as a committed Irish nationalist, and whether or not he was a 'reluctant' patriot who tended to make reference to his Irish identity only when it suited him to do so for commercial or political reasons.[79]

On the literary side, criticism of Wilde's works continues to appear in vast quantities. His writings are discussed within a myriad of intellectual, cultural, and historical contexts, and analysed and reanalysed according to changing literary fashions.[80] In 1990, the Oscar Wilde Society was founded 'to promote knowledge, appreciation and study of Wilde's life, personality and works'. This society organises 'lectures, readings and discussions about Wilde and his writings, visits to places associated with Wilde, an annual lunch in Oxford and an annual Birthday Dinner in London', and its members receive two journals: *The Wildean*, published twice a year and *Intentions*, published about six times a year.[81] Another, more bizarre manifestation of the Wilde cult is the fact that his tomb in the Père Lachaise Cemetery in Paris, designed by Jacob Epstein, has recently had to be cleaned and surrounded by a glass screen because so many visitors had imprinted their kisses on it.[82]

Such widespread interest has naturally led to further dramatisations of Wilde's life, and it is worth briefly noting three of them here. In 1985, a television mini-series, *Oscar*, starred Michael Gambon as Wilde and Robin Lermitte as Douglas. Based on Montgomery Hyde's 1976 biography, this was the first portrayal to deal directly with the 'feasting with panthers' and to depict Wilde's reunion with—and ultimate separation from—Douglas in detail.[83] Then, in 1997, appeared the highly successful movie *Wilde*, based on Ellmann's 1987 biography, starring Stephen Fry as Wilde and Jude Law as Douglas. Their ages (40 and 24 respectively) were identical with the respective ages of the protagonists during the trials and that, together with the greater sexual explicitness that was possible by 1997, added authenticity to this portrayal of the relationship.[84] Their performances, especially Law's, were generally praised, and the one criticism of Fry was that he 'toned Wilde down. There was no flamboyance, no energy, no sparkle'.[85] Most recently, Rupert Everett has written, directed and starred in *The Happy Prince* (2018), in which the 58-year-old Everett reconstructed Wilde's final years after his release from prison, interspersed with flashbacks both to his glory days and to his trial and imprisonment. Although Everett's performance tended to receive more acclaim than the film itself, this latest biopic of Wilde shows that interest in him remains undiminished.[86] No doubt further portrayals will be created in the future, adding to a gallery of film Wildes that can be traced all the way back to 1960.

In conclusion, we can see that *The Trials of Oscar Wilde* is a period piece in two senses. It depicts events that took place during the 1890s but it also reflects the values of the time in which it was made. It engaged with the sluggish public and governmental response to the Wolfenden Report by seeking to influence public opinion in favour of the legalisation of male homosexuality. Inevitably, this advocacy has a distorting effect on the film as biography. Some distortions are introduced to enhance the drama of the story but others are to communicate a particular 'message'. As Margaret Stetz has written, 'to the degree … that this biopic is true to its social agenda in the present, it cannot also afford to be true to certain aspects of its subject's life', and 'to some degree' it presents a 'defanged and denatured' Wilde.[87] There is a further problem, which is that the film highlights one issue (homosexual acts between adult males) but obscures another (sex with minors) in a way that distorts Wilde's character and life. Wilde retains his capacity to unsettle and disturb social conventions. To portray him simply as a martyr to now-defunct Victorian laws is hazardous not only because it sanitises him but also because it suggests that the issues raised by his trials are all now safely and satisfactorily resolved.[88] Although Wilde would no doubt have welcomed the legalisation of homosexuality between consenting adult males, it is also important to remember that he was addicted to 'feasting with panthers'. For him, 'the danger was half the excitement',[89] partly because they were working-class and partly because at least some of them were aged under eighteen.[90] The recent biographical works by McKenna, Edmonds, and Sturgis are particularly valuable in reconstructing this aspect of Wilde's life. They remind us of a fundamental insight that Wilde captured in one of his most brilliant aphorisms, namely that 'the truth is rarely pure and never simple'.[91]

Acknowledgements I am grateful to Tom Freeman for his helpful comments on an earlier draft of this essay.

Notes

1. Walker, 1974, p. 158.
2. Stetz, 2000, pp. 93–94; Higgins, 1996, pp. 15–58, 109–22; Dockray and Sutton, 2017, pp. 40–77.
3. Page, 1991, p. 89.
4. Higgins, 1996, pp. 116–48; Dockray and Sutton, 2017, pp. 40–56.
5. Stetz, 2000, p. 95.
6. Stetz, 2000, p. 95.
7. Stetz, 2000, p. 95; cf. Moran, 2004, p. 92.
8. Moran, 2004, pp. 80–85; Bristow, 2008, pp. 238–42; Hyde, 1948.
9. Tanitch, 1999, p. 31.
10. Moran, 2004, pp. 86–90.
11. Tanitch, 1999, p. 34.
12. Tanitch, 1999, pp. 28–29.
13. Holland, 1960; Furnell, 1960 (originally published in 1955 as *The Stringed Lute*. London: Rider).
14. Page, 1991, pp. 47, 52, 61–62.
15. Ellmann, 1987, p. 406.
16. Ellmann, 1987, p. 306; Murray, 2000, p. 32; Page, 1991, p. 44; Sturgis, 2018, p. 419.
17. Murray, 2000, p. 48; Hyde, 1984, pp. 39–41.

18. Crowther, 1960.
19. Holland and Hart-Davis, 2000, p. 758.
20. Higgins, 1996, pp. 95–104.
21. Ellmann, 1987, pp. 367–70, 418–24; Page, 1991, pp. 51–52; McKenna, 2003, pp. 284–85, 304–8, 480–81, 512–13, 521–29; Sturgis, 2018, p. 469.
22. Ellmann, 1987; McKenna, 2003; Edmonds, 2014; Sturgis, 2018.
23. Holland and Hart-Davis, 2000, pp. 683–780.
24. Holland and Hart-Davis, 2000, p. 688.
25. Ellmann, 1987, p. 403; Murray, 2000, p. 65; Page, 1991, pp. 59–60; Sturgis, 2018, pp. 522–23.
26. Murray, 2000; Wintermans, 2007.
27. Hyde, 1984.
28. Hyde, 1948.
29. Holland and Hart-Davis, 2000, pp. 559–60; original emphasis.
30. Holland and Hart-Davis, 2000, p. 594; original emphasis.
31. Holland and Hart-Davis, 2000, p. 602, where this undated letter is dated to 13 August 1894. Antony Edmonds has recently made a persuasive case that it was actually written on 10 September 1894: Edmonds, 2014, pp. 177–81.
32. Holland and Hart-Davis, 2000.
33. Ellmann, 1987, pp. 396–97, 420–21; Page, 1991, p. 57; Sturgis, 2018, pp. 507–8.
34. Hyde, 1948, p. 25; Holland, 2003, pp. 56–59.
35. Hyde, 1976, pp. 193–94; McKenna, 2003, pp. 384–85; Stratmann, 2013, pp. 185–86; Sturgis, 2018, pp. 507–8.
36. Ellmann, 1987, p. 402; McKenna, 2003, p. 429; Stratmann, 2013, pp. 199–202; Sturgis, 2018, pp. 523–25.
37. Fraser, 2004, pp. 162–63.
38. McKenna, 2003, pp. 388–89; Sturgis, 2018, p. 509.
39. Holland and Hart-Davis, 2000, p. 632; McKenna, 2003, pp. 448–51; Stratmann, 2013, p. 210; Sturgis, 2018, p. 537.
40. Ellmann, 1987, p. 346; McKenna, 2003, p. 227; Sturgis, 2018, pp. 443–44.
41. Furnell, 1960, pp. 39–65; the speech is at p. 61.
42. Holland and Hart-Davis, 2000, p. 634; Page, 1991, p. 62; Stratmann, 2013, pp. 211–12; Sturgis, 2018, pp. 539–40.
43. Holland and Hart-Davis, 2000, p. 690.
44. Hyde, 1984, p. 73.
45. Holland and Hart-Davis, 2000, p. 777.
46. Hyde, 1948, pp. 120–39, 146–52, 189–91, 233–42, 339.
47. Hyde, 1948, pp. 322–23.
48. Hyde, 1948, p. 236.

49. Hyde, 1948, pp. 191–219, 296–305.
50. Hyde, 1948, p. 150.
51. McKenna, 2003; Edmonds, 2014; Sturgis, 2018.
52. Hyde, 1948, p. 239; McKenna, 2003, p. 471; Sturgis, 2018, p. 571.
53. Edmonds, 2014, pp. 143–44.
54. Bristow, 2008, pp. 234–58.
55. Holland, 2003.
56. Holland, 2003, pp. xli, 133–44, 206–10.
57. Holland, 2003, pp. xli–xlii; Bristow, 2008, p. 257.
58. McKenna, 2003, pp. xvi–xvii, 298–99, 627; Holland, 2003, pp. 286–91.
59. McKenna, 2003, pp. xvi–xvii, 627; Edmonds, 2014, p. 159.
60. Dent, 1961, p. 78.
61. Ellmann, 1987, p. 431; Sturgis, 2018, p. 567.
62. Hyde, 1984, pp. 83–85; Murray, 2000, pp. 79–82; Fryer, 2000, pp. 103–6.
63. Holland and Hart-Davis, 2000, pp. 646–47, 650–52.
64. Ellmann, 1987, pp. 467–68; Page, 1991, p. 70; Holland and Hart-Davis, 2000, p. 652; Sturgis, 2018, pp. 604–5.
65. Holland and Hart-Davis, 2000, pp. 808, 817, 824; Sturgis, 2018, pp. 621–22.
66. Stetz, 2000, p. 100.
67. Wilde, 2007, p. 909.
68. This paragraph on Wilde's life from his release until his death is based on Page, 1991, pp. 74–89; Ellmann, 1987, pp. 495–550; McKenna, 2003, pp. 578–626; Fryer, 2000, pp. 128–70; Hyde, 1963, pp. 139–84; Frankel, 2017, pp. 85–289; Sturgis, 2018, pp. 627–715.
69. Sheridan and Galvin, 2013, p. 134; Walker, 1974, pp. 158–59.
70. Slide, 1998, pp. 139–40; Walker, 1974, p. 159.
71. Dundy, 1980, p. 249; Faulkner, 1979, p. 209.
72. Moran, 2004, p. 92.
73. Dundy, 1980, pp. 243–49, 307–14; Faulkner, 1979, pp. 209–12, 250–54.
74. Higgins, 1996, pp. 123–48; Dockray and Sutton, 2017, pp. 70–77.
75. Holland and Hart-Davis, 2000, p. 1044.
76. Roden, 2004, Chapter 1; Raby, 1997, Chapter 1.
77. Hyde, 1948, p. 323.
78. Coakley, 1994; Dudley Edwards, 2004, 2010. This theme is also explored in McCormack, 1998; Roden, 2004, pp. 246–66; Sloan, 2003, pp. 188–89.
79. For a good recent appraisal of this debate, see Killeen, 2015.
80. For useful overviews of these trends, see Roden, 2004; Sloan, 2003; Stetz, 2000; Raby, 1997; Powell and Raby, 2013.
81. http://www.oscarwildesociety.co.uk.
82. http://www.bbc.co.uk/news/entertainment-arts-15975249.

83. Tanitch, 1999, pp. 48–52.
84. Tanitch, 1999, pp. 71–73; Powell and Raby, 2013, pp. 349–50; Bristow, 2008, pp. 311–27.
85. Tanitch, 1999, p. 73.
86. See, for example, Lodge, 2018; Leader, 2018.
87. Stetz, 2000, p. 99.
88. Cf. Elfenbein, 2015; Edmonds, 2014, pp. 141–45, 148–50.
89. Holland and Hart-Davis, 2000, p. 758.
90. Kaplan, 2004, pp. 113–30.
91. Wilde, 2007, p. 671 (*The Importance of Being Earnest*, Act I).

Bibliography

Bristow, J. (ed.). 2008. *Oscar Wilde and Modern Culture: The Making of a Legend*. Athens: Ohio University Press.

Coakley, D. 1994. *Oscar Wilde: The Importance of Being Irish*. Dublin: Town House.

Crowther, B. 1960. 'Movie Review: The Trials of Oscar Wilde (1960)', *New York Times*, 28 June.

Dent, A. 1961. *Mrs Patrick Campbell*. London: Museum Press.

Dockray, K., and Sutton, A. 2017. *Politics, Society and Homosexuality in Post-War Britain: The Sexual Offences Act of 1967 and Its Significance*. Stroud: Fonthill Media.

Dudley Edwards, O. 2004. 'Wilde, Oscar Fingal O'Flahertie Wills (1854–1900), Writer', in *Oxford Dictionary of National Biography*. Oxford: Oxford University Press.

Dudley Edwards, O. 2010. 'Wilde, Oscar Fingal O'Flahertie', in *Dictionary of Irish Biography*. Cambridge: Cambridge University Press.

Dundy, E. 1980. *Finch, Bloody Finch: A Life of Peter Finch*. New York: Holt, Rinehart and Winston.

Edmonds, A. 2014. *Oscar Wilde's Scandalous Summer: The 1894 Worthing Holiday and the Aftermath*. Stroud: Amberley.

Elfenbein, A. 2015. 'On the Trials of Oscar Wilde: Myths and Realities', in D. F. Felluga (ed.), *BRANCH: Britain, Representation and Nineteenth-Century History: Extension of Romanticism and Victorianism on the Net*. http://www.branchcollective.org/?ps_articles=andrew-elfenbein-on-the-trials-of-oscar-wilde-myths-and-realities. Accessed 21 August 2016.

Ellmann, R. 1987. *Oscar Wilde*. London: Hamish Hamilton.

Faulkner, T. 1979. *Peter Finch: A Biography*. London: Angus and Robertson.

Frankel, N. 2017. *Oscar Wilde: The Unrepentant Years*. Cambridge, MA: Harvard University Press.

Fraser, J. 2004. *Close Up: An Actor Telling Tales*. London: Oberon Books.

Fryer, J. 2000. *Robbie Ross: Oscar Wilde's True Love*. London: Constable.
Furnell, J. 1960. *The Trials of Oscar Wilde*. Oadby: Ace Books. Originally published in 1955 as *The Stringed Lute*. London: Rider.
Higgins, P. 1996. *Heterosexual Dictatorship: Male Homosexuality in Post-War Britain*. London: Fourth Estate.
Holland, V. 1960. *Oscar Wilde: A Pictorial Biography*. London: Thames and Hudson.
Holland, M. 2003. *Irish Peacock and Scarlet Marquess: The Real Trial of Oscar Wilde*. London: Fourth Estate.
Holland, M., and Hart-Davis, R. (eds.). 2000. *The Complete Letters of Oscar Wilde*. New York: Henry Holt.
Hyde, H. M. 1948. *The Trials of Oscar Wilde*. London: William Hodge.
Hyde, H. M. 1963. *Oscar Wilde: The Aftermath*. London: Methuen.
Hyde, H. M. 1976. *Oscar Wilde: A Biography*. London: Penguin.
Hyde, H. M. 1984. *Lord Alfred Douglas*. London: Methuen.
Kaplan, M. B. 2004. 'Literature in the Dock: The Trials of Oscar Wilde', *Journal of Law and Society* 31 (2004), pp. 113–30.
Killeen, Jarlath. 2015. 'The Greening of Oscar Wilde: Situating Ireland in the Wilde Wars', *Irish Studies Review* 23 (2015), pp. 424–50.
Leader, Michael. 2018. 'The Happy Prince Review: Rupert Everett's Dark Wilde', *Sight & Sound*, 15 April. http://www.bfi.org.uk/news-opinion/sight-sound-magazine/reviews-recommendations/happy-prince-rupert-everett-dark-oscar-wilde. Accessed 6 June 2018.
Lodge, Guy. 2018. 'Sundance Film Review: "The Happy Prince"', *Variety*, 21 January. http://variety.com/2018/film/reviews/the-happy-prince-review-1202671527. Accessed 6 May 2018.
McCormack, J. (ed.). 1998. *Wilde the Irishman*. New Haven: Yale University Press.
McKenna, N. 2003. *The Secret Life of Oscar Wilde*. London: Arrow Books.
Moran, L. J. 2004. 'On Realism and the Law Film: The Case of Oscar Wilde', in L. J. Moran et al. (eds.), *Law's Moving Image*, pp. 77–93. London: Cavendish.
Murray, D. 2000. *Bosie: A Biography of Lord Alfred Douglas*. London: Hodder and Stoughton.
Page, N. 1991. *An Oscar Wilde Chronology*. Basingstoke: Palgrave.
Powell, K., and Raby, P. (eds.). 2013. *Oscar Wilde in Context*. Cambridge: Cambridge University Press.
Raby, P. (ed.). 1997. *The Cambridge Companion to Oscar Wilde*. Cambridge: Cambridge University Press.
Roden, F. S. (ed.). 2004. *Palgrave Advances in Oscar Wilde Studies*. Basingstoke: Palgrave.

Schroeder, H. 2002. *Additions and Corrections to Richard Ellmann's Oscar Wilde*. Braunschweig: Privately Printed.

Sheridan, M., and Galvin, A. 2013. *A Man Called Harris: The Life of Richard Harris*. Stroud: The History Press.

Slide, A. 1998. *'Banned in the USA': British Films in the United States and Their Censorship, 1933–1960*. London: I.B. Tauris.

Sloan, J. 2003. *Authors in Context: Oscar Wilde*. Oxford: Oxford University Press.

Stetz, M. D. 2000. 'Oscar Wilde at the Movies: British Sexual Politics and *The Green Carnation* (1960)', *Biography* 23 (2000), pp. 90–107.

Stratmann, L. 2013. *The Marquess of Queensberry: Wilde's Nemesis*. New Haven: Yale University Press.

Sturgis, M. 2018. *Oscar: A Life*. London: Apollo.

Tanitch, R. 1999. *Oscar Wilde on Stage and Screen*. London: Methuen.

Walker, A. 1974. *Hollywood, England: The British Film Industry in the Sixties*. London: Orion Books.

Wilde, O. 2007. *The Collected Works of Oscar Wilde*. Ware: Wordsworth Library Collection.

Wintermans, C. 2007. *Alfred Douglas: A Poet's Life and His Finest Work*. London: Peter Owen.

Infectious Enthusiasm: *The Story of Louis Pasteur* (1936)

Bart K. Holland

Introduction

Beneath the Institut Pasteur—one of the world's outstanding medical research laboratories—guests can visit an extraordinary Byzantine-style crypt decorated with resplendent mosaics (Fig. 10.1). This shrine is the final resting place of Louis Pasteur. By the time of his death in 1895 at the age of 72, Pasteur was revered as a sort of secular saint. He devoted his life to arduous scientific research, a calling which benefited all of humanity; at the same time, as Geison notes, 'Obsessed with science and its applications, Pasteur devoted little thought to religious, philosophical, or political questions.'[1]

The first section of this essay provides a synopsis of *The Story of Louis Pasteur*, noting the film's narrative as a hagiographic presentation of his struggles as a pure, ascetic, selfless scientist. The second section examines key points of difference between the film's version of the story and the actual historical facts. There I argue that the numerous alterations in the movie version serve to heighten the drama and to yield a more viable

B. K. Holland (✉)
Rutgers - New Jersey Medical School, Newark, NJ, USA
e-mail: holland@njms.rutgers.edu

T. S. Freeman and D. L. Smith (eds.), *Biography and History in Film*, Palgrave Studies in the History of the Media,
https://doi.org/10.1007/978-3-319-89408-9_10

Fig. 10.1 The crypt of Louis Pasteur (Credit Peter Olson)

commercial product, of course; but the distortions were also intended to emphasize Pasteur's saintly side, and to spread the political views of the Warner Brothers studio as well. In the third section, I show that knowledgeable critics at the film's opening were aware of its historical inaccuracies, but considered it a laudable representation nonetheless because of their reverence for Pasteur and the value they saw in the wide dissemination of this particular version of his life.

The Film's Narrative

The film is not a comprehensive biography. It covers about twenty-five years of Pasteur's life, spanning roughly 1860–1885. As it opens, Pasteur has been publicizing his theory that childbed fever is due to the lack of antiseptic technique among physicians, who thus transmit the germs that cause the disease. This 'germ theory' was an unconventional point of view at the time, and the insight certainly did not gain immediate acceptance, either in the movie or in real life. The germ theory scandalously implicated the leading physicians of the day in ignorant and deadly practices. This was a strong accusation, especially coming from Pasteur, a chemist by training rather than a physician, as is mentioned several times in the film. Some of the characters in the opening minutes of the movie agree that Pasteur's controversial views, and the strong emotions they can excite, make him 'a menace to science,' but he is actually a menace to the reputation of the medical establishment. The 'rabble' of science detest this almost inhumanly pure character whose truth points out their moral failings.

Pasteur is shown as confident that his beliefs will lead to important advances in science, and his confidence rests on the truth of observational evidence, unlike his opponents' reliance on old traditions and assumptions. He comments that Semmelweis has observed that childbed fever is found exclusively in patients who have been treated by someone who had previously been in contact with another patient with the disease. In an early scene in his laboratory, Pasteur calmly tells the small band of acolytes gathered around him, 'Find the microbe, kill the microbe' that causes childbed fever.

The controversy surrounding the germ theory of disease has reached the ear of the French Emperor, Napoleon III. A fictional character known as 'Dr Charbonnet' is visiting the royal court. He is supposedly an official of the Academy of Medicine, and serves here as a stand-in for the conservative medical establishment. Charbonnet harangues the Emperor, belittling Pasteur's theory. The Emperor, and in particular his Empress, Eugénie, want to hear the argument for the germ theory of childbed fever from Pasteur himself. The scientist is invited to appear at the Palais des Tuileries and a coachman is sent to fetch him. On the way to the palace, the coachman stops to check on his own wife, who is being attended by a midwife. The wife has just died of childbed fever, however, an event attributed passively by the midwife to an 'act of Providence.' Pasteur fiercely rejects this point of view: 'Providence? No, ignorance!'

Pasteur brings a microscope and slides of germs during his visit to the palace, to help convince those in attendance. It is not clear at the start of the scene whether Charbonnet or Pasteur will prevail. However, Pasteur's extreme devotion to the truth leads to a disastrous outcome during his audience with the emperor. It is clear in the movie that Pasteur is right, but sometimes the ardor of a saint can provoke discomfort and rejection, and that is what happens here. The midwife he has just seen in the coachman's house is going to attend the sister of the Empress, and Pasteur speaks sharply against this arrangement.

He strongly implies that the court physicians are wrong: the Empress's sister can only be safe if those attending her are required to follow Pasteur's own recommended antiseptic procedures. The Emperor is much provoked. He considers such remarks a great impertinence, angrily rejects Pasteur's point of view, and orders him to limit his microbiological research to problems with agricultural products. Pasteur is also ordered to recant: he must 'publish an immediate retraction' of the pamphlet that explained his view of germs as the cause of childbed fever. Pasteur returns home dejected and decides to move with his wife and children to Arbois, in a distant agricultural region of France, to continue his work far from the hornet's nest of the medical establishment and the contempt and interference of the court. Later, as Pasteur foretold, the Empress's sister dies of childbed fever.

Living quietly in the countryside, Pasteur develops a vaccine against anthrax which protects the local farmers from an economic disaster playing out elsewhere in France: a plague is destroying herds throughout the country. On a national level, the losses are imperiling the ability of the French government to pay the compensation demanded by Bismarck at the end of the Franco-Prussian war. Thus, French officials are eager to find out why the herds of sheep at Arbois are reported to have a very low death rate, in contrast to what is seen in the rest of France. A Dr. Radisse is the chairman of the Agricultural Board of the new Republic, a member of the Academy of Medicine, and a leading opponent of Pasteur's theories. Nonetheless, at President Thiers' request, Radisse goes to Arbois to investigate, because every head of livestock saved would represent money to 'buy back some Frenchman's liberty and self-respect,' as Thiers points out in a scene in the movie. France is in dire need of help.

Radisse is accompanied on this trip by Dr. Jean Martel, another employee of the new republican government, who had been an assistant to Charbonnet. Unlike Radisse, Martel is receptive to Pasteur's ideas. Pasteur shows him microscope slides illustrative of the life cycle of the anthrax bacterium. Pasteur has discovered that when an infected sheep dies, bacterial spores are released into the soil, where they lie in wait and later infect their next victims. Radisse ignorantly comments in the press that the sheep at Arbois are safe simply because the fields happen to be free of anthrax. The fields in the region are actually 'reeking' with anthrax, according to Pasteur, who has tested them, and they are not at all safe; it is the vaccine that is keeping the herds free of disease.

Based on what he has seen, Martel returns to Paris to argue for Pasteur's theories at a meeting at the Academy of Medicine, tangling with Charbonnet. During this meeting, Radisse suggests that Martel's support springs from an ulterior motive, a budding romance with Pasteur's daughter Annette. In a later scene, Martel does eventually marry her, but he has also honestly come to believe in the germ theory of anthrax's causation. One speaker at the Academy, Dr. Rossignol, suggests a clinical trial to settle the matter; he confidently expects the result to discredit Pasteur. Some attendees even scorn the proposed experimental test of Pasteur's vaccine as useless and ludicrous, laughingly commenting that Pasteur would be a fool to agree to such a challenge. Indeed, Charbonnet says, 'I dare him to try!' Pasteur has been silently hidden in the upper galleries of the audience, listening to the ridicule of the auditorium full of experts, and at last his two-word reaction suddenly rings out: 'I accept!'

The day has come to administer the vaccine in the clinical trial. There are crowds of farmers, doctors, and newspapermen at Rossignol's farm at Pouilly-le-Fort, where the experiment is taking place. All 50 sheep in the clinical trial have been injected with infectious blood from an anthrax-infected sheep, and half of them have been vaccinated. Pasteur believes that the unvaccinated sheep will all be dead the next morning, while the others won't even fall ill. 'At least let us hope they won't, for the sake of France,' he says. At dinner amidst Pasteur's detractors that evening, Rossignol mockingly proposes a toast, 'To the end of microbes, and their high priest, Louis Pasteur.' The visit to the sheep pens the next morning to view the results of the experiment is a momentous occasion, with the populace and the press and many dignitaries in attendance. One renowned visitor is Joseph Lister, a prominent British scientist (who did not actually attend,[2] but who did advocate the germ theory of disease as a guide to preventive measures, both in the movie and in real life). Success! The stark contrast between the deathly silence of all the unvaccinated sheep and the lively, noisy vaccinated flock astounds all in attendance, including Pasteur. The crowd and the press go wild. Rossignol, completely convinced by the experiment, begs Pasteur's pardon for having doubted him. Lister acclaims Pasteur as well.

Suddenly, the joyous moment is interrupted by shouts of 'Mad dog! Mad dog!' and a dog-bite victim is brought in. The only known treatments are applied as Pasteur watches: a witchcraft-like incantation over the suffering patient, and cauterization of the wound. The appalling suffering of the victim has a sobering effect on Pasteur, who decides on the spot to dedicate himself next to the fight against rabies, in this cinematic version of events.

Pasteur works intensely surrounded by a small group of acolytes who equal him in dedication, all laboring together selflessly day and night in pursuit of a common goal. One colleague in the lab is Martel, whose marriage to Annette, who is now pregnant, comes under strain because of the incessant work. Another colleague is Émile Roux (who later, in reality, was the founding director of one of the departments at the Institut Pasteur).[3] In one scene, it is past eleven in the evening, and the team has been granted a brief break for dinner. The meal is interrupted after just a few minutes, though, due to the delivery of an important experimental animal: a dog with rabies. The scientists run downstairs to the lab. Pasteur has his workers hold the dog steady while he uses a pipette—an instrument rather like a long, glass drinking straw—to suck up the dog's saliva with his own mouth in order to transfer the material to a culture medium. A careless moment during this procedure could result in Pasteur ingesting the infectious material, which would mean certain death from the terrible disease. Pasteur's wife Marie comes upon this scene, is horrified, and calls out for him to stop. Louis' calm and measured response to her is, 'I pledged myself to find a cure,' and he works on. The film's scenes of research on rabies all dramatically indicate the intense dedication and superhuman efforts that Pasteur has brought to his quest, toiling under physically punishing and dangerous conditions. It is as if his vow to solve a scientific problem and save humanity required him to renounce all other motivations and ignore personal risk, even the risk of an agonizing death.

Leaders of the Academy of Medicine pay a visit to Pasteur's lab due to the prompting of Dr. Zaranoff, a visiting Russian expert interested in rabies research. Pasteur shows them a small container of material which he says contains the causative microorganism of rabies, enough to kill a large population of people. Charbonnet, the doubter-in-chief, takes the bottle, rolls up his sleeve, and cheerily injects himself with its contents. He self-confidently declares that there is no risk because Pasteur's theory is wrong—rabies is not caused by organisms that can be grown in culture flasks. As it turns out, Charbonnet goes about his business unperturbed for weeks afterwards, strolling along Parisian boulevards and enjoying cafés with friends, whom he regales with tales of Pasteur's foolishness. Rossignol, a convert to Pasteur's cause since the days of the successful anthrax trial, drops by to warn Louis (and Marie) about the corrosive effect of Charbonnet's ridicule on public opinion.

In the conversation with his wife and Rossignol, Pasteur wonders aloud why the contaminated material which had transmitted rabies to formerly healthy dogs is having no effect on Charbonnet. Marie suggests that perhaps the preparation was not fresh. It was fourteen days old when Charbonnet dosed himself with it, not around a week old as it had been when it caused the dogs to become rabid. 'You may have let it stand too long. You told me once that germs grow weaker, less virulent with age,' she reminds him. This re-statement of a key concept not only gives him a satisfying explanation of the seemingly inconsistent results of his preparation, but also sparks an insight that sets him on the path to the preparation of an effective rabies vaccine. Perhaps the injection of an aged, attenuated culture of live virus might provoke a protective immune reaction, without causing disease. In principle, successively stronger doses could be administered, until the human immune system could withstand even full-strength virus without negative consequences.

Pasteur is testing this approach on dogs, when Joseph Meister, a child from Alsace, is suddenly and unexpectedly brought to him by the boy's mother and family doctor. Joseph had been bitten by a rabid dog, and there was no hope for him in conventional treatment. The doctor knew that Pasteur was famous for having devised the vaccine against anthrax, and had heard that Pasteur was working on a treatment for rabies. The visitors, hoping for a miracle, beg Pasteur to try the treatment on the boy, who stays overnight in a bedroom in Pasteur's house. Rossignol, consulted, strongly advises Pasteur not to act. Pasteur was a chemist, and to practise medicine without a license—especially if things turned out badly—could mean prison, 'perhaps the guillotine,' Pasteur muses anxiously. And even Rossignol won't help him by administering a treatment of unknown effects to a human being rather than an animal. Despite the uncertainties, however, when Pasteur is alone watching the boy's suffering, he finally injects him with the rabies vaccine, out of desperation.

Even before the cure is proven effective, word circulates around the world that the miracle-worker of Pouilly-le-Fort now has a technique that will be able to cure rabies. A mass of peasants from Russia, victims of wolf bites, is outside his house, begging to be cured by the touch of the master. He has them sent away to be held at the local hospital. Later, Meister is seen to survive, and Pasteur goes and treats them there.

When Joseph Meister is cured of rabies, the unprecedented recovery dissolves even Charbonnet's doubts. Unfortunately, during the exhausting and stressful wait for the result of the boy's treatment, Pasteur has suffered a mild stroke. He reacts by saying, 'If our efforts can save one it will be well worth it.' The Russians subsequently are cured too, and Pasteur sees the hospital ward full of recuperating patients. Meister and his party leave for home. Humbly, Pasteur refuses to let Mrs. Meister kiss his hand. He gives the child a present, and asks only to receive a letter from him each month. (In fact, Joseph Meister, ever loyal, became the concierge at the Institut Pasteur in real life, ultimately dying by suicide in the chaos of the German occupation of Paris during World War II).[4]

Marie Pasteur has the task of getting Louis to a celebration in his honor, at the Academy of Medicine. His views have been completely vindicated and he is regarded as a hero around the world. However, the self-effacing savant would never knowingly show up for an evening of awards and encomiums, so his friends and allies are secretly counting on Marie to do the trick, as requested during a visit by Roux. Trick him she does, 'casually' telling him that there is a lecture scheduled for that evening: 'By the way, Louis, Roux has just told me that a foreign scientist has a lecture at the Academy tonight. He claims to have disproven your entire germ theory.' Provoked as expected, he angrily insists on going. Diminished by the effects of his stroke, he walks in slowly, using a cane, somberly anticipating an argument. Instead, there is tumultuous applause. Lister brings him into the room saying, 'I greet you in the name of humanity.' He is heaped with honors, including a medal from the Czar's representative. Overwhelmed with emotion, and with his wife in the audience, Pasteur gives an impromptu speech that forms the closing scene of the movie and provides its final words. He addresses himself to the upper reaches of the gallery, which is filled with students. His parting remarks assert that when a scientific revelation has struck you, it is not to be abandoned, even in the face of intense opposition from doubting critics from the established order, nor should you judge those critics harshly: 'Do not let yourselves be tainted by a barren skepticism.... Do not become angry at your opponents, for no scientific theory has ever been accepted without opposition.'

Truth, Propaganda, and the Film's Narrative

The official 1936 Warner Brothers trailer for the film can be viewed online.[5] 'Every scene is a true life happening,' it declares. Of course such a claim cannot be correct, since everyday activities in the home or laboratory, not recorded at the time, must obviously be re-creations; and right from the outset there are numerous confabulations which form a prominent part of the film's narrative. For example, as mentioned before, Charbonnet is a nonexistent character personifying the medical establishment's resistance to Pasteur's discoveries. The selection of the name Charbonnet for Pasteur's opponent reflects an awareness of etymology. The French word for coal is ***charbon***, and the French expression for anthrax is consequently ***maladie du charbon***. This term refers to a black carbuncle, a coal-like lump, which forms as a result of the infection. 'Charbonnet' could be read as 'little coal lump' or perhaps in this case, 'little anthrax' or 'little carbuncle.' He rakes Pasteur over the coals, as if tormenting the saintly man with devilish tortures. Martel, on the other hand, is the nonexistent character personifying Pasteur's real-world allies in the medical field, some of whom argued forcefully in favor of Pasteur's theories at the Academy of Medicine in the 1880s.[6] They were eventually victorious, of course. Thus Pasteur's losing opponent is named after a coal lump, while Pasteur's triumphant ally Martel shares a surname with the famed Frankish warrior-king who led the Battle of Tours and preserved France from the onslaught of nonbelievers.

Many factual details are altered in the film. Louis Pasteur's wife was indeed named Marie, and the couple had five children, two of whom lived to adulthood. But the sole daughter who lived long enough to marry was named Marie-Louise, not Annette; she married René Vallery-Radot, not Martel; and Vallery-Radot was a writer, not a doctor or scientist. In fact, Vallery-Radot wrote a very thorough biography of Pasteur detailing the family's history and presenting an intimate view of years of research and discovery.[7] The romance between Annette and Martel was clearly added to provide the appealing dramatic tension from a love interest who was, fictionally, a doctor involved in the promotion of Pasteur's germ theory. The substitution of Annette for Marie-Louise was possibly motivated by a desire to avoid confusion with her mother's name, Marie, in rapid dialogue in the film.

In the movie, Pasteur witnesses the cauterization of the victim who had been bitten by a rabid dog, immediately provoking the scientist's intense quest for a potential treatment for rabies. That incident is unattested, however, and almost surely fictional. It certainly seems more than likely that Pasteur's recognition of the importance of rabies as a problem to be solved arose from his awareness of the disease in everyday European experience at the time, rather than as a result of a specific undocumented event coincidentally occurring on the date of the demonstration of the anthrax vaccine, prior to which he conducted no research on the topic. Indeed, Vallery-Radot notes that his father-in-law had witnessed the hideous suffering of rabies while growing up in the Jura region, due to 'the advent of a rabid wolf who went biting men and beasts on his way.'[8] As a child, Pasteur had seen a man survive after having been 'cauterized with a red-hot iron at the smithy near his father's house. The persons who had been bitten on the hands and head succumbed to hydrophobia, some of them amidst horrible sufferings; there were eight victims in the immediate neighbourhood.... For years the whole region remained in dread of that mad wolf.'[9] The 'mad dog' scene in the movie serves as a dramatization of the omnipresence of this disease in the European consciousness of the time and works as a segue when Pasteur turns his attention from a solved problem to his next challenge.

The disastrous interaction with Napoleon III is a more significant deviation from historical fact. Vallery-Radot's biography (1915) recollects that Pasteur was invited to spend a full week with the Emperor and Empress at the Palace of Compiègne (not at the Tuileries, by the way, and more than 80 km distant). During this visit, Pasteur reportedly discussed germs with the Empress, and with the Emperor separately. Pasteur also demonstrated the use of the microscope to view germs during a joint discussion with both of their Majesties during this visit.[10] But there is no report of any fight, nor did any discussion of childbed fever arise during the visit. Indeed, it seems that there never was any significant 'falling out' between Pasteur and the Emperor. Geison, reviewing Pasteur's collected correspondence, took note of letters appealing for support from influential friends as well as '...a number of important ministers and government officials, including Emperor Louis Napoleon and Empress Eugénie.'[11] Napoleon III in return was always thoroughly supportive and '...always took a warm interest in Pasteur's investigations.'[12] Vallery-Radot quotes a letter from the Emperor to a government minister about a delay in the construction of a laboratory for Pasteur, an interruption occasioned by Pasteur's absence due to illness.[13] Napoleon writes, 'I beg you will issue orders that the work begun should be continued.' There was never any evidence for the movie's scene with Napoleon III, or any similar debacle. (The political significance of Napoleon III will be discussed later.)

Pasteur was not at all the lone, self-effacing outsider with the French scientific establishment arrayed against him as depicted in the film. Geison notes, 'What set him aside from his rivals was the consummate success with which he deployed his polemical talents, rhetorical skills, and institutional advantages. In a highly competitive and contentious environment, he was particularly bold and successful in the art of self-advertisement. By appeal to public demonstrations...and by frequent recourse to "judiciary" commissions of the Académie des Sciences [of which he was a member], Pasteur nearly always won public and quasi-official sanction for his views.'[14] The Academy of Sciences and the Academy of Medicine were different institutions, and perhaps there was some sparring here between rival groups, with research scientists on the one hand versus practising medical doctors on the other. But Pasteur clearly had strong institutional allies and political ability and the will to use them. Note also, Pasteur was a rapidly ascending establishment figure in his own right. By age 34, he had been named director of scientific studies at the École Normale Supérieure, a very prestigious university-level institution widely known throughout France, and was overall administrator there as well.[15] The complete omission of Pasteur's broad and publicly known social and institutional support certainly seems to indicate efforts by the film's writers to heighten the drama and to sanctify Pasteur. The story-telling techniques are used to make his travails and ultimate triumph seem more heroic and virtuous. Pasteur is pictured as an innocent and unassuming man, essentially a lone voice, who selflessly battles against the establishment, with success due solely to insight followed by hard work, not involving anything so tawdry and mundane as inter-institutional politics, nor anything as potentially helpful as positive regard from a reigning monarch, and not even a job.

Perhaps the movie's most significant deviation from fact is the false depiction of Pasteur vaccinating Joseph Meister in a solo act of passion. It is true that the decision to inject a preparation of attenuated rabies virus into a person for the first time was a step fraught with difficulty from the point of view of medical ethics, as shown in the film. Moreover, the movie fails to point out that '...opposition to the application of the rabies treatment to human beings did not come only from the medical world at large, but even from Pasteur's own laboratory. Roux, in particular, felt that the method had not been sufficiently tested in animals to justify the risk of human trial and refused to sign with Pasteur the first report of treatment. He ceased to participate in the rabies study and resumed his association with the laboratory only when Pasteur became the object of bitter attacks in the Academy of Medicine….'[16] Still, when Joseph Meister arrived and the time came to put theory to the test, Pasteur was not a lone actor. 'The physiologist Vulpian and the physician Grancher assured Pasteur that the nature of the bites made it likely that the boy would contract fatal rabies, and that the evidence derived from experimentation in dogs was sufficient to justify attempting the treatment.'[17] Vulpian, not mentioned in the film, was notably the Dean of the Faculty of Medicine at Paris, and he was Pasteur's colleague at the Academy of Sciences.[18] Although a physician, Vulpian declined to give the injections because he was not in medical practice.[19] So Dr. Adrien Loir, a scientist who worked for Pasteur, was sent to fetch Grancher. In his memoir of this period, Loir writes, '*…sur l'ordre de Pasteur, j'allai chercher Grancher chez lui, rue d'Anjou et le ramenai au laboratoire. La première inoculation à l'homme fut donc faite par Grancher*'—'…on Pasteur's order, I went to look for Grancher at his home in the rue d'Anjou, and brought him back to the laboratory. *The first inoculation in man was thus performed by Grancher.*'[20] Loir was present and closely involved in the case, taking Meister's temperature several times a day and reporting on everything he said, while Pasteur visited frequently during the days of recuperation.[21] Nevertheless, 'Grancher took the medical responsibility of the case, and from then on managed the program for the treatment of rabies in human beings under Pasteur's close supervision.'[22] Grancher was an employee of Pasteur's at the time Meister arrived,[23] and went on to 'orchestrate' the successful defense of 'Pasteur's antirabies method in January 1887 in the … Academy of Medicine,' according to Gelfand's review of the extensive correspondence between Grancher and Pasteur.[24] Grancher is not mentioned in the movie, nor is there any character representing him. The omission is an important one, considering that he was the person who actually vaccinated Joseph Meister in real life.

Thus, numerous specific incidents depicted in the movie are clearly invented, and Pasteur's position in the scientific establishment is deliberately ignored. Yet the narrative arc of the film is accurate in certain general and important ways. Pasteur really did promulgate theories which met stiff opposition, but which then resulted in the revolutionary development of much-needed and effective vaccines against anthrax and rabies, eventually earning him his position as a revered figure in the history of science. Even some of the specific oppositional establishment characters presented in the film did exist. Rossignol, in real life the editor of *The Veterinary Press*, was among those who in 1882 challenged Pasteur to the public test of his anthrax vaccine. Rossignol was also one of many who engaged in vicious mockery of Pasteur, stating in a bizarre sarcastic mélange in 1881, 'Microbiolatry [sic] is the fashion, it reigns undisputed; it is a doctrine which must not even be discussed, especially when its Pontiff, the learned Monsieur Pasteur, has pronounced the sacramental words, "I have spoken." The microbe alone is and shall be the characteristic of a disease; that is understood and settled;.....the Microbe alone is true, and Pasteur is its prophet.'[25] As in the film, though, Rossignol did attend the trial of the anthrax vaccine, which he hosted on his own farm, and he was immediately converted to Pasteur's point of view by the dramatic results.

Another positive aspect of the film is that the science of microbiology, and the medical characteristics of rabies and the principles of the vaccine, are correctly represented in all material aspects.[26] And according to an unsigned 1936 review in the journal *Nature*,[27] the movie's producers also deserve '[a] word of commendation … for the excellent background representing a doctor's consulting room in pre-antiseptic times, the rural scenery and Pasteur's laboratory.'

On balance, then, does the film's narrative reflect 'what actually happened'? Like many historically based films, *The Story of Louis Pasteur* presents a caricature of reality, emphasizing the essential features so that the film provides a recognizable portrait, while telling an interesting and appealing story. Some of the alterations seem needless or innocuous, while some are understandable in the interest of personification of a point of view (e.g., the creation of Charbonnet). But there are also alterations and omissions that substantially misrepresent what happened—all serving to sharpen the distinction between Pasteur and his narrow-minded opponents, emphasize the drama of his fight against the opposition, and sanctify his single-minded and selfless dedication to the truth. In this telling, the story is simple. Pasteur and his small dedicated band of followers, after vilification and derision, overcome the establishment's opposition because they are standard-bearers for a cause that is ultimately right. The film perpetuated a view parodied by Rossignol in the quote above, and expressed in reverent architectural form by

Pasteur's crypt: Pasteur was a sacred figure, whose life's work was dedicated to relieving France and all of humanity from much misery.

What is known about the studio's preference for this altered version of reality? Of course, a movie is a commercial product, and despite the trailer's assertion that every scene was accurate, the producers at Warner Brothers were well aware that they were not producing a meticulous representation. They felt that careful historicity tended to be the enemy of good movies. Evidence for this attitude can be seen, for example, in correspondence from Hal B. Wallis, William Cagney, and Robert Buckner to the American composer, George M. Cohan.[28] The letter was written in reply to the composer's objections to the proposed script of a movie telling his life story. The script apparently had many misrepresentations of fact, and the studio was writing to convince Cohan to accept the alterations. A letter mentions a previous Warner Brothers biopic (about the life of Knute Rockne), 'which we believe you admired…. Many scenes in that picture never actually occurred as we showed them, but…when the picture was shown to his family and friends their pleasure and gratitude at the warmly humanized results overcame completely any microscopic objections to literal facts. We did the same with *Zola* and *Pasteur*….It is the only way in which a biographical picture can be made interesting and worthy.' Thus, the studio knowingly altered or deleted facts that were 'unquestionably accurate as biography and interesting as history, [if] for the time-tested purposes of motion pictures, they do not seem to us to hold or build the interest in a central theme.'[29]

The studio was not influenced solely by commercial considerations, however. At the time, fascism was on the rise in Germany; this affected the types of films produced and the scenes presented within them. Harry Warner had visited Germany on business in 1932 and been shocked to see anti-Semitic slogans plastered on walls and Brownshirts 'stalking the streets'; Jack Warner's '…annual European vacations had exposed him to Hitlerism' too.[30] Warner Brothers became an intensely political studio in the 1930s, and was especially noteworthy for the pride with which it 'wore the badge of anti-Nazism.'[31] 'Up until the outbreak of war in Europe, MGM, Paramount, RKO, and Twentieth-Century Fox figured business was business. Only Warner Brothers dissented, … it cut off relations with Germany in 1933… and injected anti-Nazi sentiments into its short subjects and feature films.'[32]

This was the context in which the studio was working, just as it was "hitting its stride," as Doherty puts it.[33] 'A series of 'great man' biopics, notably *The Story of Louis Pasteur* (1936) and the *Life of Emile Zola* (1937) lent prestige and earned Best Picture Oscars....'[34] Paul Muni played the starring role in those two films as well as in *Juarez* (1939). Muni, born to Yiddish-speaking Jewish immigrants from the Austro-Hungarian Empire,[35] was cast by Warner Brothers to play both Jewish and non-Jewish leading characters, in each case representing a man with a cause who righteously stood up against an oppressive conservative regime. Napoleon III, portrayed negatively in the movie about Pasteur, added imperialist meddling to his résumé in *Juarez* by appointing Maximilian von Habsburg, Archduke of Austria, as Emperor of Mexico (as in fact happened in 1864). That movie is a story of conflict between despot and democrat. Juarez, the elected president of Mexico who preceded Maximilian, regained his presidency after his country was liberated from foreign monarchy by the capture and execution of Maximilian in 1867.[36] The two portrayals of Napoleon III—as an authoritarian opponent of Pasteur's Truth and as the usurper of a duly elected government—fit in well with the anti-fascist politics of the studio, and with their more general anti-authoritarian stance. Even back in 1931—before the 'great man' series—Warner Brothers had produced *Little Caesar* and *Public Enemy*, films in which the hero is a gangster clawing his way to the top. In short, the studio's movies had a tendency to glorify an underdog's struggles with authority.

However, *The Story of Louis Pasteur* does not just tell the story of an underdog, nor does it portray only a decisive defeat of some generalized 'conservative establishment.' It was specifically an 'anti-Nazi parable,' according to Welky,[37] although he terms it Warner Brothers' 'most oblique' example of one. In the mid-1930s, 'The Neutrality Act, [the] Production Code Administration, and public opinion discouraged filmmakers from saying anything too courageous or divisive. The Warners instead attacked Hitlerism through metaphor, crafting productions that conveyed their point without overtly commenting on contemporary conditions,' an approach which led to framing Pasteur's 'life as a struggle between ignorance and enlightenment.'[38] In fact, I think the struggle can be seen as a fight for the values of the Enlightenment, with a capital E. Pasteur represents, and the filmmakers side with, the liberal, tolerant, scientifically oriented, open-minded values of the French philosophical movement as opposed to the fascists of Germany. In Pasteur's final speech, he exhorts the young to 'keep the flame of knowledge burning,' and to remain undaunted by those who resist the truth. This is certainly good advice for scientists, but it could certainly also be read as a subtle anti-Nazi message. Moreover, Pasteur encourages his audience not to 'let the sadness of certain hours that creep over nations' overwhelm them. That 'incongruous' phrase does not seem to relate directly to the steadfastness needed to prevail in a scientific controversy, but it 'could easily be interpreted as a swipe against Germany.'[39]

The Story of Louis Pasteur is not a historian's representation of the life of the French scientist. The substantial deviations from the truth had justifications ranging from artistic and commercial concerns to a studio's well-documented political and social outlook. The questions arise: at the film's release, were contemporary critics aware of the alterations in the story? How well-accepted were these alterations?

Critical Reception of the Film

A history of Warner Brothers' achievements in the 1930s provides a list of awards indicating the esteem in which critics held *The Story of Louis Pasteur*.[40] The Academy Award for best actor went to Paul Muni in the role of Pasteur. The movie's writers, Pierre Collings and Sheridan Gibney, won the Academy Awards for Best Writing (Original Story) and Best Writing (Screenplay). The film garnered an Academy nomination for Best Picture, as well. *Film Daily* placed it on its list of Ten Best Pictures of 1936, and rated it sixth. The National Board of Review placed it on three 'Ten Best' lists, rating it number two among 'Exceptional Photoplays,' number three in 'Popular Appeal,' and number seven among 'Young Reviewers [Ages 8–17].'

One might think that such acclaim was due to enjoyment of the movie—with the satisfying resolution of an exciting conflict in favor of the hero—primarily among the viewers ignorant of the degree to which the story had been altered. Indeed, the title and first sentences of the review in *Newsweek* indicate scant awareness of facts.[41] The article, 'Pasteur: The Scientist's Life as He Lived It, Not as Hollywood Imagined It,' starts, 'Last week the screen discarded prosaic formulas in favor of an untouched film source – straight biography. *The Story of Louis Pasteur* proves that thrilling cinema material lies in historic facts undistorted by romantic embellishments producers have piled on.' This naïve review provoked a reaction from Bert Hansen in *Picturing Medical Progress from Pasteur to Polio*: 'Historians see the film with different eyes, often bristling at [its] romantic embellishments and other distortions of fact.'[42]

Enthusiasm for the film upon its appearance in 1936 was not limited to people unaware of its inaccuracies, though. Rather, acceptance of the film's errors and contrivances seems to have affected even knowledgeable movie critics at the time. Pasteur's actual life story was explicitly and willfully ignored. In his review, a *New York Times* writer, Frank Nugent, enumerated historical errors within the movie. He then straightforwardly confessed to a belief '… that accuracy is not the most important part of biography,' acknowledging that his view was a 'heresy.' He condoned errors of time and place, as well as '… the addition of known fiction to known fact, provided these untruths are committed in the interest of a greater truth, which would be the preservation of the spirit – not the chronological letter – of a man's life.' Nugent added, 'Once you accept the essential accuracy of the conflict' depicted here, 'you should be willing to condone every factual sin the film commits.'[43] This is rather different from the view of Martin Arnold, a much more recent writer in the same newspaper, dwelling on the commitment to accuracy expected of historical representations. He contrasts the standards of scholarship with the productions of Hollywood, and mentions as an example in passing that '… in the light of scholarship, *The Story of Louis Pasteur* is absurd.'[44]

Although much is wrong with the movie, even *Nature*, one of the most rigorous scientific journals in the world, had a soft spot for it. The journal published its own 1936 review noting that the movie '…scarcely deserves the high praise given it by certain writers in the daily Press obviously unfamiliar with the details of Pasteur's life and work.' The review mentions 'many historical errors.' Yet ultimately it recommended that the public see the movie, in order to gain 'some idea of what a scientific attitude implies,' and because the audience will 'certainly realise something of the thrill of successful research, as well as the drudgery and self-sacrifice which it involves. Also, there will be no doubt left in their minds regarding the social implications of the work of the man of science.'[45]

In short, the movie is somewhat accurate: it is accurate enough to propagate an admiration for science, and to disseminate some basic scientific principles relating to microbiology and the experimental method. The moviemakers effectively spread a distorted, saintly legend of this historical figure without provoking too much opposition, because some of the main features of Pasteur's work are shown accurately, and were socially desirable. *Nature* explicitly welcomed the publicity on behalf of science and scientists, and Warner Brothers subtly embedded an anti-Nazi message. The *Nature* review concludes: 'In a film of this sort, intended for entertainment rather than instruction, it is possibly pedantic to expect absolute historical accuracy.' Does anyone really expect 'absolute' accuracy here? Or is the *Nature* writer setting up a straw man in defense of the movie, so that substantive objections can be weakened by conflation with quibbles? The historian can understand and even be sympathetic to the constraints placed on mass-market movies produced for profit, yet still conclude that this film is good as entertainment and unreliable as a history or biography.

Notes

1. Geison, 1995, pp. 42–43.
2. *Nature*, 1936, p. 1066.
3. Institut Pasteur website, 2016.
4. Dufour and Carroll, 2013, pp. 32–33.
5. Warner Brothers, 1936.
6. Especially Joseph Grancher: see Gelfand, 2002.
7. Vallery-Radot, 1915.
8. Vallery-Radot, 1915, p. 408.
9. Vallery-Radot, 1915, p. 408.
10. Vallery-Radot, 1915, pp. 125–28.
11. Geison, 1995, p. 38.
12. *Nature*, 1936, p. 1066.
13. Vallery-Radot, 1915, pp. 162–63.
14. Geison, 1995, p. 38.
15. Geison, 1995, p. 27.
16. Dubos, 1960, p. 335.
17. Dubos, 1960, p. 335.
18. Loir, 1938, p. 73.
19. Geison, 1995, p. 238; Loir, 1938, pp. 73–74.
20. Loir, 1938, p. 74, my translation, emphasis added.
21. Loir, 1938, p. 74.
22. Dubos, 1960, p. 335.
23. Geison, 1995, p. 238.
24. Gelfand, 2002, pp. 698–718.
25. Dubos, 1960, p. 337.
26. Mandell, Bennett, and Dolan, 2010, pp. 2249–58.
27. *Nature*, 1936, p. 1065.
28. Wallis, Cagney, and Buckner, 1941, in Behlmer, 1985, pp. 181–83.
29. Wallis, Cagney, and Buckner, 1941, in Behlmer, 1985, p. 182.

30. Welky, 2008, p. 42.
31. Doherty, 2013, p. 312.
32. Doherty, 2013, p. 312.
33. Doherty, 2013, p. 313.
34. Doherty, 2013, p. 313.
35. Druxman, 1974, pp. 39–42.
36. Druxman, 1974, pp. 172–74.
37. Welky, 2008, p. 42.
38. Welky, 2008, p. 42.
39. Welky, 2008, p. 43.
40. Roddick, 1983, pp. 265–66.
41. *Newsweek*, 1936, p. 27.
42. Hansen, 2009, p. 300.
43. Nugent, 1936.
44. Arnold, 2002, p. E3.
45. *Nature*, 1936, pp. 1064–65.

Bibliography

Anon. 1936. 'Louis Pasteur Film', *Nature*, 27 June, pp. 1064–65.

Anon. 1936. 'Pasteur: The Scientist's Life as He Lived It, Not as Hollywood Imagined It', *Newsweek*, 7:7, 15 February, p. 27.

Arnold, M. 2002. 'Writers Beware: History Is an Art, Not a Toaster', *The New York Times*, 28 February, pp. E1, E3.

Behlmer, R. (ed.). 1985. *Inside Warner Bros. (1935–1951)*. New York: Viking Penguin.

Doherty, T. 2013. *Hollywood and Hitler 1933–1939*. New York: Columbia University Press.

Druxman, M. B. 1974. *Paul Muni, His Life and His Films*. Cranbury, NJ: A. S. Barnes.

Dubos, R. 1960. *Louis Pasteur, Free Lance of Science*. New York: Da Capo Press.

Dufour, H., and Carroll, S. 2013. 'Great Myths Die Hard', *Nature*, 3 October, pp. 32–33.

Geison, G. L. 1995. *The Private Science of Louis Pasteur*. Princeton, NJ: Princeton University Press.

Gelfand, T. 2000. '11 January 1887, The Day Medicine Changed: Joseph Grancher's Defense of Pasteur's Treatment for Rabies', *Bulletin of the History of Medicine* 76 (4), pp. 698–718.

Hansen, B. 2009. *Picturing Medical Progress from Pasteur to Polio: A History of Mass Media Images and Popular Attitudes in America*. New Brunswick, NJ: Rutgers University Press.

Institut Pasteur. Website at http://www.pasteur.fr/en/institut-pasteur/history/story-institut-pasteur. Accessed 24 May 2016.

Loir, A. 1938. *À L'Ombre de Pasteur*. Paris: Le Mouvement Sanitaire.

Mandell, G. L., Bennett, J. E., and Dolin, R. *Mandell, Douglas, and Bennett's Principles and Practice of Infectious Diseases*. Philadelphia: Churchill Livingstone Elsevier.

Nugent, F. 1936. Available at http://www.nytimes.com/movie/review?res=9A03E2DB1630E13BBC4852DFB466838D629EDE. Accessed 26 May 2016.

Roddick, N. 1983. *A New Deal in Entertainment: Warner Brothers in the 1930s*. London: British Film Institute.

Vallery-Radot, R. 1915. *The Life of Pasteur*, trans. R. L. Devonshire. New York: Doubleday, Page, and Company.

Warner Brothers. 1936. Available at https://www.youtube.com/watch?v=WrpWv6we1jg. Accessed 17 May 2016.

Welky, D. 2008. *The Moguls and the Dictators: Hollywood and the Coming of World War II*. Baltimore: Johns Hopkins University Press.

Filming and Formatting the Explorer Hero: Captain Scott and Ealing Studios' *Scott of the Antarctic* (1948)

Klaus Dodds

Introduction

As the first director of the Scott Polar Research Institute (SPRI) at the University of Cambridge (1920–1946) and professor of geography, Frank Debenham, recalled that the idea of making a film about the late Robert Falcon Scott and his Antarctic Terra Nova Expedition (1910–1913) provoked a rather muted reaction. In a 'personal opinion' published in the Institute's journal, *Polar Record*, he noted that 'Early in 1945 a rumour was spreading round that a film was to be made of Scott's Last Expedition, and the reaction among the "survivors" – as the press choose to call us – was interesting. It was, almost universally, one of dismay and even antagonism. The arguments against were varied. The story was already sufficiently told; it was out of date; to film it would be an invasion of privacy, and so on and so forth'.[1] It was, in his

K. Dodds (✉)
Royal Holloway, London, UK
e-mail: K.Dodds@rhul.ac.uk

T. S. Freeman and D. L. Smith (eds.), *Biography and History in Film*, Palgrave Studies in the History of the Media,
https://doi.org/10.1007/978-3-319-89408-9_11

judgement, going to be a challenging film to plan, to make and to predict the reactions of those who watched it.

Debenham was a 'survivor', he was one of the geologists selected to accompany the Terra Nova expedition and explored and surveyed the mountains of Victoria Land. An injured leg prevented him from being selected to join Scott in his pursuit of the South Pole. On his return to the UK, Debenham served in World War I seeing action in France and Greece. After suffering a severe injury, he left the army and returned to Cambridge. As a fellow and lecturer in cartography, he alongside another Cambridge geologist and explorer, Raymond Priestly, were instrumental in co-founding the SPRI. The Institute's genesis lies in public donations given in the wake of the Scott tragedy. It was intended to be an enduring legacy of the Terra Nova expedition's scientific credentials and in so doing act as a very material reminder that stories about a 'dash to the pole' with Norwegian explorer Roald Amundsen should not diminish its achievements.

The former director's reflections on 'dismay' and 'antagonism' capture well the rather jaundiced views about the legacy of Robert Scott and his final expedition. Representing Scott's life and death was, by the early 1920s, already contentious subject matter. Even before the commission and production of *Scott of the Antarctic*,[2] the public engagement with the Scott expedition was varied even after the posthumous publication of Scott's expedition diaries. While many contemporaries readily accepted the idea that Scott was a heroic explorer and example for the nation, this was not shared by all. D.H. Lawrence's novel *Women in Love* (1920) serves as a reminder that Scott's achievements and even death were deeply ambiguous matters. Though allegory, Lawrence's novel questions the manner in which Scott's death was commemorated and the public outpourings of grief. Thereafter, we consider in more detail the decision by Ealing Studios to produce and the resulting time-consuming task involving delicate negotiations with surviving family members and the SPRI. Reminiscent of the sort of work that British director Paul Greengrass did with the families of those who died on flight United 93 on 11 September 2001, Ealing Studios' director Charles Frend was determined to make an 'authentic' biopic and historical film. Scott's status as a tragic yet heroic explorer figure placed some creative 'constraints' on Frend and the filming team.

As the chapter considers later, however, the timing of the film was also opportune. While there was no location filming in Antarctica, the film utilises film footage from the Antarctic Peninsula in a deliberate attempt to promote British Antarctic interests at a time of rising geopolitical tension. This is important because *Scott of the Antarctic* (1948) needs to be understood within a broader cultural, geopolitical and economic context. By the late 1940s, the Antarctic was a far more complex political space than in the midst of the so-called 'Heroic Era of exploration' (c. 1890–1914). For one thing, seven states including Britain had pressed formal territorial claims to the continent. The British claim, the Falkland Islands Dependencies, substantially overlapped with rival claims by Argentina and Chile. The United States was making its strategic and scientific presence felt across the continent. In resource terms, Britain was deeply involved with the whaling trade, working closely with Norwegian companies and individuals on South Georgia and in and around the Antarctic Peninsula. Finally, popular and literary expressions of polar commemoration helped to underwrite not only the establishment of the SPRI at Cambridge but also memorials and commemorative plaques built around the British Isles.

Debenham's aforementioned misgivings about the film project appear to be apposite. *Scott of the Antarctic* does offer a more ambivalent reading of Robert Scott and the Terra Nova expedition. Some of that critical work is done through the narrative arc and staged encounters, but there is also another element to the film which is sound. The musical score by the English composer Ralph Vaughan Williams reminds us that sound can and does shape the mood and tempo of the film, offering insights into places, times, emotional states and relationships. Ealing Studios considered Vaughan Williams to be inherently appropriate given the public reputation as a composer and contributor to the BBC including the Proms. Finally, as noted, the prevailing geopolitical context of Antarctica in the late 1940s also acts as a counterpoint to a film that ostensibly looks backwards to a Heroic Era of exploration that was largely surpassed by a new era of permanent occupation and large-scale and multinational exploration. The film's release coincided with new plans led by the United States for the future control of Antarctica.

Biopics: Ealing Studios and Scott as Explorer Hero

Film historians and other scholars have, academically speaking, neglected the sub-genre of biopic (or biographical films) as opposed to the western, gangster, thriller, drama and horror genres.[3] George Custen on

Bio/Pics: How Hollywood Constructed Public History and more recently, Dennis Bingham's *Whose Lives Are They Anyway?* are the most substantive interrogation of the sub-genre.[4] The biopic as opposed to the documentary genre uses actors to dramatise the lives of usually notable individuals. Established in the era of silent cinema, the biopic was highly popular in the 1920s and 1930s, and depending on the focus of the film they criss-cross genre types ranging from drama and epic to action-thriller and crime. Biopics also vary in whether they tackle the entire life and work of an individual or concentrate on a particular notable theme or event. In Bingham's examination of the sub-genre, he identifies distinct qualities associated with the white male biopic, which differ substantially from films about the lives of women and people of colour. In the white male biopic, Bingham argues that the wife or female partner is always secondary to the husband but nonetheless shown as integral to eventual success. While white male biopics might touch upon weakness and mistakes, they tend to present this as virtuous self-awareness and celebrate the capacity of the individual to endure and demonstrate resolve. By way of contrast, Bingham observers that female biopics often enable highly visible and successful women to be acknowledged and recognised in a prevailing American culture, which struggles to acknowledge such women in the first place.[5]

What makes Bingham's work valuable is that he is not concerned with whether a biopic is historically accurate or representative. Rather the focal point is more on generic convention and the creative role of directors and their artistic and casting interventions. So in any discussion of a biopic, it would be more fecund to think about the wider context of production, casting and reception of the biopic, which in turn might reveal evidence about authenticity and truthfulness. At that point, we might reasonably ask what might be at stake if such a biopic attracts public controversy even opprobrium. Or, alternatively, some biopics have been celebrated and most praised such as Academy and BAFTA award-winning *12 Years a Slave* (2013, directed by Steve McQueen), which was based on a nineteenth-century memoir of an American slave called Solomon Northup.

Ealing Studios' *Scott of the Antarctic* would have, at first glance, been an unlikely candidate for potential iconoclasm. In the late 1940s and early 1950s, under the leadership of Michael Balcon, the Studios enjoyed a public reputation for producing well-received comedies such as *Hue and Cry* (1947), *Kind Hearts and Coronets* (1949), *Passport to Pimlico*

(1949), *The Lavender Hill Mob* (1951) and *The Man in the White Suit* (1951). But Ealing was also associated with films that were closer to the Scott project in the sense of addressing heroism, endurance and resilience. Two prime examples bisecting the *Scott of the Antarctic* release were World War II-era dramas: *San Demetrio, London* (1943) and *The Cruel Sea* (1953). Making a historic biopic which 'narrates, exhibits, and celebrates the life of a subject in order to demonstrate, investigate, or question his or her importance in the world' was somewhat of a departure from the post-war studio norm of film comedy.[6] But it fitted nonetheless with Ealing Studios' wartime and post-war record of producing films that celebrated 'Britishness', even if in the case of Scott what was being recognised was the heroic failure of an expedition to return safely from the South Pole after reaching it in January 1912. What was going to be challenging, however, was how to confront the awkward fact that the expedition's team died only 11 miles short of One Ton depot on their return, and were earlier second place when it came to the so-called 'race to the pole'. While there was plenty of tales of hardship, steeliness and endurance, it was also a challenging story to portray because it was so well known. There was no element of narrative suspense leading perhaps other critics to conclude that the film was 'boring and [a] ridiculous undertaking'.[7]

The historic biopic can and does become more complicated when the person or persons being depicted are either still alive and/or if there are surviving family relatives and friends to consider. The decision to make a film about Scott and his last expedition was taken in 1945, and thus just over 30 years after the explorer's death. Scott's widow, Kathleen, and immediate family including his son Peter were very much alive. The relatives of the other four members of the final party were also present. Consulting with the relatives and academic authorities at the SPRI was integral to the filming production process. The decision to cast the respected English actor John Mills was also a considered one because of his public popularity in wartime films such as *We Dive at Dawn* (1943) and *Waterloo Road* (1945). His physical resemblance to the late Robert Falcon Scott was also said to have influenced casting. Balcon recalled some years later that 'My first choice to play the part of Scott was John Mills ... John worked hard ... his sincerity comes through in everything he does'.[8] After a series of auditions, popular actors Derek Bond and Kenneth More were offered the role of Captain Oates and Teddy Evans, respectively.

Ealing Studios' famous producer Sir Michael Balcon sought formal permission from surviving family relatives and the production team spent a great deal of time researching the expedition. Their support was publicly acknowledged in the closing film titles of the film, 'This film could not have been made without the generous cooperation of the survivors and the relatives of late members of Scott's Last Expedition.' Balcon was determined that the film should address the Scott expedition as sensitively as possible, recognising that the topic had been listed by the Ministry of Information in 1939 as suitable for propaganda-making about British heroes.[9] Public awareness of Scott grew substantially with the publication of some of the photographs and silent film taken by Herbert Ponting and the publication of *Scott's Last Expedition* (extracts from his journals) in a cheaper paperback edition in 1923.[10] Although edited and amended by the creator of Peter Pan, J.M. Barrie, in the form of a final 'death scene', Scott's last messages and letters were widely understood as indicative of heroism and self-sacrifice which chimed with a Britain betwixt two world wars. The Scott film contributed to a re-enchantment with the original expedition, and book sales of the journals reportedly surged in 1948–1949. The publishers, John Murray, released a special school edition in 1949.

The filmmakers worked closely with SPRI and at one stage it was hoped that the film project would offer the research institute a welcome funding boost. The partnership with Ealing Studios was not quite as profitable as anticipated. Colin Bertram, the new director of SPRI, was in regular contact with representatives of the Studios, and initially the sum of 100 guineas was paid in 1948 for 'professional services'. Later, approaches were made by the Foreign Office to try and secure further payments from the Studios for SPRI. Ealing Studios confirmed that no further payments would be possible in 1950 because of a combination of higher than expected entertainment taxes and disappointing audience figures[11] Balcon later wrote about his frustration with such an outcome given earlier hopes for recognition and success, 'Although I knew there would be enormous difficulties in making a worthy film of this great story – to say nothing of the hazards and cost – the decision to go ahead was taken at long last'.[12] While disappointing, the British government departments responsible for polar matters (in the main the Colonial and Foreign Offices) alongside specialist agencies such as FIDS and academic centres led by SPRI recognised that profile-raising needed attention. FIDS employees, for example, were encouraged to speak at the

Royal Geographical Society and contribute when invited to BBC radio broadcasting.

As part of Ealing Studios' commitment to authenticity, a former FIDS field scientist and surveyor, David James, was hired to advise on polar conditions and expeditionary techniques. James was also a former member of the Royal Navy Volunteer Reserve and involved with the evacuation of Dunkirk in 1940. Ealing hoped that James would play his part in supporting their reputation for making films that celebrated team spirit, pluckiness and public service. Scott's diaries and journals were an important primary source and other explorers and geographers were interviewed about Scott's personality and leadership style. Surviving family members of the expedition team were consulted in the pursuit of authenticity and legitimacy.[13]

It was a Royal Command film, scored by leading English composer Ralph Vaughan Williams. Balcon wanted to produce an audio-visual spectacle, 'We soon realised that colour would give enormous additional value to the picture, with a great range of exciting and colourful backgrounds'.[14] A huge sum of money was spent on the film itself, with an outlay of over £370,000 and high hopes that the movie would succeed in the UK and the United States.[15] In reality, the film was never quite as successful as Ealing had hoped or even expected. As Balcon noted ruefully, 'The American public has no interest in failure, even if it is heroic failure, and certainly they do not easily accept other people's legends'.[16] What might have hurt even further was that the production of the film was so rooted in attention to historic detail and geographical verisimilitude. Balcon appointed two scriptwriters, Walter Meade and Ivor Montagu, to work on the screenplay using expedition diaries to provide historic authenticity and interviews with survivors to gain insights into the likely interpersonal dynamics of the party. The film's sombre and respectful evaluation of the expedition spoke strongly to an austerity and ration-hit post-war Britain rather than a United States with its own 'heroic stories' to tell past and present.[17]

It was some years later that Scott and his party were to be lampooned by a post-war generation of comics, actors and writers led by Peter Cook and Monty Python. With the exception of D.H. Lawrence's *Women in Love* (1920), which features allegorical criticism of Scott's death through the demise of Gerard in the European Alps, there is little evidence prior to 1948 of Scott's reputation being traduced.[18] The English novelist, Peter Vansittart recalled in his book, *In the Fifties*, a game he used to play with his contemporaries. He would read out extracts from Scott's diaries including, 'We are showing that Englishmen can still die with a bold spirit, fighting it out to the end…'.[19] He recorded friends laughing at the performance but also amended his rendition later implying that the words had been issued at the Warsaw Ghetto of 1944. In that case of deliberate mistaken identity, he recalled his friends had applauded and nodded their approval.

For his liberal-left acquaintances at least, the Scott story no longer exercised any grip on their collective imagination. Scott's poetic musings about the expedition and its painful demise appear capable of either mockery or experimentation in a way that suggests that they might no longer be indicative of a stoical Englishness.

Screening Scott

The screenplay for *Scott of the Antarctic* does not address the broad sweep of the life and death of Robert Scott. After a prologue, which addresses the build-up to the 1910–1912 Terra Nova expedition, Scott's credentials as naval officer and polar explorer are addressed. The audience is not offered any insights into Scott's childhood in Devon and early life. Rather attention is given to how Scott gathered around him a group of men including Captain Oates, Taff Evans, Bill Wilson and Teddy Evans. What we learn is that the men were eager to fuse scientific enquiry with adventure and historic priority (i.e. being first to the South Pole) and that the expedition required powerful sponsors including the Royal Navy and the Royal Geographical Society, and a programme of events designed to raise sponsorship. Devastatingly, for the British party, they learn later that the celebrated Norwegian explorer, Roald Amundsen is also intent on reaching the South Pole. Whether Scott and his party care for it or not, the rival expeditions are in effect in a 'race to the pole'.

The remainder of the film concentrates on the arrival of the party in Antarctica and the final planning and execution of the expedition's route along the Beardmore Glacier and then over the immense polar plateau. The film depicts the arduousness of the trek, the perils and pitfalls of man-hauling and Scott's reluctance to use dogs, the arrival of the final party and their painful demise on their return from the South Pole. One challenge for the director and his team was to focus on a realist and melodramatic modality for the biopic. Audiences needed to be left with a powerful sense of the elemental qualities of Antarctica, which in 1948 was still as remote as the moon for British and international publics. While there was some controversy regarding the accuracy of Scott's contemporaneous temperature readings, there was little doubt that the party had been buffeted by extreme cold and wind. Climate scientist Susan Solomon wrote in *The Coldest March* that Scott was right to note that the coldness had been freakish. It was so cold, with temperatures below minus 40 degrees centigrade that the party's clothing froze to them, their sleeping bags provided no warmth and relief from the cold, and man-hauling became insufferable because it was so cold that the metal runners were no longer lubricating the underlying ice. The sluggish sledges were deathtraps.

What helped to convey the elemental nature of Scott's struggle with the coldness were the filming locations and the use of Technicolor. Filming was based in Norway and Switzerland, with filmed footage of Antarctica, and this commitment to authenticity helped to convey well the immense and forbidding landscapes encountered by the final party. Osmond Borradaile was responsible for the Antarctic imagery; Geoffrey Unsworth collected film from Norway and Switzerland; and Jack Cardiff was responsible for fusing on-site footage with the studio reconstruction of the final death scene. The filming of the tent interior is arguably one of the least successful moments of the film, as Cardiff struggled to secure a sense of melodramatic authenticity. By way of contrast, one of the most noteworthy qualities of *Scott* was the use of the extreme long shots of the Antarctic landscapes and seascapes, which were used effectively in order to convey to audiences what Scott and his party had to tackle: a 1600 mile return trek from Cape Evans to the South Pole perched on the polar plateau at some 9000 feet above sea level. Norwegian and Swiss footage of glaciers and mountains helped to frame the 'Antarctic' as isolated and isolating, austere yet beautiful, daunting but also beguiling. Overall, trade press reviewers such as *Monthly Film Bulletin* endorsed the artistic labour, 'Magnificent exterior photography, capturing the grandeur and beauty of the Antarctic and, in contrast, portraying its treachery and ferocity, will rank as some of the finest ever seen'.[20]

As Bingham would note, however, *Scott of the Antarctic* is unashamedly a biopic about white men. If there is another 'co-star' then it is the empty Antarctic landscapes and seascapes. By way of contrast, women play minor if largely supportive roles. Diana Churchill's portrayal of Kathleen Scott is the epitome of Bingham's observation that wives are shown as unquestionably supportive of their husbands. There is only a moment in the film where that bond of loyalty is questioned by the wife of Bill Wilson. Oriana Wilson, played by Anne Firth, is resentful that her husband agreed to accompany Scott again to the Antarctic. Sensing correctly, as it turns out, he may not return alive. But her resentment is fleeting and ultimately not sufficiently disruptive to the participation of Wilson.

There are only four female characters in the entire film and within the first thirty minutes, women disappear from the script and film itself altogether. This is a film explicitly about a small group of British men and their aspirations to explore and study Antarctica. The dynamics between the men and the homo-sociality of expedition, especially in the confines of the tent, is recurring. As Perry noted, 'As in so many Ealing films… the women are subordinated to the totally passive role – they wait patiently at home in Britain knowing they were never to see their husbands again'.[21] Even when Scott is seen lecturing across England before the expedition's departure to Antarctica, the audience is composed overwhelmingly of men. Women do not appear to be interested in the expedition and are certainly given no agency to question the wisdom or desirability of the venture itself.

What is less easy to discern though is what motivates Robert Scott's decision-making as the director steers clear of potential controversy over Scott's leadership and experimentation with mechanised vehicles and Siberian ponies. John Mills recalled some forty years later that the film was not going to probe the 'darker' elements of Scott's personality, 'He was a fascinatingly complex character – a born leader, with tremendous physical stamina and courage. He had a quick temper, which he often found difficult to control. This I was never allowed to show, because of the possibility of upsetting relations still living'.[22] Disputes with expedition members are not dwelled upon and we are never told why Scott agreed to take a party of five when pre-expedition planning had assumed there would only be four. There is no resolution to what audience members asked Scott in Yorkshire while fundraising—why would you want to go to the South Pole? It is a curious if brief scene because it introduces the spectre of doubt but then does not return with any resolution. Did Scott, for example, think that the scientific and even literary legacy of the expedition would be sufficient to resolve such matters?

The film in short concentrates its creative energies on exploring what it might have felt like to have been on that final expedition, and the immense challenges facing the men who were battling against unrelenting elemental forces. John Mills' voice-over, using extracts from Scott's diaries and journals were intended to add historical authenticity. What has often been under-estimated, however, is the role of the musical score by Ralph Vaughan Williams in creating a more ambivalent atmosphere to the film. Vaughan Williams was approached in 1947 and in her memoir of her husband his wife, Ursula, reveals that he was initially reluctant to accept the commission.[23] While she notes that he was drawn to the 'strange world of ice and storm' this was tempered by a view that 'he despised the heroism that risked lives unnecessarily'.[24] Putting personal reservations to one side, she recalled that nonetheless, 'He was excited by the demands which the setting of the film made on his invention to find musical equivalents of ice, of wind bellowing over the great, uninhabited desolation, of stubborn and impassable ridges of black and ice-covered rock, and to suggest man's endeavour to overcome the rigours of this bleak land and to match the mortal spirit against the elements'.[25]

During World War I, Ralph Vaughan Williams served in the Royal Army Medical Corp and had direct experience of the suffering of the war dead and injured. His ambivalence towards Scott's demise meant that he was not an obvious choice but it is reasonable to suspect that Ealing Studios did not appreciate his judgement about the Terra Nova expedition. Ursula Vaughan Williams was writing nearly twenty years after her late husband's composition of the musical score. What Vaughan Williams did produce, however, was widely acknowledged by film critics to add insights to the sombre even menacing nature of Antarctica. The musical score with its eerie and haunting qualities was not one that Ealing Studios was expecting because it was thought to foretell the death of Scott and his party. Vaughan Williams, working with Scott's journals, which spoke of the howling winds and unrelenting cold, was attempting to convey to audiences the terror-like qualities of the Antarctic landscape.

Although not an exercise in explicit debunking, later critics have contended that Vaughan Williams's musical score conveyed a nihilistic view of Antarctica. The musical scholar Daniel Grimley contends that 'far from being an apotheosis of the Romantic sublime, Vaughan Williams once again invokes the image of Antarctic nature as unnatural or mechanistic, a domain which operates according to systems and controls beyond the mastery or interpretative understanding of individual human agency. In this sense, Vaughan Williams's work reveals a deeper truth about the Antarctic landscape than that offered in familiar accounts of Scott's voyage, including the Ealing Studios film'.[26] Vaughan Williams's musical score, which formed the inspiration for *Sinfonia Antarctica* (1953), presents a coded warning about the limits of human capacity to master the earth. With the onset of the cold war and the nuclear age, it is possible that the musical score (despite denials from Vaughan Williams at the time) speaks to concerns beyond an Edwardian era polar expedition.

Film Critics and *Scott of the Antarctic*

Although selected as a Royal Command Film, *Scott of the Antarctic* did not receive the British Film Award of 1949. *The Fallen Idol* (1948), a murder mystery drama starring Ralph Richardson, was the top pick. Despite the impressive production budget, *Scott* only recouped around £215,000 and was in financial terms, an investment that failed to break even.[27] It was all rather galling given that post-war British cinema was more generally enjoying something of a boom in terms of participatory audiences around the UK's 4000 odd cinemas.[28] Ealing Studios' failure to turn a profit was notable and for all the commitment to authenticity and veracity, the film critics were rather divided on the film and its merits.

What becomes apparent from reading the trade press reviews is that most professional critics praised the film for its technical qualities. There was general praise for the use of Technicolor and the value overall of the on-location filming in Norway and Switzerland. Disappointingly, the actual footage from Antarctica did not attract quite the same praise, in particular the usage of polar footage at the start of the film was judged to have been poorly edited. Where there is less praise, more generally, it lies in the areas of film sequencing, plot and narrative, Scott's character and leadership style and the lack of melodrama.

The film's plot and structure was subject to particular criticism by the film critic writing for *Sunday Dispatch*. In their review published on 5 December 1948, it is observed that '*Scott of the Antarctic* is a technically competent film...but something is missing from the film that prevents it from being termed "great"... the mistake of concentrating on Scott's epic march to the South Pole and too little on the men who made it... In no way can the actors concerned be held responsible for this failure to make the men they portray seem absolutely real...[Notwithstanding that reservation] every man, women and child in the British Empire must go and see it.' What is not clear by the end of that review is why the film is sufficiently compelling. The point about delving further into the character of the party and individual personalities was something that John Mills later acknowledged as a failure of the film itself. However, at the time there was no intention to make anything but a film that conveyed a spirit and unity of purpose.

Other critics were even more robust in their criticism of the film. Writing in the *Daily Express*, Leonard Mosley remarked that, 'I felt that the Director missed the full impact of overwhelming disappointment when Scott and his men found that they had been beaten to the Pole...a good film...It is only that it seems a much more splendid story in my mind than it looked to me on screen.' In the *Daily Telegraph*, disappointment was made manifest noting, 'where imagination has filled in the gaps in the written document the effect is less happy... humour introduced at intervals to relieve polar monotony remained, for the most part, snowbound. The sight of Amundsen's flag at the Pole did not stir the emotion as it should... the story which should have had in dramatic form the power of Greek tragedy to move pity and terror, has become on the screen just another adventure story, more monotonous than most.' These reviews would have been bitterly disappointing to Ealing Studios because of their investment in producing a film that was faithful to the pioneering spirit of the expedition and a desire to represent the Scott story as uplifting to a country recovering from war.[29] It was supposed to be 'epic' in the sense of being sweeping, spectacular and supportive of Scott as a truly heroic character.

What film critics were exposing, more generally, was a failure of this epic biopic to move audiences. Rather than provoking feelings of admiration and awe, they charged Ealing Studios with producing a film that failed to capitalise on the Scott myth. After thirty years of public commemoration and exposure through the publication of Scott's journals, public recognition of the Scott story was high. Yet that also created a dilemma given that there was no obvious opportunity for suspense as it was well known that Amundsen had beaten Scott to the South Pole on 14 December 1911. Where there were opportunities to produce an 'edgier' film, the critics concluded that Ealing Studios declined to take these opportunities in the film itself. Two opportunities were identified. The first involves a seemingly trivial incident involving Edgar Evans and an accident which left him with a cut finger. Failing to heal properly, the finger became gangrenous and Evans was later further incapacitated by a head injury as the party travelled through the Beardmore Glacier. The film appears to endorse Evans's stoicism and refusal to complain about the true state of his injuries rather than consider that Evans's reluctance to admit how badly he was injured could compromise the safety of his companions.

The second example which caught the eye of the critics was where the film failed to reflect more critically on Scott's style of leadership. Earlier in the film, Oates is shown to be inept when it came to packing supplies on the sledges, and they later fell off because they were not sufficiently secure. The expedition party loses valuable time repacking the supplies. Evans is clearly cross with Oates and tells Scott that 'I can't trust myself to speak, Sir'. Scott replies 'well, don't then, Taff'. But what the film does not explore in any detail is whether Scott should have been more decisive and failed in the mind of some reviewers, such as *Sight and Sound*, to capitalise on the opportunity to ask more searching questions about what motivated Scott and how did his leadership contribute or not to the failure of the expedition to return to base camp safely. Did, for example, tensions within the party contribute in any way to that failure to endure?

Malcolm Balcon and Charles Frend were not, however, going to produce and direct a film which explored these questions in any detail. Balcon believed in an 'Arnoldian best-self', implying that it was far better to focus on how individuals can put the needs of others ahead of themselves regarding their personal wealth and class interest. As Matthew Arnold wrote in *Culture and Anarchy* in 1869, 'As he explained, "in each class there are born a certain number of natures with a curiosity about their best self, with a bent for seeing things as they are, for disentangling themselves from machinery, for simply concerning themselves with reason and the will of God, and doing their best to make these prevail;—for the pursuit, in a word, of perfection"'.[30]

While laudable in principle, the film also failed to capture the imagination of American audiences. Richard Roud, in the magazine *Sight and Sound*, observed that there was little empathy for Scott's gentlemanly and stoic character. And why would American audiences want to watch a film about British failure and death? Fortunately, the Scott film never received the opprobrium directed at the biopic about the great New York Yankees baseball star, George 'Babe' Ruth in *The Babe Ruth Story* (1948). In sharp contrast, the Ealing Studios film *The Cruel Sea* (1953) did receive a positive reaction in the United States, and what helped was its focus on World War II where the United States and UK had been successful wartime allies. The film made a star of Jack Hawkins and was the most commercially successful film of 1953, including earning over £215,000 in the United States. Notably, Malcolm Balcon remarked later that, 'I think perhaps *The Cruel Sea* because when we saw that for the first time, we realised that we really had brought it off. It seemed to just gel and be absolutely right. Sometimes you don't get that feeling, but with that one we all did'.[31]

Conclusion

Francis Spufford in his accounting of ice and the English imagination concluded quite reasonably that *Scott of the Antarctic* was intended to be 'a post-war fable of class integration'.[32] It was a film on its release in late 1948 that many British school children were taken to see as part of organised visits to the cinema. An indifferent performance at the British box office coupled with disappointing audience figures in the United States meant that the film was a damp squib for Ealing Studios. The care taken with the production of *Scott of the Antarctic* meant that Robert Scott as explorer hero was not going to be debunked until years later by revisionist historian Roland Huntford and his book *Scott and Amundsen* published in 1979.[33] What made the revisionist impulse even more unlikely in 1948 was that any viewing British public including school children had been exposed to the Scott diaries, public commemoration and the publication of other volumes including *The Worst Journey in the World* by another expedition member, Apsley Cherry-Garrard.[34] All of the above contributed to and indeed reinforced a view of Scott as a largely heroic figure and Cherry-Garrard helped to convey to audiences the emotive final resting place of Scott's party:

> Their story I am not going to try to put down. They got to this point on 21 March and on the 29th all was over. Nor will I try and put down what there was in that tent. Scott lay in the centre, Bill (Wilson) on his left, with his head towards the door, and Birdie (Bowers) on his right, lying with his feet towards the door. Bill especially had died very quietly with his hands folded over his chest. Birdie also quietly. Oates's death was a very fine one. We go on tomorrow to try and find his body. He was glad that his regiment would be proud of him. They reached the Pole a month after Amundsen.[35]

Access to the Antarctic was made possible by the British government's support for the film, via the Colonial Office. With the logistical assistance of the Falkland Islands Dependencies Survey (FIDS), an organisation created in the aftermath of a secret wartime operation called Tabarin, Ealing Studios' production was considered timely. At that point in time, Britain faced rival territorial claimants (Argentina and Chile) and increasing interest from the United States in shaping the future territorial and resource governance of the polar region.[36] The FIDS, funded by the whaling industry and managed by the British Colonial Office, enjoyed an explicit mandate—collect geographical information, produce maps and ensure that British sovereignty was as secure as possible through 'effective occupation'. FIDS's work was far removed from the 'gentlemanly' model of polar exploration of the Edwardian era. There was nothing necessarily heroic in planting plaques and signposts warning others to keep out of 'Crown Lands'. The Colonial Office had hoped that an opportunistic partnership with Ealing Studios might helpfully raise public attention on Britain's polar portfolio.

Scott of the Antarctic nonetheless contributed to the rejuvenation of an Edwardian era expedition and what it represented in terms of endurance, stoicism and ultimately heroic sacrifice.[37] We also should not under-estimate what the Scott expedition also achieved in terms of scientific advancement—while the 1948 film focussed on the fate of the South Pole party the Terra Nova expedition was also dedicated to zoological research, geology, magnetism, meteorology and the undertaking of large-scale mapping and surveying. The professional photographer Herbert Ponting captured the scientific work of the expedition members. Within seven years of the release of *Scott of the Antarctic*, a new generation of school children were watching the film in the UK and New Zealand as part of fundraising efforts dedicated to supporting the Trans-Antarctic Expedition (TAE). The TAE came to fruition in March 1958 when a British-New Zealand team led by Vivian Fuchs and Ed Hillary successfully crossed the polar continent. While Fuchs and Hillary were crossing the Antarctic, *Scott of the Antarctic* lead actor John Mills was starring in a World War II movie called *Dunkirk* (1958). Even if the TAE did not capture the artistic imagination and commercial planning of Ealing Studios, it did prove that a British-led polar expedition did not have to end in disaster.

Notes

1. Debenham, 1949, p. 311.
2. Frend, 1948.
3. Langford, 2005, p. 14.
4. Custen, 1992; Bingham, 2010.
5. Bingham, 2010, pp. 9–10.
6. Bingham, 2010, p. 10.
7. Bazin, 1967, p. 157.
8. Balcon, 1969, p. 175.
9. Richards, 1993.
10. Jones, 2003.
11. Dodds, 2002.
12. Balcon, 1969, p. 171.
13. Balcon, 1948, pp. 153–55.
14. Balcon, 1948, p. 154.
15. Chapman, 2005, p. 150.
16. Balcon, 1969, p. 174.
17. Chapman, 2005.
18. Jones, 2014.
19. Vansittart, 1995, cited in Wheeler, 2010, p. 57.
20. *Monthly Film Bulletin*, 1949, p. 4.
21. Perry, 1981, p. 109.
22. Mills, 1980, p. 295.
23. Vaughan Williams, 1964.
24. Vaughan Williams, 1964, p. 279.
25. Vaughan Williams, 1964, p. 135.
26. Grimley, 2008, p. 140.
27. Cited in Chapman, 2005, p. 155.
28. Harper and Porter, 1999, p. 67.
29. Chapman, 2005, p. 147.
30. Original 1869, 1960, p. 144.
31. Cited in BBC, 2017.
32. Spufford, 1996, p. 4; Paget, 1990.
33. Huntford, 1979.
34. Cherry-Garrard, 1922.
35. Cherry-Garrard, 1922, 2010, p. 496.
36. Dodds, 2002.
37. Durgnat, 2011.

Bibliography

Anon. 1949. 'Scott of the Antarctic', *Monthly Film Bulletin* 16 (181), p. 4.

Arnold, M. 1960. *Culture and Anarchy. The Complete Prose Works of Matthew Arnold*. Ann Arbor: University of Michigan Press.

Balcon, M. 1948. 'The Technical Problems of Scott of the Antarctic', *Sight and Sound* 17 (68), pp. 153–55.

Balcon, M. 1969. *Michael Balcon Presents... A Lifetime of Films*. London: Hutchinson.

Barr, C. 1977. *Ealing Studios*. London: Cameron and Taylor.

Bazin, A. 1967. *What Is Cinema Volume 1*. Berkeley: University of California Press.

BBC. 2017. *Fifties British War Films: Days of Glory*. Available at http://www.bbc.co.uk/programmes/b01pkj2m.

Bingham, D. 2010. *Whose Lives Are They Anyway? The Biopic as Contemporary Film Genre*. London: Rutgers University Press.

Chapman, J. 2005. *Past and Present: National Identity and the British Historical Film*. London: I.B. Tauris.

Chapman, J. 2006. 'Cinemas of Empire', *History Compass* 4 (5), pp. 814–19.

Cherry-Gerrard, A. 1922. *The Worst Journey in the World: Antarctica 1910–1913* (Reprinted by Oxford University Press 2010).

Cherry-Garrard, A. 2010. *The Worst Journey of the World*. London: Vintage.

Custen, G. 1992. *Bio/Pics: How Hollywood Constructs Public History*. Rutgers: Rutgers University Press.

Debenham, F. 1949. 'Scott of the Antarctic: A Personal Opinion', *Polar Record*, 5, pp. 37–38.

Dodds, K. 2002. *Pink Ice: Britain and the South Atlantic Empire*. London: I.B. Tauris.

Drazin, C. 1998. *The Finest Years: British Cinema of the 1940s*. London: André Deutsch.

Durgnat, R. 2011. *A Mirror for England: British Movies from Austerity to Affluence*. 2nd edition. London: BFI.

Frend, C. (Director) 1948. *Scott of the Antarctic*. Ealing Studios.

Grimley, D. 2008. 'Music, Ice and the "Geometry of Fear": The Landscapes of Vaughan Williams' Sinfonia Antarctica', *Musical Quarterly* 91 (1), pp. 116–50.

Harper, S., and Porter, V. 1999. 'Cinema Audience Tastes in 1950s Britain', *Journal of Popular British Cinema* 2, pp. 66–82.

Huntford, R. 1979. *Scott and Amundsen*. London: Hodder and Stoughton.

Jones, M. 2003. *The Last Great Quest*. Oxford: Oxford University Press.

Jones, M. 2014. 'The Truth About Captain Scott': The Last Place on Earth, Debunking, Sexuality and Decline in the 1980s', *Journal of Imperial and Commonwealth History* 42, 857–881.

Langford, B. 2005. *Film Genre*. Edinburgh: Edinburgh University Press.
Lawrence, D. H. 1920. *Women in Love*. London: Thomas Seltzer.
Mills, J. 1980. *Up in the Clouds, Gentlemen Please*. London: Orion.
Paget, D. 1990. *True Stories? Documentary Drama on Radio, Screen and Stage*. Manchester: Manchester University Press.
Perry, G. 1981. *Forever Ealing*. London: Pavilion.
Richards, J. 1993. *Film and British National Identity*. Manchester: Manchester University Press.
Spicer, A. 2001. *Typical Men: The Representation of Masculinity in Popular British Cinema*. London: I.B. Tauris.
Spufford, F. 1996. *I May be Some Time: Ice and the English Imagination*. London: Faber and Faber.
Stubbs, J. 2013. *Historical Film: A Critical Introduction*. London: Bloomsbury Academic.
Variety. 1947. 'Review: Scott of the Antarctic', *Variety* [Online]. 31 December. Available from http://variety.com/1947/film/reviews/scott-of-the-antarctic-1200415779/.
Vaughan Williams, U. 1964. *RVW*. Oxford: Oxford University Press.
Wheeler, S. 2010. *Terra Incognita: Travels in Antarctica*. London: Vintage.

Inside JFK's White House: The Myth of John F. Kennedy and *Thirteen Days* (2000)

Andrew Priest

John Fitzgerald Kennedy (JFK) was the first movie star president. He was handsome, telegenic, and eloquent. He had a beautiful wife and together they cultivated an image, which Jacqueline Kennedy later termed 'Camelot'.[1] He was then struck down in his prime, forever fixed in the popular imagination as the shining symbol of unfulfilled hope for America and the world.

As if to underline his film star qualities, Kennedy was also the first sitting President of the United States to be the subject of a Hollywood movie.[2] In June 1963, just five months before he was assassinated, Warner Brothers released *PT-109*, a motion picture based on Kennedy's experiences during World War II. Directed by Leslie H. Martinson, Cliff Robertson played the young naval officer although at just six years younger than Kennedy, Robertson was almost 15 years older than the president had been during his wartime experiences in the Pacific. If Robertson was miscast, this was nothing compared to the financial

A. Priest (✉)
University of Essex, Colchester, UK
e-mail: apriest@essex.ac.uk

T. S. Freeman and D. L. Smith (eds.), *Biography and History in Film*, Palgrave Studies in the History of the Media,
https://doi.org/10.1007/978-3-319-89408-9_12

problems, production delays, and interference from the White House and Kennedy family that bedevilled the making of the film. Kennedy confidantes were particularly keen to ensure that the movie portrayed the president favourably (the president himself apparently helped pick Robertson), and this caused numerous tensions with the production company. While the film in no-way turned out to be disparaging of the president, *PT-109* was a disaster when it was released. Critically panned and a box office flop, it disappeared almost without trace.[3]

Since then, many actors have played President Kennedy in Hollywood productions, often more successfully than Robertson did. These include Martin Sheen (twice in *The Missiles of October* in 1974 and the 1983 *Kennedy* miniseries), Patrick Dempsey in 1993s *JFK: Reckless Youth*, and James Marsden in *The Butler* released in 2013. With the recent film *Jackie* (2016) starring Natalie Portman as Jacqueline Bouvier Kennedy trying to come to terms with her husband's death, it seems there is no let-up in the public's hunger for depictions of the thirty-fifth president and those close to him.

One of the most successful Kennedy portrayals is Bruce Greenwood's in Roger Donaldson's film *Thirteen Days.* Released at the end of 2000, *Thirteen Days* follows the inner workings of the White House during the tense and tumultuous stand-off between the United States and the Soviet Union over the stationing of Soviet missiles in Cuba, the so-called Cuban Missile Crisis, in late 1962. Greenwood's sensitive portrayal of the president along with the fascinating depiction of the discussions by members of his Executive Committee (ExComm) during these crucial days helped make the movie a critical and commercial success. Added to this, the fact that the film was based on the secret tapes that Kennedy himself had made of these meetings and the subsequent book of those tapes by two leading historians of the missile crisis and the film looked something like the perfect historical movie: a cracking story, a great cast, *and* historical accuracy.[4]

The film has not been without its controversies, however. In particular, some historians have faulted its focus on the figure of Kenneth O'Donnell, played by Kevin Costner. O'Donnell was a Kennedy family friend from Harvard and a special advisor to the president, effectively his appointments secretary. During the film, Costner's character is always at the centre of the action, whether in private conference with the Kennedy brothers, helping Kennedy to restrain the hawkish Joint Chiefs of Staff (JCS), or facilitating a back channel to the Kremlin. There is just one problem—O'Donnell was not involved in many of these scenarios, only occasionally attending and rarely speaking during the ExComm meetings.[5] Robert McNamara, Kennedy's Secretary of Defense, was blunt in an interview shortly after the film was released. The figure of O'Donnell as portrayed by Costner was 'Totally fictional… Kenny O'Donnell didn't have any role whatsoever in the missile crisis'.[6] A group of experts on the events of late 1962 was even more dismissive in the wake of the film's release: O'Donnell 'did little more during the crisis than make sure the coffee was fresh'.[7]

As Raluca Lucia Cimpean has recently suggested, historical inaccuracies on a 'minimal scale', including using composite or fictionalised characters and invented scenes, are all-but inevitable in Hollywood movies, even in docudramas such as this one that purport to inform. This is in large part because of the complexities of the subject matters they examine.[8] Placing O'Donnell's character at the centre of the narrative is clearly meant to serve at least two important purposes for viewers of the film who are likely only to have hazy notions of missiles in Cuba decades after the events it depicts. The first is to provide something of an everyman's perspective on the crisis. Because O'Donnell was not a central figure in the administration, his character operates as an outsider watching the proceedings, even if he is involved in them in this fictionalised version. Secondly, it gives the viewer an insight into the informal policy process outside of the meeting room, and beyond the reach of the tape recorder. Costner's O'Donnell has personal access to the president and offers the ultimate insider's account of how JFK handled what many regard as the greatest post-war crisis in international politics. These perspectives—outsider and insider—at first glance in tension with one another but actually complementary, are important innovations of the film's narrative, and, despite the overplaying of his role in the discussions, largely jibe with O'Donnell's recollections in his sympathetic memoir of JFK.[9]

In other ways, however, *Thirteen Days* does what most, if not all, portrayals of Kennedy on film do, reaffirming his mystique and framing him as the most alluring and tragic of presidents, and as national and international icon. As this chapter suggests, this mystique is essential to the Hollywood Kennedy. Of course, not everyone views Kennedy in the same way, but, as Paul H. Santa Cruz argues, 'Americans all remember him' because he already represents what French historian Pierre Nora has termed a site of memory (*lieu de mémoire*) in American history.[10]

Because of this, however much any fictionalised account of Kennedy appears to provide new insights, it must conform to pre-existing, popular notions of his character and politics, burnishing his image as a cerebral, wise, and ultimately heroic figure.[11]

Thirteen Days primarily associates Kennedy with a particular view of the time in which he lived. For the filmmakers, to borrow Bernard von Bothmer's phrase, he represents the 'good sixties'. This is the mythical period that many Americans regard either as a prolongation of the quiet, safe, and conservative 1950s (itself, of course, a myth) or the promise of a liberal future that never came to pass amidst the destruction of American cities and the Vietnam War in the second half of the decade (the 'bad sixties').[12]

Here, the moment in which the film was made, during the last gasps of the administration of Democrat Bill Clinton, is significant. Clinton utilised and manipulated extant public understandings of Kennedy—the man and the politician—during his presidential bid and term of office to suggest there was a connection between them. Perhaps most obviously, the forty-second president made prodigious use of an image of himself as a young man meeting the thirty-fifth president at the White House in July 1963. In developing such conscious links, Clinton suggested that both men were liberal on relatively uncontentious issues—especially the promotion of equal rights for African Americans—while simultaneously distancing himself from the ones that had become more controversial in the years since Kennedy's death, especially the War on Poverty. This War was a policy initiative that had been supported by Kennedy but only enacted later by his successor, Lyndon Johnson, and which President Ronald Reagan had famously declared lost by the 1980s amid the rise of conservatism and the rollback of much of its legislation.[13] Such a distinction between contentious and uncontentious issues was especially important as Clinton dealt with the Republican Party's resurgence in Congress from the mid-1990s, a further backlash against much of the liberalism that Kennedy had espoused.[14] *Thirteen Days* thus reflects something of the bipartisan spirit that, by this time, pervaded popular views of Kennedy and his times, uniting Republicans and Democrats in their admiration for the man and what they respectively believed he represented.[15]

The film also reaches back to a time of supposed American innocence before the Vietnam War, showing Kennedy's resolution of a major foreign policy crisis in a deft diplomatic manner that many Americans felt was lacking in the confusing post-Cold War 1990s. More than just its tone, therefore, the film's view of the recent past is reflected in its very subject matter and the events it portrays, and the film is as significant for what it omits as for what it chooses to include. Vietnam, for example, is mentioned only once at the beginning of the film, a reference that rightly suggests it was one among a number of foreign policy problems that Kennedy was attending to at that time (and, from his perspective, minor in comparison to the one in Cuba), but with no attention to the Kennedy administration's massive expansion of the American commitment there. More importantly on the topic of the film, there is nothing on why Fidel Castro might have wanted to place nuclear missiles in Cuba or why Soviet premier Nikita Khrushchev was willing to supply them. Of course, as in their dalliances with fiction, historical films have to be selective in the events they represent and it is often the case that political context is lacking in Hollywood accounts of past events. However, in the case of *Thirteen Days*, the *Cuban* missile crisis is recast largely as an *American* affair, omitting most of the global dimensions, which is significant in a film that purports to be about international politics. It does make reference to the status of Berlin and potential retribution that the Soviets might take there, but only to emphasise the enormous nuclear threat that this would pose to the United States, ignoring almost entirely the perspectives of the Soviet Union and Cuba and making only fleeting reference to US allies.

The exception to this lack of international context is contained in several allusions to the Bay of Pigs invasion. This infamous episode when Central Intelligence Agency (CIA) trained exiles attempted to invade Cuba and topple Castro's government in April 1961, just weeks into Kennedy's presidency, crops up a number of times in the protagonists' discussions. Yet even here the scope is limited. The filmmakers make no attempt to explain this event or tell us how it might help us understand developments in Cuba in October 1962. The film merely begins with footage of nuclear explosions (suggesting what might have been had Kennedy not been as resolute as he was) followed by U2 spy planes photographing the Soviet missile sites before they are shown to the president. There is virtually nothing at all on the measures Kennedy took against the Castro regime, including the attempted destabilisation of the government there and assassination attempts against Castro himself in the wake of the Bay of Pigs humiliation, or the ongoing US embargo on Cuba.[16]

Instead, the film recasts the Bay of Pigs episode as a personal learning experience for Kennedy, a rooky presidential error that taught him important lessons about overseas intervention and international diplomacy which he then applied during the missile crisis. While there is certainly something to this idea, its importance here is in presenting Kennedy as a person who is willing to learn from his mistakes and grow as a person as he finesses his understanding of the presidency. This notion of growth is an important component of the Kennedy myth because it suggests that, while benefitting from his prestigious position in US society, he overcame serious challenges to his privileged life. These were often health-related and his chronic illnesses along with the sometimes-terrible ways his doctors treated them have been recounted in uncomfortable detail by recent biographers. (They are referenced obliquely in *Thirteen Days* when he takes pills, implied to be for his back pain, before wincing as he proceeds to sit in his favourite rocking chair).[17] They were also moral and intellectual, suggesting that Kennedy's political career was one in which he came to understand the importance of America's position in the world and the need for social progress at home. This continued and advanced during his time in the highest office as he faced further challenges, whether in the guise of Soviet adventurism abroad or segregation in the southern United States. The film therefore advances the idea of the Cuban missile crisis as the ultimate personal challenge for Kennedy, a quest for knowledge and growth, which he successfully surmounted.[18]

By far the most important lesson that JFK learned from the Bay of Pigs fiasco, *Thirteen Days* suggests, was to stand up to the JCS and especially Air Force Chief Curtis LeMay, in the movie a bug-eyed warmonger played by Kevin Conway. LeMay regards Kennedy and his brother, Attorney General Robert F. Kennedy (Steven Culp), as effete and weak. As he puts it at one point: 'Those goddamn Kennedys are gonna destroy this country if we don't do something about this!' This tension between Kennedy and the military is established early in the narrative when O'Donnell tells the president that the situation is 'starting to smell like the Bay of Pigs all over again'. Kennedy responds to this by complaining that when listening to his more hawkish advisors 'I kept seeing Lemnitzer and Dulles, telling me all I had to do was sign on the dotted line, and the invasion would succeed… and Castro would be gone, just, easy, just like that'. In recalling the advice he received from former chairman of JCS Lyman Lemnitzer and erstwhile Secretary of State John

Foster Dulles, the film simultaneously implies he was tricked into the Bay of Pigs invasion by the previous Eisenhower administration while establishing the supposed tension between the Kennedys and the politico-military-intelligence establishment. This is subsequently developed and reinforced, especially by O'Donnell: 'What did you think Congress was gonna do? Offer you unconditional support? Kiss your Catholic ass? They don't think we even deserve to be here', he tells the president at one point. The narrative arc of the film is therefore less about the conflict between the United States and the Soviet Union and more concerned with the struggles within the Kennedy administration, between those advocating a blockade and air strikes, and between the Kennedy clan and the others who are perceived to be jealous of its power.[19] In this way, the film conforms to other popular accounts of Kennedy suggesting that he was an anti-establishment figure overcoming various forces reined against him.

This also applies to the other historical touchstone of the film: the memory of Munich. On this issue, Kennedy's personal story and recent international history are, once again, intertwined but in a different way from the Bay of Pigs. During the early stages of his struggle with what to do about the missiles in Cuba, sceptics focus on the Kennedy family brand, which is tainted by association with the appeasement of Nazi Germany, rather than Kennedy himself. References to Munich—of which there are several—are thus double-edged in this retelling of the Cuban crisis. On the one hand, they represent the American view of the Soviets as being like Hitler in the 1930s, suggesting that putting off the day of reckoning will simply make it worse when that day comes (Secretary of State Dean Rusk tells the president: 'Appeasement only makes the aggressor more aggressive. And the Soviets will be emboldened to push us even harder'). On the other, they target Kennedy because of his father's accommodation of the Nazis when he was ambassador in London during the 1930s (presidential advisor Dean Acheson muses: 'Let's hope appeasement doesn't run in families. I fear weakness does').[20] Again, the fact that Kennedy proves all these cynics to be wrong demonstrates his ability to grow and mature, fitting with the film's dominant theme.

In fact, *Thirteen Days* distorts Kennedy's early attitudes toward the nuclear crisis in Cuba in 1962, at the very least downplaying, if not outright ignoring, his initially hawkish response. Rather than being cowed by the memory of Munich and the Bay of Pigs, Kennedy seriously considered an invasion of the territory to remove the missiles during the first days. Thus his position was much closer to that of the JCS than the film suggests. Similarly, and taking its lead from Robert Kennedy's subsequent account of the missile crisis, it also significantly overplays his later role in the decision to strike a secret deal with the Soviets to trade the removal of Jupiter missiles in Turkey for those in Cuba, alongside a promise not to invade. Certainly, it misrepresents the extent to which this idea originated with him.[21]

The significance here is not that the film alters the historical record per se—this is often the case in Hollywood movies—but that the subject matter and the way the filmmakers present it is designed to paint a particular portrait of Kennedy. His success as president can hardly be said to have been in his legislative achievements, which were slight during his short term, so his half-hearted attempts at civil rights reforms and faltering responses to domestic crises are rarely the stuff of Kennedy biopics. Instead, Kennedy's real success is shown to have been in foreign policy and in remaking the office of the presidency.

This is especially important in the ways he interacts with those around him. The film shows Kennedy drawing out key traits of those individuals in his administration who journalist David Halberstam dubbed the 'Best and the Brightest'.[22] This process, it implies, may be wasted on the JCS—who are old and stuck in their ways—but it is an important part of the president's relationship with his civilian staff. All of these characters are sketched briefly and according to hazy, popular notions of their chief character traits, whether it is technocrat McNamara, bland Dean Rusk, lily-livered National Security Advisor McGeorge Bundy, or ageing United Nations (UN) Ambassador Adlai Stevenson. All, to a greater or lesser degree, are brought up to a higher level over the course of the film by the president. Both Bundy and Stevenson are unfairly maligned in the movie, especially Stevenson. He is initially portrayed as a pusillanimous has been who then comes good during encounters with his opposite number, Valerian Zorin, at the UN. This, the film makes clear, is under Kennedy's careful tutelage, dragging Stevenson into the modern age ('You call Adlai—you tell him to stick it to this son of a bitch!'). Here, there is no doubt that Kennedy is the benign patriarch of a bureaucratic family that historian Robert Dean has called an 'Imperial Brotherhood'; a hyper-masculine political elite driving United States Cold War policy in the 1950s and 1960s.[23]

Indeed, the actual family life for which Kennedy was famed and that still forms an important part of his image is relegated to a few fleeting scenes in *Thirteen Days.* It comprises a brief cameo by his wife, Jacqueline (played by Stephanie Romanov) at the beginning of the movie, the Kennedy and O'Donnell clans' attendance at church on the middle Sunday of the crisis, and a pensive stare through a window at his two children, Caroline and John Jr., playing in the garden at the height of the drama. The 'nuclear family' at the centre of the drama is actually O'Donnell's: scenes in the O'Donnell household bookend the movie, while telephone calls from Costner's character to his long-suffering wife, his attendance at his son's football game, and his wistful stares at a photograph of all his children punctuate the narrative.[24] This focus even implies that Kennedy—and his brother Robert who is the only other Kennedy family member central to this story—is making the ultimate sacrifice by performing bureaucratic miracles for others more than for the good of his own loved ones. While, as Mark White suggests, the film's brief depictions of the Kennedys and O'Donnell as family men are intended to demonstrate their morality—especially so because several scenes have references to their Catholicism—they are also designed to give a human dimension to a film that is about the male-dominated world of Washington politics.[25] This gendered perspective is driven home in the final scene as we see the Kennedy brothers talking on the porch of the White House with the president holding a football that he then hands to O'Donnell as they walk back inside.

In presenting Kennedy's family as an essentially male, bureaucratic one the director is also able to skirt controversial issues that would potentially sully JFK's image. Although something on the president's voracious womanising was apparently included in the original script (written in 1997), there are no allusions to it in the final version. The only reference to presidential indiscretions is a somewhat esoteric one early in the film to President Warren G. Harding—hardly the most prominent of chief executives—smuggling his mistresses into the White House.[26] White has also pointed out that Kennedy's promiscuity was not irrelevant to the Cuban Missile Crisis. The president's two-year affair with Judith Campbell Exner was significant because of her close links to Chicago mafia bosses John Roselli and Sam Giancana, both of whom were involved in CIA plots to assassinate Castro. Whether Kennedy knew about Campbell's close relationship with these men is open to question, despite her later unsubstantiated (and likely false) claims that she was a

Kennedy-Giancana go-between.[27] Yet it is difficult to see how the writer could have broached this subject in a film that portrayed Kennedy in this way, especially given its almost exclusive attention to the relationships between middle-aged, white men.

Thirteen Days thus reflects the broader difficulty of delving deeply into Kennedy family life in that they significantly complicate the Kennedy image. While such depictions do sometimes feature in longer treatments, such as the 1983 miniseries *Kennedy* and the more recent, controversial, and critically maligned *The Kennedys* (2011, with Greg Kinnear as JFK), the main focus of such productions tends to be the dramas that place Kennedy at the centre of a family saga, more soap opera than political cinema. They too, however, must conform to accepted ideas about the House of Kennedy. In addition to its melodramatic tone and questionable reconstructions of certain events, for example, *The Kennedys* was controversial because it encompassed some of the less palatable aspects of the family's life—including sexual indiscretions, drug-taking, and connections to the mafia—to the extent that it was dropped by The History Channel and then allegedly had to be edited to be shown elsewhere. Keepers of the Kennedy flame were at the forefront of protests against the show, including speechwriter Theodore Sorenson who had already done so much to protect the legacy since the president's death in November 1963.[28]

And it is always that death that sits at the centre of all Kennedy dramas, including *Thirteen Days*. Even if it is not shown on screen, it overshadows all that he did in his life and shapes his public image even in biographical depictions of that life. In some other films, this means that Kennedy's absence is his presence: he is there but not there, the events and the people around him a sad reminder that he is gone. In part, this is because of his omniscience in the popular imagination, especially on television, which makes playing him on screen such a task—he is so well known that it is difficult to recreate him in a semi-fictional setting. But it is also important because of what his absence represents, whether this is through close family members mourning him as in *Jackie*, the ordinary citizens of Dallas briefly thrust centre stage in *Parkland* (2013), or the unanswered questions about his death in Oliver Stone's *JFK* (1991). In all of these productions, and several others, Kennedy is central to the story but missing from the picture; his absence rather than his presence remembered, his loss mourned, and his memory celebrated. Moreover, as Cimpean notes, several other films about subsequent political events conform to similar ideas, relying on Kennedy's death to inform and even drive their narratives. In particular, John Frankenheimer's TV movie *Path to War* (2002) about Lyndon B. Johnson's Vietnam decision making and Oliver Stone's *Nixon* (1995) feature two of Kennedy's successors dealing with the travails of the later 1960s and 1970s with obvious reference to their fallen predecessor and the lost time he represents.[29]

Such portrayals also suggest—either implicitly or explicitly—that Kennedy was the right man in the right place at the right time. They thus tap an important theme in portrayals of post-war presidents, mirroring popular attitudes, which laud some of them (Kennedy and Ronald Reagan especially) while being critical of others (notably Johnson and Richard Nixon). At one point, *Thirteen Days* even makes this explicit by contrasting the smooth, urbane president with his Vice President, Lyndon Johnson. In a scene in the Oval Office in the midst of the crisis when Kennedy complains that things cannot get much worse O'Donnell comments drily, 'Oh, I don't know; we could have to go down to Lyndon's ranch again, dressed up as cowboys, shoot deer out of the back of his convertible'. Smiling at the thought of Johnson the Texan hick, the president replies 'That *was* a bad day'. As this scene infers on an almost Shakespearean level, Johnson's aesthetic shortcomings explain his (later) political ones. These are brought into sharper relief by another contrast between the setting of the discussion in the White House—Camelot itself—and the reference to Johnson's backwater home in Texas. The writers have no doubt that many in the audience will understand too—we are in on Kennedy's private joke.

Thus, television and cinema reinforce extant notions of presidential achievement and failure. As Douglas Kellner has suggested, the modern presidency has to be understood in terms of the way it crafts narrative and spectacle in order to frame it. Successful presidents make 'good movies' that the public responds to positively, something Kennedy accomplished during his time in office but which his acolytes have done with even more success in the decades since.[30] Of course, one could say that these attitudes towards particular presidents are entirely fair—Kennedy was wise and cautious during the missile crisis and Reagan supposedly ended the Cold War while Johnson mired the United States in Vietnam and Nixon resigned in disgrace—but there are important meanings in such cultural representations because this makes them amenable to public consumption in particular ways. This allows—but also constrains—filmmakers to craft and maintain popular public portraits of these leaders, focusing on certain aspects of their presidencies. Kennedy's role as the first cinematic president makes him particularly compelling for Hollywood directors in this respect. This is why Kennedy biopics tend to be about the Cuban triumph and the assassination while the less savoury elements, whether they relate to his personal or political life, are relegated. Such depictions of Kennedy cast him as something close to the perfect president, akin to the fictional Josiah Bartlett in the Aaron Sorkin television show *The West Wing* (which ran from 1999 to 2006); a man of his time. Kennedy's actions during the 13 days of October 1962 thus make him the ultimate Hollywood leading man: calm and cautious but also strong and resolute when necessary.

Such views are reaffirmed at the end of *Thirteen Days*, which has original footage of John F. Kennedy (not Bruce Greenwood playing him) giving an address at the American University in Washington in June 1963. In his most impressive foreign policy speech as president, made just five months before he died, Kennedy focused on the need for common understanding between east and west, arguing that both sides needed to search for peace if they were to prevent catastrophe. As he suggested in the segment played in the film, 'in the final analysis, our most basic common link is that we all inhabit this small planet. We all breathe the same air. We all cherish our children's future. And we are all mortal'.[31] Ending the film in this way makes it clear that the missile crisis has changed aspects of the Cold War and demonstrated Kennedy's continued capacity to grow and learn the lessons of the presidency. By focusing on a speech made so close to the end of his life, the selection of his reference to our collective mortality clearly alluding to his own, it also implies that this hope for the future was snatched away by the assassin's bullet.

While this speech is thus a convenient way to illustrate classic traits of the Kennedy myth, it is also significant for another reason: because it mirrors perhaps the most notorious and culturally impactful Kennedy film of all time, Oliver Stone's *JFK*. As noted above, *JFK* is about Kennedy's assassination and takes as its main source material a book by New Orleans District Attorney, Jim Garrison, played in the film by the Kennedy film stalwart Kevin Costner, about his efforts to prosecute individuals he believed had been involved in killing the president and then concealing their crime. Leaving aside many of the controversies that the film generated, it was a major cinematic event. It made enormous sums at the box office, generated a new generation of Kennedy conspiracy theorists, and even persuaded the US government to release additional documents relating to the assassination.[32] In contrast to *Thirteen Days*, the American University speech is used at the beginning of *JFK*, the culmination of a brief, highly tendentious opening montage of the history of the late 1950s and early 1960s that includes the Cuban Missile Crisis. While Stone uses the speech in a different manner to Donaldson—to open up questions about the reasons for Kennedy's death rather than just to illustrate the successes of his life—and the tone of *JFK* wildly diverges from *Thirteen Days*, the reception of his film shaped and embellished public ideas about Kennedy and the period in which he governed. Most notably it suggested that under Kennedy's leadership at this particular time almost anything was possible. Kennedy's death thus ushered in a period of decline in America, a downward spiral from which it has not fully recovered. This helped to enlarge an artistic environment that has almost universally revered his legacy.[33]

Thirteen Days was made in this environment. As White has pointed out, beyond merely using the American University speech, both films have much in common; particularly in the way they portray Kennedy as struggling against his aggressive generals and trying to lessen Cold War tensions.[34] More than this, both films take the end of Kennedy's life—either poring over it in *JFK* or lightly referencing it in *Thirteen Days*—to suggest that Kennedy was the lost hope for America. As *JFK* so aptly illustrates, the events surrounding his assassination—the images of that bright day in Dallas, the carefully-crafted symbolism of his funeral, and the endless conspiracy theories that many continue to propound—are cultural touchstones that speak to far broader concerns about the United States. Many American citizens see Kennedy's death as heralding a period of decline in America, during which, among many other things, the population became more deeply divided over the political solutions required for the nation's problems. All could agree that his demise was a tragedy, but many also implicitly suggested that it was in part responsible for this precipitous decline, with Kennedy's life, personality, and image becoming associated with all that was great about America in the previous era.[35] Oliver Stone's thesis that almost every calamity in recent American history, but especially the Vietnam War, has been because of JFK's death may be an extreme retelling of the myth, but it has echoes in the numerous other screen representations of him, including *Thirteen Days*. While Donaldson's movie is ostensibly about Kennedy preventing catastrophe in October 1962, it also implies that Kennedy would have saved the United States from its subsequent traumas.[36] If Kennedy had survived, it suggests, the 'good sixties' could have endured.

This also helps explain why other presidents have generally fared so badly on screen when contrasted with the cinematic John F. Kennedy, and also something of why Kennedy's popularity remains so strong among the American public. There is a symbiotic relationship in Hollywood between the Hollywood image of JFK as a wise and tragic figure whose loss cannot be calculated and the enlargement of that image in popular culture over the last half-century. This view has remained remarkably impervious to the creeping revelations since Kennedy's death about his private life, and an increasingly sceptical scholarly community that questions the extent of his political achievements.[37] On film, Kennedy is the essence of the presidency against which others are measured and he is sometimes strikingly juxtaposed with his successors, most notably Lyndon Johnson, to demonstrate this. Despite a growing number of films explicitly about Johnson and the achievements of his presidency, including the recent Home Box Office movie *All the Way* (2016) and Rob Reiner's *LBJ* (2017), as well as a large number of revisionist academic studies, Hollywood's approach to the thirty-sixth president continues to present him as the antithesis of the thirty-fifth. Most egregiously, as in Lee Daniel's *The Butler* (2013) for example, Johnson is portrayed as an obscene caricature, in stark contrast to a fuller and much more positive representation of Kennedy in the same film. Even much more sophisticated studies such as Ava DuVernay's *Selma* (2014) have been accused of anti-Johnson bias.[38] Such portrayals both reflect and reinforce popular views of presidents as successes or failures, with Kennedy almost always the former and Johnson the latter.

Thus, for all its technical merits *Thirteen Days* fails to break free from the traditions of the Kennedy movie. To be sure, as compelling as he is for Hollywood, portraying Kennedy on screen remains a challenge for filmmakers. This is because he was so telegenic but also so heavily photographed and recorded in his lifetime that he remains instantly recognisable even to those born long after his death. So while Greenwood does an admirable job of depicting him, unlike the participants of the negotiations to end the Cuban Missile Crisis, Donaldson's film takes few chances. By removing much of the international and historical context, it reaffirms Americans' conception of the episode as almost exclusively American, an existential threat to the United States resolved by the embodiment of the nation, the president, in the form of a man most

Americans see as one of the greatest occupants of the office, Kennedy. The character of O'Donnell aside, therefore, the historical inaccuracies seem less to do with artistic licence and more about the projection of the Kennedy myth. While like all myths there is some reality to it, its persistence has been because it was nurtured by a Kennedy industry consisting of his supporters and members of the creative community. Donaldson's projections of ideas about Kennedy's growth and maturation before he was snatched away as he was about to reach the height of his powers are crucial elements of this.

Of course, one could argue that it is impossible to do otherwise in a commercial venture that must chime with what audiences will find acceptable. It is, it seems, all-but impossible even to imply significant criticism of Kennedy under such circumstances. Yet this means that regardless of their differences in focus, form, and tone, celluloid studies of the thirty-fifth president of the United States—from *PT-109* to *Thirteen Days* and beyond—have remained remarkably consistent in the ways that they portray him.

Notes

1. White, 1963, pp. 158–59.
2. The Michael Curtiz film *Yankee Doodle Dandy* (1942) starring James Cagney does feature an actor (Jack Young) playing Franklin D. Roosevelt, but Roosevelt is not the focus of the movie and only appears from behind with his voice provided by impersonator Art Gilmore.
3. For an account of the troubled production, see Cull, 2012, pp. 138–64.
4. May and Zelikow, 1997. For a balanced review of the film by one of these authors, see May, 2001, p. 34. May stresses that he had virtually nothing to do with the making of the film.
5. Although May and Zelikow speculate that O'Donnell may have attended other meetings, he spoke for the first time during the morning meeting of 22 October, the seventh day of the crisis, and then only very briefly, and at one other meeting later the same day. See May and Zelikow, 1997, pp. 204–27.
6. PBS Online NewsHour, 2001.
7. Allyn, Blight, and Walch, 2002, p. 414. For further discussion of the film as historical narrative, see, for example, Doherty, 2001, pp. 1211–13; Doherty, 2002, pp. 13–15; Waters, 2001, pp. 69–70.
8. Cimpean, 2015, p. 98.
9. O'Donnell and Powers with McCarthy, 1972, especially pp. 312–13.

10. Santa Cruz, 2015, pp. 15–17.
11. For a discussion that compares the film to the historical record and also covers the Kennedy image, see White, 2011, pp. 131–50. For further discussion of Kennedy's image and the Kennedy Myth, see especially Brown, 1988; Hellmann, 1997; Frame, 2016, pp. 21–34; Hogan, 2017.
12. Von Bothmer, 2010.
13. Reagan, 1988.
14. Von Bothmer, 2010, pp. 131–41.
15. It was, for example, the first film President George W. Bush saw in the White House as president, an event to which he invited the late president's younger brother, Edward. Cook, 2002, pp. 757–58.
16. White, 2011, pp. 139–40; Brenner, 2002. At one point, CIA Director John McCone responds to Robert Kennedy's refusal to agree to a sneak attack on Cuba because it would be unethical by telling him '[Y]ou weren't so ethically particular when we were talking about options for removing Castro over at CIA'.
17. See especially Dallek, 2003.
18. Brown, 1988, pp. 20–23.
19. Cimpean, 2015, p. 90.
20. Cimpean, 2015, pp. 87–88.
21. White, 2011, pp. 144–46.
22. Halberstam, 1969.
23. Dean, 2001.
24. For further development of the significance of what he calls the 'nuclear family' in this film, see Simon, 2001, pp. 43–44.
25. White, 2011, pp. 141.
26. On the original reference to Kennedy's promiscuity, see Cimpean, 2015, pp. 101–2.
27. White, 2011, pp. 144–45. Journalist Seymour Hersh relayed many of the most salacious parts of the Exner affair based on his uncorroborated interviews with her. See Hersh, 1997, pp. 294–325. For a brief, and more balanced, account of the affair and its implications, see O'Brien, pp. 36–40.
28. See, Itzkoff, 2001; Frame, 2016, pp. 21–22.
29. Cimpean, 2015, pp. 146–62.
30. Kellner, 2002, pp. 467–86.
31. Kennedy, 1963.
32. Weiner, 1993.
33. Stokes, 2013, pp. 219–29.
34. White, 2001, p. 147.
35. On the idea of Kennedy as national symbol, see Brown, 1988, especially pp. 1–5, 100–101.

36. Brown, 1988, pp. 20–23.
37. See especially White, 134–35.
38. Most notably, Johnson's assistant for domestic affairs, Joseph A. Califano, Jr., criticised the way the movie portrayed Johnson as reticent to press for the Voting Rights Act in 1965. See Califano, 2015. For a balanced response, see, for example, Sorkin, 2015.

Bibliography

Allyn, B. J., Blight, J. G., and Walch, D. A. 2002. *Cuba on the Brink: Castro, the Missile Crisis, and the Soviet Collapse; Revised for the Fortieth Anniversary.* Lanham, MD: Rowman & Littlefield.

Brenner, P. 2002. 'Turning History on Its Head', *National Security Archive*, 2002, http://nsarchive.gwu.edu/nsa/cuba_mis_cri/brenner.htm. Accessed 1 August 2017.

Brown, T. 1988. *JFK: History of an Image*. London: I.B. Tauris.

Califano, J. A., Jr. 2015. 'The Movie "Selma" Has a Glaring Flaw', *Washington Post*, 26 December.

Cimpean, R. L. 2015. *The JFK Image: Profiles in Docudrama*. London: Rowman & Littlefield.

Cook, C. 2002. 'The Permanence of the "Permanent Campaign": George W. Bush's Public Presidency', *Presidential Studies Quarterly* 32 (4), pp. 757–58.

Cull, N. J. 2012. 'Anatomy of a Shipwreck: Warner Bros., the White House and the Celluloid Sinking of *PT 109*', in J. E. Smythe (ed.), *Hollywood and the American Historical Film*, pp. 138–64. Basingstoke: Palgrave.

Dallek, R. 2003. *John F. Kennedy: An Unfinished Life*. London: Allen Lane.

Dean, R. D. 2001. *Imperial Brotherhood: Gender and the Making of Cold War Foreign Policy*. Amherst: University of Massachusetts Press.

Doherty, T. 2001. 'Thirteen Days', *Journal of American History* 88 (3), pp. 1211–13.

Doherty, T. 2002. 'Film and History, Foxes and Hedgehogs', *OAH Magazine of History* 16 (4), pp. 13–15.

Frame, G. 2016. 'The Myth of John F. Kennedy in Film and Television', *Film & History* 46 (2), pp. 21–34.

Halberstam, D. 1969. *The Best and the Brightest*. New York: Random House.

Hellmann, J. 1997. *The Kennedy Obsession: The American Myth of JFK*. New York: Columbia University Press.

Hersh, S. 1997. *The Dark Side of Camelot*. London: HarperCollins.

Hogan, M. J. 2017. *The Afterlife of John F. Kennedy: A Biography*. New York: Cambridge University Press.

Itzkoff, D. 2001. 'Dramatizing Camelot', *New York Times*, 18 January, C1.

Kellner, D. 2002. 'Presidential Politics: The Movie', *American Behavioral Scientist* 46, no. 4, pp. 467–86.

Kennedy, J. F. 1963. 'Commencement Address at American University in Washington', *The American Presidency Project*, 10 June. http://www.presidency.ucsb.edu/ws/?pid=9266. Accessed 1 August 2017.

May, E. R. 2001. 'Thirteen Days in 145 Minutes', *The American Prospect*, 1–15 January, p. 34.

May, E. R., and Zelikow, P. D. (eds.). 1997. *The Kennedy Tapes: Inside the White House During the Cuban Missile Crisis.* Cambridge, MA and London: Belknap Press.

O'Brien, M. 1999. 'The Exner File: Truth and Fantasy from a President's Mistress', *Washington Monthly*, December, pp. 36–40.

O'Donnell, K. P., and Powers, D. F. with McCarthy, J. 1972. *Johnny, We Hardly Knew Ye: Memories of John Fitzgerald Kennedy.* Boston and Toronto: Little, Brown.

PBS Online NewsHour. 2001. 'Thirteen Days'. https://web.archive.org/web/20010905114944/, http://www.pbs.org:80/newshour/forum/february01/thirteendays3.html. Accessed 12 July 2017.

Reagan, R. 1988. 'Address Before a Joint Session of Congress on the State of the Union', *The American Presidency Project*, 25 January. http://www.presidency.ucsb.edu/ws/?pid=36035. Accessed 1 August 2017.

Santa Cruz, P. H. 2015. *Making JFK Matter: Popular Memory and the Thirty-Fifth President.* Denton: University of North Texas Press.

Simon, A. 2001. 'Thirteen Days', *Cinéaste* 26 (2), pp. 43–44.

Sorkin, A. D. 2015. 'Why "Selma" Is More Than Fair to L.B.J.', *New Yorker*, 22 January.

Stokes, M. 2013. *American History Through Hollywood Film: From the Revolution to the 1960s.* London: Bloomsbury.

Von Bothmer, B. 2010. *Framing the Sixties: The Use and Abuse of a Decade from Ronald Reagan to George W. Bush.* Amherst and Boston: University of Massachusetts Press.

Waters, R. 2001. 'Thirteen Days', *Film & History* 31 (1), pp. 69–70.

Weiner, T. 1993. 'Papers on Kennedy Assassination Are Unsealed, and '63 Is Revisited', *New York Times*, 24 August, A1.

White, M. 2011. 'The Cinematic Kennedy: *Thirteen Days* and the Burnishing of an Image', in I. W. Morgan (ed.), *Presidents in the Movies: American History and Politics on Screen*, pp. 131–50. New York: Palgrave Macmillan.

White, T. H. 1963. 'For President Kennedy: An Epilogue', *Life*, 6 December, pp. 158–59.

Power and Its Loss in *The Iron Lady*

Florence Sutcliffe-Braithwaite and Jon Lawrence

Introduction

The Iron Lady appeared in 2011, written by Abi Morgan (one of the writers on the 2007 film *Brick Lane*, and subsequently writer of *Suffragette* [2015]), and directed by Phyllida Lloyd. Meryl Streep won an Oscar for Best Actress for the film (and Mark Coulier and J. Roy Helland won another for best make-up, for transforming Streep into the aged Margaret Thatcher). The film appeared two years before Thatcher's death in 2013, but when its subject was already suffering from dementia, and much of the media coverage focused on the potential insensitivity of portraying Thatcher thus. Arguably the furore over dementia says more about the preoccupations of British society in 2011 than it does about the film. Many of the key symptoms of dementia are not shown, and often Thatcher is politically sharp, if forgetful. Instead, the film is really about grief and the price Thatcher paid in her personal life for her determined pursuit of power.

F. Sutcliffe-Braithwaite (✉)
University College, London, UK
e-mail: f.sutcliffe-braithwaite@ucl.ac.uk

J. Lawrence
University of Exeter, Exeter, UK
e-mail: J.Lawrence3@exeter.ac.uk

T. S. Freeman and D. L. Smith (eds.), *Biography and History in Film*, Palgrave Studies in the History of the Media,
https://doi.org/10.1007/978-3-319-89408-9_13

In its attempt to cover a long and eventful political life in less than two hours, *The Iron Lady* makes narrative choices which together create some impressions that are not borne out by historical analysis. The film squeezes Thatcher's public life into a simple narrative arc of adversity, triumph, hubris, and downfall, rather than acknowledge that politics, and indeed life, are rather messier than this. The Falklands War figures out of sequence in order to make it appear the 'crowning achievement' of Thatcher's one-woman crusade. The central problem with this is that it lumps together all the problems and opposition Thatcher faced, and, correspondingly, all her moments of triumph. One consequence is that the film ends up replicating the 'declinist' narrative of postwar Britain that Thatcher herself peddled, implying that once a leader came along who was willing to take the 'hard choices', the re-establishment of Britain's self-respect in the world *and* economic prowess inevitably followed. The contested nature of Thatcher's achievements and the complex nature of historical causation are, in this way, obscured. In its treatment of gender, the film is in places sophisticated, showing difficult compromises rather than a woman 'having it all'. However, in other places the film falls back on a simplistic narrative that presents us with a plucky young woman fighting against the chauvinist establishment, and viewers are invited to root for her on that basis. Perhaps inevitably, there is little space to explore the complexity of the political goals that drove Thatcher. The film relies on its narrative framing, and the pathos of frail old age, to try to get the audience to identify with Thatcher. It is, ultimately, far more compelling as an exploration of the price of power in Thatcher's personal life than as a political biography.

Narrative and Timeline

The Iron Lady works through the device of flashback, showing an aged Thatcher, suffering from dementia, remembering her early life. The narrative demands of a feature film require, however, that the episodic story of Thatcher's political and personal life be condensed and fitted into a simple narrative arc: struggle, success, setback and adversity, triumph, and finally hubris and downfall. The early part of Thatcher's career is truncated: the film moves straight from her unsuccessful candidacy in Dartford in 1950 to her election as MP for Finchley in 1959, and from there, straight to 1974, when Thatcher is shown in Ted Heath's Cabinet (with little sense of how she got there). The film truncates the complicated events of the 1970s: Heath's Cabinet is shown debating the miners' strike of 1974, and viewers are told that the miners are demanding a 35 per cent increase in wages (this was, in fact, what they achieved under the Wilson government that followed the February 1974 General Election). Outside in the streets of London, we have just been shown pavements piled high with rubbish bags, the most striking imagery of the 1979 'Winter of Discontent'. That winter saw a protracted wave of public and private sector strikes, including refuse collectors and gravediggers. In the film, the imagery of the Winter of Discontent is rolled into a general picture of chaos and public sector strikes in the 1970s. The film also moves Denis Thatcher's nervous breakdown from 1964 to 1974, so that it occurs not when Thatcher was slowly advancing her ministerial career, but at the point when the film has Thatcher deciding to run for the leadership of her party. Personal crisis and political crisis must coincide, but this image of the 1970s is distorted and distorting, and reduces most of the decade's problems to one simple diagnosis: it was the unions' fault.

Of course, Thatcher did not, in fact, challenge Heath for the leadership until 1975; the film cuts out the two General Elections of 1974, which Heath lost. Thatcher is shown campaigning for the leadership of her party with pro-business and anti-trade union rhetoric, and Airey Neave and Gordon Reece are now shown taking in hand her image. In fact, Reece first coached Thatcher while she was still a member of Heath's shadow cabinet, first during the General Election of 1970 and again in 1974.[1] Reece continued this assistance during Thatcher's campaign for the party leadership, and the film shows her agreeing to give up her hats, but defending her wearing of pearls (in fact, she had refused to give up the pearls during the famous 'milk snatcher' row of 1972).[2]

The film does try to get details like the pearls and hat correct. However, such fidelity masks the fact that the film's account of Thatcher's campaign for the leadership of the party downplays or obscures certain important—and dramatic—elements of the campaign. When telling Denis that she will run for the leadership, she tells him she must run to 'make them reaffirm the principles on which the Conservative Party stands'. In this statement, the film presumably intends to hint at the idea that Thatcher—and others within the party, particularly on its backbenches—were developing a narrative that held that the Conservative Party in the 1950s and 1960s had lost its way, and needed to be returned to its proper principles. E.H.H. Green and

Mark Wickham-Jones have convincingly argued that this was, indeed the case.[3] It is also the case, though, that Airey Neave, as Thatcher's campaign manager, ran a brilliant and cunning campaign for her, telling many people that it was vital for Thatcher to win the first ballot against Heath. This would ensure that Heath stood down, opening the path for some of his loyal supporters and more appropriate leaders (like William Whitelaw) to stand in the second round of the ballot. However, Thatcher's success in the first round was so convincing that she had the momentum—and the support from restive backbenchers—to upset the predictable succession of Whitelaw or another of Heath's lieutenants. This behind-the-scenes plotting was important, but is obscured in the film's brief account of Thatcher's campaign for the leadership.

The film jumps directly from 1974/1975 to 1979, to show the death of Airey Neave, killed by a car bomb planted by the INLA, an Irish Republican splinter group, which detonated as he drove out of the Palace of Westminster car park. Thatcher is placed at the scene of the atrocity and has to be restrained from running up to Neave's burning car. This is entirely invented, in order to drive home the film's suggestion that in Neave, Thatcher found a second father figure; a guide and inspiration. His death, therefore, comes as a bitter blow to Thatcher. Carol Thatcher did, indeed, record in her memoir that 'my brother once said that, of all the trials and tribulations Mum had to face in her long political career, losing Airey Neave was the hardest for her to bear. She said she felt "like a puppet whose strings have been cut"'.[4] The film implies, however, that Neave was more than a political maneuverer—he is an ideological inspiration, telling Thatcher to 'lead' the party and the country in order to change things. But Neave was, in John Campbell's words, 'no right-winger … but a traditional One Nation Conservative who spent most of the next four years [from 1975 to 1979] striving to counter the influence of her more radical advisors'.[5] This complexity is ironed out in favour of a simple story of the Thatcherite ideological crusade.

It is in its depiction of Thatcher's eleven years in power that *The Iron Lady* is most free with its timeline. Through its use of flashback the film constructs two periods: in the first, Thatcher is shown beset by problems and enemies. She is shown in 1980/1981 telling ministers that she will not do a U-turn on her leaked budget, despite its unpopularity. A montage then depicts the Brixton disorders (1981), the People's March for Jobs (1983), and the miners' strike (1984–1985). These are three very different events. The Brixton disorders (or 'riots' as Thatcher and the press tended to call them) took place over 10–12 April 1981, in Brixton, an inner-city area of London characterised by a high proportion of black residents and high levels of poverty and unemployment. Involving black and white rioters, the disorders were sparked by anger at heavy and discriminatory policing, but the socio-economic context was key to creating a situation that erupted into violent conflict with police, arson, and looting. The People's March for Jobs and the miners' strike, by contrast, were both related to the trade union movement. There were two marches, in 1981 and 1983, called the People's March for Jobs, both protesting against the high levels of unemployment that the Thatcher government was apparently willing to tolerate. The miners' strike of 1984–1985 was a year-long industrial action pursued by the National Union of Mineworkers, in opposition to plans from the National Coal Board to close mines deemed 'unproductive'.

After a clip of Thatcher arguing that 'we shall never waver, even for a second, in our determination to see this country prosper again', we return to the montage, with imagery relating to Irish Republicans' armed struggle against the British state in the 1980s: hunger strikers (1980–1981), the Harrods IRA car bomb (1983), the Hyde Park and Regents' Park IRA bombs (1982), and the Brighton hotel bomb which targeted the Conservative leadership during the party's annual conference in 1984. Finally, the film turns to the events it sets up as Thatcher's greatest test and greatest triumph: the invasion of the Falkland Islands by Argentina, and the British action to re-take the islands (1982). The elision of these very different political events creates a problematic effect. The viewer is given no sense of why the IRA was contesting Westminster rule of Northern Ireland. The miners' strike and the People's March for Jobs are shown alongside the Brixton disorders with no explication of the reasons for these events. The images are used simply as exemplars of chaos, violence, and disorder. Though we hear a voiceover charging that 'the miners are being starved back to work, their need is desperate', the links between government policy and high unemployment, the closing of coal mines, inner-city deprivation, and institutional racism in the Metropolitan Police are not made. All these challenges and threats to Thatcher's leadership are lumped into one, their distinctive causes and different natures flattened.

Finally, after Thatcher's bold course in the Falklands is rewarded by victory, the film uses a second montage to show the viewer the results of Thatcher's unwavering strength in the face of adversity: it shows

Thatcher dancing with Ronald Reagan and Nelson Mandela (she did meet the latter in June 1990, though without dancing), the Berlin Wall falling, and a series of headlines—'Business is Booming', 'Maggie's Millionaires'—and of images—money, computer terminals—designed to evoke the Big Bang in the City of London (1986) and the explosion of wealth associated with the 'Lawson boom' of the mid-to-late 1980s. This montage seems to imply that once Britain had shown itself able to stand up to foreign aggressors, economic success and the ending of the Cold War were the logical results. This entirely ignores the real structural factors lying behind the boom of the late 1980s. Indeed, it almost seems to present the viewer with a Nietzschean lesson in the power of strength of will. The ebb and flow of events is truncated into a more cinema-friendly narrative of struggle, adversity, and triumph which profoundly distorts causation.

One justification for these muddled and truncated timelines might be that *The Iron Lady* views events through the perspective of Thatcher herself. She did tend to lump together all her enemies, and the perspective of the ageing Thatcher, suffering from dementia and looking back on a long career, might well iron out complexity and present events in Manichean blocs. Nevertheless, the impression that the film gives is misleading. It is possible to use cinematic techniques to show that the world is being viewed through the eyes of one character: the camera angles taking in the Gothic architecture when Thatcher first enters the Palace of Westminster, for example, convey the sense of awe she is feeling. By contrast, in the montage flashback scenes we frequently see Thatcher in short, documentary news style. These recreated scenes, spliced with powerful contemporary news images, tend to give an aura of objectivity to the film's representation of history. *The Iron Lady*, in the end, leaves the viewer with the impression that Thatcher's view of the world is normative, rather than contested, and obscures important elements of historical causation.

Failing Powers

Morgan and Lloyd's portrayal of Thatcher attracted considerable controversy for representing the former premier battling against the effects of dementia in old age. Indeed, critics and commentators were already attacking the film for its insensitivity on this score, and its disregard for Thatcher's privacy, even before its UK release in January 2012.[6] Long before the film had been finished, sections of the media also highlighted attacks on it by Thatcher's twin children, Mark and Carol, who were reported to be 'appalled' at reports that the screenplay would portray their mother 'as a dementia sufferer looking back at her life with sadness', and who apparently denounced the film's plot as a 'left-wing fantasy'.[7] It had been Carol Thatcher's 2008 memoir *A Swim-on Part in the Goldfish Bowl* that had first drawn attention to Margaret Thatcher's illness, and so early reports of the family's disquiet may have predisposed many commentators to see *The Iron Lady*'s representation of a frail and forgetful Baroness Thatcher almost exclusively in relation to taboos around the depiction of dementia.[8] Earlier in 2011, there had been considerable controversy about revelations in the French press that former President Jacques Chirac was suffering from Alzheimer's disease, and the idea of drawing further attention to Thatcher's condition was undoubtedly anathema to many.[9]

But was Max Pemberton right to denounce the film's portrayal of Lady Thatcher's 'decline into dementia' as 'lamentable, vile and shameful' in the *Daily Telegraph*?[10] Pemberton was in no doubt that Streep had set out to capture the symptoms of dementia, and he was morally outraged that the film could be made and released while Thatcher was still alive and grappling with the debilitating effects of her illness. On the second point it is hard to disagree with him—there can be no doubt that the film's makers knew of Thatcher's condition and discounted the moral objections to making a film about her frailty and decline while she was still alive.[11] But arguably Streep's portrayal of Thatcher is first and foremost an attempt to convey the poignancy of power lost, rather than a study of dementia as such. Yes, Thatcher is portrayed as forgetful and at times muddled, but the focus of the film is primarily on grief and loss, with Thatcher mourning the loss of Denis and the loss of power in almost equal measure (and crucially being forced, in the process, to appraise which mattered most to her).

Once one knows that the real Margaret Thatcher was already struggling with dementia in 2008, when the film is set, it becomes difficult to view the Streep-as-Thatcher of *The Iron Lady* as simply an old woman struggling to accept the ebbing of her powers. But unlike Carol Thatcher's memoir, the film makes no explicit attempt to signal that Thatcher's problem is dementia, rather than simply short-term memory loss compounded by the disorientating effects of bereavement. For instance, Thatcher is shown running rings around the doctor asked to assess her mental powers. She deflects the doctor's questions about bereavement by bluntly telling him, 'my husband has been gone for years; cancer'. And when he responds by sympathetically intoning that she is 'bound to feel …' she cuts him off in mid-flow:

> What? What am I bound to be feeling? People don't think any more, they feel. Do you know, one of the great problems of our age is that we are governed by people who care more about feelings than thoughts and ideas. Now thoughts and ideas, that interests me – ask me what I'm thinking.

Thatcher, we are shown, remains sufficiently abreast of contemporary politics to have a finely honed critique of her successors' mediated politics of 'spin' and 'narrative'. Similarly, though she may not always be able to remember the names of her guests at a dinner party, she is shown summoning up her old rhetoric to denounce the evils of global terrorism, raising a laugh by characterising the Prime Minister as a 'clever man, quite a smoothy', and capturing the essence of modern politics in a pithy sentence: 'it used to be about trying to do something, now it's about trying to be someone'.[12]

In *The Iron Lady*, Thatcher is haunted by bereavement and doubt, more than by dementia. She sees Jim Broadbent's Denis at every turn not because she is losing her mind (as she herself fears), but because she cannot reconcile herself to his loss. Just as his clothes still fill the house, so does his conversation; both are coping mechanisms thrown up by Thatcher's grief. In fact the dialogues between Margaret and Denis that structure the film only really make sense when they are viewed as Margaret's two-part internal monologues. Sometimes the imaginary Denis stokes Margaret's feelings, as when he echoes her fury at the 'vacillators' who conspired to overthrow her in 1990, but more often his role is that of a mildly chiding alter ego; questioning her motives, highlighting her weaknesses (including her failing powers of memory). Still bitter at the 'weak men' who forced her out eighteen years earlier, Margaret consoles herself by declaring, 'if you take the tough decisions, yes, people will hate you today, but they will thank you for generations'. But the imaginary Denis immediately undercuts her grandiloquence by observing wryly, 'or forget you entirely and chuck you out with the rubbish'. He voices the frustrations of the ageing Thatcher, no longer able to command power and authority as she once did.

Indeed, the key purpose of the imaginary Denis as Margaret's alter ego is to allow her to weigh up her life and ask herself if the sacrifices required to fulfil her confident, youthful ambition that 'one's life must matter' had been worth it. In an important scene near the end of the film we see Margaret looking at old family photographs, pictures by her children and memorabilia from her early election campaigns. The incongruous juxtaposition prompts her to tell the imaginary Denis that she always wanted him to be happy; 'were you?' she asks him plaintively, 'tell me the truth'. For once there is no response from Denis—she does not know how he would answer that question. Strikingly, during this exchange we hear Thatcher speaking while her lips remain visibly sealed—the film-makers are showing us that this is an interior dialogue, not a conversation with a ghost or hallucination.

In real life, Margaret Thatcher may have struggled to comprehend that Denis was dead,[13] but in *The Iron Lady* she struggles to accept it—the distinction is important. We see her haunted by doubts about whether her single-minded determination to make an impact in public life undermined the happiness of those who mattered most to her: Denis and her children Carol and Mark. In the scene where she asks Denis if he was happy, we also hear her intone the two ambitions at the heart of her conflicted identity. As she picks up a blue rosette and a Margaret Roberts election leaflet we hear her declare: 'all I wanted was to make a difference in the world'. A few seconds later, as she picks up a hand-drawn card made by Carol and Mark for their father's birthday, she declares 'all I wanted was for my children to be well and to grow up happy—happier than I was certainly'. Interviewed in 2011, writer Abi Morgan commented that she had been struck by the fact that there was 'a lot of sentiment in her [Thatcher's] life. For a woman who could be so brutal in her policies, I think she could be very sentimental in her personal life' (as an example she points to the pearls that Thatcher refused to give up wearing because, as we are told in the film, they had been a gift from Denis).[14] Thatcher's imaginary Denis is Morgan's device for showing this dimension of Thatcher's personality, and putting it in direct dialogue with the more familiar public Thatcher: the strong-willed figure always determined to change the world by taking the 'tough decisions' from which others shied away. But in its presentation of those 'tough decisions', the film finds it hard to give a nuanced account of Thatcher's political ideology.

Thatcher's Political Ideology

The Iron Lady makes some interesting suggestions about what Thatcher's political beliefs really were, and where their roots lay. While not inaccurate, they are, nevertheless, partial. The film shows us early on—and later returns to—a scene of Thatcher's father, Alderman Roberts, speaking at a political meeting in the mid-1940s. Roberts tells his listeners that business, small as well as big, is the 'lifeblood' of any community; small business-people are 'self-reliant' and 'plain bloody minded', refusing to take state handouts. In a later flashback to Roberts' speech, he says 'there's no good in pretending we're all equal; we're not all the same, never have been. We should encourage our children to aspire to achieve more than we have'. Thatcher is shown learning her politics from her father, as well as in Roberts' shop, where she diligently serves customers (and profit margins).

Thatcher certainly did absorb a large part of her politics—and her assumptions about the 'bourgeois virtues' of hard work, thrift and self-reliance which she thought made for a prosperous society—from her upbringing as the daughter of a provincial, Methodist grocer.[15] Alfred Roberts was an Independent Alderman on Grantham town council between 1927 and 1943, but this reflected the fact that the convention was, in the interwar period, to keep party labels out of local politics. The Labour Party began to disrupt this in the late 1920s, and ran a Labour candidate against Roberts in 1927. Roberts represented the Chamber of Trade, against 'socialism', the labour movement, and more specifically against the Co-operative movement. The Independents on the council did not have to declare themselves to be Liberals or Conservatives, but Roberts certainly supported the Conservative candidates in Grantham in the 1935 and 1945 General Elections. In the 1950 General Election, when his daughter contested the constituency of Dartford, Roberts came to support her, and was held up as an example of one-time Liberals who, over the course of the interwar period, had realised their beliefs had migrated into the Conservative Party.[16] This distinctive type of Conservatism—drawing on older Liberal ideas about free trade, Methodist individualism and interwar anti-socialism—was certainly a key part of Thatcher's politics.

Much historical debate has centred on the question of the impact of 'neoliberal' political economists like Friedrich von Hayek and Milton Friedman in shaping Thatcher's political project. Historians like Richard

Cockett have suggested that it was these neoliberal ideas that really made Thatcherism distinctive.[17] Others, like Richard Vinen and John Campbell, have argued that Thatcher plucked from this body of thinking, magpie-like, when it was useful to justify her ideas.[18] Vinen suggests that Thatcherism was really rooted in the drive for power, and the need to respond to changing circumstances.[19] The answers to these questions of ideological formation are not clear-cut. Sutcliffe-Braithwaite, Grimley, and others have suggested that her small-town upbringing and Methodism were, in fact, more important formative influences on Thatcher than neoliberal theorising.[20] Even if this is the case, however, it is still significant that in *The Iron Lady* we get no hint that the ideas of this important group of neoliberal thinkers have been accorded a significant place in many accounts of the formation of Thatcher's political project.

Indeed, almost the only time the term 'free market' appears in the film is when Michael Foot is depicted in the early 1980s, addressing Thatcher across the despatch box, arguing that her free-market economics are designed to make the rich richer and the poor poorer. Thatcher is depicted as 'pro-business': when campaigning for the leadership of the Conservative Party in the mid-1970s, she argues that business is the 'backbone of the nation'. But there is little sense of what this means in practice. The clearest message the film gives is that Thatcher is anti-trade unionism: campaigning for the leadership, she argues that the union movement was founded to 'protect' workers but is now 'killing jobs'. Trade unions are consistently depicted as being at the bottom of the nation's problems, with striking images of rubbish uncollected and power cuts, as well as references to Thatcher's well-known struggle with the National Union of Mineworkers in 1984–85. Such images tend to reinforce the idea that the unions really were at the bottom of the nation's supposed problems in the 1970s, ignoring other powerful explanations for the economic challenges Britain faced in the decade—for example, persistent under-investment in industry, or the long process of deindustrialisation. Indeed, where other Conservatives argued the unions were to blame for inflation (through cost-push factors driven by high wage claims), Thatcher turned to monetarist theory to explain inflation—and monetarism insisted that it was uncontrolled expansion of the supply of money that was to blame. The film also entirely fails to mention the other key driver of inflation during the 1970s: the repeated oil price hikes, particularly those linked to the Yom Kippur War of 1973 and the Iranian revolution of 1979.

The image of Thatcher as a politician obsessed with inflation recurs throughout the film. Its opening shots show the aged Thatcher in 2008 surprised by the price of milk. Later in the film, in 1980/1981 when Thatcher is being urged to change track, and abandon the monetarist 'medicine' she has prescribed for the country, one of her ministers suggests that she is out of touch, and she sharply recites the prices of Lurpack butter, Anchor butter, and Flora margarine. She—the housewife and mother—is the one who is 'in touch' with the cost of living. She tells her ministers that 'we did not seek election and win in order to manage the decline of a great nation'. Thatcher certainly did see her political mission to be the restoration of British 'greatness', as in a speech entitled 'Britain Awake', given as Leader of the Opposition in 1976, where she argued:

> we in the Conservative Party believe that Britain is still great. The decline of our relative power in the world was partly inevitable—with the rise of the super powers with their vast reserves of manpower and resources. But it was partly avoidable too—the result of our economic decline accelerated by Socialism. We must reverse that decline when we are returned to Government.[21]

To the extent that the film gives Thatcher's own perspective on her political project, this is fair enough.

However, one of the key problems with Thatcher's statement in the film that 'we did not seek election and win in order to manage the decline of a great nation' is that it appears to endorse her point of view. This impassioned declaration encapsulates how the film presents Thatcher's political project. Later the film shows the viewer her supposed 'reversal' of British decline in depicting victory in the Falklands War and the mid-1980s economic boom. This entire narrative arc depends upon a straightforward acceptance of Thatcher's own rhetoric—which was constructed for her own political purposes and, historians would argue, needs to be deconstructed if we are to adequately assess Thatcherism.[22] The idea of postwar decline was an increasingly prevalent one from the late 1950s onwards, fuelled by fears that other economies—particularly that of West Germany—were overtaking 'the workshop of the world', as well as by decolonization and the loss of the Empire that had once sustained Britain's political and economic reach. But historians for many years have recognised that 'decline' is not an adequate narrative to describe postwar Britain, though 'declinist' narratives were increasingly pervasive. Rather, Jim Tomlinson has suggested, we should understand postwar British economic history through the master-narrative of deindustrialisation.[23] In replicating declinism, *The Iron Lady* obscures an important part of the *politics* as well as the economics of the postwar period.

Another problem with this framing of Thatcher is that it flattens and obscures the reasons that different groups—within and outside the Conservative Party—had for opposing her. Thatcher is presented as almost the only MP in her party who understands the financial pressures that ordinary household budgets are under, and thus as the real mouthpiece of 'common sense'. Thatcher did, indeed, think of herself as the purveyor of 'common sense' in 1970s and 1980s Britain. But the film has little space to show that 'common sense' is always a contested—and political—construction. Indeed, film is perhaps ill-suited to articulating this point. Historical work on the Conservative Party in the interwar period has often focused on the way that its leaders managed to construct their ideological vision as 'national', and as 'common sense'.[24] The same has been said of Thatcher. This insight is lost in the film. So is the fact that many within the Conservative Party disputed the idea that Thatcher was returning the party to its 'true' roots, and argued that they were the true inheritors of the longstanding 'One Nation' strand of the party's history which emphasised class conciliation and concern for the working classes.[25]

Indeed, the film increasingly frames Thatcher's battles as not so much *for* a set of political goals as *against* 'weakness' in the Conservative Party. In the Cabinet meeting in 1974 where Heath argues that conciliation with the miners is necessary, Thatcher, sat at the end of the table, is the only one to dissent from his view. The term 'conciliation' echoes in the air as she contemplates the dangers of Heath's approach, and recalls her father, speaking about not being beaten during the Second World War. Unbending strength in the face of enemies—an unwillingness to conciliate—are presented as Thatcher's strengths, and what sets her apart from the men around her. During the Falklands crisis she even says that she will never 'appease' the Argentinians, recalling the appeasement of Hitler in the 1930s. The Second World War analogy is repeated several times in the film. In 1974, when Thatcher is shown giving Carol a driving lesson, a radio broadcast is heard likening the blackouts and power cuts caused by the miners' strike to the blackout during the Second World War. Later that day, when telling Denis she will run to be leader, Thatcher says, 'someone must force the point. Someone must say the unsayable'. Her bravery and strength are presented in the film as impressive; when her ministers are urging her to change tack in 1980/81, she holds her course, telling them that her 'nerve' will not fail. She pulls them up on their self-interested approach to politics: they are worried about losing their seats at the next election; she, by contrast, is only concerned with doing the right thing. Since it is hard to imagine many viewers feeling that they should be on the side of weak and self-interested leadership (or appeasement), this frames Thatcher, again, as on the right side: the film invites the viewer to root for her against the 'weak', spineless men she is battling.

This presentation, however, ignores the question of *what*, precisely, Thatcher wanted to do politically. Was it really a good idea to reject conciliation with the unions? Did Thatcher really make Britain a successful and prosperous nation once more? This appears to be the conclusion of the montage near the film's end which shows Thatcher dancing with Reagan and Mandela, and images of the late 1980s boom. The film does briefly suggest alternative perspectives on Thatcher's achievements: in a news broadcast shown early in the film, the aged Thatcher listens as she is described as a controversial figure, credited with helping to end the Cold War and reversing postwar British economic decline, but also with overseeing savage public sector cuts and privatisations. Film is not necessarily a medium that lends itself to the weighing of evidence on either side of a complex question. It might be argued that *The Iron Lady* attempts to give Thatcher's point of view, and her point of view was—very clearly—that she had transformed Britain for the better. But plenty of evidence—rocketing inequality, growing poverty and insecurity at the bottom, increasingly visible homelessness, failing public services, and the recession that hit in the early 1990s, for example—could be adduced to suggest that it is too simplistic to suggest that Thatcher made Britain more prosperous. And the latter is the overriding impression that the film gives.

Not that the film is entirely lacking in complexity in its depiction of Thatcher as a bold and strong leader rooting out weakness. In the scenes near the end of the film where Thatcher and the imagined Denis lambast the 'weak men' who ejected her from the leadership, Denis voices her inner doubts about whether it was all worth it. Were the sacrifices she made in her personal life justified, given that her own colleagues, in the end, rejected her leadership and ejected her from No. 10? This question dominates the film, leaving little space for an assessment of what Thatcher's political ideology really achieved in practice. The impression we are left with is Thatcher's own, one-sided take: that she reversed post-war British decline and thus did 'make a difference in the world'.

Gender and Class in *The Iron Lady*

Morgan said that she wanted ***The Iron Lady*** to show how women pay a different—and greater—price for success than do men.[26] The film returns repeatedly to the relationships Thatcher allowed to wither and the happy family experiences she sacrificed for her political career. As Denis tells her while she watches a video of a happy family holiday in 1959, just before she first entered Parliament, 'you can rewind it, but you can't change it'. Gender is, thus, at the heart of the film. In almost every political scene, Thatcher is the only woman. When she watches her father addressing a political meeting during the Second World War, she is the only woman in the crowd, except for her mother, who tells her to fetch the cups for the tea. When she is shown at dinner with the Dartford Conservative Association in 1950, the men and women separate after dinner. When Thatcher enters Parliament, we see images of male statues, men in the corridors, men's shoes; the 'Members' toilet is for men, and the 'Lady Members' toilet has an ironing board in it. There is never, throughout the film, another female figure shown on either Government or Opposition benches. While Thatcher was in a tiny minority—there were only 25 female MPs elected in 1959 and only 19 in 1979—it is, nevertheless, implausible that Thatcher would never have spotted another female MP. The film over-exaggerates her isolation as a woman in Parliament to emphasise the barriers she had to overcome; but in suggesting she was unique, it erases the other women who struggled to make it possible for women to forge political careers.

The moment when Margaret Thatcher claims, wide-eyed, while running for the leadership of her party, that there will be 'no female Prime Minister here, not in my lifetime' is also implausible. Thatcher did, indeed, claim several times in the early 1970s that she did not think there would be a female Prime Minister 'in her lifetime': in 1970 she suggested that this was down to the fact that 'the male population is too prejudiced'.[27] But to present Thatcher as a political naif, nobly running without even a thought that she might take the leadership of her party from Heath, is hardly credible, given her political ambition. Her chances of winning might not have been secure in 1975 when she challenged Heath, but she would not have done it had she not contemplated winning.

The film does capture some of the complexity in Thatcher's attitude towards her own gender. Margaret Roberts is poignantly distanced from other women growing up. Fashionably dressed young women in Grantham laugh at Margaret as a swot, and when she gets into Oxford, her own mother does not know how to respond, refusing to take the letter from her, and saying simply 'me hands are still damp' (the second time that the imagery of making tea and washing up is used to indicate 'traditional femininity'). The aged Thatcher tells Carol, 'I've always preferred the company of men'. We are given a hint of the way that she flirted with ministers—documented, most obviously, in Alan Clark's diaries—in her interaction with Richard E. Grant as Michael Heseltine, during their Cabinet photo.[28] As well as feeling shut out of the male worlds of politics, Thatcher did also thrive in the company of men.

It is also the case that Thatcher publicly emphasised her ability to fulfil some of the traditional markers of femininity. This comes out in the film when she is shown having a button sewn back on to a full-length evening gown while her ministers stand around in dinner jackets, and again when she chides Denis for attempting to cook his own breakfast. Thatcher was not afraid to emphasise her femininity as leader of her party and as Prime Minister, making a performance of shopping trips and of giving Denis his breakfast.[29] As Laura Beers argues, '[a]gain and again throughout her premiership, Thatcher emphasised that she was Mrs Thatcher first and foremost, a housewife and a mother, and that as a wife and mother she was able to understand the concerns of ordinary women'.[30] Particularly as leader of her party, Thatcher leveraged her femininity to cultivate support. She also publicly endorsed the idea that for most women, home and family would be the first priority, and if they worked, it would be a secondary pursuit, aimed at improving their family's quality of life, often part-time. Furthermore, she dismissed the post-1968 feminist movement which argued for a thoroughgoing transformation of gender roles, disparaging them using the stereotypes of strident and dungaree-wearing women.[31]

Yet one of the most important moments in the film is when Thatcher accepts Denis's proposal of marriage—which, as he says, would profoundly help her political career—and tells him:

> I love you so much, but I will never be one of those women, Denis, who stays silent and pretty on the arm of her husband, or remote and alone in the kitchen doing the washing up, for that matter ... no, one's life must matter Denis. Beyond all the cooking, and the cleaning, and the children, one's life must mean more than that. I cannot die washing up a teacup!

This captures some of the sentiments that Thatcher expressed early on in her political career. In a 1954 article for the magazine *Onward*, published by Conservative Central Office for the Young Conservatives, Thatcher wrote that:

> For a short while after our twins were born I was without help and had to do everything myself including three-hourly feeds day and night, so I know how exhausting children and housework can be! As well as being exhausted, however, I felt nothing more than a drudge. I had little to talk about when my husband came home in the evening and all the time I was consciously looking forward to what I called 'getting back to work'—namely, to using some of the mental resources which I had been expressly trained to use for years. I was indeed 'on the go' literally for 24 hours a day but I wasn't doing the kind of work that made full use of my own faculties.[32]

This statement echoes ideas that grew up in the 1950s and 1960s about the need not to waste the talents of highly educated women, and to give them possibilities for fulfilment outside the limited rounds of home-making. As Helen McCarthy has shown, these arguments were largely dismissed by post-1968 feminists, but nevertheless were central in the decades before 1968 to justifying married women's pursuit of work and intellectual pursuits outside the home.[33] In voicing the desire to be more than just a 'drudge', to work and use her education, Thatcher was in tune with the emerging liberal feminist discourses of her time.

The Iron Lady has some justification for showing us a female dinner guest telling the aged Thatcher that she was an 'inspiration' to women 'like me'. Thatcher was taken as a 'feminist icon' by some younger women in the 1980s and 1990s.[34] But the film does not do full justice to the complexity of Thatcher's attitudes towards gender, in failing to show how hostile she was to the post-1968 feminist movement, and how many of her policies—cutting funding for local authority-provided child-care, for example—harmed the ability of other women to do as she did. In addition, the film constantly emphasises that Thatcher's struggle was the struggle of a plucky woman against dismissive and sexist men who belittled and underestimated her. When speaking to the luminaries of the Dartford Conservative Association in 1950, the men are hostile or sceptical, and as she leaves, she hears one of them remark sardonically, 'well, that's told us'. She herself tells Airey Neave and Gordon Reece, when discussing running for the leadership, that for many of her colleagues, being led by a woman would be like 'being led into battle by their chambermaid'. Again and again, Thatcher is underestimated by men, from those in her own party to US Secretary of State Alexander Haig, with whom she deals during the Falklands War. Ultimately, she is toppled as leader by a backroom plot created by the men in her own party. The impression this creates is of Thatcher as more of a gender warrior than she really was. The audience at some points in the film is invited, it seems, to root for the plucky Thatcher simply on the grounds that she is a woman being put down and held back by men.

In fact, in the film, it is not only her gender but also her class background which is seen to hold her back. Thatcher's comment that her colleagues would not like to be led into battle by 'their chambermaid' refers to class as well as gender, and Thatcher follows it up by saying 'it's my background and my sex'. The men grilling Thatcher on behalf of the Dartford Conservative Association make several references to her background as a grocer's daughter, which she proudly defends. Though she came firmly from the lower-middle classes, and had in many ways a privileged upbringing in interwar Britain, Thatcher was certainly distant from the upper-middle- and upper-class men who dominated the upper ranks of the Conservative Party in the interwar and postwar decades. Nevertheless, the film can be anachronistic in its efforts to highlight Thatcher's class difference. In her dinner with the Dartford Conservative Association, the young Margaret Roberts looks with covert horror at the items of cutlery arrayed on either side of her plate; Denis covertly instructs her to 'start on the outside, work your way in'. This is a nice double entendre but it could hardly be the case that an Oxford graduate, even one who matriculated during wartime, could have missed out on learning how to manage cutlery at a formal dinner, even had Thatcher not learned this in Grantham.

Throughout the film, the prejudice Thatcher had to face on class grounds is emphasised again and again. After Howe resigns from her Cabinet, whispers in the corridors of the Palace of Westminster accuse her of bullying, and one MP says, 'I wouldn't have spoken to my gamekeeper like that'. The implication is that Thatcher is a jumped-up commoner who has none of the innate patrician breeding needed to rule. Such sentiments certainly ran through the corridors of Westminster in the 1980s. At the height of the Falklands invasion crisis, Alan Clark records right-winger Nick Budgen denouncing Thatcher as 'a vulgar, middle-class Reaganite'.[35] But even so, the film ignores the fact that under Thatcher, many MPs from humbler backgrounds—often lower-middle-class backgrounds like her own—obtained more prominent positions in the Conservative Party. MPs like John Major, Norman Fowler, Norman Tebbit, and John Biffen came from similarly 'unprivileged' backgrounds, and some suggested that they formed a 'new Thatcherite class' within the Conservative Party.[36] Tim Bale has shown that even if the transformation was far from complete, it was significant.[37] The film also ignores the fact that Heath, like Thatcher, came from a provincial and lower-middle-class family, growing up in Broadstairs, the son of a builder and successful small businessman who had begun life as a carpenter. Perhaps more importantly, the film seems to invite the viewer to back Thatcher against the old, wealthy, privileged men who disdain her. As late as 1990 we see her telling her cabinet colleagues, in justification of the Poll Tax, 'you haven't had to fight hard for anything. It's all been given to you. And you feel guilty about it. Well may I say on behalf of those who have had to fight their way up and don't feel guilty about it, we resent those slackers who take, take, take and contribute nothing to the community.' Again the consequence is to obscure the nature—and the highly controversial effects—of Thatcher's political ideology.

Conclusion

In this essay, we have argued that *The Iron Lady*, while paying considerable attention to detail (for example, in its focus on Thatcher's image and how she altered it over time), creates a number of impressions that are historically problematic. It plays around with dates in order to create a simple narrative arc appropriate to film. This means Thatcher's enemies—and her triumphs—are conflated. We see a nation in decline, 'held to ransom' by trade unions, crying out for a leader willing to take them on. Thatcher is just such a leader, though she has to battle privileged, weak-willed men in her own party in order to take the leadership—and to take the 'hard choices' that ultimately restore Britain's self-respect and economic health (the two are, it is implied, inextricably linked). Perhaps there is simply too much material to fit into one feature film; but, though the film does suggest to the viewer that Thatcher was 'controversial', the reasons for that controversy—rocketing inequality and poverty, the wholesale collapse of manufacturing, the destruction of the mining industry, for example—cannot be explored in a rounded way in a film that often presents the world through Thatcher's eyes. In a medium that tends to produce the impression of objective observation, the arguments on the other side are not represented.

From the point of view of its gender politics, the final scenes of *The Iron Lady* are hard to read. Thatcher has been trying to let go of—or lay the ghost of—Denis throughout the film. Near the end, Thatcher muses that 'all I wanted was to make a difference in the world', and Denis reassures her that she did. But when, moments later, she reflects that she wanted her children to be well and happy, and asks Denis if he was happy, he gives her no answer. Finally, Thatcher packs his clothes and shoes into bin liners, calls him and says goodbye. Wavering, she asks Denis to stay, but, walking away, he tells her, 'you're going to be fine on your own love. You always have been.' In the final scenes of the film, Thatcher sits alone in her kitchen. She drinks a cup of tea, then goes to the sink, telling her assistant that she'll wash it up. The woman who vowed she would not die at the kitchen sink ends the film smiling as she washes. Is it because she has dementia, or because she has finally dealt with her grief at losing Denis? Is it because she's made peace with the sacrifices she made in her family life in order to pursue her goal of 'making a difference', or (conversely) because she accepts her role as washer-up now? It's not clear the film knows which of these interpretations it wants to favour.

Notes

1. Campbell, 2000, pp. 207, 276.
2. Campbell, 2000, p. 297.
3. Green, 2002; Wickham-Jones, 1997.
4. Thatcher, 2008, pp. 67–68.

5. Campbell, 2000, p. 323.
6. 'Director Defends Iron Lady Film,' *Daily Telegraph*, 14 November 2011; *The Times*, 24 December 2011, p. 3.
7. T. Walker, 'Margaret Thatcher's Family Are "Appalled" at Meryl Streep Film,' *Daily Telegraph*, 17 July 2010.
8. Thatcher, 2008, pp. 259–65.
9. *The Times*, 31 January 2011, p. 27.
10. M. Pemberton, 'The Iron Lady and Margaret Thatcher's Dementia: Why This Despicable Film Makes Voyeurs of Us All,' *Daily Telegraph*, 14 January 2012.
11. See interviews with Phyllida Lloyd and Meryl Streep in 2011 such as those for IndieWire at http://www.indiewire.com/2011/12/director-phyllida-lloyd-says-she-thought-of-the-iron-lady-as-king-lear-for-girls-254724/ and http://www.indiewire.com/2011/12/interview-with-phyllida-lloyd-director-of-the-iron-lady-240968/, where Lloyd says 'We are all interested in dementia and in the insignificance of an old lady'.
12. Although Gordon Brown was Prime Minister by 2008 one imagines the audience is expected to think of Tony Blair when she makes her quip about being a 'smoothy' (or possibly even David Cameron, since only the keen-eyed would notice that the background historical events in the film occurred in September 2008).
13. Thatcher, 2008, p. 265.
14. M. Silverstein, 'Interview with Abi Morgan—Writer of *The Iron Lady*,' at http://www.indiewire.com/2011/12/interview-with-abi-morgan-writer-of-the-iron-lady-240976/.
15. Lawrence and Sutcliffe-Braithwaite, 2012.
16. Campbell, 2000, pp. 11–12.
17. Cockett, 1994.
18. Vinen, 2009; Campbell, 2000.
19. Vinen, 2009.
20. Sutcliffe-Braithwaite, 2012; Grimley, 2012.
21. Thatcher, Speech at Kensington Town Hall, 19 January 1976, http://www.margaretthatcher.org/document/102939.
22. Saunders, 2012.
23. Tomlinson, 2016.
24. McKibbin, 1990; Williamson, 1999; Jarvis, 1996.
25. Seawright (2005).
26. M. Silverstein, 'Interview with Abi Morgan—Writer of *The Iron Lady*' at http://www.indiewire.com/2011/12/interview-with-abi-morgan-writer-of-the-iron-lady-240976/.
27. Thatcher, Interview for *Finchley Press*, 23 June 1970, http://www.margaretthatcher.org/document/101765; Thatcher, TV Interview for BBC1

Val Meets the VIPs, 5 March 1973, http://www.margaretthatcher.org/document/101992.
28. Clark, 2001.
29. Harris, 2013, p. 18.
30. Beers, 2012, p. 119.
31. Beers, 2012, p. 119.
32. Thatcher, 'Finding Time,' *Onward*, April 1954, http://www.margaretthatcher.org/document/100939.
33. McCarthy, 2016.
34. Walter, 1998.
35. Clark, 2001, p. 305, 2 March 1982.
36. Ranelagh, 1991, pp. 51, 47.
37. Bale, 2012, p. 246.

Bibliography

Bale, T. 2012. *The Conservatives Since 1945: The Drivers of Party Change*. Oxford: Oxford University Press.

Beers, L. 2012. 'Thatcher and the Women's Vote', in B. Jackson and R. Saunders (eds.), *Making Thatcher's Britain*, pp. 113–31. Cambridge: Cambridge University Press.

Campbell, J. 2000. *Margaret Thatcher. 1. The Grocer's Daughter*. London: Cape.

Clark, A. 2001. *Diaries: Into Politics*. London: Phoenix.

Cockett, R. 1994. *Thinking the Unthinkable: Think-Tanks and the Economic Counter-Revolution, 1931–1983*. London: HarperCollins.

Green, E. H. H. 2002. 'Thatcherism: A Historical Perspective', in E. H. H. Green (ed.), *Ideologies of Conservatism: Conservative Political Ideas in the Twentieth Century*, pp. 214–240. Oxford: Oxford University Press.

Grimley, M. 2012. 'Thatcherism, Morality and Religion', in B. Jackson and R. Saunders (eds.), *Making Thatcher's Britain*, pp. 78–94. Cambridge: Cambridge University Press.

Harris, R. 2013. *Not for Turning: The Life of Margaret Thatcher*. London: Bantam Press.

Jarvis, D. 1996. 'British Conservatism and Class Politics in the 1920s', *English Historical Review* 111 (1996), pp. 59–84.

Lawrence, J., and F. Sutcliffe-Braithwaite. 2012. 'Margaret Thatcher and the Decline of Class Politics', in B. Jackson and R. Saunders (eds.), *Making Thatcher's Britain*, pp. 132–48. Cambridge: Cambridge University Press.

McCarthy, H. 2016. 'Social Science and Married Women's Employment in Post-War Britain', *Past & Present* 233, (2016), pp. 269–305.

McKibbin, R. 1990. 'Class and Conventional Wisdom: The Conservative Party and the "Public" in Inter-war Britain', in R. McKibbin (ed.), *The Ideologies of Class: Social Relations in Britain, 1880–1950*, pp. 259–94. Oxford: Oxford University Press.

Ranelagh, J. 1991. *Thatcher's People*. London: HarperCollins.

Saunders, R. 2012. '"Crisis? What Crisis?" Thatcherism and the Seventies', in B. Jackson and R. Saunders (eds.), *Making Thatcher's Britain*, pp. 25–42. Cambridge: Cambridge University Press.

Seawright, D. 2005. 'One Nation', in Kevin Hickson (ed.), *The Political Thought of the Conservative Party Since 1945*, pp. 69–92. Basingstoke: Palgrave Macmillan.

Sutcliffe-Braithwaite, F. 2012. 'Neo-liberalism and Morality in the Making of Thatcherite Social Policy', *Historical Journal* 55 (2012), pp. 497–520.

Thatcher, C. 2008. *A Swim-on Part in the Goldfish Bowl*. London: Headline.

Tomlinson, J. 2016. 'De-industrialization Not Decline: A New Meta-narrative for Post-war British History', *Twentieth-Century British History* 27 (2016), pp. 76–99.

Vinen, R. 2009. *Thatcher's Britain: The Politics and Social Upheaval of the Thatcher Era*. London: Simon & Schuster.

Walter, N. 1998. *The New Feminism*. London: Little, Brown.

Wickham-Jones, M. 1997. 'Right Turn: A Revisionist Account of the 1975 Conservative Party Leadership Election', *Twentieth Century British History* 8 (1997), pp. 74–89.

Williamson, P. 1999. *Stanley Baldwin: Conservative Leadership and National Values*. Cambridge: Cambridge University Press.

Index

T. S. Freeman and D. L. Smith (eds.), *Biography and History in Film*, Palgrave Studies in the History of the Media,
https://doi.org/10.1007/978-3-319-89408-9

B

U

V

W

X

Y

Z